The Roman Castrati

Also available from Bloomsbury

Gender and the Interpretation of Classical Myth, Lillian Doherty
Greek Homosexuality, K. J. Dover
Women's Life in Greece and Rome, Maureen B. Fant and Mary R. Lefkowitz

The Roman Castrati

Eunuchs in the Roman Empire

Shaun Tougher

BLOOMSBURY ACADEMIC
LONDON • NEW YORK • OXFORD • NEW DELHI • SYDNEY

BLOOMSBURY ACADEMIC
Bloomsbury Publishing Plc
50 Bedford Square, London, WC1B 3DP, UK
1385 Broadway, New York, NY 10018, USA
29 Earlsfort Terrace, Dublin 2, Ireland

BLOOMSBURY, BLOOMSBURY ACADEMIC and the Diana logo are trademarks of
Bloomsbury Publishing Plc

First published in Great Britain 2021
This paperback edition published in 2022

Copyright © Shaun Tougher, 2021

Shaun Tougher has asserted his right under the Copyright, Designs and Patents Act, 1988,
to be identified as Author of this work.

For legal purposes the Acknowledgements on p. ix constitute an extension
of this copyright page.

Cover design: Terry Woodley
Cover image © Vatican Apostolic Library

All rights reserved. No part of this publication may be reproduced or transmitted in any form or by any means, electronic or mechanical, including photocopying, recording, or any information storage or retrieval system, without prior permission in writing from the publishers.

Bloomsbury Publishing Plc does not have any control over, or responsibility for, any third-party websites referred to or in this book. All internet addresses given in this book were correct at the time of going to press. The author and publisher regret any inconvenience caused if addresses have changed or sites have ceased to exist, but can accept no responsibility for any such changes.

A catalogue record for this book is available from the British Library.

Library of Congress Cataloging-in-Publication Data
Names: Tougher, Shaun, author.
Title: The Roman castrati : eunuchs in the Roman Empire / Shaun Tougher.
Description: London ; New York : Bloomsbury Academic, 2021. | Includes bibliographical references and index. | Summary: "Eunuchs tend to be associated with eastern courts, popularly perceived as harem personnel. However, the Roman empire was also distinguished by eunuchs – they existed as slaves, court officials, religious figures and free men. This book is the first to be devoted to the range of Roman eunuchs. Across seven chapters (spanning the third century BC to the sixth century AD), Shaun Tougher examines the history of Roman eunuchs, focusing on key texts and specific individuals. Subjects met include the Galli (the self-castrating devotees of the goddess the Great Mother), Terence's comedy The Eunuch (the earliest surviving Latin text to use the word 'eunuch'), Sporus and Earinus the eunuch favourites of the emperors Nero and Domitian, the 'Ethiopian eunuch' of the Acts of the Apostles (an early convert to Christianity), Favorinus of Arles (a superstar intersex philosopher), the Grand Chamberlain Eutropius (the only eunuch ever to be consul), and Narses the eunuch general who defeated the Ostrogoths and restored Italy to Roman rule. A key theme of the chapters is gender, inescapable when studying castrated males. Ultimately this book is as much about the eunuch in the Roman imagination as it is the reality of the eunuch in the Roman empire"– Provided by publisher.
Identifiers: LCCN 2020022264 (print) | LCCN 2020022265 (ebook) | ISBN 9781847251688 (hardback) | ISBN 9781350188235 (paperback) | ISBN 9781441174413 (ebook) | ISBN 9781350164048 (epub)
Subjects: LCSH: Castrati–Rome. | Eunuchs–Rome. | Rome–Civilization. | Rome–History–Empire, 30 B.C.–476 A.D.
Classification: LCC HQ449 .T683 2021 (print) | LCC HQ449 (ebook) | DDC 305.90937—dc23
LC record available at https://lccn.loc.gov/2020022264
LC ebook record available at https://lccn.loc.gov/2020022265

ISBN:	HB:	978-1-8472-5168-8
	PB:	978-1-3501-8823-5
	ePDF:	978-1-4411-7441-3
	eBook:	978-1-3501-6404-8

Typeset by RefineCatch Limited, Bungay, Suffolk

To find out more about our authors and books visit www.bloomsbury.com
and sign up for our Newsletters

For Mum

Contents

Preface		viii
Acknowledgements		ix
List of Abbreviations		x
Introduction: Eunuchs in the Roman Empire		1
1	Eunuchs of the Great Mother: The Galli in Rome	7
2	Greeks Bearing Gifts: Terence's *The Eunuch*	21
3	Of Seed and Spring: Eunuch Slaves of Imperial Rome	33
4	Born Eunuchs: The Case of Favorinus of Arles	55
5	Eusebius and His Kind: Court Eunuchs of the Later Roman Empire	79
6	'Eunuchs for the Kingdom of Heaven': Self-Castration and Eunuchs in Early Christianity	99
7	Military Eunuchs: The Case of Narses	119
Notes		137
References		181
Index		207

Preface

This book is a prequel. Having written a book on the eunuchs of the Byzantine Empire it seemed natural to write one on the eunuchs of the Roman Empire. The original intention was to write a book that was accessible to a broad audience, not one that was just for other academics and students. To this end the book focuses on case studies of individuals as well as examining discrete aspects of the history of Roman eunuchs from the third century BC to the sixth century AD. I hope also that the book fosters further study of eunuchs, a subject which has witnessed increasing research interest, fed no doubt by the centrality of the question of gender identity in their history. Gender naturally surfaces in this book but it is not a book about gender; rather it is primarily concerned with the lives and roles of eunuchs found in the Roman empire. The book has taken longer to complete than originally envisaged, not least because of heavy administrative burdens. It is a great pleasure finally to be able to acknowledge the debts incurred in the writing of it. I am extremely grateful for the enormous patience and support extended by the editors involved in the project, first Michael Greenwood and then Alice Wright. They have made the experience much less stressful than it might otherwise have been and have demonstrated great understanding of the pressures faced by academics today. I would also like to thank the anonymous reader who provided much-appreciated feedback. At Cardiff University colleagues provided specific advice and general support. In particular I thank Nicholas Baker-Brian, Guy Bradley, Eve MacDonald, Alex McAuley and Laurence Totelin, as well as the staff of the Arts and Social Sciences Library who went beyond the call of duty to assist me. Other academics beyond Cardiff provided invaluable material and guidance, and I thank especially Chris de Wet, Juan Lewis, Mark Humphries, Liz James, Shushma Malik, Lynn Roller, Ulrike Roth, Nancy Ševčenko and Jamie Wood. Finally, friends in Cardiff and elsewhere provided much-needed support and comfort, in particular Vicki Cummings, Kate Gilliver, Shelley Hales, Mary Harlow, Scott Hieger, Ian Kinsella, Lloyd Llewellyn-Jones, Janett Morgan and Keir Waddington, and the gang of William, Jay, Rupert, Hester and Charlie.

Shaun Tougher
Cardiff, 17 March 2020

Acknowledgements

Biblioteca Apostolica Vaticana for permission to reproduce *Codex Vaticanus Latinus* 3868, folio 25v.

Harvard University Press for permission to reproduce material from: *Philostratus and Eunapius* translated by Wilmer C. Wright, Loeb Classical Library volume 234, Cambridge, Mass.: Harvard University Press, First published 1921. Loeb Classical Library ® is a registered trademark of the President and Fellows of Harvard College.

Statius, vol. 1 translated by D.R. Shackleton Bailey, Loeb Classical Library volume 206, Cambridge, Mass.: Harvard University Press, Copyright © 2003, 2015 by the President and Fellows of Harvard College. Loeb Classical Library ® is a registered trademark of the President and Fellows of Harvard College.

Abbreviations

AASS	Acta Sanctorum
AJP	American Journal of Philology
AnBoll	Analecta Bollandiana
ANRW	Aufstieg und Niedergang der römischen Welt
BF	Byzantinische Forschungen
BHG	Bibliotheca Hagiographica Graeca
BHL	Bibliotheca Hagiographica Latina
BMCR	Bryn Mawr Classical Review
Byz	Byzantion
CIL	Corpus inscriptionum latinarum
CP	Classical Philology
CQ	Classical Quarterly
DOP	Dumbarton Oaks Papers
JHS	Journal of Hellenic Studies
JLA	Journal of Late Antiquity
JRS	Journal of Roman Studies
PBSR	Papers of the British School at Rome
PCPS	Proceedings of the Cambridge Philological Society
PG	Patrologia graeca
PLRE	A.H.M. Jones et al. (eds), *The Prosopography of the Later Roman Empire*, 3 vols (Cambridge: Cambridge University Press, 1971–92)
P&P	Past and Present
REB	Revue des études byzantines
YCS	Yale Classical Studies
ZPE	Zeitschrift für Papyrologie und Epigraphik

Introduction:
Eunuchs in the Roman Empire

Cleopatra's eunuchs

CLEOPATRA	Thou, eunuch Mardian!
MARDIAN	What's your highness' pleasure?
CLEOPATRA	Not now to hear thee sing. I take no pleasure
	In aught an eunuch has. 'Tis well for thee
	That, being unseminared, thy freer thoughts
	May not fly forth of Egypt. Hast thou affections?
MARDIAN	Yes, gracious madam.
CLEOPATRA	Indeed?
MARDIAN	Not in deed, madam, for I can do nothing
	But what indeed is honest to be done.
	Yet have I fierce affections, and think
	What Venus did with Mars.

Thus runs an exchange between Cleopatra, the famous queen of Egypt, and her eunuch Mardian in William Shakespeare's *Antony and Cleopatra*.[1] Shakespeare did not simply invent this detail of a eunuch at Cleopatra's court but was led by the ancient text he depended on, Plutarch's *Life of Antony*, written in the early-second century AD.[2] Although Plutarch was a Greek, he was led by texts written by Romans and closer in time to the conflict between Octavian (the adopted son and heir of Julius Caesar and subsequently effectively the first Roman emperor, Augustus) and Antony and Cleopatra which emphasized the foreignness and femaleness of the queen, in which the figure of the eunuch could be deployed.[3] Plutarch echoes this Roman propaganda when he writes:

> As soon as Octavius Caesar had completed his preparations, he had a decree passed declaring war on Cleopatra and depriving Antony of the authority which he had allowed a woman to exercise in his place. Octavius Caesar also gave it out that Antony had allowed himself to fall under the influence of drugs, that he was no longer responsible for his actions, and that the Romans were fighting this war

against Mardian the eunuch, Potheinus, Iras, who was Cleopatra's hairdresser, and Charmian, her waiting-woman, since it was they who were mainly responsible for the direction of affairs.[4]

The Roman poet Lucan's depiction of the court of Cleopatra and her brother Ptolemy XIII at the time of Julius Caesar, written in the mid-first century AD, also deploys these orientalist tropes:

> There was also a swarm of attendants, and a multitude to serve the banqueters, differing from one another in race or age. Some had the hair of Africa, and others were so fair-haired that Caesar said he had never seen hair so red in the Rhine country; some had dark skins and woolly heads, with hair receding from the forehead. There too were hapless boys who had lost their manhood by the knife (Nec non infelix ferro mollita iuventis/Atque exsecta virum); and opposite them stood youths, whose cheeks, in spite of their age, were scarce darkened by any down. There the sovereigns sat down, and with them Caesar, greater than they. Cleopatra, not content with a crown of her own and her brother for a husband, was there, with her baleful beauty painted up beyond all measure: covered with the spoils of the Red Sea, she carried a fortune round her neck and in her hair, and was weighed down by her ornaments.[5]

Despite the sensationalist depiction of the court there was a reality here. Eunuchs were a feature of the Ptolemaic kingdom, established in Egypt by the general Ptolemy after the death of Alexander the Great in 323 BC, the Macedonian king who conquered the Persian empire and became Lord of Asia. For instance, it was Pothinus a eunuch of Ptolemy XIII who was said to be responsible for the killing of Julius Caesar's rival Pompey the Great when he fled to Egypt after his defeat at the Battle of Pharsalus in 48 BC.[6] The eunuch Eulaeus was a leading minister of the young Ptolemy VI in the second century BC.[7] Aristonicus was a celebrated eunuch of Ptolemy V (204–181 BC).[8] Eunuchs can be found in other Hellenistic kingdoms which were established in the wake of the death of Alexander the Great.[9] Alexander the Great himself was reputed to have taken as his lover the eunuch Bagoas (who previously served the Persian king Darius III), a relationship immortalized in Mary Renault's *The Persian Boy*.[10] Alexander the Great and his successors thus adopted an eastern custom of utilizing eunuchs at court, a custom not just of Persia but of other eastern cultures too, including Assyria.[11] In the later Roman Empire there is expressed the notion that it was the Assyrian queen Semiramis who was responsible for 'inventing' eunuchs.[12] Significantly, and despite wishing to create the impression that eunuchs were something eastern and alien, the Roman Empire itself did experience and utilize eunuchs.

Roman eunuchs

The commonplace existence of eunuchs within the Roman Empire is strikingly conveyed by the Christian author Tertullian, writing in North Africa in the late-second century AD; in his *Exhortation to Chastity* he lists as examples of unmarried men soldiers, celibate bachelors and eunuchs.[13] Despite this arresting remark, Roman eunuchs have not previously had a monograph devoted to them. The closest there has been is Peter Guyot's *Eunuchen als Sklaven und Freigelassene in der griechisch-römischen Antike*, published in 1980. Guyot's book highlights the main reason for why eunuchs are found in the Roman Empire – slavery – but is not just concerned with Rome, and only extends to the end of the fourth century AD despite the fact that the sixth century AD would constitute a more natural end point. His coverage of Roman eunuchs is particularly devoted to those who are found at the imperial court.[14] It is the court eunuchs of the later Roman Empire who have attracted the most attention and generated much study, for it was in this period that eunuchs became an institutional feature of the court as chamberlains (*cubicularii*) and are understood to have become politically powerful.[15] It was a court eunuch, Chrysaphius, who in the fifth century devised the plan to assassinate Attila the Hun.[16]

Eunuchs were found at the imperial court prior to the institutional changes so associated with the Emperor Diocletian (284–305). Famous examples of eunuch favourites are Earinus the 'cupbearer' of Domitian (81–96), and Sporus the 'wife' of Nero (54–68).[17] Further, eunuch slaves at Rome evidently predate the age of emperors, though details are elusive. It is likely that with Rome's conquest of Macedon in 168 BC, and her expansion into the Greek east, eunuch slaves – luxury items – made their way to the centre of the empire. The earliest surviving use of the word *eunuchus* is in a play that was staged in Rome in 161 BC. This was Terence's *The Eunuch*, adapted from a Greek play of the same name written over a century earlier by Menander, and which kept its setting of Hellenistic Athens but set before a Roman audience rich ideas about the nature, understanding and roles of eunuchs.[18] Its central conceit is that a young Athenian citizen takes the place of a eunuch slave to gain access to a young woman (seemingly a slave) he has seen and desired. The play thus foregrounds a common perception of eunuchs, that they were guardians of women in domestic settings. Indeed, an etymology of the Greek word eunuch was 'guardian of the bed', though it could also be understood as 'well-disposed towards'; evidently why the Greek word 'eunuch' signified a castrated man was unknown.[19] The notion that eunuchs as castrated males lacked desire, and were thus safe to be put in charge of women, is reflected by the existence of the so-called 'eunuch's lettuce', or 'anti-aphrodisiac lettuce', known for its great efficacy in quelling desire.[20] However, eunuch slaves were as much in the company of men as women, if not more so. Terence's play is also revealing in that it was a huge success; it had to be staged twice in one day and was the highest-grossing Roman play up to that date. This suggests that it was enjoyable but also that its subject matter was of interest to a Roman audience.

Terence's play was staged in Rome for the Megalensian Games, part of the April festival for the goddess known as the Great Mother (Magna Mater). Her cult had been formally introduced to Rome in 204 BC when the sacred stone representing her had been brought from the Greek east.[21] She was installed on the Palatine Hill, and there a temple was dedicated to her in 191 BC. Her cult provides another reason for the existence of eunuchs in the Roman Empire for it featured self-castrating devotees, called the Galli. One theory why the Galli embraced castration voluntarily is that they were imitating the figure of Attis, a young man associated with the goddess who castrated himself in a frenzy, though possibly this aspect of the myth was invented to explain the actions of the Galli themselves. Such self-castrates differed from slave eunuchs in several ways. They embraced castration willingly, rather than having it forced upon them as victims of the slave trade. They would castrate themselves when they had already reached maturity, whereas slave eunuchs were created before they had attained puberty and thus had the distinctive physical features of 'true' eunuchs: high voices, beardlessness, and longer limbs.[22] One thing that they did have in common, however, was that they tended not to be Roman citizens; the source of slaves and Galli was non-Romans.

Voluntary castration for religious reasons was not just confined to the cult of the Great Mother. It featured in other pagan cults too, but also in early Christianity.[23] In the Gospel of Matthew, Jesus asserts 'For there are eunuchs (εὐνοῦχοι) who have been born so from their mother's womb, and there are eunuchs who have been made eunuchs by men, and there are eunuchs who have made themselves eunuchs for the sake of the kingdom of heaven.'[24] Some Christians understood the last category of eunuchs to be an injunction that they should castrate themselves for their faith. Generally, however, the words were taken metaphorically, indicating that Christians should be chaste like eunuchs. In AD 325 the first church council, the Council of Nicaea, ruled that men who had voluntarily castrated themselves could not be clergy, though it allowed that those were castrated against their will or on medical grounds could be.[25]

The words ascribed to Jesus thus reveal that the term 'eunuch' did not necessarily mean someone who was literally castrated; it could be understood metaphorically, indicating someone who was like a eunuch in their behaviour. Further, the category of 'born eunuch' reveals that individuals could be understood to be eunuch-like because of their physical condition; the term *spado* could also encompass both castrated eunuchs and non-castrated 'eunuchs'.[26] In the present day the term 'intersex' can be used to describe some people who would fit the category of 'born eunuch', such as the South African athlete Caster Semenya, but they existed in the Roman Empire too. An instance is Favorinus of Arles, a celebrated orator and intellectual from the second century AD – he is particularly associated with the Emperor Hadrian (117–138) – who has been likened to Oscar Wilde.[27] Favorinus, who referred to himself as a eunuch, was evidently born intersex, even if his exact condition is not known. Although born in Arles he became adept in Greek, and performed in the Greek east and even in Rome itself. Statues were set up to him, reflecting his celebrity status. Favorinus blurred gender lines but also other identities. Not only was he a westerner known for his expertise in Greek, he was a Roman citizen and a eunuch. Indeed, Christians could be citizens and eunuchs too. Thus, eunuchs in the Roman Empire were not necessarily foreigners.

Span, scope and significance

All these ways in which eunuchs existed, were experienced, and utilized in the Roman empire are explored in this book. Its chronological span stretches from the introduction of the Great Mother into Rome in 204 BC to the death of the eunuch chamberlain and general Narses in Italy at the end of the sixth century AD, a century that can be taken as marking the transition from the Roman Empire to the Byzantine Empire. The book consists of seven chapters, which generally progress chronologically. Each chapter is devoted to a particular aspect of the history of eunuchs in the Roman Empire, often organizing the discussion by focusing on a specific individual or individuals. Throughout I follow the linguistic gender ascribed to eunuchs by the ancient texts – that is the masculine 'he' – though of course recognize that gender is socially constructed and that the gender identity of eunuchs was a matter of debate in the ancient world. Indeed, in the early twenty-first century we are more conscious than ever that multiple gender identities can exist, that the male/female binary system does not suffice. Eunuchs of the ancient world reflect this fact, and this contributes to modern interest in them.

Chapter 1 addresses the cult of the Great Mother. Focusing especially on significant texts written in the first century BC and the first century AD, the chapter considers how and why the Great Mother was adopted by Rome, her association with Attis (her self-castrating consort), and the place of the Galli within the cult, which was in fact much more overt in Rome than in the Greek world. Roman writings about the cult reveal much about concepts of eunuchs, notably the understanding of the gender implications of castration. Chapter 2 examines the first Roman text to deal with eunuchs, Terence's *The Eunuch*. The chapter identifies and comments on a range of issues that surface in the play, such as perceptions of eunuchs, the roles they played, their dress and their voice, as well as castration as a form of punishment. Further, it considers whether the play reveals anything about the reality of eunuchs in Rome around 161 BC. Chapter 3 moves on to more definite territory, considering the evidence for known eunuch slaves in Rome in the late Republic and early Empire. The high-profile examples of Sporus and Earinus take centre stage, and what is known of their lives and careers is examined. It emerges that in the first century of the Roman Empire eunuchs were already seen as a significant imperial accoutrement and speak of the nature and perception of Roman imperial power. Chapter 4 explores 'born eunuchs' through the case of Favorinus of Arles. A comparative wealth of information survives relating to him which provides insight into how such individuals could be perceived. Favorinus also serves as an unusual example of a eunuch who was both free and of significant social standing, compounding his historical interest. Chapter 5 addresses one of the most well-studied aspects of eunuchs in the Roman Empire, their emergence as an institutional element of the later Roman court as chamberlains (*cubicularii*), and as apparently politically powerful, especially in the role of Grand Chamberlain (*praepositus sacri cubiculi*). The chapter focuses on two specific Grand Chamberlains, Eusebius and Eutropius, both from the fourth century AD. Despite the hostile presentation of Eusebius and Eutropius in Roman texts these writings can be utilized to understand both the roles they played in the imperial system and why they were so valued by their imperial masters. Chapter 6 explores why self-castration arose as a practice in early Christianity, what the response to this was, and how eunuchs had a conspicuous place in Christianity even if they were not self-castrates. They are found as converts (witness the case of the 'Ethiopian Eunuch' in the Acts of the Apostles), martyrs, patrons, clergy, saints and monks. Like other

Christian men, eunuchs could struggle to control their passions, graphically demonstrated by the case of the servant-turned-abbot Eutropius in the sixth century AD. Finally, Chapter 7 returns to court eunuchs but considers a particular – and perhaps unexpected – role that they could play, that of military commander. This role came to prominence in the sixth century AD, most famously in the shape of Narses, the chamberlain-turned-general of the Emperor Justinian I (527–565). It was Narses rather than the celebrated Belisarius who manged to secure the reconquest of Italy for the emperor, defeating the Ostrogoths in two pitched battles in the 550s. The chapter is especially concerned to explore the issues of why Narses was appointed general in the first place and how his identity as a eunuch affected the understanding of his role as general. Chapter 7 serves as an appropriate conclusion for the book, not just chronologically but also because Narses marks the peak of the position of eunuchs within the Roman Empire, for he was effectively ruler of Roman Italy.

Although devoted to discrete aspects of the history of eunuchs in the Roman Empire the chapters share large themes, central to the history of Rome itself. These include slavery, power, religion and identity, the latter encompassing ethnicity and gender. This means that this book is as much about the idea of the eunuch – the eunuch in Roman imagination – as it is about the historical reality of eunuchs in the Roman Empire. Indeed, one of the great joys of studying Roman eunuchs is engaging with the rich and arresting texts written about eunuchs in the Roman empire. Terence's *The Eunuch* has already been singled out, but other notable examples are Catullus' poem on a self-castrating Gallus named Attis, Statius' poem on the dedication of locks of Earinus' hair, Lucian's dialogue *Eunuch* concerning a eunuch competing for a chair of philosophy in Athens, Aulus Gellius' memoirs of cultural life entitled *Attic Nights* in which Favorinus is the main recurring character and a Doctor Johnson figure, Ammianus Marcellinus' history which dwells on the eunuchs of the Emperor Constantius II, and Claudian's invectives on the Grand Chamberlain Eutropius. Rome undoubtedly produced a great wealth of significant literature about eunuchs. This fact makes it all the more strange that this book is the first monograph devoted to the whole range of Roman eunuchs across the history of the empire. Perhaps there was a reluctance to acknowledge the general significance of eunuchs in the Roman Empire, an unwillingness grounded in long-lived orientalist attitudes. The fact that eunuchs were a feature of the Greco-Roman world cannot be denied and should not be forgotten. As this book demonstrates, eunuchs were part of the history of the Roman Empire long before the advent of the court eunuchs of the later Roman Empire, and not just as devotees of the Great Mother but as slaves and court favourites as well as free individuals. The advantage of taking a longer view of the history of eunuchs in the Roman Empire is that one can track the increasing prominence and significance of eunuchs within it and appreciate that Rome needs to be situated within the wider Mediterranean world. Ultimately, Rome is revealed to be another Hellenistic kingdom, as familiar with eunuchs as Cleopatra.

1

Eunuchs of the Great Mother: The Galli in Rome

Introduction

When Romans thought of eunuchs what seems to have come to mind automatically is the Galli, the supposedly self-castrating devotees of the Great Mother (Magna Mater). As late as the end of the fourth century AD, in the time of the Christian Roman Empire, the poet Claudian references the Great Mother when writing about the prominent court eunuch Eutropius, declaring that it would be more appropriate for him to be a Gallus and a devotee of the goddess.[1] The cult of the Great Mother was formally introduced to Rome from Asia Minor in 204 BC at the time of the empire's conflict with the famous Hannibal the Carthaginian.[2] The goddess established a central place in Roman thinking about the security and well-being of the empire; she was, for instance, one of two deities who were the subject of 'hymns' by the last pagan emperor Julian in the middle of the fourth century AD.[3] Indeed, the Great Mother and her cult must be one of the most written about elements of Roman religion. The objective of this chapter, however, is not to provide a comprehensive account of the cult throughout the span of the history of the Roman Empire but to address particular aspects of it and consider Roman ideas about the Galli rather than attempt to pin down their reality; for instance, while it is a matter of debate whether the Galli really were self-castrates it is still important that the Romans were fixated with the notion that they were.[4] Focusing in particular on significant texts written in the first century BC and the first century AD, the chapter considers how and why the Great Mother was adopted by Rome, her association with Attis (her self-castrating consort), and the place of the Galli within the cult, which was in fact much more overt in Rome than in the Greek world.[5] Roman writings about the cult reveal much about their concepts of eunuchs, notably their understanding of the gender implications of castration.

The Great Mother comes to Rome

While the cult of the Great Mother may be one of the most written about aspects of Roman religion it is also one of the most elusive.[6] For knowledge of the introduction of her cult to Rome, historians are primarily dependent on several texts dating to the age of Augustus (the late-first century BC to the early-first century AD), while reconstructions of the cult and its rites are based on very fragmentary and late evidence, including Christian polemic.[7] Nevertheless, the Great Mother and her cult exert a potent fascination; this was ostensibly a foreign import to Rome which flourished, and it seemingly entailed the placing at the heart of the empire, on the Palatine Hill, the dramatic prospect of self-castrating religious personnel.

The cult of the Great Mother (also referred to as Cybele and the Mother of the Gods) originated in Anatolia – centred on Phrygia – from where it spread to Greece and then to Rome.[8] The cult began as early as 1000 BC, and from the end of the third century BC a major shrine to the goddess was established at Pessinus in Phrygia. A narrative of the importation of the Great Mother to Rome is found in Book 29 of Livy's vast account of the history of Rome from its foundation down to his own time, terminating in 9 BC.[9] He describes how in 205 BC an oracle was discovered in the Sibylline Books which stated that 'if ever a foreign foe should invade that land of Italy, he could be driven out of Italy and defeated if the Idaean Mother should be brought from Pessinus to Rome'. Thus, the Senate despatched a delegation to Attalus the king of Pergamum (241–197 BC) to seek his assistance, the delegation receiving further divine support for their mission when on the journey they visited the oracle of Apollo at Delphi in Greece, which told them that 'they should gain what they sought with the help of King Attalus; that after conveying the goddess to Rome they were then to make sure that the best man at Rome should hospitably welcome her'. The Roman envoys were well received by Attalus, who escorted them to Pessinus in Phrygia where they were entrusted with a sacred stone (the effigy of the Mother of the Gods). Travelling by ship to Rome's harbour city of Ostia, the goddess was met there by the best man (Publius Cornelius Scipio Nasica had been chosen, though Livy says there was no written record of why such a young man had been selected) in the company of the leading matrons of the city. Having received the stone from the goddess's priests, Scipio handed it over to the matrons who then carried it into the city. Amongst the matrons Livy singles out Claudia Quinta, whose 'repute, previously not unquestioned, as tradition reports it, has made her purity the more celebrated amongst posterity by a service so devout'. The goddess was conveyed to the temple of Victory on the Palatine Hill, on the day preceding the Ides of April, a holy day. Then '[t]he people thronged to the Palatine bearing gifts for the goddess, and there was a banquet of the gods, and games also, called the Megalesia'.[10]

Livy's account of the importation of the Great Mother testifies to the significance and popularity of the goddess and her cult, but it is clear that aspects of it are problematic; for instance, other texts reflect variant traditions, and Livy fails to address some key questions and provide a fully satisfying narrative (he himself is frustrated about the lack of explanation of the selection of Scipio as the best man).[11] He even fails to mention apparently vital aspects of the cult, the figures of Attis and the Galli. He presents Attalus as acquiescent in the wishes of the Romans, but in Ovid's *On the Roman Calendar* (*Fasti*, dated to AD 8) the king initially refuses the Roman request and is only persuaded when an earthquake expressed divine disapproval and the goddess declared that she wanted to go to Rome.[12] However, since Rome and Attalus had a common enemy in the shape of Philip V of Macedon (221–179 BC), it is likely that the king of Pergamum was keen to establish good relations with Rome and was thus a willing participant in this religious transaction. As to the site of the shrine from which the goddess was taken, Varro (writing in the middle of the first century BC) locates it in Pergamum rather than Pessinus, saying that the festival of the Great Mother (the Megalesia) was named after the Megalesion, her temple (near the city wall of Pergamum) from which she was brought to Rome.[13] It has been argued that the naming of Pessinus as the site was an anachronism, for in 205 BC Pergamum did not have power over Pessinus.[14] As Livy and other sources make clear anyway, the Great Mother was particularly associated with Ida, a mountain in the Troad, in proximity to the ancient city of Troy. Although Livy does not mention the factor of Troy in his narrative other writers do, such as Ovid. When the poet asks where the goddess came from the muse Erato answers '"The Mother Goddess ever loved Dindymus, and Cybele, and Ida, with its delightful springs, and the realm of Ilium. When Aeneas carried Troy to the Italian fields, the goddess almost followed the ships that bore the sacred things"'.[15] The belief that the Romans were descended from Trojans would certainly explain why at the end of the third century BC Rome was interested in the Mother Goddess at all, a fact that is hard to fathom from Livy's account. Another poet writing during the reign of Augustus emphasizes the connections between Rome, Troy and the Great Mother.[16] This is Virgil, who in his famous poem the *Aeneid* relates the coming to Italy of the Trojan Aeneas and his role in the foundation of Rome. The Great Mother features prominently in the poem, and serves as the protector of Aeneas.[17] For example, Aeneas having built his fleet from the pines on Mount Ida the Great Mother beseeched Jupiter to keep the ships safe, which he agreed to do once they had reached Laurentum in Italy, when they were transformed into sea nymphs.[18] Aeneas then addressed a prayer to the goddess: "'Kindly Mother of the Gods, dweller on Ida, who takes delight in Mount Dindymus, in cities crowned with towers and in the lion pair responsive to your chariot reins, be now my leader in the battle. Bring near to us the due fulfilment of your omen. Stand by the side of your Phrygians and give us your divine blessing."'[19] The subject matter of the *Aeneid* was in tune with the concerns of Augustus (the poem was written after his defeat of Antony and Cleopatra at Actium in 31 BC and before 19 BC, the year of Virgil's death), who claimed descent from Aeneas and was keen to revere the Great Mother who had come from Troy too.[20] When the temple of the Great Mother on the Palatine, which was originally dedicated in 191 BC,[21] burnt down (not for the first time) in AD 3 Augustus had it rebuilt.[22] This temple was located opposite Augustus' house on the Palatine.[23] The goddess had links not just with the Julian family through Troy, but also with the Claudians because of the story of Claudia Quinta.[24] It seems that Augustus' wife Livia, a Claudian, identified with the Great Mother; for instance, she is portrayed as the goddess on a cameo.[25]

The Claudia Quinta element of the story mentioned by Livy is also commented on by other authors.[26] The role of the matron in the narrative was obviously of great interest to Ovid.[27] In Livy, Claudia was a beautiful noble, with an incorrect reputation for being unchaste. When the ship carrying the goddess ran aground she alone was able to move it when she pulled on the rope attached to it, and this was a sign from the goddess that Claudia was innocent of the accusations against her. Ovid testifies to the truth of the story by having Erato remark 'My story is a strange one, but it is attested by the stage' (mira, sed et scaena testificata loquar).[28] By the time Herodian wrote his *History* in the third century AD, Claudia had become a Vestal Virgin 'who was under a vow of chastity but was being charged with adultery', and who used her sash (rather than a rope) to pull the ship; making Claudia a Vestal has the effect of emphasizing the significance of her intact chastity.[29] The figure of Claudia features in material culture too. An altar from Rome dating to the first or second century AD shows the goddess seated on the boat being pulled by Claudia, the altar being dedicated by another Claudia, Claudia Synthyche, who inscribed on the altar 'To the Mother of the Gods and to the Saviour Saviour Ship, having undertaken a vow, Claudia Synthyche gave this altar'.[30] In his *Memorable Doings and Sayings*, compiled in the reign of Augustus' successor Tiberius (AD 14–37), Valerius Maximus records that there was a statue of Claudia Quinta in the vestibule of the temple of the Great Mother, and that it survived unscathed two fires which consumed the shrine (in 111 BC and AD 3).[31] In the fourth century AD, Julian also highlights the significance of material evidence, declaring that bronze statues in Rome prove the story of the miracle of the ship.[32]

The Great Mother and Attis

In relation to the subject of eunuchs, however, there are two elements completely absent from Livy's narrative: the figures of Attis and the Galli. In the variant myths about the Great Mother, Attis appears as the mortal consort of the goddess,[33] and the existence of the Galli in the cult is often associated with him. In contrast to Livy, Ovid mentions both Attis and the Galli.[34] Erato narrates the story of Attis and the goddess to him. Attis was a good-looking Phrygian boy who shared a 'chaste passion' (*casto ... amore*) with the Great Mother. He promised always to be a boy and guard her temple, and that if he broke his oath the love for which he did so would be his last. However, he fell in love with the nymph Sagaritis, which brought down the goddess's revenge. She damaged the tree of the Naiad, who thus died, and Attis went mad and fled to the top of Mount Dindymus. There he swore that the Furies were upon him, and 'mangled ... his body with a sharp stone, and trailed his long hair in the filthy dust; and his cry was, "I have deserved it! With my blood I pay the penalty that is my due. Ah, perish the parts that were my ruin"', then rid himself of his genitals 'and of a sudden was bereft of every sign of manhood'.[35] This version of the myth of Attis is common in both Greek and Roman authors, suggesting that it was well known,[36] but there were different versions too. The Greek writer Pausanias in his *Description of Greece*, written in the mid-second century AD, gives the following account of the origins and life of Attis:

> Zeus, it is said, let fall in his sleep seed upon the ground, which in course of time sent up a demon, with two sexual organs, male and female. They call the demon Agdistis. But the gods, fearing Agdistis, cut off the male organ. There grew up from it an almond-tree with its fruit ripe, and a daughter of the river Sangarius, they say, took of the fruit and laid it in her bosom, when it at once disappeared, but she was

with child. A child was born, and exposed, but was tended by a he-goat. As he grew up, his beauty was more then human, and Agdistis fell in love with him. When he had grown up, Attis was sent by his relatives to Pessinus, that he might wed the king's daughter. The marriage-song was being sung, when Agdistis appeared, and Attis went mad and cut off his genitals, as also did he who was giving him his daughter in marriage. But Agdistis repented of what he had done to Attis, and persuaded Zeus to grant that the body of Attis should neither rot at all nor decay.[37]

A fuller version of this story is found in a Latin Christian work dating to the early-fourth century, Arnobius of Sicca's *Against the Pagans*.[38] In this attack on paganism, Arnobius says he presents the myth of the Great Mother as narrated by a certain Timotheus (who may date to the third century BC).[39] This version runs as follows:

> 5. In Timotheus, who was no mean mythologist, and also in others equally well informed, the birth of the Great Mother of the gods, and the origin of her rites, are thus detailed, being derived – as he himself writes and suggests – from learned books of antiquities, and from his acquaintance with the most secret mysteries: – Within the confines of Phrygia, he says, there is a rock of unheard-of wildness in every respect, the name of which is Agdus, so named by the natives of that district. Stones taken from it, as Themis by her oracle had enjoined, Deucalion and Pyrrha threw upon the earth, at that time emptied of men; from which this Great Mother, too, as she is called, was fashioned along with the others, and animated by the deity. Her, given over to rest and sleep on the very summit of the rock, Jupiter assailed with lewdest desires. But when, after long strife, he could not accomplish what he had proposed to himself, he, baffled, spent his lust on the stone. This the rock received, and with many groanings Acdestis is born in the tenth month, being named from his mother rock. In him there had been resistless might, and a fierceness of disposition beyond control, a lust made furious, and derived from both sexes. He violently plundered and laid waste; he scattered destruction wherever the ferocity of his disposition had led him; he regarded not gods nor men, nor did he think anything more powerful than himself; he contemned earth, heaven, and the stars. 6. Now, when it had been often considered in the councils of the gods, by what means it might be possible either to weaken or to curb his audacity, Liber, the rest hanging back, takes upon himself this task. With the strongest wine he drugs a spring much resorted to by Acdestis where he had been wont to assuage the heat and burning thirst roused in him by sport and hunting. Hither runs Acdestis to drink when he felt the need; he gulps down the draught too greedily into his gaping veins. Overcome by what he is quite unaccustomed to, he is in consequence sent fast asleep. Liber is near the snare which he had set; over his foot he throws one end of a halter formed of hairs, woven together very skilfully; with the other end he lays hold of his privy members. When the fumes of the wine passed off, Acdestis starts up furiously, and his foot dragging the noose, by his own strength he robs himself of his sex; with the tearing asunder of these parts there is an immense flow of blood; both are carried off and swallowed up by the earth; from them there suddenly springs up, covered with fruit, a pomegranate tree,

seeing the beauty of which, with admiration, Nana, daughter of the king or river Sangarius, gathers and places in her bosom some of the fruit. By this she becomes pregnant; her father shuts her up, supposing that she had been debauched, and seeks to have her starved to death; she is kept alive by the mother of the gods with apples, and other food, and brings forth a child, but Sangarius orders it to be exposed. One Phorbas having found the child, takes it home, brings it up on goats' milk; and as handsome fellows are so named in Lydia, or because the Phrygians in their own way of speaking call their goats *attagi*, it happened in consequence that the boy obtained the name Attis. Him the mother of the gods loved exceedingly, because he was of most surpassing beauty; and Acdestis, who was his companion, as he grew up fondling him, and bound to him by wicked compliance with his lust in the only way now possible, leading him through wooded glades, and presenting him with the spoils of many wild beats, which the boy Attis at first said boastfully were won by his own toil and labour. Afterwards, under the influence of wine, he admits that he is both loved by Acdestis, and honoured by him with the gifts brought from the forest; whence it is unlawful for those polluted by drinking wine to enter into his sanctuary, because it discovered his secret. 7. Then Midas, king of Pessinus, wishing to withdraw the youth from so disgraceful an intimacy, resolves to give him his own daughter in marriage, and caused the gates of the town to be closed, that no one of evil omen might disturb their marriage joys. But the mother of the gods, knowing the fate of the youth, and that he would live among men in safety only so long as he was free from the ties of marriage, that no disaster might occur, enters the closed city, raising its walls with her head, which began to be crowned with towers in consequence. Acdestis, bursting with rage because of the boy's being torn from himself, and brought to seek a wife, fills all the guests with frenzied madness: the Phrygians shriek aloud, panic-stricken at the appearance of the gods; a daughter of adulterous Gallus cuts off her breasts; Attis snatches the pipe borne by him who was goading them to frenzy; and he, too, now filled with furious passion, raving frantically and tossed about, throws himself down at last, and under a pine tree mutilates himself, saying, 'Take these, Acdestis, for which you have stirred up so great and terribly perilous commotions.' With the streaming blood his life flies; but the Great Mother of the gods gathers the parts which had been cut off, and throws earth on them, having first covered them, and wrapped them in the garment of the dead. From the blood which had flowed springs a flower, the violet, and with this the tree is girt. Thence the custom began and arose, whereby you even now veil and wreath with flowers the sacred pine. The virgin who had been the bride, whose name, as Valerius the pontifex relates, was Ia, veils the breast of the lifeless youth with soft wool, sheds tears with Acdestis, and slays herself. After her death her blood is changed into purple violets. The mother of the gods sheds tears also, from which springs an almond tree, signifying the bitterness of death. Then she bears away to her cave the pine tree, beneath which Attis had unmanned himself; and Acdestis joining in her wailings, she beats and wounds her breast, pacing round the trunk of the tree now at rest. Jupiter is begged by Acdestis that Attis may be restored to life: he does not permit it. What, however, fate allowed, he readily grants, that his body should not decay, that his hairs should always grow, that the least of his fingers should live, and should be kept ever in motion; content with which favours, it is said that Acdestis consecrated the body in Pessinus, and honoured it with yearly rites and priestly services.[40]

One of the most famous Roman material images of Attis is a statue found at the sanctuary of the Great Mother at Ostia, where he had his own shrine as part of the complex; he reclines languidly in a state of near undress, his head crowned with a garland of fruit and pine cones and a Phrygian cap surrounded by sun rays and topped by a crescent moon, and his left arm resting on a bearded head, perhaps representing the river Sangarius or Gallus.[41] This celebrated statue perhaps dates to the reign of Hadrian (117–138). It used to be asserted that images of Attis were also associated with the Great Mother from soon after her introduction to Rome, for offerings of figurines identified as Attis were found on the site of her temple on the Palatine.[42] However, this identification has been challenged by some, who suggest that they are simply male children or personifications of penises.[43] Further, it is generally stated that the place of Attis within the Roman cult of the Great Mother only became significant from the first century AD onwards.[44] It is argued that this is apparent from the reorganization of the festival for the cult dated to the reign of Claudius (41–54) on the strength of a reference in a sixth-century text, the *On the Months* of John the Lydian.[45] He says that Claudius developed the March festival, which relates to the figure of Attis; the April festival was focused on the goddess herself.

Details of the March and April festivals are known from a fourth-century calendar created for Furius Dionysus Philocalus in AD 354, in the reign of Constantius II.[46] The March festival is listed as comprising:

15 March: The Entry of the Reed. This may refer to Attis' abandonment in reeds on the river bank, and his castration because of the cutting of reeds.
22 March: The Entry of the Tree. This refers to the pine tree, prominent in the story of Attis, and it symbolizes his dead body. Mourning accompanied the entry of the tree, and it continued into 23 March.
24 March: The Day of Blood (discussed below).
25 March: The Day of Rejoicing (*Hilaria*). This celebrated the rebirth of Attis.
26 March: The Day of Rest.
27 March: The Day of Ablution (*Lavatio*). On this day the cult statue of the goddess and other cult artefacts were transported to the river Almo and washed there.[47]

It is generally agreed that Claudius was not responsible for all the elements of the March festival listed in the Calendar of Philocalus; it is argued that the Entry of the Reed and the *Hilaria* were introduced in the second century AD, under Antoninus Pius (138–161) at the earliest.[48] It is posited that Claudius instituted a festival of mourning while Antoninus Pius one of celebration, reflecting the change in status of Attis from consort of the goddess to god in his own right, a god of rebirth. Thus, Livy's lack of mention of Attis may reflect that he was initially not such a significant part of the cult of the Great Mother, but alternatively it could be that Livy did not want to distract from the main focus of his narrative.

The Great Mother and the Galli

The other element of the cult not mentioned by Livy is the Galli themselves, the infamous supposedly self-castrating devotees of the goddess, who, as Mary Beard has remarked, '[w]ith their flowing hair, extravagant jewelry, and long yellow silken robes ... stalk the pages of Roman literature as mad, frenzied, foreign eunuchs'.[49] While Livy does not mention them in his account of the introduction of the cult, in Ovid's reflections on the festival of the Mother Goddess, the Megalensian festival, begun on 4 April (the anniversary of her entry into Rome) and continuing until 10 April,[50] they feature from the beginning: 'Eunuchs (*semimares*) will march and thump their hollow drums, and cymbals clashed on cymbals will give out their tinkling noises: seated on the unmanly necks of her attendants (*molli comitum cervice*), the goddess herself will be borne with howls through the streets in the city's midst.'[51] Ovid also asks Erato why the attendants of the goddess cut their members, and why those who castrate themselves (*se excidere*) for her are called Galli.[52] In addition, Ovid includes the castrated attendants in his account of the arrival of the Great Mother in Rome; as she is brought into the city 'The attendants howled, the mad flute blew, and hands unmanly (*molles ... manus*) beat the leathern drums.'[53]

Thus for Ovid, the Galli were an integral feature of the cult of the Mother Goddess, yet Livy does not mention them. Perhaps, as with Attis, he deemed it unnecessary to include this element, or perhaps the Galli (and Attis also) did not feature in the events of 204 BC. According to Dionysius of Halicarnassus, a Greek who wrote a history of Rome and lived in the city in the time of Augustus, the Romans could be very circumspect about the more outlandish elements of foreign religions that they imported into their city; he comments:

> The rites of the Idaean goddess are a case in point; for the praetors perform sacrifices and celebrate games in her honour every year according to the Roman customs, but the priest and priestess of the goddess are Phrygians, and it is they who carry her image in procession through the city, begging alms in her name according to their custom,[54] and wearing figures upon their breasts and striking their timbrels while their followers play tunes upon their flutes in honour of the Mother of the Gods. But by a law and decree of the senate no native Roman walks in procession through the city arrayed in a parti-coloured robe, begging alms or escorted by flute-players, or worships the goddess with the Phrygian ceremonies. So cautious are they about admitting any foreign religious customs and so great is their aversion to all pompous display that is wanting in decorum.[55]

Perhaps, then, Livy did not wish to dwell on the non-Roman aspects of the cult of the Great Mother.

It is notable that in the remarks of Dionysius he does not identify the priest of the goddess as a eunuch, or use the term Gallus either. It is common for modern translators of Latin texts to translate 'Gallus' as meaning 'eunuch priest', but this may not necessarily be correct.[56] The renowned scholar of ancient religion Arthur Darby Nock already observed in 1925 that 'Under the [Roman] Empire, if not earlier, [the Galli] were sharply distinguished from the *sacerdotes* proper'.[57] More recently, Hugh Bowden has argued that the term Gallus was originally used in the Greek east of priests of the goddess but did not signify that they were eunuchs; he argues that the eunuchs associated with the goddess were rather wandering devotees, *metragyrtai* (meaning 'beggars for the Mother').[58] He asserts that it is Roman poets who use the term Gallus to mean eunuchs. However, other Roman authors could use the term Gallus and mean a eunuch, as is clear from an episode in Valerius Maximus' *Memorable Doings and Sayings*.[59] This is the story of Genucius who in 77 BC was not allowed to inherit a legacy because he was a self-castrate and therefore neither male nor female.[60] Further, Valerius Maximus says Genucius was a Gallus of the Great Mother (*Matris Magnae Gallus*). Thus in the Roman world, the term Gallus could be used of eunuch devotees of the goddess, but they were not necessarily priests.

There is also the question of whether the Galli were necessarily castrated. Genucius is clearly presented as being so. Also at the end of the second century BC there is encountered a slave who castrated himself for the goddess, and was exiled from Rome for his pains.[61] Pliny the Elder in his *Natural History*, written in the late 70s AD, cites an otherwise unknown Marcus Caelius for the 'fact' that the Galli castrate themselves with a shard of Samian pottery.[62] A satire of Juvenal, who wrote in the late-first and early-second centuries AD, refers to the practice of self-castration associated with the cult.[63] Some modern commentators assume that during the March festival on the Day of Blood devotees castrated themselves, though others are more circumspect and refer to self-flagellation and laceration.[64] It is obviously difficult to be sure if a Gallus was indeed a castrate. Stories of the self-castration of Attis suggest that it was an important feature of the cult, and indeed some commentators think that these stories about Attis were in fact invented in order to explain why there were self-castrating followers of the goddess.[65] Tertullian, a Christian from North Africa writing at the end of the second century AD, refers to having seen in the amphitheatre the castration of a criminal dressed up as Attis, which reflects that the castration of Attis was well known but not necessarily that the Galli did castrate themselves.[66] A later development of the Roman cult and it rituals emphasizes the significance of the shedding of blood; this is the introduction of the taurobolium, the sacrificing of a bull.[67] This is testified to in inscriptions on votive altars, in particular those at the Phrygianum – a sanctuary of the Great Mother and Attis – on the Vatican Hill in Rome, which date primarily to the fourth century AD.[68] Some of the inscriptions mention the dedication of powers (*vires*), understood to be a reference to the genitals of the animal, and a substitute for self-castration.[69] Notably, these inscriptions are not products of the Galli themselves, but rather the Roman elite. This is taken to reflect the opening up of the cult to participation of Roman citizens, who would be extremely unlikely to castrate themselves or embrace the role of the Galli. This is further emphasized by the fact that there was introduced in Rome the position of Archigallus, that is Chief Gallus, who is considered to have been a Roman citizen and thus not a castrate; it is generally believed that this occurred as part of the imperial reorganization of the cult.[70] The material images of Archigalli that survive are thus considered not to be depictions of (possible) eunuchs but of Roman citizens.[71]

Regarding whether the Galli were castrates, it can be noted that self-castration is also found in other religious contexts. It features not only in other eastern ancient pagan cults,[72] but also in early Christianity (discussed in Chapter 6). Christian self-castration could continue beyond the ancient world, witness the modern case of the Skoptsy in Russia.[73] The Skoptsy (literally 'the castrated ones' or 'self-castrators') were Christians who embraced castration to secure purity and salvation. They came to light in the 1770s and survived into the 1930s. As justification of their practice they appealed, like early Christians, to Matthew 19.12. Male Skoptsy could undergo the removal of just the testicles ('minor seal') or of the penis too ('major seal'). Female members of the community could also endure genital mutilation, encompassing the removal of nipples, breasts and external parts of the vagina. Probably the most famous comparative case for the Galli is the Hijras of Southern Asia.[74] The practice of self-castration for the Hijras forms part of their dedication to the Hindu goddess Bahuchara Mata, a version of the Indian mother goddess. The Hijras dress and act like women, taking female names and using female kinship terms to describe the relationships between them. They form well-organized hierarchical communities and live in houses headed by a guru. They are associated with begging. A traditional role of Hijras is to perform at weddings and celebrations for the birth of a child, for which they are paid. They sing and dance and are believed to have the power to bless the couple or child, imparting fertility. Significantly though, not all Skoptsy or Hijras necessarily were/are castrated, despite the value attached to the act as marking the true devotee.[75] Thus in the case of the Galli, self-castration is probable but it cannot be assumed that every Gallus was a castrate.[76]

A key question about the Galli is why were they a feature of the Roman cult of the Great Mother at all? Amongst the questions Ovid poses to Erato about the cult (why does the goddess delight in a perpetual din; why do lions submit to her; why does she wear a turreted crown; where did she come from, was she always in Rome; why does she collect money in small coins; why do people invite others to so many feasts and banquets at the time of her festival; why is the Megalesia the first games of the year in Rome; why are herbs offered to her) is why do the Galli castrate themselves (as well as why are they called Galli)? Erato's response is that the Galli are imitating Attis: "'His madness (*furor*) set an example, and still his unmanly minsters (*mollesque ministri*) cut their vile members (*vilia membra*) while they toss their hair'".[77] The very name of the Galli emphasizes the madness of their (and Attis') act, for it is derived from a Phrygian river, the Gallus, "'a river of mad water ... Who drinks of it goes mad'".[78] Modern commentators often resort to the example of Attis to explain the Galli's supposed self-castration, but it is important to appreciate that in addition to madness the embracing of chastity was a motive factor for Attis in Ovid's tale (and there is also an element of punishment in the young man's castration, for this could be deemed the appropriate penalty for sexual misdemeanours). Attis had sworn to be chastely faithful to the Great Mother, so it was entirely apposite that he should castrate himself having strayed with the nymph: he was making himself a literal eunuch for the goddess. Nock argues that continence was the explanation for religious castration.[79] That chastity is as important a motif for Ovid as madness (or an even more important one) is indicated by the fact that he dwells on the figure of Claudia Quinta, whose chastity is suspect but is vindicated by the goddess, who granted her the power to pull the ship in order to demonstrate her innocence.[80]

In his discussion of the issue, Nock rejects other theories explaining the self-castration of the Galli (assimilation with the goddess; granting their *vires* to the goddess) and emphasizes that the act was an indication of the degree of devotion to the Great Mother. However, it is worth considering further explanations too, especially those provided by other Roman authors. For instance, in an account of the festival of the Mother of the Gods in his *On the Nature of Things*, the poet Lucretius (an Epicurean who lived in the first half of the first century BC) declares that the goddess was given Galli by her followers 'to indicate that those who have violated the majesty of the Mother, and have been found ungrateful to their parents, should be thought unworthy to bring living offspring into the regions of light'.[81] As James Jope observes, this makes one think of the case of Attis also but Lucretius does not name him and is concerned rather 'with the general admonition against impiety which he ascribes to the cult'; Jope asserts that the Galli are 'interpreted as an expression of contempt for filial ingratitude; their castration is a veiled threat of punishment'.[82] Other interpretations are given by Varro and the Stoic philosopher Cornutus, writing in the first century BC and the first century AD respectively.[83] Varro relates the Galli to the earth (the goddess herself), saying that they signify 'that those who lack seed should devote themselves to the earth'.[84] Cornutus presents them in cosmogonic terms, relating them to the myth of Uranus who was castrated by Cronus.[85] The Christian author Justin Martyr, writing in the second century AD, asserts that the self-castration was sexually motivated.[86] Thus it seems that Roman commentators felt free to explain the behaviour of the Galli as they thought fit or as suited their interests. One has the impression that they are faced with a pre-existing cult with its symbols and rites and they seek to provide explanations for them. Thus Roller was led to her suggestion that the story of the castration of Attis was invented to explain the existence of the Galli, rather than the existence of the Galli being explained by the castration of Attis.[87] One might also wonder, however, if the castration of the Galli signified the extent of the power of the Great Mother herself, as protector and supporter of the Roman empire; her power was so great that her devotees were emasculated.[88] This might also reflect notions of eastern queens being surrounded by eunuchs.

Roman views of the Galli

Thus, the history of the cult of the Great Mother in Rome presents very challenging questions for historians because of the character and complexity of the sources, which can be fragmentary, late and hostile. Debate continues to surround the cult, including the questions of the role and nature of the Galli. Another way to approach the Galli, however, is to focus on the image of them created in the Roman texts and analyse what this suggests about attitudes to, and understandings of, them, rather than trying to reconstruct their reality.[89] The remainder of this chapter adopts such an approach, examining particular texts primarily from the first century BC and the first century AD to identify what they reveal about Roman attitudes to the Galli as castrated individuals.

One of the most famous literary depictions of a self-castrating devotee of the Mother Goddess dates to the first century BC. It is one of the poems of Catullus, who was active in Rome in the middle of the century.⁹⁰ Significantly, the subject of the poem goes by the name of Attis. Once Attis has castrated himself in Phrygia he becomes feminized.⁹¹ Cornish's translation of Catullus chooses to make this even more explicit by using the female pronoun rather than the male one:

> [G]oaded by raging madness, bewildered in mind, he cast down from him with sharp flint-stone the burden of his members. So when *she* felt her limbs to have lost their manhood (*viro*), still with fresh blood dabbling the face of the ground, swiftly with snowy hands she seized the light timbrel (*tympanum*), your timbrel, Cybele, thy mysteries, Mother, and shaking with soft fingers the hollow oxhide thus began she to sing to her companions tremulously.⁹²

Not only has Attis become feminized, but he has also become a leader of the Galli, exhorting them to follow him into the Phrygian forests of Cybele, '"where the noise of cymbals sounds, where timbrels re-echo, where the Phrygian flute-player blows a deep note on his curved reed, where the Maenads ivy-crowned toss their heads violently, where with shrill yells they shake the holy emblems"'.⁹³ Interestingly, when his frenzy has passed Attis reflects on what he has done, and laments his former life and his status as a beautiful youth:

> "I, shall I from my own home be borne far away into these forests? from my country, my possessions, my friends, my parents, shall I be absent? absent from the market, the wrestling-place, the racecourse, the playground? unhappy, ah unhappy heart, again, again must thou complain. For what form of human figure is there which I had not? I, to be a woman (*ego mulier*) – I who was a stripling (*adolescens*), I a youth (*ephebus*), I a boy (*puer*), I was the flower of the playground, I was once the glory of the palaestra: mine were the crowded doorways, mine the warm thresholds, mine the flowery garlands to deck my house when I was to leave my chamber at sunrise. I, shall I now be called – what? a handmaid of the gods, a ministress of Cybele?"⁹⁴

Attis is no longer a boy, but a feminine servant of the Great Mother. He also refers to himself as a 'barren man' (*vir sterilis*), while the poet observes that he is 'woman but no true one' (*notha mulier*).⁹⁵

This last remark about the ambiguous gender identity of Attis finds echo in the depiction of the Gallus Genucius already encountered in Valerius Maximus' *Memorable Doings and Sayings*. This text was dedicated to the emperor Tiberius in the first century AD, but the episode dates to 77 BC. As already noted, Genucius was not allowed to inherit his legacy since as a self-castrate he 'should not be reckoned among either men or women' (neque virorum neque mulierum numero haberi debere).⁹⁶ Further, however, Valerius Maximus presents Genucius as indecent and contaminated; he is forbidden to attend the tribunal so that it 'should not be defiled by [his] obscene presence and tainted voice' (obscena Genucii praesentia inquinataque voce).⁹⁷ As a eunuch not only is his gender identity at issue, so is his very status as a human being.⁹⁸ The distaste for eunuchs is palpable.

Finally, rich texts for the analysis of the image of the Galli are presented by the works of the Roman satirists Juvenal and Martial, both active in the late-first century AD, with Juvenal continuing into the second century.[99] In his sixth satire, on Roman women as wives, Juvenal comes to the topic of the superstitious nature of women, in which he describes how a eunuch of the Great Mother warns a woman of impending trouble 'unless she purifies herself with a hundred eggs and presents him with her old russet-coloured dresses' (alluding to the feminine attire of the Galli).[100] Juvenal introduces the eunuch to alarming and unattractive effect:

> Look! In comes the troupe of frenzied Bellona and the Mother of the Gods (*matrisque deum*), along with an enormous eunuch (*ingens semivir*), a face his perverted (*obsceno*) sidekick must revere. A long time ago now he picked up a shard and cut off his soft (*mollia*) genitals. The noisy band and the common drums (*tympana*) fall quiet in his presence and his cheeks are clothed in the Phrygian cap.[101]

The satire touches quickly on many familiar motifs associated with the Galli: frenzy, perversion, effeminacy, noisy music, easternness.[102]

Martial deals with the Galli (and Attis) several times in his epigrams, and tends to dwell on their effeminacy.[103] He describes a certain Dindymus as 'more emasculate than a flabby eunuch, more womanish than the catamite of Celaenae [i.e. Attis],[104] whose name the [gelded] [Gallus] of the mad Mother howls' (Spadone cum sis eviratior fluxo, et concubine mollior Celaenaeo, quem sectus ululat Matris entheae Gallus).[105] The softness[106] of Attis is also mentioned when he is compared unfavourably with a beautiful boy called Cestus, whom Martial declares Cybele would have preferred to 'her womanish Phrygian' (te Cybele molli mallet habere Phryge).[107] The musical role of the Galli surfaces also; an epigram referring to a Gallus selling bronzes mourning Attis is titled 'Cymbals'.[108] The sterility of the Galli is emphasized in an engaging epigram relating how a discharged soldier travelling home to Ravenna with a beautiful boy called Achillas fell in with some eunuchs of Cybele (*semiviro Cybeles*); these 'sterile men' (*steriles ... viri*) wanted to castrate the boy, but he tricks them and they end up castrating the soldier instead.[109]

Thus, Martial tends to describe Galli in familiar ways, and especially as feminized men. This seems to have been the major Roman concern with the Galli (and eunuchs in general), since they provided such a contrast to the ideal of the Roman man as masculine, encompassing the role of being a father.[110] However, Martial can also play with the stereotypical presentation of Galli, in one very explicit and memorable epigram. It runs:

> What, licking women down inside there, Gallus?
> The thing you should be sucking is a phallus.
> They cut your cock off, but not so to bed,
> Cunt-lover: what needs doctoring now's your head.
> For while your missing member can't but fail,
> Your tongue still breaks Cybele's rule: it's male.[111]

Martial graphically asserts that the eunuch remains male in his desires, confounding expectations.

Notably, the issue of gender ambiguity can also surface in relation to material evidence for the Galli. Discussing a tomb portrait discovered near Rome, dated to the second century AD, and identified as a Gallus, Mary Beard, John North and Simon Price note that the figure (also decorated with objects relating to the cult) is wearing '[s]wathed dress – reminiscent of female, rather than male, clothing'.[112] Hugh Bowden, however, is of the view that it depicts a priest rather than a Gallus, but the point still stands regarding the dress of the personnel of the cult.[113]

Conclusion

Introduced to Rome at the end of the third century BC, the cult of the Great Mother became firmly established within the history and identity of the Roman Empire. The Great Mother was considered a powerful protector of the Roman Empire, installed on the Palatine Hill and celebrated annually in April. Her associate Attis and her devotees the Galli were also a critical part of her cult. Despite the rhetoric of the foreignness of the cult and its practices it was embraced by the Romans, even more so than in the Greek world.[114] Whether or not they were castrated, and whatever their precise role in the cult, there is no doubt that Roman authors engaged strongly with the figure of the Galli and presented them as self-castrates. This led them to reflect on issues of sex, gender and identity, issues crucial for the understanding of eunuchs in general.

2

Greeks Bearing Gifts: Terence's *The Eunuch*

Introduction

Although the cult of the Great Mother was introduced to Rome in 204 BC the earliest surviving Roman text to deal with eunuchs, and the first to use the word 'eunuch',[1] is Terence's play *The Eunuch*, dated to 161 BC. The play was adapted from a Greek play of the same name by the Athenian Menander, a leading figure in New Comedy who was active in the late-fourth and early-third centuries BC. *The Eunuch* revolves around a young Athenian man called Chaerea posing as a eunuch so he can gain access to a young girl called Pamphila with whom he has fallen in love; taken into her household and entrusted with her care he then rapes her. Despite the interest of the play for the subject of eunuchs, attention has tended to focus on two particular aspects of the drama: how Terence adapted the play from Menander (though only a few fragments of Menander's original survive), and the issue of the rape, which modern readers have found problematic. With regard to adaptation, for instance, Terence himself confesses in his prologue to the play that he introduced into it two characters (a soldier and a sponger) taken from another of Menander's plays, *The Toady*.[2] On the modern anxiety about the rape, Sander Goldberg, when reviewing the commentary on the play by John Barsby published in 1999, observed that 'The last English commentary on *Eunuchus* was Sidney Ashmore's of 1908, surely one measure of the discomfort the play has produced over the years'.[3] It is indeed notable that the play has been the subject of several commentaries and translations in recent years, a reflection of the increasing interest in Terence rather than *The Eunuch* in particular, witness for instance the publication in 2013 of Wiley-Blackwell's *A Companion to Terence*.[4] As referred to, Barsby published a commentary on the play in 1999, and in 2001 he also published a translation as part of the new Terence volumes in the Loeb Classical Library series.[5] In 2000, Tony Brothers also published a translation and commentary, with Aris and Phillips who have produced a series of translations of Greek and Roman plays.[6] In 2006, another new translation of the plays of Terence, by Peter Brown, was published by Oxford University Press.[7]

In spite of this surge of study, the eunuch aspect of the play still continues to be comparatively neglected. Brown's comments are limited, his focus being on the translations which he hopes will 'restore [Terence's] reputation, and above all ... will encourage actors and directors to put on performances of his plays'.[8] Barsby and Brothers make some interesting comments, but they are scattered and individual. There is no discussion of the real eunuch Dorus as a character in Brothers' Introduction, and Barsby does not consider Dorus' personality in the commentary.[9] Granted, Dorus' appearance on stage is brief and his dialogue minimal, but the lack of attention given to him seems symbolic of a general lack of engagement with a fundamental aspect of the play. Indeed, in 1995 Cynthia Dessen, in an important study foregrounding the eunuch theme of the play, remarked acutely 'modern critics have consistently avoided discussing the eunuch'.[10] For Dessen, the figure of the eunuch is vital for understanding the play, which 'offers the eunuch as a controlling metaphor to mediate conflicting claims of service and desire in social relationships'.[11] She asserts that the eunuch 'As the controlling metaphor ... inspires much of the character development, action, and language in the play'.[12] Unfortunately, her study did not have the impact it should have done; Brothers does not cite it, and while Barsby does he only refers briefly to her ideas.[13] I certainly agree with Dessen that the central subject of the eunuch needs to be addressed, though my own emphasis is on the reality, rather than the metaphor, of the eunuch.[14] This chapter identifies and comments on a range of issues relating to eunuchs that the play features but which modern commentaries have dealt with inadequately. These issues encompass perceptions of eunuchs, the roles they played, their dress and their voice, as well as castration as a form of punishment. A further concern will then be to consider what the play reveals about eunuchs in Rome around 161 BC.

Terence: a life?

On the face of it a lot is known about Terence, as the biographer Suetonius (c. 70–c. 130 AD), more famous for his lives of the Caesars from Julius Caesar to Domitian, composed a life of the playwright, included in his *Lives of the Poets*. The life was preserved in the commentary on the plays of Terence produced by the grammarian Aelius Donatus in the fourth century AD.[15] Suetonius' life indicates that Terence lived from 184–159 BC, recording that he left Rome when he was still twenty-four and a tradition that he died during the consulship of Gnaeus Cornelius Dolabella and Marcus Fulvius Nobilior. Suetonius relates that Publius Terentius Afer was from Carthage in North Africa but became a slave. In Rome, he was in the service of the senator Terentius Lucanus, who educated him and freed him 'because of the young man's talent and good looks' (*ingenium et formam*). Terence is reported to have had close relationships with several elite Roman men, including Scipio Africanus the Younger and his confidant Gaius Laelius. It was rumoured that these two men in fact assisted Terence with his writing, a rumour that the playwright refers to himself in the prologue to his *The Brothers*. Some even suggested that the plays were Scipio's (shades of the debate about the authorship of the plays of Shakespeare). Of Terence's career as a playwright, Suetonius relates that he wrote six comedies, the first of which was *The Girl from Andros*.[16] Terence proved a hit in Rome, his *The Eunuch* being particularly successful: it was performed twice in one day 'and earned more money than any previous comedy of any writer'.[17]

Dramatically, after Terence had published his six plays, and when he was only twenty-four years old, he quit Rome for the Greek world and never came back. The details of his death varied: one report said that he perished at sea when journeying back from Greece (with 108 new plays!), but others asserted that he died in Greece before setting sail, 'having fallen ill from grief and annoyance at losing his baggage, which he had sent on to the ship, and with it the new plays'. Suetonius concludes his life of Terence with a brief description of his appearance ('moderate height, slender and of dark complexion'), what he left behind him (a daughter and extensive gardens on the Appian Way), and an assessment of his reputation as a writer.

Suetonius' 'facts' about Terence and his life are problematic, of course, as he composed the biography over two hundred years after the death of his subject.[18] Thus there was extensive opportunity for information about the life of Terence to become corrupted and elaborated. Suetonius draws on a range of sources dating from the later-second century BC to the first century AD, from the playwright Lucius Afranius to the annalist Fenestella. His most prominent sources are the poet Porcius Licinius (writing at the end of the second century BC, and no lover of Terence), the poet Volcacius (writing in the early-first century BC, and who placed Terence sixth in his top ten of comedy writers), the biographer Cornelius Nepos (writing in the second half of the first century BC), the grammarian Quintus Cosconius (first century BC), and the annalist Fenestella (who spanned the second half of the first century BC and the early-first century AD).[19] Suetonius is quick to observe that details of Terence's biography were contested, and that opinions about his work varied. For instance, in addition to the different reports of his death, some thought that Terence had become a slave when made a prisoner of war though others (Fenestella) rejected this idea as impossible. Fenestella also rejected the notion that Scipio and Laelius favoured Terence because of his 'youthful beauty'. The wealth of Terence at the time of his death was also disputed, Porcius having him reduced to penury. Such problematic evidence led Barsby to declare 'There is very little about Terence's life that can be asserted as a fact'.[20]

In addition to Suetonius' *Life of Terence*, however, there exist the prologues of his plays (in which he addressed the audience about his work through a mouthpiece) as well as the production notices (*didascaliae*) attached to the plays. It seems that the prologues themselves supplied details which were then elaborated in stories about Terence.[21] For instance, in the prologues to *The Self-Tormentor* and *The Brothers*, Terence alludes to the allegations that he was 'assisted' in his writing of the plays.[22] The fact, recorded in the production notes, that *The Mother-in-Law* and *The Brothers* were both performed in 160 BC for the funeral games of Aemilius Paullus (the biological father of Scipio, who was adopted by Cornelius Scipio) no doubt encouraged the belief that Terence was of the 'Scipionic Circle'.[23] So much for the life of Terence; what of the play itself?

The Eunuch: a summary

From Suetonius' account it appears that *The Eunuch* was a very popular and financially rewarding play. It was first performed in April 161 BC on the occasion of the

Megalensian Games. It was adapted from the play of the same title by the Athenian Menander (c. 342–c. 291 BC), a leading figure in the New Comedy of the Hellenistic era, after the death of Alexander the Great in 323 BC. The Latin version of the play is set in Hellenistic Athens: the soldier Thraso alludes to his service with a king, probably a king of the Seleucid dynasty judging by the reference to war elephants of the Indian variety;[24] and Phaedria, the lover of the courtesan Thais, recalls that she wanted a eunuch 'because only queens (*reginae*) have them in their households'.[25] The play pivots around the conceit of a young Athenian gentleman (Chaerea, the younger brother of Phaedria) gaining access to the house of Thais (a non-Athenian courtesan, and lover of Phaedria) by disguising himself as a eunuch (called Dorus, whom Phaedria had given to Thais as a gift) in order to seduce Pamphila (a young girl who has been taken into Thais' household as a slave, gifted to her by another lover, the soldier Thraso).

Following the prologue, the play opens in the street between the houses of Thais and the father of Phaedria and Chaerea. Phaedria is tormented with love for Thais, but Thais asks Phaedria to let her other lover Thraso take precedence with her for a few days, as she wishes to secure from him the gift of a female slave who was actually brought up with her on Rhodes as her sister, so that she can restore the girl to her family in Attica (where she originally hailed from) and thus secure friends for herself. Phaedria reluctantly agrees to her proposal, intending to retreat to the country for two days, but before he does so he instructs his slave Parmeno to give to Thais a gift of two slaves he has bought for her, a slave girl from Ethiopia and a eunuch. Thais enters her house to await the brother of the girl, and Phaedria departs. Then, observed by Parmeno, Gnatho (the sponger who is attached to Thraso) arrives with the girl, called Pamphila, to give her to Thais. After Gnatho has delivered Pamphila and a maid into the house, Chaerea, Phaedria's brother, arrives in haste. Chaerea has become infatuated with a girl whom he saw walking in the street but lost sight of her when he was monopolized by a relation of his father. Parmeno realizes that the girl is Pamphila, and suggests that Chaerea takes the place of the eunuch by putting on his clothes. To Parmeno's shock Chaerea enthusiastically embraces the plan, and they go inside to get ready. Thraso and Gnatho arrive at Thais' house, and Thais comes out to go to supper with them. Before they depart, Parmeno hands over the gifts of the slave girl and the eunuch to Thais, who is impressed by the good looks of 'Dorus'. Thais takes the slaves into the house before emerging again to depart with Thraso, Gnatho having gone ahead. Before she leaves, Thais tells her maid Pythias to await the arrival of Chremes, the brother of Pamphila, and to look after Pamphila. Chremes then arrives, though he is deeply suspicious of why Thais has asked him to come. Pythias instructs Dorias, another maid, to take Chremes to Thais, then Pythias goes into the house.

In the street there arrives Antipho, looking for his friend Chaerea. At that moment Chaerea comes out of Thais' house, exultant with joy. He is delighted to see Antipho and tells him what has happened.[26] Chaerea reports that he was entrusted with Pamphila and inspired by a picture of Jupiter descending on Danae as a shower of golden rain he had sex with her. Chaerea then departs with Antipho to the latter's house, in order to get changed. He also wants to ask Antipho for 'advice about how I can have the girl to myself in future'.[27] Dorias returns to Thais' house, bringing her mistress's jewels, musing on how the arrival of Chremes had put Thraso's nose out of joint (thinking Chremes another lover of Thais) and caused a row. Phaedria also arrives, having been unable to bear not seeing Thais. Their arrival coincides with Pythias rushing out of Thais' house in great alarm, seeking 'Dorus' after the discovery of his rape of Pamphila. She also reports to Phaedria and Dorias that she suspects the 'eunuch' stole something from the house. Phaedria fetches the real Dorus out of his house, but Pythias does not recognize him as the eunuch who entered Thais' house. Dorus tells them about the substitution effected by Parmeno and Chaerea. To protect his brother, Phaedria tells Dorus to change his story, and they go inside, but Pythias and Dorias are not deceived. Dorias advises Pythias to tell Thais nothing of what has happened, only that the eunuch has disappeared. Dorias goes into the house with the jewels, while Pythias intercepts a drunken Chremes. Thais arrives too and explains that she wants to restore Chremes' sister to him but that Thraso has misunderstood the situation and is coming to take Pamphila back. Thais sends Pythias indoors to fetch a little box containing Pamphila's keepsakes. These are then shown to Chremes to prove that the girl is his sister.

At that moment Thraso arrives with Gnatho and other supporters, intending to storm the house and seize Pamphila. Thraso confronts Thais, but is rebuked and repelled by Chremes, despite his initial fear. He tells Thraso that Pamphila is his sister, and departs to fetch the nurse Sophrona in order to prove it. Thais slips inside her house, slamming the door. Thraso and his men depart, Gnatho advising the soldier that Thais will 'soon be back of her own accord, begging your forgiveness'.[28] Thais and Pythias emerge from the house, discussing what happened between the 'eunuch' and Pamphila. Pythias reveals that Chaerea was disguised as Dorus, just as Chaerea returns, still wearing the clothes of the eunuch, having been unable to get changed. Thais talks to him, pretending to think that he is Dorus. It is revealed to him that Pamphila is not a slave but free-born. Thais also reveals that she knows that she is talking to Chaerea. She tells Chaerea that her plans to restore the girl to her family and thus benefit herself have gone awry because of him, but he hopes that there will now be friendship between them. He asserts that he did what he did because he loved Pamphila and asks Thais if he can marry the girl. He and Thais go indoors to await the arrival of Chremes, though Pythias is still mistrustful of Chaerea and wants revenge on Parmeno for suggesting the substitution scheme.

Chremes returns with the nurse, who has recognized the keepsakes of Pamphila. They enter Thais' house, followed by Pythias. She quickly returns to talk to Parmeno, working her revenge. She pretends that the imposter is to be punished for raping a freeborn Athenian, the punishment to take the form usually inflicted on adulterers (probably meaning castration).[29] Pythias declares that Parmeno is being blamed for having devised the deception. Parmeno is desperate to help Chaerea, and so determines to tell the father of Chaerea everything, the old man arriving on stage as Pythias goes back indoors, her work done. Parmeno summarizes what has happened, and in consternation the father dashes into the house of Thais. Pythias re-emerges, revelling in the joke she has played. She confesses her trick to Parmeno, but warns him that he will have to face the wrath of Chaerea and his father, declaring 'This is the reward you've got for that gift you brought us', then she goes back inside.[30] Thraso and Gnatho return, the soldier prepared to submit to Thais. Chaerea emerges from the house in a state of joy, delighted that he is engaged to Pamphila but also that 'Thais has entrusted herself to my father's care and put herself under our guardianship and protection'; he exults 'we're all one household now' (*una est domus*).[31] Parmeno goes to fetch Phaedria to tell him the good news that Thais is now all his. Phaedria joins his brother, sharing his delight, but Thraso still loves Thais and asks Gnatho to secure for him contact with her in the future. Gnatho talks to Phaedria and Chaerea alone, and persuades Phaedria to allow Thraso to continue to see Thais since the soldier will be able to supply her material needs, as well as theirs. Gnatho wins their agreement that he can join their entourage and abandon Thraso. Gnatho reports his success to Thraso, and they all head into Thais' house together.

Eunuchs in *The Eunuch*: aspects and attitudes

Although the real eunuch Dorus only appears briefly in *The Eunuch*, and does not say very much, a wide range of issues relating to eunuchs are dealt with in the play. Their status as slaves, the roles they play in households, their dress, and their sex lives, are all addressed, as well as the attitudes and beliefs that society held about them.

Slavery defines Dorus, as he was bought by Phaedria as a gift for Thais. The status of the eunuch as a gift appears to be symbolized by his very name; Barsby asserts that Dorus is 'probably related to the Greek word' for gift, δῶρον.[32] Phaedria seems pleased with the presents he has acquired for Thais, who had been wanting a eunuch as well as an Ethiopian slave girl. He tells her that he paid 'twenty minae for them both',[33] though later on Parmeno tells Phaedria's father that the eunuch alone cost twenty minae (a third of a talent).[34] It seems that Thais is meant to be impressed with how much Phaedria spent on his gift, though modern commentators disagree about whether this was an expensive gift or whether there is a joke here in that the slaves cost so little.[35] There are indeed remarks made about how unimpressive Dorus is as a specimen (discussed below), but it is possible that he was still expensive as a rare commodity. A eunuch is certainly presented as a luxury item and a status symbol, for it is related by Phaedria that Thais wanted a eunuch because it was queens (or wealthy women in general) who had them in their households.[36]

The association of eunuchs with the service of women is further emphasized in the play by discussion of what roles Dorus is to play in the household. Chaerea is envious of the proximity that the eunuch will have with Pamphila, observing 'He'll always be seeing that exquisite fellow-slave of his ... he'll talk to her, be under the same roof with her, sometimes have his meals with her, and now and then sleep next to her'.[37] Parmeno reinforces these ideas when he proposes (in jest) that Chaerea should take the place of Dorus and elaborates the benefits that will be won: 'you could have your meals with her, be with her, touch her, play games with her, sleep next to her'.[38] Chaerea details the tasks he had to perform as a eunuch, when he tells Antipho what occurred in Thais' house.[39] He was entrusted with the care of Pamphila by Thais, who 'gave orders that no man was to go near her, and told me not to leave her, but to stay in the inner rooms of the house – just me and her'.[40] Some maids remained with the girl, and Chaerea urged them to be quick about preparing a bath for Pamphila. On her return from the bath, Pamphila lay on a couch, and the maids instructed Chaerea to fan her. Barsby and Brothers do not comment on the task of fanning (nor do they remark on the issues of roles and intimacy in general), but it is one that could have strong associations with eunuchs. Neo-Assyrian reliefs depict eunuchs (if one accepts this identification) fanning their masters, and in the Athenian playwright Euripides' *Orestes* (dating to the late-fifth century BC) Helen of Troy's Phrygian slave, probably a eunuch, recalls how he fanned her.[41] Possibly another aspect of the roles eunuchs could play in households is referred to when Parmeno is handing 'Dorus' over to Thais, for he challenges 'Test him on literature, gymnastics, music; I'll prove he's skilled in everything a young gentleman should know'.[42] Perhaps this alludes to the fact that eunuchs (and other slaves) could play a role as teachers, or perhaps Parmeno is just teasing as the 'eunuch' really is 'a young gentleman'.

Primarily then the play emphasizes the strong association and intimacy eunuchs could have with women. The degree of trust that was placed in eunuchs as attendants of women is explicable as it was believed that eunuchs did not experience desire, or if they did, they could not enact it, beliefs also addressed by the play. Chaerea tells Antipho that if he had resisted raping Pamphila then he really would have been a eunuch.[43] When Pythias tells Phaedria that Dorus has raped Pamphila he responds 'You're off your head. How could a eunuch do that?'[44] Pythias confides in Dorias that she had heard that eunuchs 'were really great lovers of women, but that they couldn't manage it'.[45] Brothers does not comment on this concept, while Barsby notes that post-pubertal eunuchs were 'capable of sexual intercourse'.[46] In relation to sex, the play also alludes to the fact that eunuchs themselves could be the object of sexual desire, for both women and men. When Thais sees 'Dorus' for the first time she exclaims how good-looking he is, and Thraso intimates that he would fuck him, even if he wasn't drunk.[47] Of course, they are both really responding to Chaerea, but the fact remains that they think he is a eunuch and that young eunuchs could be considered beautiful and desirable.[48]

Significantly, when Parmeno first suggests the duplication scheme to Chaerea he observes 'you look just right, and you're the right age; you can easily pass yourself off as a eunuch'.[49] This indicates that eunuchs were indeed stereotypically thought of as young and beautiful. Interestingly Brothers translates Parmeno's remark as 'you've got the looks and age to pass as *the* eunuch easily' (my emphasis).[50] However, this is at odds with other descriptions of Dorus. Earlier, Parmeno refers to Dorus disparagingly as 'this decrepit old eunuch' (*decrepito hoc eunucho*),[51] and Chaerea calls him a 'wretched-looking fellow' and an 'effeminate old man' (*illum, obsecro, inhonestum hominem ... senem mulierem*).[52] When Pythias reports that 'Dorus' has made off after the rape and the theft, Phaedria comments 'I'd be very surprised if that wretched specimen (*ille ... ignavos*) could go anywhere very far'.[53] When the real Dorus is brought before Pythias she is perplexed, and declares 'But there's no comparison between this one and the other one. The other one had handsome, gentlemanly looks ... This one's a wrinkled, ancient, spent old man with the colour of a weasel' (*hic est vietus vetus veternosus senex colore mustelino*).[54] This description of the shrivelled fossil of a eunuch has elicited much comment, especially for its reference to a weasel. The late antique grammarian Aelius Donatus, who wrote a commentary on Terence in the fourth century AD, remarked that Terence had here misunderstood the Greek of Menander, who had described the eunuch rather as 'a spotted lizard of an old man', alluding to the freckled skin of eunuchs.[55] Notably, the contrast of the ideal of the beautiful young eunuch with the grim image of a eunuch whom old age has caught up with is also exploited in late antiquity by the poet Claudian in his first invective against Eutropius, for he conjures up an horrific image of the aged Grand Chamberlain, more effective for its juxtaposition with his early love life when he was an object of desire.[56] Of course, Terence (or Menander) is not just reflecting on the transience of beauty or making a point about the nature of eunuchs; for the purposes of the plot it is vital that Dorus and Chaerea can be distinguished from one another so that the deception can be exposed. Thus, it is useful for the eunuch to be old and decrepit so that he can be told apart from the young and handsome Athenian.[57]

Another aspect of the eunuch emphasized by the play is the nature of his attire, though Brothers does not engage with the topic and Barsby only touches on it briefly.[58] The main method Chaerea adopts to disguise himself as the eunuch is to put on his clothes, which are clearly distinctive.[59] When Pythias does not recognize Dorus, Phaedria says this is because 'he was all dressed up in coloured clothes (varia veste exornatus). He looks ugly (foedus) to you now as he hasn't got them on'.[60] There is some evidence that eunuchs did indeed wear distinctive clothing. Barsby notes that Eugraphius in his commentary (written after that of Donatus, and usually dated to the sixth century) records that multicoloured clothing was worn by eunuchs, and that the illustrated manuscripts of Terence's plays do depict Chaearea in clothing of varicoloured stripes.[61] Whether eunuchs did wear such dress in reality requires further reflection, but for the purposes of the play it was certainly useful to have the 'eunuch' easily recognized by his costume, and further it had, of course, great comic potential.[62] One thinks also of how for Antipho Chaerea mimes peeking through the eunuch's fan to gaze on Pamphila.[63] The issue of the dress of the eunuch touches too on issues of status and shame. After he has raped Pamphila and emerged from Thais' house Chaerea is set on getting changed out of the eunuch dress at Antipho's but is thwarted and is still wearing the outfit when he returns and meets Thais.[64] He confesses to Thais that he feels ashamed at the thought of being seen by his father dressed in such a fashion in the street.[65] The humiliation is stressed again when Pythias reports to Parmeno that Chaerea's father did see him in Dorus' clothes in Thais' house.[66] Clearly, as a free male, Chaerea did not want to be seen in the apparel of not just a slave but a castrated slave. Gender concerns are at play here.

While dress of eunuchs, real or imagined, is engaged with by the play, one famous aspect of eunuchs is not obviously addressed: what they sounded like. Ancient sources frequently comment on the higher pitch of the eunuch voice, caused by the lack of growth of the vocal cords after castration.[67] As noted above, Dorus does not have much dialogue anyway, but the characters on stage with him do not comment on what he sounds like. However, perhaps there are some indications that there is awareness of the nature of the eunuch voice. When Chaerea relates to Antipho what happened in Thais' house when he was posing as a eunuch he asserts that when Thais gave him his instructions 'I nodded my agreement (adnuo), staring modestly (modeste) at the floor'.[68] Barsby comments that 'Chaerea submissively refrains from speaking,'[69] but perhaps there is more to it than this; perhaps Chaerea also avoided speaking so that he would not give himself away. Chaerea does have to speak as Dorus later, when he encounters Thais on returning to his street still dressed as the eunuch. As Barsby observes, Chaerea's responses to Thais' questions are 'appropriately ... brief and deferential'.[70] Certainly Dorus' own responses to Phaedria and Pythias are marked by brevity (at one point he just shakes his head) and a desire to co-operate and please, and he obeys Phaedria's command that he should lie. Thus, the play uses key characteristics to define eunuch speech and behaviour rather than dwelling on the sound of the voice, as far as can be judged. It is, however, perfectly possible that the actors did adopt a higher voice when playing a eunuch or playing a character pretending to be a eunuch. As with eunuch dress, this could have had significant comic potential, as when Chaerea is interviewed by Thais as Dorus but then switches to his true identity when she reveals that she knows who he is.[71] There is one clear indication, however, that gendered speech could also be used to signify the acting of a eunuch. Barsby notes that when talking to Antipho Chaerea uses the 'predominantly female oath' of '*pol*' ('by Pollux') and suggests this may signify that at this point he is 'imitating the voice and gestures of a eunuch'.[72] Alternatively, perhaps it is being suggested that Chaerea has become feminized by impersonating a eunuch, or it is reinforcing the contrast between the impotent eunuch and the potent man, for this is where Chaerea exclaims that he really would have been a eunuch if he hadn't raped Pamphila. Dessen also comments on the characteristics of Chaerea's speech after he emerges from the house after the rape, and asserts that these 'suggest fluctuating ego boundaries as masculine and feminine qualities merge'.[73] Interestingly J.N. Adams notes that when Chaerea describes for Antipho what happened in the house he mentions that one of the maids addressed him '"Hey you"' ('"*heus tu*"'); Adams comments '*Heus* was inappropriate in the mouth of a member of the weaker sex, but here the *ancilla* is addressing someone of no distinct sex. The addressee is so sexually inferior that she can adopt a masculine role towards him'.[74]

The view that eunuchs were feminized beings was certainly a common one, and is touched on elsewhere, when Chaerea dismisses Dorus as an 'effeminate old man' (*senem mulierem*), which Barsby declares is 'a bold phrase'.[75] It forms a package of negative opinions about eunuchs in the play. Perhaps there is more to the dismissal of Dorus as a decrepit old man than his actual age. Eunuchs and old men could be associated because of the perception that they lacked sex drive. Further, the attribute of lethargy (*veternosus*) associated with Dorus was one commonly ascribed to elderly eunuchs, according to the commentary of Donatus, as Barsby notes.[76] There is also the view that eunuchs constituted monsters, because of their altered physical natures and their perceived characters.[77] This is expressed when Phaedria questions Dorus after the discovery of the rape of Pamphila, for he calls the eunuch 'you monster of a man' (*monstrum hominis*).[78] Barsby observes that this is 'with reference to his behaviour as well as to his state as a eunuch',[79] but the emphasis should be on the latter as by this stage there is already doubt that Dorus did commit the rape as Pythias did not recognize him as the eunuch who came to Thais' house.[80] Pythias' earlier castigations of Dorus as accursed (*scelerosum*), villainous (*scelus*), wicked (*impium*) and poisonous (*venefico*) are in the immediate aftermath of her discovery of the rape, but may also refer to his condition as a eunuch.[81] Pythias' accusation that Dorus also stole something from the house (a matter never referred to again) may also allude to the stereotypical views of eunuchs as greedy and untrustworthy, rather than just being a straightforward remark.[82] Thus, the play sets beside the ideal of the beautiful and youthful eunuch (possession of which reflected elevated social status) the less attractive perceptions of eunuchs as debased and corrupt. In regard to this Dessen observes that Dorus and Chaerea 'express the double social construct of the eunuch. Old and young, ugly and attractive, impotent yet oversexed, physically powerless yet mentally powerful – the eunuch holds all these contradictions within himself, but for this very reason he could never be enacted as one character'.[83]

The final aspect of eunuchs touched on by the play is the utilization of castration as punishment for sex crimes.[84] Although Pythias is both allusive and elusive about the exact nature of the penalty that is to befall Chaerea (and maybe she is deliberately so in order to heighten the anxiety of Parmeno), it seems likely that castration is meant; in Plautus' *The Braggart Soldier* (a Roman play written decades before Terence's *The Eunuch*) the soldier is threatened with castration for committing adultery.[85] Pythias coyly and teasingly remarks that Chremes is 'threatening to do to him what's usually done to adulterers. I've never seen it done, and wouldn't want to either',[86] and Parmeno is suitably horrified. The prospect of Chaerea, who has posed as a eunuch, being turned into a real eunuch would certainly be very fitting.

Rome and *The Eunuch*

Thus, Terence's *The Eunuch* conveys much about aspects of and attitudes to eunuchs. The question that remains is, does the play tell us anything about eunuchs in Rome itself rather than in Hellenistic Athens and the Hellenistic east more broadly? More directly put, did Rome have direct experience of eunuchs by 161 BC? In his survey of eunuch slaves and freedmen in the Greco-Roman world, Guyot opined that Terence's experience of eunuchs was just literary.[87] Dessen disagrees with this, since there would have been in Rome eunuchs associated with the Great Mother, the Galli.[88] As seen in the previous chapter, the cult was installed in Rome in 204 BC, and a temple for the Great Mother established on the Palatine Hill in 191 BC. Indeed, Dessen notes the fact that *The Eunuch* was performed at the Megalensian Games, part of the festivities for the Great Mother in April, might indicate that its subject matter was chosen in relation to the presence in Rome of eunuchs as part of the cult of the goddess.[89] The association of the play with self-castrating devotees of the Great Mother is appealingly neat, but as discussed in the previous chapter, there is debate about whether the Galli did come with the goddess to Rome and whether they were self-castrates in actuality. It may be that the Galli keep Terence's experience of eunuchs purely literary.

There could, however, have been other ways that Romans were familiar with eunuchs. It is possible that eunuchs came to Rome as part of embassies from the Hellenistic world. Delegates of the Seleucid king Antiochus IV Epiphanes (175–164 BC) were in Rome in 173 BC, including leading minister Apollonius.[90] Antiochus himself was a hostage in Rome for about ten years, then his nephew Demetrius replaced him prior to 178/7 BC, before escaping in 162 BC.⁹¹ In 171 BC, there were both Ptolemaic and Seleucid ambassadors in Rome.⁹² In 168 BC, there was in Rome an audience with Ptolemaic emissaries.⁹³ It is also of note that one of the chief ministers of Ptolemy VI Philometor (186–145 BC) was a eunuch, Eulaeus (he was regent from 176 BC when Cleopatra I died, and he disappears in 169 BC).⁹⁴

Further, could there have been eunuch slaves in Rome by 161 BC? Barsby asserts that '[t]here is no evidence that they were familiar figures of everyday life in T[erence]'s day; in the context of the play the eunuch is an extravagant and exotic gift'.⁹⁵ Conversely, Lynn Roller avows the commonness of eunuch slaves in Rome ('eunuchs ... were regularly used as slaves and must have been familiar to most people'), citing Terence's *The Eunuch* itself, which she says 'certainly seems to take their presence for granted'.⁹⁶ The problem is one of evidence; until the late republican and early imperial period there is not definite proof of eunuch slaves in Rome. However, this does not mean that they were not there. Given the political and cultural context of the period is it not possible that eunuch slaves were indeed already being consumed in Rome? Barsby himself emphasizes that the period was marked by the growing Hellenization of Rome and Rome's increasing contact with, and presence in, the Hellenistic east.⁹⁷ Matthew Leigh's *Comedy and the Rise of Rome*, published in 2004, seeks to 'investigate the comedies of Plautus and Terence in the light of Roman history and Roman history in the light of Plautus and Terence', noting that 'The crucial phenomenon of the age of Plautus and Terence is the rise of Rome from regional power to effective master of the Mediterranean world'.⁹⁸ Leigh's work is part of a wider 'attempt to think historically about Roman comedy', exemplified also by John Starks' chapter '*opera in bello, in otio, in negotio*: Terence and Rome in the 160s BCE', in the 2013 *A Companion to Terence*.⁹⁹ For instance, Starks discusses Roman relations with the Seleucids, jumping off from the reference in *The Eunuch* to Thraso serving the king and his exchange with the commander of the elephants, and he considers the career of Aemilius Paullus as part of the military and political activities of the 'great men' of Terence's day, culminating in his triumph in Rome in 167 BC for the defeat of Macedon in the Third Macedonian War, at the Battle of Pydna (168 BC).¹⁰⁰ Starks declares that 'Paullus' most substantial legacy was a stream of Macedonian wealth so great that all Roman citizens were relieved of direct taxation for the next 125 years'.¹⁰¹ Barsby also comments on the flood of slaves into Rome after the conquest of Macedon.¹⁰² In this context of the increasing power, wealth and Hellenization of Rome and her eastern expansion and presence it is surely not impossible that eunuch slaves were in Rome by 161 BC; indeed, it is likely that they were. Terence's *The Eunuch* may thus speak directly to actual Roman experience.

Conclusion

For the history of the eunuch in the Roman Empire Terence's *The Eunuch* is a text of great interest and importance. It is the first extant Latin text to use the term 'eunuch', and although adapted from a Greek play and set in Hellenistic Athens it laid before an audience in Rome a wealth of ideas about eunuchs. It conveys both assumptions about the roles played by eunuchs and perceptions of them; eunuchs were presented as expensive slaves suitable for attendance on women, and as feminized and impotent. The fact that the play was successful and popular is suggestive of Roman interest in the subject. By the middle of the second century BC Romans were clearly familiar with the concept of the eunuch, and possibly with the reality too.

3

Of Seed and Spring: Eunuch Slaves of Imperial Rome

Introduction

Terence's *The Eunuch* reveals that Romans were familiar with the concept of eunuchs as slaves by at least 161 BC. Whether actual eunuch slaves were part of the landscape of Rome during the Republic is hard to know because of the lack of definite evidence, but with the establishment of the Principate under Augustus (27 BC–AD 14) the fog begins to clear. Texts relating to the first two Roman dynasties, the 'Julio-Claudians' (27 BC–68 AD) and the Flavians (69–96), regularly refer to their possession of eunuchs (as well as the possession of eunuchs by the elite in general). Two imperial eunuch slaves of the first century AD are particularly prominent in the historical record: Sporus and Earinus.[1] Sporus is especially associated with Nero (54–68), though he was deployed by subsequent emperors too. Earinus was owned by Domitian (81–96), ironically an emperor celebrated for his law banning castration.[2] In both cases, the sexual nature of the relationship of the eunuch with his emperor is emphasized by the sources. This chapter analyses the cases of Sporus and Earinus in depth, considering what texts record about them, the nature of these texts, modern discussion of their cases, and what Sporus and Earinus reveal more generally about eunuchs and the roles they played in Roman society in the first century AD. To this end, the chapter also explores the wider context of the presence of eunuchs in Rome, for it is vital not to treat Sporus and Earinus in isolation. It emerges that already in the first century of the Roman empire eunuchs were seen as a significant imperial accoutrement and speak of the nature and perception of Roman imperial power.

Sporus: the texts

The major text for Sporus is Suetonius' biography of Nero in his *Lives of the Caesars*, which dates to early in the reign of the Emperor Hadrian (117–138). Suetonius worked for Hadrian as his minister for correspondence (*ab epistulis*), and had previously served as minister in charge of the imperial libraries in Rome (*a bibliothecis*) and minister in charge of the imperial archives (*a studiis*). Sporus is first mentioned in a chapter dealing with Nero's sexual activities.[3] Suetonius relates that the emperor had the boy Sporus castrated and 'attempted to transform him into a woman' (in muliebrem naturam transfigurare conatus).[4] Nero married him 'with dowry and bridal veil and all due ceremony', after which escorted by a large crowd of people he took him home, where he treated him as if he was his wife.[5] It is clear that this event is situated in Greece (which Nero toured in 66–67), for Suetonius adds that Sporus (dressed as an empress and transported in a litter) accompanied Nero 'around the meeting places and markets (*conventus mercatusque*) of Greece and later, at Rome, around the Sigillaria', the emperor kissing the eunuch affectionately and repeatedly.[6] In the context of the 'wedding' of Nero and Sporus, Suetonius also records a contemporary witticism still current in his day, 'that it would have been a good thing for humanity if Nero's father had taken such a wife' (i.e. that Nero had never been born). The subsequent episodes featuring Sporus relate to the fall and suicide of Nero. One of the portents foretelling the emperor's end was the eunuch giving him on New Year's Day, while Nero was taking the auspices, a ring engraved with the rape of Prosperina; this could be interpreted as ominous as she had been abducted by Pluto, the god of the underworld.[7] When the emperor fled Rome for the villa of his freedman Phaon, Sporus was one of the four attendants who went with him.[8] As Nero contemplated suicide in the villa he exhorted Sporus to begin to lament and to wail.[9]

Other texts supplement the details supplied by Suetonius. Plutarch (who died in 126) refers to Sporus in his *Life of Galba*, reporting that after the death of Nero Nymphidius (his Praetorian Prefect who had imperial aspirations) took possession of Sporus (having sent for him while Nero's body was still burning on the pyre), and treated him like his consort and called him Poppaea (the name of Nero's wife, who had died in 65; notably Suetonius himself does not record the Poppaea association).[10] There are several references to Sporus in the *Roman History* of Cassius Dio, more in fact than in any other text.[11] Cassius Dio was a Greek from Nicaea in Bithynia who had a distinguished senatorial career in the late second and early third centuries and who is especially associated with the Severan dynasty (193–235).[12] Unfortunately, his eighty-book history does not survive intact, and for the Books which featured Sporus (62 and 63) one has to depend on excerpts and epitomes produced in the time of the Byzantine Empire. Nevertheless, these expand on what Suetonius related. The castration and feminization of Sporus (identified as a freedman whom Nero called by this name) is presented in terms of Nero pining for his dead wife Sabina (Poppaea), for Sporus resembled her.[13] Again, the emperor is said to treat the eunuch like a wife, even marrying him, and it is noted that the Romans (and others) celebrated the wedding publicly. It is recorded that the wedding occurred in Greece, Tigellinus (the Praetorian Prefect of Nero) giving the 'bride' away.[14] In their celebration of the marriage, the Greeks are said to have uttered 'all the customary good wishes, even to the extent of praying that legitimate children might be born to them'.[15] The fact that Nero married Sporus in Greece is given as another reason why the emperor called the eunuch Sabina, for it was in Greece that he had married the real Sabina. Once again, Nero is said to have treated Sporus as his wife, the eunuch also being called 'lady and empress and mistress'.[16] A certain Calvia Crispinilla, a socially distinguished woman, was charged with the care of the eunuch, as well as his wardrobe.[17] The quip that if only Nero's father had had such a wife is recorded again. The story then also turns to the fall and suicide of Nero. It is noted that he fled with Sporus as well as Phaon and Epaphroditus to Phaon's estate.[18] Some of the Byzantine texts assert that Nero also wanted his companions to kill themselves and when they refused he wished to kill Sporus but was unable to do so.[19] Like Plutarch, Cassius Dio touches on what happened to Sporus after the death of Nero. Like Nymphidius, the Emperor Otho (69) associated with Sporus too, as well as other favourites of Nero.[20] Finally, when Vitellius (69) succeeded Otho, as part of the gladiatorial contests he was organizing he planned to have Sporus put on stage 'in the rôle of a maiden being ravished', but the eunuch 'would not endure the shame and committed suicide'.[21]

The story of Sporus and Nero thus became a staple of later histories of Rome, being found also, for instance, in Aurelius Victor's *De Caesaribus*, a brief history of the rulers of Rome from Augustus to Constantius II (337–361), completed in 360. Aurelius Victor observes that at the end 'Nero was deserted on all sides except by a eunuch, whom he had once tried to make into a woman by surgery' (desertus undique nisi ab spadone, quem quondam exsectum formare in mulierem tentaverat).[22] Yet it was not just biographies and histories that mentioned Sporus, for he is alluded to in a discourse *On Beauty* by the orator Dio Chrysostom.[23] Dio was a Greek from Prusa who lived from the mid-first century to the early-second century AD. He studied and worked in Rome, though he found himself exiled by the Emperor Domitian. It seems that he wrote *On Beauty* while Domitian was alive, for he observes that everyone wishes Nero was still alive (the implication being that the present emperor is worse).[24] In the discourse he develops the proposition that masculine beauty is dying out while feminine beauty is increasingly appreciated. He observes that the Persians thought feminine beauty superior to masculine beauty, witness their making eunuchs of beautiful males, motivated by lust.[25] This brings him to Nero and Sporus. He asserts 'we all know how in our time that he not only castrated the youth whom he loved, but also changed his name for a woman's', and that the eunuch 'actually wore his hair parted, young women attended him whenever he went for a walk, he wore women's clothes, and was forced to do everything else a woman does in the same way'.[26] It is added that Nero even offered to reward with honours and money anyone who managed to make Sporus a woman.[27] The fate of Nero is once again alluded to in connection with the eunuch, though with a rather different slant in this case. Dio observes that it was Nero's treatment of Sporus that caused his downfall, for the eunuch was angry and revealed the emperor's intentions to his entourage, who revolted and forced him to commit suicide.[28]

Earinus: the texts

Unlike Sporus, who was written about after his death and mainly in biographies and histories, Earinus was written about while he was alive, and in poetry. The two Latin poets who wrote about him were Statius and Martial, authors strongly associated with Domitian and his reign.[29] Earinus is the subject of one of Statius' poems in his collection of occasional poetry, the *Silvae*, while he features in several of Martial's epigrams.[30] Statius was born in the mid-first century AD (between 45 and the early 50s) in Naples, a city of Greek origin which continued to be a centre for Greek culture. His father was a poet and also a teacher, and Statius had a thorough grounding in Greek literature. He went on to become a celebrated poet himself, publishing his epic poem the *Thebaid* at the beginning of the 90s. His *Silvae* was published in three instalments: Books 1–3 in 93, Book 4 in 95, and Book 5 after his death. Having moved to Rome he returned home to Naples, and it is thought that he had died by the time of Domitian's own death in 96. Martial was born slightly earlier than Statius, and briefly outlived him too (c. 38–c. 104). He was from Bilbilis in Spain, and, like Statius, he returned home again after a successful career in Rome. He came to the imperial city in the mid 60s and went on to establish himself as a celebrated poet. He published his epigrams from 86 onwards, resulting in a collection of twelve books. Book 9, which includes his six epigrams on Earinus, appeared in 94. Also, like Statius, Martial had particular connections with Domitian and his court, and returned to Spain only a few years after the death of the emperor. Of the two authors, the work of Statius is the more significant for the eunuch,[31] for not only does the 106 line poem commemorate the dedication of Earinus' hair at the temple of Asclepius at Pergamum (where the poem says he came from) it also reflects on the eunuch's history and relationship with the emperor.[32] Further, the preface to Book 3 (dedicated to Statius' friend Pollius Felix, a retired local government dignitary of Puteoli and Naples)[33] declares that the eunuch himself (identified as a freedman – *libertus* – of Domitian) had asked Statius 'to dedicate in verse the hair that he was sending to Pergamene Asclepius along with a jewelled box and mirror'.[34] Such is the length and the interest of the poem that it is worth providing a full translation:[35]

The Hair of Flavius Earinus
Go, locks, and speed, I pray, across a favouring sea, go,
lying softly on the garlanded gold, go! Gentle Cytherea shall
give you fair voyage and calm the south winds. Perhaps she
will take you from the perilous craft and lead you over the
waters in her shell.
  Accept, son of Phoebus, the lauded tresses that Caesar's
lad presents to you; accept them gladly and show them
to your unshorn father. Let him compare them how they
shine, and long think they are from his brother Lyaeus.
Perhaps he will in turn sever the beauty of his own unfailing
hair and place it for you enclosed in other gold.
  Pergamus, more fortunate by far than pine-clad Ida,
though Ida pride herself on the cloud of a holy rape –
for surely she gave the High Ones him [Ganymede] at whom Juno
ever looks askance, recoiling from his hand and refusing
the nectar: but you have the gods' favour, specially
commended by your fair nurseling. You sent to Latium a
servant whom Ausonian Jupiter [Domitian] and Roman Juno [Domitia
    Longina] alike
regard with kindly brow, both approving; and not without
the will of the gods is the lord of the earth so well pleased.

'Tis said that as golden Venus was driving her soft swans
on her way from Eryx' height to the Idalian groves, she entered
the Pergamene dwelling where the gentle god [Asclepius] is
present to aid the sick, their greatest helper, staying the
hastening Fates and brooding over his health-giving serpent.
She sees a boy, shining with star of peerless beauty, as
he plays before the altar of the very god. Deceived at first
for a little while by the sudden apparition, she fancies him
one of her many sons; but he had no bow and no shades
springing from his radiant shoulders. She wonders at his
boyish grace, gazing at his face and hair, and 'Shall you go,'
she says, 'to the Ausonian towers neglected of Venus? Shall
you bear a mean dwelling and common yoke of servitude?
Far be it! I shall give this beauty the master it deserves. Come
now with me, boy, come! I shall fly you through
the stars in my winged chariot to the leader, a gift of gifts.
No common bondage shall await you: you are destined to
serve dignity in the Palace (*Palatino*). Nothing so sweet in all the
world have I seen or given birth to, I own it. The boys of
Latmos [Endymion] and Sangaros [Attis] shall freely yield to you, and he that a
vain image in a fountain and a barren love consumed [Narcissus]. The
cerulean Naiad would have preferred you [to Hylas] and seized your
urn in a stronger grip to drag you down. Boy, you are beyond
them all; more beautiful he only to whom you shall be
given.'
    So saying, she lifts him by her side through the light
air and tells him to take a seat in the swan-drawn car. In a
trice, there are the Latian Hills and the home of ancient
Evander, that Germanicus [Domitian], renowned father of the world,
adorns with new masonry and levels with the topmost stars.
Then it becomes the goddess' closer care how best to
arrange his locks, what dress is meet to kindle his rosy
countenance, what gold is worthiest on his fingers, what on
his neck. Well she knew the leader's celestial eyes; she herself
had joined the marriage torches and given him his
bride with bounteous hand.[36] So she decks the hair, so
drapes him with Tyrian raiment, gives him beams of her
own fire. Former favourites retire, the flocks of servitors;
he bears first cups to the great leader, weighty murrhine
and crystal, with a hand more fair. New grace enhances the
wine.
    Boy dear to the High Ones, chosen to sip first the reverenced
nectar and touch so often that mighty hand, the
hand the Getae seek to know, and Persians, Armenians, Indians
to touch! O born under a lucky star, greatly have

the gods favoured you. Once too your country's god himself
left lofty Pergamus to cross the sea, lest the first down mar
your shining cheeks and darken your beauty's joys. None
other was entrusted with the power to soften the boy, but
with silent skill Phoebus' son [Asclepius] gently bade this body leave
its sex (*de sexu transire*), not shocked by any gash. Yet Cytherea is gnawed
by worry, fearing the boy might suffer. Not yet had the
leader's noble clemency begun to keep male children
intact from birth. Now 'tis forbidden to mollify sex (*frangere sexum*) and
change manhood; rejoicing Nature sees only those she
created. No more under an evil law do slave mothers fear
to bear the burden of sons.

    You too, had you been born later, would now be a young
man, with shaded cheeks and limbs full-grown, stronger.
More gifts than one you would have sent rejoicing to
Phoebus' shrine: as it is, let only the tress sail to your native shores.
The Paphian used to steep it in plenteous perfume,
a kindly Grace used to comb it. The severed lock of purple
Nisus will yield to it, and that which proud Achilles was
keeping for Sperchis. When first it was decreed to crop
your snow-white brow and unveil your gleaming shoulders,
the tender winged ones with their Paphian mother
run up and make ready your tresses and place a silken robe
over your breast. Then they cut the lock with linked arrows
and place it on gold and gems. Mother Cytherea herself
catches it as it falls and anoints it once again with her secret
essences. Then spoke a boy from the throng who had
chanced to carry in upturned hands the mirror resplendent
with jewelled gold: 'Let us give this too. No gift will be
more welcome to his native temple; it will be more potent (*potentius*)
than the gold itself. Only do you fix a look therein and leave
your face there forever.' So he spoke and shut in the mirror,
catching the likeness.

    But the peerless boy, stretching his hands to the stars:
'In return for these gifts, gentlest guardian of mankind,
may you long wish, if I have so deserved, to renew our
lord's youth and preserve him for the world. The stars ask
this with me, and the waters and the lands. Let him, I pray,
pass through Ilian and Pylian years both, rejoicing that his
own home and the Tarpeian temple grow old along with
himself.'

    So he spoke, and Pergamus wondered that the altars
shook.

Three of Martial's epigrams also deal with the dedication of the eunuch's hair (9.16, 17 and 36), while the other three (9.11, 12, and 13) concern Earinus' name itself.[37] Earinus derives from the Greek word for spring (ἔαρ), and in 9.11 Martial makes the most of the sweet and sensuous associations of that season:

> Name born together with violets and roses, by
> which is named the best part of the year, which has
> the flavour of Hybla and Attic flowers and the
> fragrance of the proud bird's [the Phoenix] nest: name sweeter
> than blessed nectar, by which Cybele's boy [Attis] and he
> who mixes the Thunderer's cups [Ganymede] would rather be
> called, to which, if you sound it in the Parrhasian
> palace, Venuses and Cupids answer: that noble,
> soft (*molle*), and dainty (*delicatum*) name I wished to put into polished verse.[38]

The epigram then concludes with Martial commenting on the fact that although Greek poets could make the eunuch's name fit their metre it was not possible for Latin poets to do so.[39] Epigram 9.12 (or 13 – the order is debated)[40] also dwells on the associations of the name with spring, but also the honour due to it:

> You have a name that designates a tender season
> of the year, when Cecropian bees raid the short-lived
> spring (*ver*), a name that deserved to be painted
> with Acidalian reed, that Cytherea rejoices to
> inscribe with her own needle, a name to be traced in
> letters made of Erythraean pearls or the Heliad's
> jewel [amber] thumb-rubbed, one that cranes might raise
> to the stars with scribal feather, one that belongs only
> in Caesar's house.[41]

Epigram 9.13 (or 12) is in the form of a riddle about the name of the eunuch, and is spoken by Earinus himself:

> If autumn gave me my name, I should be Oporinos;
> if the shivering stars of winter, Chimerinos; named
> from summer's season you would call me Therinos;
> who is he to whom springtime (*verna*) gave a name?[42]

The remainder of the epigrams deal with the dedication of the hair of Earinus to Asclepius, the initial two alluding to the gift of the mirror as well. The first (9.16) refers again to the derivation of Earinus' name:

> The boy, his master's favourite (*gratissimus*) in all the palace,
> whose name means spring time (*tempora verna*), has dedicated his
> mirror, beauty's counsellor, and his sweet locks (*dulcisque capillos*) as
> hallowed offerings to the god of Pergamum. Happy
> the land appraised by such a gift! It would not
> rather possess the hair of Ganymede.[43]

The second (9.17) addresses Asclepius himself:

> Revered grandson of Latona, who with gentle herbs
> prevail upon the threads and short distaffs of the
> Fates, your boy has sent you from Latium's city
> these locks his master praised, a vow fulfilled. And
> to his dedicated tresses he has added the bright disk
> whose judgement made his blooming countenance
> secure. Do you preserve his youthful loveliness (*iuvenale decus*); let
> him be no less comely now that his hair is short
> than when it was long.[44]

The final epigram (9.36) conjures up another scenario, imagining Ganymede's reaction to the action of Earinus:[45]

> The Phrygian boy, famed joy of the other Jupiter,
> had seen the Ausonian page (*ministrum*) with his hair newly
> shorn: 'What your Caesar (look!) has allowed his
> young man (*ephebo*), please allow yours, greatest of rulers,'
> said he. 'Already the first down lies hidden by my
> long locks; already your Juno laughs at me and calls
> me a man.' To him said the Heavenly Father:
> 'Sweetest (*dulcissime*) boy, not I but the case itself denies you
> what you ask. My Caesar has a thousand pages (*mille ministros*) like
> yourself; the vast palace has scarcely room for so
> many star-like youths. But if shorn hair gives you a
> manly look (*vultus . . . viriles*), whom else shall I have to mix the nectar?'[46]

One further text mentions Earinus too, the history of Cassius Dio.[47] Earinus surfaces in observations about how Domitian hated the friends of Vespasian (69–79) and Titus (78–81) because he hated his father and brother. It is remarked that although Domitian 'himself loved a certain eunuch Earinius he nevertheless . . . forbade for anyone in the Roman empire to be castrated henceforth' with the object of insulting Titus' memory, for he too had been a keen eunuch enthusiast.[48]

Interpretations of Sporus and Earinus

Thus, on the face of it, there are two famous court eunuchs in the first century AD; for instance, in the eighteenth century Alexander Pope satirized Lord Hervey as Sporus,[49] and there exist blog posts on Sporus and Earinus titled 'The eunuch that would be empress' and 'Earinus: a Roman civil rights activist?'[50] However, there is a risk of becoming carried away in reconstructing the reality of the lives and histories of these two eunuchs: the nature and status of the texts that deal with Sporus and Earinus must be borne in mind. It is instructive to consider here an examination of both eunuchs in

Caroline Vout's *Power and Eroticism in Imperial Rome*.[51] Vout declares that her study is 'neither social history nor straight historical narrative';[52] rather, it is an examination of why stories about the sex lives of the emperors were recorded and what they reveal about imperial power, for 'Sex is a way to talk about *imperium*'.[53] Essentially, the truth or otherwise of the stories is not relevant, she is concerned with the 'construction of feelings, as opposed to facts'.[54] In her study, Sporus and Earinus merit a chapter each, that on Sporus focusing on the issue of male-male marriage and that on Earinus being concerned with the poets themselves.[55] In the case of Sporus, she notes that the main texts (she specifies Suetonius and Cassius Dio) are not contemporary with the eunuch,[56] and she remarks too that Tacitus – the Roman historian (*c.* 56–*c.* 120) who wrote about the Julio-Claudians from Tiberius to Nero in his *Annals* – 'is strangely silent' about the marriage of Sporus and Nero.[57] She also observes that stories about Sporus and Nero are usually either dismissed as sensationalist or are taken to prove the existence of marriage between males in Rome, both of which approaches 'collude in the premise that History must be true'. For her, the figure of Sporus is bound up with the casting of Nero as a tyrannical ruler, so the story of the eunuch 'cannot be divorced from its context' (meaning the literary context as well as the context of Hadrian's reign, when Suetonius was writing). She argues that the right question to ask is 'what Sporus *means* in, and for, Neronian *and* Hadrianic Rome'.[58] She draws attention to Suetonius' placing Sporus in the context of the Sigillaria, 'this being both a period of time and an area of the city devoted to selling gifts for the Saturnalia, a festival that promoted the temporary swapping of social hierarchies ... Norms were reinforced and celebrated by way of controlled inversion.'[59] The figure of Sporus, then, would emphasize the negative image of Nero as an emperor overturning the natural order, whose reign made the inversions of the Saturnalia the norm. Vout further perceives that Sporus' imitation of Poppaea is sinister for she 'is already a symbol of tyranny and ... this tyranny informs his own characterisation in the sources'.[60] Although acting the wife of Nero, Sporus cannot provide the emperor with an heir, just as Poppaea had been unable to do. Further, Poppaea's construction as eastern and non-Roman (like Cleopatra) is echoed by the eunuch too. Ultimately, Vout concludes 'It is against this broader background of image-making that we have to contextualise Sporus: a world in which Romans are cast as aliens, men as women, and the emperor as tyrant'.[61]

Regarding Earinus, Vout emphasizes that the main texts for him (Statius and Martial) are contemporary with the reign of Domitian,[62] and thus predate the stories about Sporus recorded in Suetonius and Cassius Dio. Statius and Martial therefore offer images of Domitian not informed by the tyrannical tradition that developed about him, but ostensibly they praise him (though there may be implied criticism).[63] She argues that for the poets, writing about Earinus and Domitian is a way of writing about Domitian but also a way of writing about themselves as poets seeking patronage, for 'the power differential inherent within the relationship, and the sacrifice and devotion implied by the act of castration, offer them a drawing board on which to map their own complicated feelings in writing about and for an imperial patron'.[64] She observes that the Greekness of Earinus is also of relevance to them as poets, for it raises the issue of their use of Greek literary models, such as Callimachus' *Lock of Berenice*,[65] as well as the influence of Latin authors inspired by Greek models, especially Catullus.[66]

Ultimately, Statius and Martial, through Earinus, are exploring issues of identity in imperial Rome.[67] It is appreciated that Statius (as well as Martial) can be cast as an outsider, commenting on the nature of Roman culture (and society) in a period of transformation.[68]

However, despite her avowal that she is not writing social history, and despite the fact that eunuchs per se are not her concern, Vout touches on several interesting topics relating to eunuchs in early imperial Rome. She observes the changing political context, with the traditional elite losing their authority and freedmen and eunuchs gaining influence through the imperial court.[69] She considers Domitian's anti-castration legislation.[70] Further, she cannot help addressing the vital topic of Roman attitudes to, and perceptions of, eunuchs. For instance, on the question of the sexual desirability of eunuchs she notes that in Rome 'eunuchs are not normally praised with the same palette as pretty boys', but are usually presented in negative terms 'as hideously made-up and flabby, deformed even', and that if they are considered in sexual terms 'it is usually as objects of derision and disgust rather than as objects of desire'.[71] She contemplates the suggestion of John Garthwaite that Martial's struggle with naming Earinus is also a reflection of his discomfort with the fact of the eunuch's castration (and notably Martial does not make explicit that Earinus is a eunuch,[72] although Statius addresses it head on).[73] It terms of the gender identity of Earinus as a eunuch she notes that in Statius he is feminized, as the feminine gifts of the mirror and the jewelled box underline,[74] and also reflected by the fact that one of Statius' models, Callimachus' *Lock of Berenice*, concerns the dedication of hair by the Hellenistic queen for the salvation of her husband-brother Ptolemy III (246–221 BC), Earinus thus becoming wife and empress.[75] Earinus is arrested in youth too, unable to attain manhood;[76] he may be able to engage in the Greek ritual of hair dedication, but he cannot participate in the Roman custom of dedicating the first beard.[77] Nonetheless, Vout's literary sensibilities are uppermost and she eschews history as truth and fact. For instance, in her final conclusion she asserts 'Whatever [Earinus'] actual status within Domitian's court, the complexities of his written personae are a crucial component of the patronage dynamic'.[78]

However, not everyone is so chary of attempting to reconstruct the reality of the histories of the eunuchs. Vout herself alludes to 'a brave attempt to extricate "real" Earinus from the poems' by Christer Henriksén.[79] He asserts that Earinus came to Rome from Pergamum when he was a boy at a time when Domitian was already emperor (as Statius presents the youth as destined to serve the emperor), that he was castrated when he arrived, then acted as cupbearer and attendant for Domitian. As for the castration, he is of the view that this was probably done by compression rather than excision, as Statius declares that it entailed no wound, and thus Earinus must still have been 'a little boy ... but [not] younger than three'.[80] He accepts that Earinus was indeed beautiful, and that there was a sexual aspect to his relationship with the emperor. He dates the clipping of the hair to 94 (between the publication dates of Books 8 and 9 of Martial), an act he had to be given permission for, and which signified his transition from youth (as Statius notes that if he had not been castrated he could also have sent clippings from his beard), but perhaps also his manumission (long hair was a marker of slaves and they cut it when they were freed, though they could cut it earlier if allowed). He notes, however, that neither Statius nor Martial refer to the freeing of Earinus in their poems so concludes that he must have been freed after their composition.[81] He interprets the mirror as an insignia of Earinus' boyhood, which he was leaving behind. He estimates that the eunuch was at least sixteen at the time of the dedication in 94, so if he was castrated in 81 he would have been at least three years old then; ultimately he observes that 'it is most likely that he was castrated in 81–83 at the age of 3–5, and that he was 16–18 years old at the time of the hair offering in 94'.[82] He accepts that Earinus had some influence with Domitian, given that he was the emperor's favourite, assuming that it was the eunuch's desire to have his hair cut and be freed. The hair was then sent to Asclepius' temple in Pergamum in a jewelled gold box ('the usual practice...though the use of such a precious box was restricted to the imperial family and the very rich'), and was 'consecrated to the god, presumably with some dedicatory verse accompanying it'.[83] Returning to the question of Earinus' manumission (when he took the name Flavius Earinus, possibly with the praenomen Titus), he notes that this was done at an unusually early stage (a minimum age in law was thirty, and reasons for early manumission did not apply to imperial slaves), and asserts that this 'demonstrates that Domitian's affection for him was sincere'.[84] Henriksén also devotes particular attention to why Earinus chose to dedicate his hair at the temple of Asclepius, declaring that 'there must surely be an explanation better established in reality' than the 'fictitious and mythological explanation' given by Statius.[85] He finds a reason for Earinus' devotion to Asclepius (the god of medicine) in the fact of the medical operation he had undergone to make him a eunuch. He observes that the cachet of the temple at Pergamum had risen by the end of the first century AD, eclipsing the shrine at Epidaurus, noting the suggestions of Christian Habicht in *Die Inschriften des Asklepieions* that the very poems of Statius and Martial 'played a part in the process by divulging the connection with the imperial palace', and that Domitian's own promotion of Pergamene Asclepius reflects the influence of Earinus himself.[86] On the issue of the influence of the eunuch with the emperor he also notes John Sullivan's suggestion that Earinus induced (either actively or passively) Domitian's decision to ban castration, which he accepts was introduced after Earinus had been castrated.[87] He accepts, too, that Earinus requested the poem, though this amounted to an indirect request by the emperor.[88]

As for Sporus, the work of Edward Champlin and David Woods is noteworthy for attempting to reconstruct the reality of his life.[89] Champlin appears to take the sources for Sporus at face value.[90] He asserts that Nero married the eunuch in 66 or 67, that he was with the emperor at his death, and that Nero 'turned [to Sporus] to begin the ritual lamentation before he took his own life'.[91] He notes that Suetonius does not acknowledge the Sabina factor in his account of the creation of Sporus, and opines 'For once, Dio's narrative is superior', observing that Dio Chrysostom supports Cassius Dio's story. He also accepts the stories about Sporus' life after the death of Nero, being the partner of Nymphidius and probably also Otho, and committing suicide under Vitellius when required to play 'in the title role of the Rape of Persephone'.[92] He suggests that at the time of his death, Sporus had not yet reached the age of twenty. Champlin does ponder the relationship further, remarking that Nero's love is not for Sporus but the dead Sabina. Considering the situation from the eunuch's point of view he wonders 'Did he

... grow to love the man who had castrated him, who forced him to dress and act like a woman, and who longed to transform him surgically from male to female', and notes 'No one thought to record his feelings'.[93] For his part, he finds it telling that Sporus fled when Nero asked him to kill himself too, and that Dio Chrysostom indicates that the eunuch betrayed the emperor. Further, he comments on Sporus' gift of the ring to Nero that 'It was a singularly ill-timed gesture ... and, unlike the many other portents of the coming disaster, this gesture was premeditated'.[94] He connects the image on the ring to how Nero had treated Sporus as well as to the role the eunuch was intended to play on stage under Vitellius. Regarding the motivations for Nero creating and transforming Sporus, he suggests that these might have included 'sexual pleasure (rather unlikely ...) and the chance to upset the moral majority (highly probable)'.[95] He emphasizes, however, that Nero was having fun. In his view '[t]he wedding ... must have played as farce'; the parading of the eunuch dressed as empress at the Sigillaria indicates that 'Sporus ... was a joke for Saturnalia'; the very selection of Sporus' name for the castrated freedman by Nero himself (as asserted by Cassius Dio) is a witticism, for in Greek the name 'means "seed," "semen."'[96]

David Woods' response to the story of Nero and Sporus is rather different, as he questions the sources but reconstructs a different reality for the relationship between the emperor and his eunuch. Like Champlin he questions the love (or lust) aspect of the relationship, though he accepts that Sporus did resemble Poppaea Sabina. He then suggests that Nero would have thought the physical similarity between his dead wife and the eunuch meant that they were related, and since (he argues) that the emperor thought Poppaea was of imperial blood (as she had persuaded him that she was a daughter of Tiberius) that would have meant that he could have considered that Sporus too was related to the imperial family (a grandchild of Tiberius). Thus, he believes that there was a political reason for Nero's treatment of Sporus, a potential dynastic rival: he castrated him to prevent him having children and humiliated him sexually, as he is reported to have done to other male rivals. He finds support for this argument also in the attitude of Nymphidius and Otho to Sporus, which he says makes sense if they thought that Sporus 'represented some form of continuation with the Julio-Claudian dynasty quite apart from his non-legal "marriage" to Nero, that is, that he was of imperial descent himself'.[97] He argues that the name Sporus itself is significant (for 'spurius' was an adjective derived from a Sabine word which was used in a derogatory fashion to mean a mother's illegitimate child), and suggests that Nero was alluding to this (or less likely that the name given to the eunuch was Spurius and that it was not spelt correctly in the Greek source drawn on by Suetonius and Cassius Dio). Like Champlin, Woods detects hostility in Sporus' attitude to Nero (the gift of the ominous ring; the story of the betrayal), and argues that if the eunuch did indeed flee with the emperor in 68 (and the story is not just fiction) this was more to do with self-preservation than love.

The approaches of Henriksén, Champlin and Woods are certainly not without their problems, especially with regard to the question of how hard texts can be pressed to yield 'facts'. In the case of Earinus, the main sources are poems, and the most significant one, Statius', is ostensibly panegyrical with a strong mythological character.[98] Can it really be assumed that Domitian must already have been emperor when Earinus arrived in Rome as Venus says he was destined to serve the Roman ruler? It is perfectly possible that Earinus was already in the service of Domitian before the death of Titus in 81 (or even in the service of Titus himself). It does seem that Earinus must have been castrated in Rome under Domitian (for surely if this had not been the case Statius would have been only too happy to declare it), but again, how far can one press the assertion that the castration conducted by Asclepius left no wound? Does this really mean that Earinus was eunuchized by the compression method, or is this poetic licence? And even if the compression argument is accepted, are Henriksén's assertions about the age at which Earinus was operated on convincing? There is no reason to believe that he was castrated at such a young age, or as soon as he had arrived in Rome. Surely one has to allow time for the bond between emperor and slave to form before the decision is taken to prolong the youthful beauty of the boy by castrating him? On the question of Earinus' role at the court, can one really be sure that he was a cupbearer to the emperor? Perhaps this function is no more than a deliberate allusion to Ganymede's relationship with Jupiter.[99] If he had been a cupbearer, would he not have dedicated a cup to Asclepius rather than a mirror as a vestige of his past life if he was marking his transition from youth? On the dating of the hair clipping, Henriksén is guided by the publication dates of Martial's Books 8 and 9 of epigrams, yet Martial must have written the poems earlier than 94, for Statius indicates there was a delay between the dedication of the hair and the writing of his poem, which was published in 93. Thus, there remains chronological uncertainty not just about when Earinus came to Rome and when he was castrated but about when the dedication rite occurred, though it must have taken place in 93 at the latest. Henriksén must be right, however, to argue that Earinus had a particular reason to dedicate his hair to Asclepius, but it seems odd that he ascribes this to the medical operation (which happened after the boy had left Pergamum), for Statius' indication that there was a pre-existing link with the god's temple in his home city is surely significant.

As for Sporus, the key issue is the lateness of the evidence, mainly biography and history. Champlin takes a very positivist view of the stories about Sporus, which is however clarified by his discussion of the main sources elsewhere in his book but not referred to in the specific consideration of the eunuch. He is right to emphasize the significance of Dio Chrysostom's evidence for Sporus (the earliest surviving mention of the eunuch), but he also makes the case for the lost histories of Pliny the Elder and Cluvius Rufus, especially the latter who was close to Nero and his court, and was on the tour of Greece. Nevertheless, he is too ready to accept every detail. Can one really be sure that Sporus did give the emperor a ring with the image of the rape of Prosperina on it? The fact that the gift reflects on the eunuch's own treatment by Nero as well as foreshadowing his intended treatment at the hands of Vitellius seems all too neat, and one suspects that a literary construct is at work. He accepts without blinking the story that Sporus fled from Nero, even though it is only recorded in one of the Byzantine epitomes of Cassius Dio. Clearly Champlin's focus is Nero himself, rather than his eunuch, as is evident in his quest to consider what motivated the emperor to act in the way he did. This results in Nero creating the joke of Sporus (his name, the wedding, the trip to the Sigillaria), but one can still ask, is this image of Nero any more accurate than the one created by the later authors, the one of Nero as tyrant? Woods himself is indebted to Champlin's vision of Nero and Sporus (detecting hostility in the relationship rather than love) but pursues his own path to understand it in political terms. The main problem with his interpretation is that it rests on his hypothesis that Poppaea had convinced Nero that she was a daughter of Tiberius. For this there is no evidence, and without it Woods' theories remain just that. There are also other elements to his argument that fail to convince. He himself poses the question that if Sporus really was a dynastic threat why didn't Nero just kill him? His answer is that Sporus was a lesser threat than other male rivals, and that Nero might have killed him in the end anyway. One also has to wonder that if Nero did think Sporus was of imperial blood and this was known by others why was this not recorded by the sources. As for the fact that Nymphidius and Otho supposedly showed an interest in Sporus, this can be understood without recourse to proposing that the eunuch was of imperial blood; he could have been seen as a vital symbol of Nero's regime (an 'imperial mascot', as Vout memorably has it),[100] or a status symbol in his own right, or they might have had personal reasons for their interest in him (it is alleged that Nymphidius took Sporus as his consort, and Otho had been married to Poppaea too), or perhaps the sources are suggesting that these figures were tyrannical also. Regarding the name Sporus, no doubt its selection is important, but since the argument that the eunuch was an illegitimate member of the dynasty fails to convince, if it was intended to evoke his status as a bastard this must have been for other reasons.

It is clear, then, that attempting to reconstruct the reality of these eunuch lives has its pitfalls. Conversely, however, the approach taken by Vout can also be interrogated. On the matter of texts about Sporus she places most emphasis on Suetonius (naturally, given her interest in Hadrian), but obscures the fact that the biographer does not even mention the supposed resemblance between Sporus and Poppaea, which is a key element in her analysis. She draws mainly on Cassius Dio (though she could have deployed Dio Chrysostom and Plutarch here), which surely raises questions about the meaning of the relationship between Sporus and Nero for Severan Rome (or Byzantine Constantinople) but this is not on her radar. Indeed, she could have made more use of Dio Chrysostom's reference to Nero and Sporus, for this is the earliest surviving testimony about the relationship and also dates to the reign of Domitian, so may be informed by reaction to the relationship between that emperor and Earinus. As noted, she emphasizes that Tacitus does not mention Sporus, which perhaps creates an impression of uncertainty about the existence of the eunuch, but it needs to be remembered that Tacitus' account of the reign of Nero in his *Annals* (Books 13–16) is incomplete, for the manuscript breaks off in 66 with the suicide of Thrasea Paetus, before having reached Nero's visit to Greece.[101] True, Tacitus' *Histories* (which begins in 69 when Galba was already emperor) does not mention Sporus, but perhaps this is not so surprising, and he does refer to eunuchs in general joining Vitellius.[102] With regard to her exploration of the poems about Earinus there are some elements that she does not comment on, especially in Statius' poem. For instance, John Garthwaite observes that the mention of Venus' conch shell serves to recall 'the goddess' birth in the ocean from the severed genitals of Uranos, and her own journey across the waters in the *concha*'.[103] She does not refer to the fact that Earinus' prayer beseeches youth for the emperor, which is significant given the eunuch's status as a being who will remain preternaturally youthful, making his request entirely fitting. She minimizes the fact of Earinus' own patronage of the poem, throwing the focus back on to the emperor. The association of Earinus with the series of famed doomed pretty boys (Endymion, Attis, Narcissus, Hylas) merited further comment, especially given her own remarks about 'powerful *pueri*' and the 'impact of dying beautiful and young'.[104] Garthwaite reads these allusions (as well as those to Nisus and Achilles) in a sinister light,[105] but the trade-off of tragic early death for blessed eternal youth is recognized and valued (one thinks, for instance, of the modern immortal James Dean).

There are also some particular peculiarities in Vout's discussion. One is her lack of engagement with the model of Alexander the Great and his eunuch lover Bagoas. Vout relegates this pair to a footnote, and, Martial-like, she does not even name the famous eunuch.[106] Her justification for doing so is that this case is different to Roman sexual attitudes to eunuchs (she asserts that eunuchs are generally not seen as attractive or sexual, and if they are 'it is usually as objects of derision and disgust rather than as objects of desire'[107]) as it is placed in a Macedonian context. In the first instance, one can argue that there was Roman resonance in the story of Alexander and his eunuch, for probably in the first century AD (most likely either in the reign of Claudius or that of Vespasian) Quintus Curtius Rufus wrote in Latin a history of the famous Macedonian monarch (indeed, the only life of Alexander in Latin), who is depicted as a ruler who becomes corrupted and sinks into tyranny.[108] There is no doubt that the history is meant to speak to a Roman audience about imperial rule. Further, even if Vout is right that Roman sexual attitudes to eunuchs are different (and this point can be debated, as shown below), in Curtius there is much more to the relationship between Alexander and Bagoas than just sex, for the real issue is the question of the influence that the eunuch wields over the king. When Bagoas entered the service of Alexander (having previously been the lover of the Persian king Darius III) he wins pardon for the chiliarch Nabarzanes, but more significantly secures the destruction of the Persian Orxines, the satrap of Persis.[109] Orxines is depicted as an innocent victim of the eunuch, whose enmity he had earned by not paying him court. Orxines had refused to do so, declaring 'he paid his respects to the king's friends, not his whores [*non scorta*], and that it was not the Persian custom to regard as men those who allowed themselves to be sexually used as women'.[110] Thus, Bagoas hatches a plot to destroy Orxines, using his influence with Alexander gained though his sexual services. Eventually Orxines is condemned to death for having plundered the tomb of Cyrus the Great. Going to his death, Orxines rebukes Bagoas to his face, declaring 'I had heard that women were once rulers in Asia but this really is something new – a *eunuch* as king!'[111] Curtius then remarks on the deterioration of Alexander's character, observing that 'At the end of his life, his degeneration from his former self was so complete that, though earlier possessed of unassailable self-control, he followed a male whore's judgement to give some men kingdoms and deprive others of their lives.'[112] Thus, Curtius' presentation of Alexander and Bagoas is of relevance for Vout's examination of sex and *imperium*. Curtius certainly dwells on the sexual attractiveness of Bagoas. He describes him as 'an exceptionally good-looking eunuch in the very flower of his youth' (specie singulari spado atque in ipso flore pueritate).[113] He emphasizes that it is the eunuch's sexual hold over the king which gives him his power, asserting for instance that he would slander

Orxines whilst having sex with Alexander.[114] Plutarch also mentions the relationship between Bagoas and Alexander in his biography of the Macedonian king, 'likely ... published between 110 and 115'.[115] Describing an incident where Alexander attended singing and dancing contests in which his favourite Bagoas was awarded the prize, he reports that the eunuch then came and sat beside the king, at which the Macedonians applauded and urged Alexander to kiss the winner, which the king did, embracing and kissing the eunuch tenderly.[116] One is put in mind of Nero kissing Sporus in public. It is telling also that the advocate and rhetorician Quintilian, in his *Training in Oratory* which was written under Domitian, refers to a Bagoas in his discussion of shifting ideals of male beauty in relation to oratorical tastes of the late-first century AD. An advocate of virility, he remarks:

> When the masters of sculpture and painting desired to carve or paint forms of ideal beauty, they never fell into the error of taking some Bagoas or Megabyzus as models, but rightly selected the well-known Doryphorus, equally adapted either for the fields of war or for the wrestling school, and other warlike and athletic youths as types of physical beauty. Shall we then, who are endeavouring to mould the ideal orator, equip eloquence not with weapons but with timbrels?[117]

As noted above, Vout opines that in Roman thought eunuchs were not usually considered as attractive and desirable (and thus Earinus constitutes an unusual case). She asserts that they were typically 'described as hideously made up and flabby, deformed even' and that if they were 'thought of as sexual' (for they were generally considered 'non-sexual' and thus 'suitable companions for wives and children') 'it is usually as objects of derision and disgust rather than as objects of desire'.[118] Such assertions, however, can be questioned.[119] In the first place, it appears that Vout (and also Carole Newlands) equates the Galli with eunuchs in general, but there are important distinctions. Galli were seen as males who had chosen to have themselves castrated (typically after they had attained puberty), and who in their devotion to the Great Mother dressed and acted in a female fashion. This is rather different to the run of the mill slaves who were eunuchs, for they were castrated before puberty and against their will, and there can be the impression that beauty was a factor in considering which slaves to castrate. The Roman abhorrence of self-castration must be appreciated, for it adds to the revulsion they could feel for the Galli. Thus, one needs to distinguish between Roman comments on Galli in particular and on eunuchs in general. Further, one needs to recognize that there could be competing views of eunuchs: as has already been seen in Terence's *The Eunuch* there co-exist the ideal of the beautiful youthful eunuch that one would want to fuck and the disappointing specimen of Dorus. Certainly some of Martial's other epigrams, for instance, comment in a mocking way on the sexual activities of eunuchs (such as the cases of the Gallus Baeticus who has a taste for cunnilingus rather than cock-sucking, and the eunuch Dindymus involved in a threesome with an old man and an unsatisfied girl Aegle),[120] but this does not mean that his (and Statius') celebration of the sensuous beauty of Earinus is necessarily unusual: all would depend on the aims of the writer. Clearly, Sporus is presented as beautiful and desirable too, as is Quintus Curtius Rufus' Bagoas. Other beautiful and desirable eunuchs will be met below.

Sporus and Earinus: a view

Thus, both the approach that seeks truth and reality and that which eschews these and seeks concepts and feelings can have their problems and limitations, as well as their virtues. It is evident that one must be sensitive to the literary and historical context of the texts and not just accept them at face value, while also recognizing that they can convey hard detail both about the existence of eunuchs in Rome and how they were perceived. It is important also to pose questions about specific eunuchs (as well as eunuchs in general) even if definite answers cannot be provided, for recognition of the issues at stake is as important as the establishment of 'reality'. The cases of the eunuchs Sporus and Earinus present different problems in relation to the evidence, for on the one hand there are sources (mostly historiographical and biographical) which were written later than the events they refer to and are written in a tradition that denigrates Nero as a tyrant, and on the other there are mainly contemporary poems which are ostensibly celebrating the eunuch and his emperor. As a first step one can surely agree that both Sporus and Earinus existed; the fact of the latter was not in question, but a question mark had hung over the actuality of the former. One can argue that the lack of mention of Sporus by Tacitus is not necessarily problematic, as the relevant part of the account of the reign of Nero has been lost (or was never completed) and the lack of mention of his story in the narrative of the reigns of Galba, Otho and Vitellius could be explained by Tacitus thinking that it was not important enough to include. More positively, it should be emphasized that Dio Chrysostom's oration *On Beauty* is the earliest text to refer to Sporus (probably written in the reign of Domitian, so at least fourteen years after the death of Nero), and Dio himself stresses that he can remember Nero and his reign.[121] Further, even though Suetonius and Cassius Dio were writing later they were able to draw on texts written by contemporaries, not the least of which was the narrative by Cluvius Rufus, an intimate of the court of Nero who had accompanied the emperor on his tour of Greece.[122] In addition, Plutarch was old enough to remember Nero's visit to Greece since he was a young man at the time.[123] As for Suetonius himself, although he was born just after the death of Nero his father had served under Otho and was a source of information for his son.[124] At the very least, then, Sporus and Earinus serve as examples of the taste for eunuchs at the Roman imperial court in the first century AD. Both were slaves who were subsequently freed (though Suetonius implies that Sporus was castrated after being freed), and both were castrated at the wishes of their imperial masters. Their slave status also seems to be reflected by their names, which were given to them for the meanings they had (Earinus evoking spring and thus youth and beauty; Sporus, meaning 'seed', is discussed further below). Both seem to have had sexual relationships with their masters, Earinus being depicted as Ganymede to Domitian's Jupiter, and Sporus more unusually as the 'wife' of the emperor (and thus he is presented more as a transvestite or even a transsexual).

How much further the texts can be pressed for hard detail varies in each case. It seems likely that Nero and Sporus did go through some through some form of ceremonial union in Greece and that the eunuch did dress up as a woman, probably recalling Poppaea Sabina.[125] Again, it is likely that Sporus was with Nero when he fled and at his death, together with other freedmen in the emperor's entourage. One should be more cautious of accepting that the eunuch gave Nero a present of a ring featuring an image of the rape of Prosperina and that he betrayed the emperor, given that these are such loaded stories. Regarding his career after the death of Nero, it is possible that he was taken up and utilized by other men for a variety of reasons (as a luxury item, as an imperial symbol, as a sexual partner, as a notorious figure), but there is also the possibility that such stories exist to reflect on the character of the men who aspired to succeed Nero. Regarding the origins of Sporus, some assume that he was Greek but this is not definite.[126] It is probable that he was still youthful when he was castrated, given his feminine appearance, so Champlin's suggestion that he was not yet twenty at the time of his death is fair.[127] There remains the issue of his name. To read it as a joke is a possibility but seems rather forced. Presumably it could be read in a more positive way, suggesting plant life.[128]

Regarding Earinus, it seems clear that he was originally from Pergamum and had come to Rome as a slave and ended up in the service of Domitian. How he had become a slave in the first place is not revealed, but if the discovery of him as a child by Venus at the temple of Asclepius has any germ of reality, perhaps he had been abandoned there.[129] The dedication of his hair at the temple of Asclepius merits a more compelling explanation than the fact that he had been castrated (probably by compression, though excision cannot be ruled out), and one answer could be that he did have a pre-existing connection with the temple. As for his role at court, it evidently entailed proximity to the emperor, but whether he fulfilled the actual function of cupbearer must be open to question as it serves the purpose of emphasizing the parallel with Ganymede and Jupiter. Regarding issues of chronology, the most that can be said for certain is that at the time of the hair clipping (before 93) Earinus was of an age when he would be expected also to dedicate his first beard. Something of the social status of the eunuch is conveyed too by the fact the he was the patron of Statius' poem, which should not be neglected in favour of its imperial aspect, important though that is. Unlike Vout, Newlands emphasizes the role of Earinus as patron and recipient of the poem and imagines his reaction to it.[130]

The texts, however, are equally valuable for what they reveal about concepts of, and attitudes to, eunuchs in Roman society. Key, of course, is gender. The view of eunuchs as feminized beings is particularly evident, especially in the case of Sporus, who looks like a woman, dresses like a woman, and is virtually turned into a woman.[131] Earinus is described in terms of softness, delicacy and luxury, and the gift of the mirror evokes femininity, as well as beauty in general. This is the beauty of male youth, too, as the comparison of Earinus with Ganymede, Attis, Endymion, Narcissus, Hylas and Cupid reflects. Statius conveys the idea that Earinus will be eternally youthful, unable to grow a beard. In this respect, Martial seems to offer a rather different take on Earinus, for he depicts Ganymede as the one trapped in eternal youth, unable to cut his hair and become an ephebe like Domitian's eunuch. It is important to appreciate that different authors could deploy different concepts in relation to the same subject matter, highlighting that contrasting perceptions could co-exist. In relation to gender, the presentation of both eunuchs as sexual partners for older men indicates their passivity too. As Vout notes, however, passivity could equate to power, and the texts convey something of the Roman realization of the power and status eunuchs could achieve.

Although Sporus can be seen as a passive victim, the interest shown in him by Nymphidius, Otho and Vitellius suggests something of his significance and worth as a symbol of imperial status. The role he plays as empress also indicates that his status and position were of consequence. Power is more forcibly conveyed in the case of Earinus. Not only is he close to the Roman emperor (and the empress), this intimacy is the envy of nations. Further, his dedication to Pergamum is seen as an honour, and when he speaks his prayer for Domitian the altars in his home city shake. Another aspect of eunuchs addressed explicitly by Statius is castration, and he communicates the Roman distaste for the operation. While he asserts that the castration of Earinus, effected by Asclepius, caused no pain and left no scar, he leaves one in no doubt that this was not normally the case. Not only does Venus' anxiety convey this, but his description of castration as the shattering of sex (*frangere sexum*) creates a strong impact.[132] The fact that Domitian himself had outlawed castration (as Statius makes explicit in the poem, being quick to assert that the law came into being after the castration of Earinus himself) reflects this Roman attitude too. The action of the emperor is reported amongst his innovations in Suetonius' *Life of Domitian*, which includes the detail that in addition the price of eunuchs still in the possession of slave dealers was capped.[133] Such was the approval of the measure of an emperor who was subsequently denigrated as a tyrant that he still earned praise for it, witness the remarks of the later Roman historian Ammianus Marcellinus, writing at the end of the fourth century AD: 'I take pleasure in praising Domitian of old, for although, unlike his father and his brother, he drenched the memory of his name with indelible detestation, yet he won distinction by a most highly approved law, by which he had under heavy penalties forbidden anyone within the bounds of the Roman jurisdiction to geld a boy (castraret quisquam puerum)'.[134] As Ammianus makes explicit, this ban related to males within the Roman Empire, so eunuchs could be created and supplied from beyond the frontiers of Rome, as later Roman legislation reveals (see Chapter 5). The concern was clearly about the castration of citizens and other inhabitants of the empire, rather than about castration per se. Suetonius' assertion that the prices of eunuchs were capped too indicates that they were an expensive luxury item. Martial also refers to Domitian's law in other of his epigrams, including two in Book Nine itself.[135] It is notable that in these two (especially 9.7: Domitian recently 'succoured tender youths to stop cruel lust from sterilizing males')[136] he presents the practice of castrating boys as being associated with lust, reinforcing the impression that eunuchs in Roman society could be considered sexually desirable.

The wider picture

Thus, the cases of Sporus and Earinus reveal something of the reality of eunuchs at the imperial court, as well as of the attitudes to and conceptions of eunuchs that existed in Roman society. However, it is vital not to see Sporus and Earinus in isolation, for there is a much wider picture of eunuchs in the imperial service in the first century AD (and in elite Roman society in general), as the survey of Guyot has shown.[137] Both Suetonius and Tacitus refer to other eunuchs in the service of emperors of the first century AD, as far back as Tiberius. Domitian's brother, Titus, was known for his taste for eunuchs; commenting on Titus' reputation for lustfulness Suetonius records that he owned a troop of eunuchs and was considered a second Nero.[138] Likewise, Tacitus records that during his progress to Rome, Vitellius was joined by herds of eunuchs (*spadonum gregibus*) and all the other particular personnel of Nero's court.[139] More concrete examples are provided too. Nero had a eunuch Pelago, who in 62 oversaw the men sent to kill Plautus (the great-grandson of Tiberius) 'like a king's minion over his satellites' (quasi satellitibus ministrum regium).[140] Claudius had a eunuch food-taster named Halotus, who also served Nero and ended up being protected by Galba and made a procurator.[141] Claudius' freedman Posides was a eunuch, and at the emperor's British triumph he was awarded the decoration of a headless spear.[142] Tacitus records the existence of the eunuch Lygdus during the reign of Tiberius, serving in the household of the emperor's son Drusus, noting that Lygdus' 'years and looks had won him the affection of his master and a prominent place among his attendants'.[143] The focus of the narrative is the role of the eunuch in the death of Drusus in 23, supposedly by poisoning in a plot devised by the Praetorian Prefect Sejanus, who is said to have seduced Lygdus.[144] Pliny the Elder in his *Natural History* refers to a eunuch who was owned by Sejanus and sold after his fall and execution in 31; this is the eunuch Paezon (specified as just one of the eunuchs owned by Sejanus, so he had more) who was bought by Clutorius Priscus for 50,000,000 sesterces, payment 'for lust and not for beauty' (quam libidinis, non formae) says Pliny.[145] Pliny also mentions in the context of the reign of Claudius a wealthy eunuch of Thessalian origin, a freedman of Marcus Aeserninus, who chose to enrol himself among the freedmen of the emperor to obtain power.[146] Scathing about the rewards that could be gained from influence at court or in government, Plutarch includes amongst these sitting in front seats amongst eunuchs and concubines (παρ' εὐνούχοις καὶ παλλακαῖς).[147]

Other authors refer to the existence of eunuch slaves in Roman society more generally, though one of these associates eunuchs with one of Octavian's right hand man, Maecenas. Quintilian in his *Training in Oratory* alludes to 'slave-dealers who castrate boys in order to increase the attractions of their beauty', asserting that '[a] false resemblance to the female sex may in itself delight lust', reminding one of Dio Chrysostom's comment on the vogue for male feminine beauty.[148] Writing in the reign of Nero, Petronius in his *Satyricon* endows the wealthy freedman Trimalchio with two eunuch attendants, one of them holding a silver chamber pot and the other counting balls that fell to the ground during a game played by their master.[149] Also from the reign of Nero, Seneca the Younger in one of his *Moral Letters to Lucilius* refers to Octavian's friend and ally Maecenas (he died in 8 BC) as having had two eunuchs; writing on style as a mirror of character, Seneca says of Maecenas 'this was the man who, at the very time when the state was embroiled in civil strife, when the city was in difficulties and under martial law, was attended in public by two eunuchs – both of them more men than himself' (Hunc esse, cui tunc maxime civilibus bellis strepemtibus et sollicita urbe et armata comitatus hic fuerit in publico spadones duo, magis tamen viri quam ipse).[150] This letter of Seneca, if credited, indicates that there were indeed already eunuchs in Rome by the time of the late Republic. Even if its historical accuracy is doubted it is clear that there were eunuch slaves owned by the elite and members of the imperial family during the reign of Tiberius, and given that this fact is treated as a matter of course it is likely that such a situation predated Tiberius' coming to power in AD 14.

Conclusion

By the first century AD, eunuch slaves were a fact of life in Rome. Sporus and Earinus just happen to be very famous examples, their lives intertwined with infamous emperors and conveyed in arresting stories and texts. They speak vividly of the existence of eunuchs as part of the slave trade, and of the roles played by them in Roman society and the views that (elite male) Roman society held of them. They were expensive and beautiful possessions, who could develop close relations with their masters and even acquire status and authority. Such facts anticipate the institutionalized court eunuchs of the later Roman Empire.[151] It is telling that when in AD 399 the poet Claudian reviews the life, career and power of the eunuch Eutropius, Grand Chamberlain of the emperor Arcadius, he compares him to Chrysogonus (freedman of Sulla) and Narcissus (freedman of Claudius).[152] Although neither of these men was a eunuch – as far as is known – their assumed power through their relationship with their masters spoke to a late Roman audience used to court eunuchs. Equally telling is that the Christian poet Prudentius at the start of the fifth century imagines Antinous, the famous doomed lover of the Emperor Hadrian, as a castrate.[153] Eunuch slaves who served the Roman emperors had a long history before the later Roman Empire, stretching as far back it seems as the time of Augustus himself.

4

Born Eunuchs:
The Case of Favorinus of Arles

Introduction

It would be a common – and entirely understandable – assumption that eunuchs had to be created. However, this is not necessarily the case, as words ascribed to Jesus Christ usefully reveal. In the Gospel of Matthew, when Jesus has been quizzed about his views on divorce and marriage by the Pharisees, and his disciples wonder if it is better not to marry, he responds by declaring 'For there are eunuchs who have been born so from their mother's womb, and there are eunuchs who have been made eunuchs by men, and there are eunuchs who have made themselves eunuchs for the sake of the kingdom of Heaven' (Matthew 19.12).[1] Thus, the term eunuch could be employed not just in its literal sense (to denote a castrated male), but also in a metaphorical sense (to denote someone who embraced celibacy), and additionally to denote those whose physical nature rendered them distinct (and akin to a man-made eunuch). In recent years, the term 'intersex' has been used to describe such people, those born sexually ambiguous, but in antiquity the phrase 'born eunuch' could be utilized.[2] This chapter focuses primarily on the case of one such born eunuch from the Roman Empire, the Gallic sophist Favorinus of Arles. Favorinus existed from the late-first to the mid-second centuries AD (c. 80–c. 160), thus living through the reign of the Roman Emperor Hadrian with whom he is especially associated.[3] A comparative wealth of information survives relating to him which also provides insight into how such individuals could be perceived, making Favorinus an important subject for study. Further, he also serves as an unusual example of a eunuch who was both free and of significant social standing, which compounds his historical interest. This chapter establishes what is known of his life and career, then explores what his case reveals about attitudes towards people in the Roman Empire who would now be categorized as intersex. Favorinus provides an arresting example of such a person from antiquity, and his case deserves to be much more widely known.

Life and career of Favorinus

Favorinus was certainly a very celebrated – even controversial – figure in his own day. Stephen Beall has described him as 'a prototypical popstar: effeminate in voice and appearance, elaborately dressed, morally suspect, superlatively clever, profoundly incongruous',[4] while Walter Stevenson, noting the modern day example of Michael Jackson, has suggested that the androgyny of eunuchs in general may have contributed to their appeal.[5] Maud Gleason raises the figure of another modern icon to compare Favorinus with: that 'arch-poseur of another age', Oscar Wilde.[6] Favorinus was certainly wildly popular as a performer in Rome and the Greek world; he had statues erected to him, and associated with the great and the good of his day, including other intellectuals as well as the Roman emperor himself. Naturally, he had his rivals and critics too – notably the sophist Polemo – a further sign of his cultural and social pre-eminence.[7] It is no surprise then that a host of texts mention him, such as the *Attic Nights* of his 'disciple' Aulus Gellius, a miscellany of reports about the cultural life of his time, and so named after the fact that he began the collection of these intellectual notes on winter nights spent on an estate in Attica. Favorinus was a prolific author himself, and some of his writings survive, such as his oration on his statue at Corinth. Particularly useful, however, for supplying an account of Favorinus' life and career, and a foundation from which to explore it further, is the chapter on Favorinus in Philostratus' *Lives of the Sophists*.[8] Philostratus was himself a sophist of the late-second to mid-third centuries AD, and published his *Lives* of previous greats in the 230s.[9] His entry on Favorinus runs as follows:

> Favorinus the philosopher, no less than Dio [of Prusa], was proclaimed a sophist by the charm and beauty of his eloquence. He came from the Gauls of the West, from the city of Arelate which is situated on the river Rhone. He was born double-sexed, a hermaphrodite (διφυὴς δὲ ἐτέχθη καὶ ἀνδρόθηλυς), and this was plainly shown in his appearance; for even when he grew old he had no beard; it was evident too from his voice which sounded thin, shrill, and high-pitched, with the modulations that nature bestows on eunuchs also. Yet he was so ardent in love that he was actually charged with adultery by a man of consular rank. Though he quarrelled with the Emperor Hadrian, he suffered no ill consequences. Hence he used to say in the ambiguous style of an oracle, that there were in the story of his life these three paradoxes: Though he was a Gaul he led the life of a Hellene; a eunuch, he had been tried for adultery; he had quarrelled with an Emperor and was still alive. But this must rather be set down to the credit of Hadrian, seeing that, though he was Emperor, he disagreed on terms of equality with one whom it was in his power to put to death. For a prince is really superior if he controls his anger 'When he is wrath with a lesser man,' and 'Mighty is the anger of Zeus-nurtured kings,' if only it be kept in check by reason. Those who endeavour to guide and amend the morals of princes would do well to add this saying to the sentiments expressed by the poets.
>
> He was appointed high priest, whereupon he appealed to the established usage of his birthplace, pleading that, according to the laws on such matters, he was exempt from public services because he was a philosopher. But when he saw that the Emperor intended to vote against him on the ground that he was not a philosopher, he forestalled him in the following way. 'O Emperor,' he cried, 'I have had a dream of which you ought to be informed. My teacher Dio appeared to me,

and with respect to this suit admonished and reminded me that we come into the world not for ourselves alone, but also for the country of our birth. Therefore, O Emperor, I obey my teacher, and I undertake this public service.' Now the Emperor had acted thus merely for his own diversion, for by turning his mind to philosopher[s] and sophists he used to lighten the responsibilities of Empire. The Athenians however took the affair seriously, and, especially the Athenian magistrates themselves, hastened in a body to throw down the bronze statue of Favorinus as though he were the Emperor's bitterest enemy. Yet on hearing of it Favorinus showed no resentment or anger at the insult, but observed: 'Socrates himself would have been the gainer, if the Athenians had merely deprived him of a bronze statue, instead of making him drink hemlock.'

He was very intimate with Herodes [Atticus] the sophist who regarded him as his teacher and father, and wrote to him: 'When shall I see you, and when shall I lick the honey from your lips?'[10] Accordingly at his death he bequeathed to Herodes all the books that he had collected, his house in Rome, and Autolecythus.[11] This was an Indian, entirely black, a pet of Herodes and Favorinus, for as they drank their wine together he used to divert them by sprinkling his Indian dialect with Attic words and by speaking barbarous Greek with a tongue that stammered and faltered.

The quarrel that arose between Polemo and Favorinus began in Ionia, where the Ephesians favoured Favorinus, while Smyrna admired Polemo; and it became more bitter in Rome; for there consulars and sons of consulars by applauding either one or the other started between them a rivalry such as kindles the keenest envy and malice even in the hearts of wise men. However they may be forgiven for that rivalry, since human nature holds that the love of glory never grows old; but they are to be blamed for the speeches that they composed assailing one another; for personal abuse is brutal, and even if it be true, that does not acquit of disgrace even the man who speaks about such things. And so when people called Favorinus a sophist, the mere fact that he had quarrelled with a sophist was evidence enough; for that spirit of rivalry of which I spoke is always directed against one's competitors in the same craft.

His style of eloquence was careless in construction, but it was both learned and pleasing. It is said that he improvised with ease and fluency. As for the speeches against Proxenus, we must conclude that Favorinus would neither have conceived nor composed them, but that they are the work of an immature youth who was intoxicated at the time, or rather he vomited them. But the speeches *On One Untimely Dead*,[12] and *For the Gladiators*, and *For the Baths*, I judge to be genuine and well written; and this is far more true of his dissertations on philosophy, of which the best are those on the doctrines of Pyrrho; for he concedes to the followers of Pyrrho the ability to make a legal decision, though in other matters they suspend their judgement.[13]

When he delivered discourses in Rome, the interest in them was universal, so much so that even those in his audience who did not understand the Greek language shared in the pleasure that he gave; for he fascinated even them by the tones of his voice, by his expressive glance and the rhythm of his speech. They were also enchanted by the epilogue of his orations, which they called 'The Ode,' though I call it mere affectation, since it is arbitrarily added at the close of an argument that has been logically proved. He is said to have been a pupil of Dio, but he is as different from Dio as any who never were his pupils. This is all I have to say about the men who, though they pursued philosophy, had the reputation of sophists.[14]

This third-century account of Favorinus' life and career can serve as the basis for analysis and discussion, informed by other surviving texts.[15] Hailing from the city of Arles in Gaul (in the province of Gallia Narbonensis), Favorinus clearly belonged to a comparatively socially distinguished family.[16] His advanced education itself indicates this. Born in the Latin west he developed a gift for Greek, and was able to travel to Greece for his studies and apparently to become a pupil of Dio Chrysostom, one of the most celebrated orators of the day.[17] Further, in the reign of Hadrian he went on to become a high priest for his province of origin, a role that reflected his social status and economic advantages.[18] In addition, strikingly, despite his physical condition (discussed below), he was able to maintain a privileged lifestyle; one imagines that such individuals who were born into peasant families, for instance, had a very different experience of life.

Of course, it was partly as a result of his very condition that Favorinus was able to maintain his elite lifestyle, by carving out a successful career for himself as a philosopher cum sophist with a unique selling point.[19] His status as a eunuch seems to have lent him to a certain extent a distinctive style. Philostratus emphasizes the delightful sound and manner of Favorinus' performances, and while other sophists no doubt were able to achieve such effects too there is the sense that his physical status contributed to his art.[20] For instance, he looked and sounded different: he lacked the beard one would expect the philosopher to have, and also his voice remained at a higher pitch. Favorinus proved popular both in Rome itself and the Greek world, witness the response of the Ephesians to him and the statue erected in his honour in Athens, a tribute also offered by the Corinthians.[21] In Aulus Gellius' *Attic Nights*, Favorinus is a major character, appearing twenty-seven times and being referred to a further six times;[22] he is, as Beall observes, quite simply 'the "star" of the work',[23] and one of the Doctor Johnsons to Gellius' Boswell.[24] Beall notes that Favorinus 'appears in the initial chapters of several books, disappears, and occasionally resurfaces', but it is worth expanding on this remark in order to emphasize further the centrality of Favorinus in the text.[25] Favorinus appears in seventeen of the twenty Books of the *Attic Nights* (only not in Books 6, 7 and 15), and features at the start of seven (for details of the episodes see the Appendix at the end of this chapter).[26] The significance of Favorinus in the text has been stressed also by Joseph Howley, who describes him as the 'internal avatar' of the *Attic Nights* and as 'the most visible and explicit Socrates of the entire work'.[27] The view of Wytse Keulen that Aulus Gellius' presentation of Favorinus is 'double-edged', both praising and undermining the notoriously hellenophile eunuch (who serves as a 'jester-hero' and 'comic authority figure') to enhance Gellius' own authority in pursuit of a Roman cultural programme, has not met with acceptance; as Leofranc Holford-Strevens observes, Keulen's 'persistent theme is that Gellius at once defends Favorinus against his detractors and warns against making him a role-model; but who, if not Gellius himself, was presenting him as such?'²⁸ Keulen's understanding of the work of Aulus Gellius still leaves Favorinus as its Socrates. The *Historia Augusta* (a series of imperial biographies seemingly produced in the fourth century) declares that many considered Favorinus pre-eminent among the philosophers, grammarians, rhetoricians and other artists of his day.²⁹ While discussing Varus of Perge, Philostratus notes that this sophist's teacher was Quadratus (proconsul of Asia *c.* AD 156/7) 'who used to argue extempore on abstract philosophical themes, and as a sophist followed the fashion set by Favorinus'.³⁰ Favorinus did not just perform, however; he was also a writer. As Philostratus indicates, there was some debate about which texts were authentic works (notably his surviving speech about his statue at Corinth, the *Corinthian Oration*, was preserved with the works of Dio Chrysostom as *Oration* 37, and Dio's *Oration* 64, *On Fortune*, is ascribed to Favorinus as well), but he clearly wrote much more than exists today.³¹ There survives also an oration *On Exile* (discovered in 1931), but the works mentioned by Philostratus are lost.³² The entry on Favorinus in the tenth-century Byzantine encyclopedia known as the *Souda* (meaning 'Stronghold') asserts that he competed with Plutarch in the number of books he wrote, giving as examples of his work *On Homer's Philosophy*, *On Socrates and his Art of Love*, *On Plato*, and *On the Philosophers' Way of Life*, and reports that he also produced a collection of maxims.³³ Aulus Gellius mentions his ten-book work on Pyrrhonian philosophy, referred to in Philostratus.³⁴

Favorinus' status as a celebrated intellectual and orator is reflected by the company he kept. Dio Chrysostom was his master, and he was friends with Plutarch, the orator and advocate Fronto, and the Athenian sophist Herodes Atticus.³⁵ Plutarch and Favorinus met in Greece, visiting Thermopylae and Delphi together. Plutarch dedicated his *On Primordial Cold* to Favorinus, as well as writing him a letter *On Friendship* and having him appear in his *Sympotic Questions*. Atticus was a pupil of Favorinus, and he had others too. Philostratus tells us that Favorinus was one of the teachers of Alexander the Cilician and that it was from him 'above all that he caught the charm and beauty of his eloquence'.³⁶ Aulus Gellius refers to other pupils of Favorinus (one of whom is identified as being of senatorial rank), and also relates that Favorinus visited Fronto when he was ill, and that one of the consuls was a friend of the eunuch.³⁷ Aulus Gellius was clearly a fan of Favorinus and spent much time in the company of the object of his affection, from the 140s onwards.³⁸ Favorinus also had contact with Roman emperors, notably Hadrian, but also his successor Antoninus Pius (138–161), attending salutations of this emperor.³⁹ Having dealings with the emperor could have its dangers though, and Favorinus had his difficulties with Hadrian, perhaps fed or exploited by his rival Polemo.⁴⁰ Philostratus asserts that Favorinus quarrelled with Hadrian, and mentions that the emperor opposed him being exempted from serving as a priest on the grounds that he was a philosopher. The tension between Hadrian and Favorinus is also mentioned in the epitome of Cassius Dio's *Roman History*, though this presents it as being due to the emperor's jealousy on account of his own intellectual aspirations. It asserts that 'inasmuch as [Hadrian] wished to surpass everybody in everything, he hated those who attained eminence in any direction. It was this feeling that led him to undertake to overthrow two sophists, Favorinus the Gaul, and Dionysius of Miletus, by various methods, but chiefly by elevating their antagonists, who were of little or no worth at all'.[41] Intellectual conflict is also suggested by an episode in the life of Hadrian in the *Historia Augusta*. It relates that 'once Favorinus, when he had yielded to Hadrian's criticism of a word which he had used, raised a merry laugh among his friends. For when they reproached him for having done wrong in yielding to Hadrian in the matter of a word used by reputable authors, he replied: "You are urging a wrong course, my friends, when you do not suffer me to regard as the most learned man the one who has thirty legions"'.[42] The epitome of Cassius Dio also includes an incident where Favorinus conceded defeat to the emperor, anticipating his opposition:

> And Favorinus, who was about to plead a case before the emperor in regard to exemption from taxes, a privilege which he desired to secure in his native land, suspected that he should be unsuccessful and receive insults besides, and so merely entered the court-room and made this brief statement: 'My teacher stood beside me last night in a dream and bade me serve my country, as having been born for her.'[43]

Whether this is related to the question of Favorinus becoming a priest is unclear, but either way, both the *Historia Augusta* and the epitome of Cassius Dio seem not to do justice to the idea of a quarrel between Favorinus and Hadrian. There are signs that something much more serious was at stake.[44] Both the Athenians and the Corinthians took down the statues that had been set up in honour of Favorinus, which indicates that he had been disgraced, and perhaps he was even punished by being exiled to Chios, if his oration *On Exile* is taken to refer to an actual event.[45] Possibly the accusation of adultery referred to in Philostratus is relevant here (and the speech to the Corinthians seems to point to an accusation of sexual impropriety).[46] Ultimately, however, it is not known. Simon Swain suggests that Favorinus' difficulty with the emperor was simply due to the fact that Hadrian was irritated by, and jealous of, Favorinus.[47] Eugenio Amato and Yvette Julien propose that Hadrian simply became exasperated by the combination of issues with Favorinus and thus exiled him, suggesting this occurred in 133.[48] Holford-Strevens sees the adultery episode as key, and proposes that Hadrian made clear to Favorinus that he should leave Rome even if acquitted.[49] Gleason ultimately opines that because of 'the inconsistent narratives of Philostratus and Dio ... and the inconsistent behavior of Hadrian himself, the complete story of Favorinus' quarrels with the emperor will never be told'.[50]

Favorinus certainly had tensions with other individuals too. In Lucian's life of the Cynic philosopher Demonax of Cyprus there are included a couple of barbed exchanges between Favorinus and the Cynic, the former coming off worst; these (discussed further below) make fun of Favorinus' status as a eunuch but also his status as a philosopher.[51] Galen of Pergamum, the famous physician and polymath, attacked Favorinus in his *On the Best Form of Education*, taking issue with the eunuch's view that 'the best form of education is arguing on both sides of a question'.[52] Favorinus himself wrote a work against the Stoic Epictetus, defending Plutarch from his attacks.[53] Favorinus' most notorious difficult relationship beyond that with Hadrian was with the sophist Polemo, and perhaps this is related to the quarrel with the emperor.[54] As the epitome of Cassius Dio asserts, the emperor sought to undermine the eminent sophist by promoting others of less ability. It may be significant that Hadrian selected Polemo to give the speech at the inauguration of the temple of Olympian Zeus in Athens in 130 or 131.[55] It sounds as if the spat between Favorinus and Polemo became very intense and bitter. Philostratus also records that Polemo was reprimanded for his speeches attacking Favorinus by one of his teachers, the philosopher Timocrates, Polemo cowering 'before him in awe and submission, like boys who fear blows from their teachers when they have been disobedient'.[56] Traces of these hostile speeches surface in a physiognomic text ascribed to Polemo which has been preserved in an Arabic translation.[57] This viciously attacks Favorinus for his physical characteristics and his concomitant moral qualities, asserting that he was 'greedy and immoral beyond all description' (discussed further below). However, despite these problems and setbacks, including possibly being exiled, Favorinus seems to have ended his career well. He outlived Hadrian, was re-established in Rome, and passed his mantle on to his heir Herodes Atticus. Furthermore, his subsequent reputation was high. Notably, his friend Aulus Gellius promoted him in his *Attic Nights*, which does not breathe a word about Favorinus' difficulties with Hadrian or Polemo,[58] and is notable for its 'absence of any vitriolic attacks ... on Favorinus' unique and uncertain gender and sexuality'.[59] Above all, Favorinus secured the accolade of being remembered as a sophist who was more of a philosopher.

Favorinus as eunuch

While Favorinus is interesting and important as a figure in the cultural history of the Greco-Roman world in the second century AD, it is his status as a eunuch that is the particular concern of this chapter (though the two aspects are not unconnected). He clearly was a 'born eunuch', Philostratus declaring that he was 'born double sexed, a hermaphrodite'. Favorinus seems to have self-identified as a eunuch, one of the paradoxes of his life being that although he was a eunuch he was tried for adultery (thus confounding the conception that eunuchs were naturally chaste). Philostratus also asserts that Favorinus had physical features typical of a eunuch: he did not have a beard and his voice was high. Other stories about Favorinus, and two key texts, Polemo's *Physiognomy* and Lucian's *Eunuch*, dwell on his condition as a eunuch and how this was expressed in his character and behaviour, and these need to be considered at length.

Of chief importance is the text of Polemo, whose animosity towards Favorinus has already been noted. This is testified to by Philostratus also in his life of Polemo. He records that when the philosopher Timocrates told Polemo that 'Favorinus had become a chatterbox, Polemo said wittily: "And so is every old woman," thus making fun of him for being like a eunuch'.[60] Polemo's testimony is found in the Arabic translation of his treatise on physiognomy. In the course of discussing eyes and what they indicate the text launches into a virulent attack on Favorinus:

> If you see an eye that is always open and dark, with some moistness in it, then the owner of this has great desire. If the gaze is soft together with this description, then its owner is good. If the eye is open, and it has brilliance like that of marble and

sharp sight, this indicates a lack of modesty. This nature is in the eyes of men who are not like the other men, like the eunuch who is not a eunuch but who was born without testicles.

I do not know if I have seen any of this description except for one man. He was from a land called Celtas. He was greedy and immoral beyond all description. His eyes were those of the most evil of people, and his eyes were of this description. I shall describe his body to you. He had puffed-up eyes, his cheeks were slack, his mouth was broad, his neck was long and thin, his ankles were thick, with much flesh on the legs. His neck was similar to the neck of a woman, and likewise all the rest of his limbs, and all his extremities were moist, and he would not walk erect, and his limbs and members were flaccid. He would take great care of himself and his abundant hair, and he would apply medicaments to his body afterwards. (He would give in) to every cause that incited a passion for desire and sexual intercourse. He had a voice resembling the voice of a woman and slim lips. I never before saw looks like his in the general populace or such eyes. Despite his form he would poke fun at everything and he would do whatever came into his mind. He had learnt the Greek language and its discourse by virtue of speaking a great deal, and he was called a sophist. He was an itinerant visitor in the towns and markets, gathering the people so that he could display his wickedness, and he sought out immorality. He was also a deceitful magician, and would swindle, telling people that he could give life and bring death, and thereby he would dupe a group of people until the crowds of women and men around him increased. He would tell the men that he had the power to compel women to come to them, and likewise the men to the women. He would corroborate that by his words about the occult. He was a leader in evil and a teacher of it. He would collect kinds of fatal poisons, and the whole sum of his intellect was engaged in one of these matters.[61]

If there was any doubt that this text has Favorinus in mind, it is confirmed by another work on physiognomy (anonymous, and written in Latin), which has been dated to the third or fourth century A.D.[62] This *Book of Physiognomy* also addresses the topic of eyes, and regarding those that are wide open and flashing it notes:

The eyes of a certain Celt were reported to have been like this by our authority Polemon, who described this man as a eunuch (*eunuchum*) of his own time. He did not write down his name, but it is understood that he was talking about Favorinus. He assigned the other signs of a body of this type to this man: a tense brow, soft cheeks, a loose mouth, a thin neck, thick legs, thick feet as if congested with flesh, a feminine voice, womanly words, limbs, and all his joints without strength, loose and badly connected (tensam frontem, genas molles, os laxum, cervicem tenuem, crassa crura, pedes plenos tanquam congestis pulpis, vocem femineam, verba muliebria, membra et articulos omnes sine vigore, laxos et dissolutus).[63]

In Polemo's treatment of Favorinus what leaps immediately to the eye is the association of him with the qualities ascribed to women. Favorinus' body is soft and moist, and his voice is high. He also behaves like a woman, being overly attentive to his appearance, lacking self-control, and talking too much. Further, the accusations of magic (notably erotic magic), using poisons and being untrustworthy could be gender-loaded too, as well as raising the spectre of treason in relation to Favorinus' possible exile. Thus Polemo, to a great extent, follows the typical path of categorizing (and attacking) a eunuch as a feminized being. However, it is notable that he emphasizes that Favorinus was not just an ordinary eunuch, one created by castration, but was a born eunuch. The uniqueness of this eunuch is conveyed further by the declaration that Polemo had only ever seen one such eunuch. This raises the issue of born eunuchs being a distinct category from created eunuchs, which will be returned to after a consideration of Lucian's allusions to Favorinus and his general attitude to eunuchs expressed in his dialogue titled *Eunuch*.

Lucian, a prolific writer of the second century AD, hailed from Samosata in Syria and was born around 120.[64] He is best known for the satirical nature of his writing, and one of his works generates much humour from the competition for a chair of Peripatetic philosophy in Athens towards the end of the century, around 179. This is his *Eunuch*, so-called because one of the candidates for the chair was (supposedly) a eunuch, and much of the amusement of the text derives from this fact.[65] The chair was one of several pairs established by imperial patronage (that of Marcus Aurelius, 161–180), in the fields of Stoic, Platonic, Epicurean as well as Peripatetic philosophy, and had become vacant when the holder of the chair had died. The account of the competition is presented in the form of a dialogue between two men, Pamphilus and Lycinus, the latter having been in attendance in the agora at the trial for the post and then reporting what had occurred to the former. The chair was hotly contested (it came with a salary of ten thousand drachma a year), and there were two leading candidates, Diocles and Bagoas. Diocles is identified as 'the dialectician' while Bagoas (if his name was not enough of a clue) is described as 'the one who is reputed to be a eunuch' (ὁ εὐνοῦχος εἶναι δοκῶν).[66] Having each proved their own worth for the post, they then began to attack one another on the grounds of their private lives. At the culmination of this Diocles asserted that the very fact that Bagoas was a eunuch disqualified him for the chair, Lycinus reporting that he said:

> such people ought to be excluded ... not simply from all that but even from temples and holy-water bowls and all the places of public assembly, and he declared it an ill-omened, ill-met sight if on first leaving home in the morning, one should set eyes on any such person. He had a great deal to say, too, on that score, observing that a eunuch was neither man nor woman, but something composite, hybrid, and monstrous, alien to human nature (οὔτε ἄνδρα οὔτε γυναῖκα εἶναι τὸν εὐνοῦχον λέγοντος, ἀλλά τι σύνθετον καὶ μικτὸν καὶ τερατῶδες, ἔξω τῆς ἀνθρωπείας φύσεως).[67]

Lycinus then details Bagoas' reply, in the course of which the eunuch refers to the case of Favorinus himself, as a eunuch who had been a philosopher:

> At first, through shame and cowardice – for that sort of behaviour is natural to them – he remained silent a long while and blushed and was plainly in a sweat, but

finally in a weak, effeminate (λεπτόν τι καὶ γυναικεῖον) voice he said that Diocles was acting unjustly in trying to exclude a eunuch from philosophy, in which even women had a part; and he brought in Aspasia, Diotima, and Thargelia to support him; also a certain Academic eunuch hailing from among the Pelasgians, who shortly before our time achieved a high reputation among the Greeks.[68]

According to Lycinus, the appeal to Favorinus cut no ice with Dicoles, who said he would have excluded him also, 'undismayed by his reputation among the common sort; and he repeated a number of humorous remarks made to the man by Stoics and Cynics regarding his physical imperfection'.[69]

Diocles having put the issue of Bagoas' eunuchood on the agenda, the debate continued before the judges. Lycinus reports:

> [Diocles] said that presence and a fine physical endowment should be among the attributes of a philosopher, and that above all else he should have a long beard that would inspire confidence in those who visited him and sought to become his pupils, one that would befit the ten thousand drachmas which he was to receive from the Emperor, whereas a eunuch was in worse case than a cut priest (τῶν βακήλων), for the latter had at least known manhood once, but the former had been marred from the very first and was an ambiguous sort of creature like a crow, which cannot be reckoned either with doves or with ravens. [Bagoas] pleaded that this was not a physical examination; that there should be an investigation of soul and mind and knowledge of doctrines. Then Aristotle was cited as a witness to support his case, since he tremendously admired the eunuch Hermias, the tyrant of Atarneus, to the point of celebrating sacrifices to him in the same way as to the gods.[70] Moreover, Bagoas ventured to add an observation to the effect that a eunuch was a far more suitable teacher for the young, since he could not incur any blame as regards them and would not incur that charge against Socrates of leading the youngsters astray. And as he had been ridiculed especially for his beardlessness, he despatched this shaft to good effect – he thought so, anyhow: 'If it is by length of beard that philosophers are to be judged, a he-goat would with greater justice be given preference to all of them!'

At this point, the debate took an unexpected direction, for someone (perhaps Lucian himself, if the episode was real) raised the possibility that Bagoas was not a real eunuch, interjecting 'if this fellow, so smooth of jowl, effeminate in voice, and otherwise similar to a eunuch, should strip, you would find him very masculine. Unless those who talk about him are lying, he was once taken in adultery' (thus again recalling the example of Favorinus).[71] This person admits that Bagoas had been acquitted, the judges accepting that he was indeed a real eunuch, but wonders if Bagoas will now declare himself a real man given the prize in prospect. Lycinus describes Bagoas' consternation at this turn of events, for he was now placed in a quandary:

> Upon those remarks everyone began to laugh, as was natural, while Bagoas fell into greater confusion and was beside himself, turning all colours of the rainbow and

dripping with cold sweat. On the one hand, he did not think it seemly to plead guilty to the charge of adultery; yet, on the other, he thought that this accusation would not be without its usefulness for the case then in progress.[72]

Lycinus then describes how the case descended very quickly into mirth, some judges suggesting that Bagoas should be stripped and inspected and others that women should be brought in to see if Bagoas would have sex with them, watched over by 'one of the judges, the eldest and most trustworthy ... [to] see whether he could practise philosophy'.[73] Amidst the laughter it was decided to refer the case to Italy, to the imperial court. Lycinus adds that Diocles, amongst his subsequent preparations, is seeking to revive the charge of adultery against Bagoas, though this might work against him as it could establish the supposed eunuch as a real man and thus able to be a philosopher (according to the terms of his own argument). As for Bagoas, he was concentrating on proving that he was expert enough to win the post. Lycinus ends by remarking humorously 'I may well pray that my son (who is still quite young) may be suitably endowed for the practise of philosophy with other tools than brain or tongue'.[74]

Thus, Lucian's *Eunuch*, although a satirical work, presents a fascinating reflection of certain attitudes that existed towards eunuchs in the late-second century AD, as well as providing allusions to historical examples of actual eunuchs. Focusing on the negative attitudes towards eunuchs first, there is the familiar view that they are feminized beings, a view voiced both by Diocles and Lycinus. There are the references to Bagoas' 'weak, effeminate voice', his 'shame and cowardice', his blushing and his lack of a beard. Diocles' key point becomes that Bagoas is not a man and thus is not qualified to be a philosopher. Bagoas is able to counter these points and make a virtue of the fact that he is a eunuch. He observes that women could be philosophers, so there is no reason why eunuchs could not be too, and indeed there was the historical case of Favorinus. He also draws attention to the historical case of Hermias the tyrant of Atarneus, to prove that eunuchs could be well thought of, even by the likes of Aristotle, who was Hermias' son-in-law. He argues that possession of a beard does not make a philosopher.[75] Bagoas, too, draws on the concept that eunuchs were chaste beings, for he argues that the young males he would be teaching would be entirely safe in his company. It is this last point that brings up the question of whether Bagoas really was a genuine eunuch, for he had previously been charged with adultery, though he had been acquitted at the time. This, of course, intensifies the parallel between Bagoas and Favorinus, and it is of interest that Diocles alludes to jokes made at Favorinus' expense by Stoics and Cynics, for, as referred to above, in Lucian's life of the Cynic philosopher Demonax of Cyprus there are included a couple of exchanges between the eunuch and the Cynic:

> I should like to cite a few of his well-directed and witty remarks, and may as well begin with Favorinus and what he said to him. When Favorinus was told by someone that Demonax was making fun of his lectures and particularly of the melodies in them (τῶν ἐν αὐταῖς μελῶν),[76] saying that it was vulgar and effeminate (ἀγεννὲς καὶ γυναικεῖον) and not by any means appropriate to philosophy, he went to Demonax and asked him: 'Who are you to libel my compositions?' 'A man with an ear that is not easy to cheat,' said he. The sophist kept at him and asked: 'What

qualifications had you, Demonax, to leave school and commence philosophy?' 'Balls ("Ορχεις),' he retorted.

Another time the same man went to him and asked what philosophical school he favoured most. Demonax replied: 'Why, who told you that I was a philosopher?' As he left, he broke into a very hearty laugh; and when Favorinus asked him what he was laughing at, he replied: 'It seemed to me ridiculous that you should think a philosopher can be told by his beard when you yourself have none.'[77]

Here again there are common themes and ideas. Favorinus is feminized (his style is sweet) and he lacks the male accoutrements of balls and a beard. His status as a philosopher is questioned, and he is made an object of fun.

However, in Lucian's *Eunuch* there are also the more intriguing comments about the ambiguity of eunuchs and their status as monsters and ill-omened creatures, and the indication that there is a sliding scale of the terribleness of eunuchs. Eunuchs may be conceived of as feminized beings, as not male, but there is also the view voiced by Diocles that they are neither male nor female but something different entirely, a point reinforced by the comparison with crows which are neither doves nor ravens. This gives eunuchs a sinister complexion, and Diocles asserts that they should not be allowed in public locations, conveying the idea that they could contaminate the community. For Diocles, eunuchs are ill-omened and also monstrous, outside human nature itself. He also indicates that some eunuchs are worse than others, the devotees of Cybele having at least once been men whereas a eunuch 'had been marred from the very first and was an ambiguous sort of creature'. One might assume that the comparison here is between those who were castrated after passing through puberty and those who were castrated before passing through puberty, yet it is also possible that Lucian has in mind the difference between those who are turned into eunuchs by castration and those who are born eunuchs. Given that the case of Bagoas is paralleled with that of Favorinus it indeed seems probable that it is a question of born eunuchs here. The alternative would be that Bagoas was an ex-slave, which, although suggested by his name, is not addressed at all in the dialogue, and surely would have been if that was the case, as it would have assisted Diocles' attack on his rival. Thus, Lucian's *Eunuch*, like Polemo's *Physiognomy*, indicates that born eunuchs were viewed in an even dimmer light than man-made eunuchs, and this attitude will be considered at greater length to see how widespread it was and why it was held.

Favorinus as born eunuch

It is clear that Favorinus was indeed a born eunuch, in that his condition was known from his birth. It seems that he was born with undescended testicles. However, his exact condition has been a matter of speculation. The most sustained analysis is that of Hugh Mason.[78] Drawing on the surviving sources, Mason compiles a list of the symptoms of Favorinus and comparing these with various medical conditions he favours the view that Favorinus' condition was Reifenstein's syndrome, a form of male pseudo-hermaphroditism. Key for Mason's diagnosis is the testimony that Favorinus had a normal male sex drive. Mason does identify a potential problem in his diagnosis, for no source mentions gynaecomastia (enlarged breasts) in relation to Favorinus, but ultimately this difficulty can be surmounted for it could be considered 'part of ... general obesity'.[79] He also notes that some of the symptoms mentioned by Polemo ('such as the flashing eyes, long thin neck, and fleshy legs') are not explained by Reifenstein's syndrome, but concludes that 'the bulk of Polemo's details' can be ascribed 'to no very specific medical conditions'.[80] One wonders, however, whether Mason puts too much faith in the references to Favorinus' active sex life. The texts of Polemo and Lucian are hostile, and even if Bagoas is based on Favorinus it is notable that Bagoas was acquitted of the charge of adultery and his being a real man is not proved by the end. More problematic perhaps is the testimony of Philostratus who records the paradox that Favorinus was charged with adultery and asserts that the eunuch was 'ardent in love'. Yet there is no proof that Favorinus was found guilty, and it was one of the assumptions about eunuchs that they could still feel desire and attempt to act on it. The details of Favorinus' sex life must remain open to question, and thus the identification of his condition as Reifenstein's syndrome can be questioned. Further, it is clear from Mason's own table of 'Distinctive Features of Sexual Disorders' that the features of Reifenstein's syndrome can match those of true hermaphroditism. Tellingly, in their own consideration of Favorinus' condition, although F.P. Retief and J.F.G. Cilliers think it likely that Favorinus was a congenital eunuch and 'agree that [Reifenstein's syndrome] is a strong possibility', they are open to the option that Favorinus was a true hermaphrodite.[81]

Ultimately, it is does not matter what Favorinus' true medical condition was; what matters is what contemporaries thought about his identity.[82] For them, he was a born eunuch. Such individuals could be considered monsters and met with extreme hostility.[83] Luc Brisson notes that '[a] whole series of Greek and Roman laws ordered parents to expose abnormal children'.[84] Drawing on Livy's history of Rome (written in the time of Augustus) and the *Book of Prodigies* produced by Julius Obsequens in the fourth century AD (and which used Livy's history as its source), Brisson compiled a list of sixteen prodigies relating to the birth or discovery of androgynous beings between the years 209–92 BC.[85] He observes that most of these individuals were dealt with by being consigned to water. For instance, amongst the prodigies at the start of the year 209 BC Livy records that at Sinuessa 'a child was born of uncertain sex, as between male and female – the populace call them hermaphrodites' (natum ambiguo inter marem ac feminam sexu infantem, quos androgynos volgus ... appellat).[86] Of a similar prodigy two years later, Livy gives details of the expiation required, recording that 'the soothsayers summoned from Etruria said it was a terrible and loathsome portent (foedum ac turpe prodigium); it must be removed from Roman territory, far from contact with earth, and drowned in the sea'.[87] Brisson asserts that in the imperial period there was a shift in attitude to such individuals, to a less cruel and more enlightened stance.[88] To illustrate this he cites episodes from the universal history of Diodorus Siculus, the *Historical Library* produced in the first century BC. Here are met individuals whose bodies changed sex after they had married: Herais a half-Arabian half-Macedonian woman who became a man and changed her name to Diophantus (her father's name), and thirty years later Callo a woman from Epidaurus who became a man and took the name Callon.[89] Both these episodes are placed in the context of the Hellenistic east in the second half of the second century BC, but Diodorus then notes and observes:

> Likewise in Naples and a good many other places sudden changes of this sort are said to have occurred. Not that the male and female natures have been united to form a truly bisexual type (δίμορφον τύπον), for that is impossible, but that Nature, to mankind's consternation and mystification, has through the bodily parts falsely given this impression. And this is the reason why we have considered these shifts of sex worthy of record, not for the entertainment, but for the improvement of our readers. For many men, thinking such things to be portents (τέρατα), fall into superstition, and not merely isolated individuals, but even nations and cities.[90]

He then records the burning near Rome of an androgyne (who was married to an Italian man) at the time of the Marsian War (Social War, 91–88 BC); he comments '[t]hus did one whose nature was like ours and who was not, in reality, a monster (τέρας), meet an unsuitable end through misunderstanding of his malady'.[91] Brisson observes that 'Under the Empire... "hermaphrodites" appear no longer to have been considered as terrifying prodigies, no doubt thanks to a rationalist reaction against superstition, of the type manifested by Diodorus'.[92] As he notes, Pliny the Elder in his *Natural History* reflects this rather different view, stating 'Persons are also born of both sexes combined – what we call Hermaphrodites, formerly called *androgyni* and considered as portents, but now as entertainments' (Gignuntur et utriusque sexus quos Hermaphroditos vocamus, olim androgynous vocatos et in prodigiis habitos, nunc vero in deliciis).[93] Notably, Aulus Gellius quotes this passage himself in his *Attic Nights*;[94] Baldwin wonders if there is a dig at Favorinus here ('a touch of sly humour'), but given Aulus Gellius' general attitude to Favorinus this seems unlikely.[95] Pliny's observations clearly became fundamental to Roman views on intersex individuals, for they are also referenced in late antiquity by Augustine in his *City of God*.[96] Discussing the origins of monstrous men (whether from Adam or the sons of Noah) he includes those that are 'bisexual by nature' (*utriusque sexus*) and asserts that they are all are God's creations and are all descended from Adam. He remarks '[a]lthough androgyni, whom men also call hermaphrodites, are very rare, yet it is difficult to find periods when they do not occur. In them the marks of both sexes appear together in such a way that it is uncertain from which they should properly receive their name. However, our established manner of speaking has given them the gender of the better sex, calling them masculine. For no one ever called them in the feminine *androgynaecae* or *hermaphroditae*'.[97]

This shifting attitude might explain one of the puzzles of the life of Favorinus, why he himself was not exposed, a puzzle Gleason raises but does not answer: she remarks that '[t]he infant...could have been exposed as a *monstrum*... but for reasons lost to history the family decided to rear it as a male'.[98] Perhaps at the time in which he was born such a response would no longer have been automatic. Nevertheless, it still seems somewhat surprising that Favorinus' family, despite their evident social standing, raised such a child so publicly, fostering his education to a high degree. Free born elite eunuchs are much less commonly met in the ancient world; eunuchs tend to originate as part of the slave trade or as self-castrating religious devotees. A rare comparative case might be that of Otes the eunuch who in the third century AD was depicted in the frescoes at Dura-Europos, the frontier garrison town in Syria, at the time when it was in Roman hands.[99] He was shown sacrificing with another man (the councillor Iabsumsos the son of Abdaathes; their names and identities are known from inscriptions written in Greek) to five Palmyrene deities, in the 'Temple of Bel' in the town's northwest corner, in a room that Otes himself founded ('Οτῆς εὐνοῦχος ὁ κτίσας τὴν ἐξέδραν).[100] Some have understood Otes as a self-castrating priest, though others have rejected this in favour of considering him a slave or freedman, either of the Parthian empire or of the councillor.[101] However, perhaps Otes was always a free individual. His lack of a patronym might be due to him being well known as 'the eunuch' (one thinks of Favorinus' apparent self-identification as a eunuch). The fact that the inscription identifies him as the founder of the room might suggest his social distinction, not just wealth from a career as a slave (he also seems to be attended by his own servant, Gorsak).[102] Certainly in terms of his dress there is nothing to distinguish him from the councillor. In terms of size he is actually larger; this might reflect his greater social significance or his physique as a eunuch, or perhaps both. Definite cases of freeborn eunuchs are Dorotheus the educated presbyter of Antioch from the late third century and the general Solomon from the reign of Justinian I (527–565). Dorotheus was known to Eusebius of Caesarea, who records in his *Church History* that 'he was by nature a eunuch, having been so from his very birth (τὴν φύσιν δὲ ἄλλως εὐνοῦχος, οὕτω πεφυκὼς ἐξ αὐτῆς γενέσεως), so that even the emperor, accounting this as a sort of miracle (παράδοξον), took him into his friendship and honoured him with the charge of the purple dye-works at Tyre'.[103] While Dorotheus was, like Favorinus, a born eunuch, Solomon was apparently an accidental eunuch, as recorded by the historian Procopius who knew him; he writes that Solomon was born near Daras on the eastern frontier and suffered some injury when he was still a baby which made him a eunuch.[104] Solomon went on to carve out a military career for himself, being one of the commanders of the federates and manager (*domesticus*) for the famous general Belisarius for the expedition to North Africa in 533, before becoming the leading general there after the defeat of the Vandals, as well as Praetorian Prefect.[105] Pliny refers to the possibility of accidental eunuchs in his *Natural History*, writing 'In man only [testicles] may be crushed owing to an injury or from natural causes, and this forms a third class, in distinction from hermaphrodites and eunuchs, the impotent' (homini tantum iniuria aut sponte naturae franguntur, idque tertium ab hermaphroditis et spadonibus semiviri genus habent).[106] Thus free born eunuchs could exist, though they are clearly much less common. In the case of Favorinus, one wonders if the decision of his parents to foster his education, especially in Greek, was a tacit recognition that as a born eunuch he was not going to have the usual career of a provincial elite male. Gleason observes that 'Favorinus' decision to concentrate on Greek was unusual',[107] while Amato and Julien associate Favorinus' devotion to his studies with his physical condition, reflecting 'on peut seulement imaginer que Favorinos s'efforça de compenser ce défaut naturel en se consacrant activement à ses cours et conférences publiques dans tout l'Empire, ce qui explique son succès rapide'.[108]

However, even though there seems to have been a shift in attitude towards born eunuchs, it is clear that hostility towards them – and eunuchs in general – could still exist. For instance, general antipathy is seen also in Lucian's *The Mistaken Critic*; he declares:

> We avoid those who are lame in the right foot, especially if we should see them early in the morning; and if anyone should see a cut priest or a eunuch (βάκηλον ἢ εὐνοῦχον) or a monkey immediately upon leaving the house, he returns upon his tracks and goes back, auguring that his daily business for that day will not be successful, thanks to the bad and inauspicious omen at the start.[109]

The inauspiciousness of eunuchs is also expressed in the dreambook of Artemidorus, which dates to the second century AD, during the Antonine era. Discussing people whom one can and cannot trust when they appear in dreams, Artemidorus declares 'Sophists, poor men, priests of Cybele, castrated men, and eunuchs (γάλλοι καὶ ἀπόκοποι καὶ σπάδοντες) are also untrustworthy. For these men, even if they say nothing, indicate false expectations, since they cannot be numbered either among men or among women (μήτε ἐν ἀνδράσι μήτε ἐν γυναιξὶν) due to their physical condition'.[110] In Claudian's invectives on the Grand Chamberlain Eutropius at the end of the fourth century, he plays on the notion of Eutropius being designated as consul for 399 as monstrous and a prodigy, with the eunuch's death being required for expiation. He exclaims 'Let the world cease to wonder at the births of creatures half human, half bestial, at monstrous babes that affright their own mothers (metuendaque pignora matri) ... All portents pale before the eunuch consul (omnia cesserunt eunucho consule monstra)', and declares 'The consul's own blood must cleanse the consular insignia, the monster itself must be sacrificed (consule lustrandi fasces ipsoque litandum prodigio)'.[111] As seen in the case of Favorinus, the texts hostile towards him emphasize the terribleness of the fact that he is a born eunuch; his uniqueness makes him much worse than other eunuchs.

The view that born eunuchs were worse than castrated eunuchs is also met in other texts, suggesting that it was a more widespread notion. In another physiognomic text, Adamantius the Sophist (who probably lived in the first half of the fourth century AD) asserts 'Those who are naturally eunuchs have worse signs than other men and are largely savage-minded, deceitful, and villainous, some more than others. Some signs of those who are eunuchs by castration change with the castration, but most of the congenital nature remains'.[112] Given Adamantius' debt to the work of Polemo he may simply have been echoing his views, but there are other earlier texts which share them. In his *Training in Oratory*, written towards the end of the first century AD, the rhetorician Quintilian discusses eunuchs in relation to the current style of declamations, which he says that 'owing to the fact that they are composed solely with the design of giving pleasure, have become flaccid and nerveless' (atque ad solam compositae voluptatem nervis carent).[113] He argues that:

> declaimers are guilty of exactly the same offence as slave-dealers who castrate boys in order to increase the attractions of their beauty. For just as the slave-dealer regards strength and muscle, and above all, the beard and other natural

characteristics of manhood as blemishes, and softens down all that would be sturdy if allowed to grow, on the ground that it would be harsh and hard, even so we conceal the manly form of eloquence and power of speaking closely and forcibly by giving it a delicate complexion of style and, so long as what we say is smooth and polished, are absolutely indifferent as to whether our words have any power or no.[114]

Quintilian is clearly unhappy with this development, and declares:

But I take Nature for my guide and regard any man whatsoever as fairer to view than a eunuch (*spadone*), nor can I believe that Providence is ever so indifferent to what itself has created as to allow weakness (*debilitas*) to be an excellence, nor again can I think that the knife can render beautiful that which, if produced in the natural course of birth (*si nasceretur*), would be regarded as a monster (*monstrum*).[115]

Quintilian thus clearly articulates the distinction between created eunuchs, which are found beautiful (by some), and born eunuchs, which would be considered monsters, aberrations of nature. One can imagine all too well what Quintilian would have made of Favorinus and his style.

Conclusion

In the history of eunuchs of the Roman Empire, Favorinus marks a very arresting and significant case. He is not a slave eunuch or a religious self-castrate, but a born eunuch and a free and socially distinguished individual. As such, he is a more unusual albeit not unique case, though the extent of his fame and popularity does set him apart from most other Roman eunuchs. His identity as a born eunuch gives him particular currency in the early-twenty-first century, when intersex identity is recognized and much discussed. Favorinus provides a fascinating example of an intersex individual from antiquity; he deserves to regain his fame.

Appendix: Appearances and mentions of Favorinus in Aulus Gellius' *Attic Nights*

Listed below are the twenty-seven appearances and six mentions of Favorinus in Aulus Gellius' *Attic Nights*, which consisted of twenty Books (for a list and summary of the episodes see also Baldwin (1975: 21–8)). Favorinus appears in seventeen of the twenty Books. At times Gellius uses Greek to quote Favorinus, and it is thought that when he does so he is citing from writings of the eunuch (Holford-Strevens (1988: 80) and (2003: 109)). Howley (2018: 240) notes that '[b]y effectively playing the role of Favorinus, who made his own career in the roleplay-rich world of sophistic declamation, Gellius claims his teacher's authority, and asserts his own authorial control over the text'. The episodes convey well the range of expertise of Favorinus, his wit, and his interest in and facility with Latin too, despite being a notorious hellenophile. In the summaries below the translations are from Rolfe (1927).

1.3.27 (vol. 1: 20–1)

Reflecting on whether one ever ought to do wrong to assist a friend (starting from the example of Chilo the Spartan) Gellius cites a range of relevant opinions, including Favorinus' remark (in Greek) that '"That which among men is called a favour is the relaxing of strictness in time of need."'

1.10 (vol. 1: 50–1)

Favorinus reprimands a young man for using archaic words and phrases, exhorting him to use the language of the present day.

1.15.17 (vol. 1: 78–9)

Gellius reports that he heard Favorinus say that Euripides' lines 'Of unrestrained mouth/And of lawless folly/Is disaster the end,' should be understood to refer not just to those who speak impiously or lawlessly but also to windbags.

1.21 (vol. 1: 94–7)

When Gellius reports the grammarian Julius Hyginus' correction of a line in Virgil's *Georgics* (Hyginus saying in his *Commentaries* on Virgil that he discovered the true text in a version belonging to the family of the poet), Favorinus agrees with the amendment but tells Gellius that he is prepared to swear that Virgil did not coin the word '*amaror*' but copied it from the poet Lucretius.

2.1 (vol. 1: 122–3)

Discussing Socrates' capacity for physical endurance and his temperance, Gellius cites (in Greek) from Favorinus' discussion of the fortitude and virtues of Socrates, '"He often stood from sun to sun, more rigid than the tree trunks."'

2.5 (vol. 1: 132–3)

Favorinus contrasts the writing of Plato and Lysias, saying that if you carefully change a word in Plato you impair his elegance but if you do the same with Lysias you affect his meaning.

2.12.5-6 (vol. 1: 156–9)

Favorinus comments on a law of Solon concerning civil dissent, saying it should also be applied to brothers or friends who are in disagreement.

2.22 (vol. 1: 182–93)

Gellius recalls what Favorinus said about the Iapyx wind and the names and quarters of others, when dining with friends at home. Gellius reports that usually at such dinners 'there was ... read either an old song of one of the lyric poets, or something from history, now in Greek and now in Latin'. Gellius (2.22.27, p. 191) notes that Favorinus spoke 'with extreme elegance of diction and in a delightful and graceful style throughout' (cum elegantia verborum totiusque sermonis comitate atque gratia denarravit).

2.26 (vol. 1: 210–17)

Favorinus pays a visit to Fronto (now ex-consul) when he was suffering from gout, taking Gellius with him. At Fronto's there are other intellectuals present, and there is a discussion between Favorinus and Fronto concerning colours and their names, and the range of shades of colours that exist. Fronto notes that Favorinus seems to prefer the Greek language (2.26.7).

3.1 (vol. 1: 234–9)

In late winter Favorinus and Gellius walk in the sunshine in the court of the Baths of Titus, and discuss with others (including a disciple of Favorinus) why Sallust asserts in his *Catiline* (11.3), which a friend was reading to them, that avarice makes a man effeminate not just in soul but also in body. Favorinus appears perplexed by the notion, even after the discussion, and wonders if Sallust overstated the case.

3.3.6 (vol. 1: 246–9)

Favorinus is delighted by a line from Plautus' *Nervularia* which Gellius was reading, and says the single line reveals the author to be Plautus.

3.16.17 (vol. 1: 294–5)

Favorinus elucidates for Gellius the meaning of a phrase in Homer's *Odyssey* which he had found puzzling.

3.19 (vol. 1: 302–5)

After a dinner at Favorinus' there was a reading from Gavius Bassus' *On the Origin of Verbs and Substantives*, and Favorinus disputed Bassus' etymology of the word *parcus*.

4.1 (vol. 1: 308–17)

In the vestibule of the Palatine palace, while waiting with others to greet the emperor (probably Antoninus Pius), Favorinus responds to a boastful grammarian's discussion of the word *penus* and wittily bests him.[116] Gellius observes 'Thus Favorinus used to lead ordinary conversation of this kind from insignificant and trivial topics to those which were better worth hearing and knowing, topics not lugged in irrelevantly, nor by way of display, but springing from and suggested by the conversations themselves' (4.1.19).

5.11.8–14 (vol. 1: 410–13)

Favorinus takes issue with Bias' assertion that one should not marry as a beautiful wife will be unfaithful and an ugly one a punishment, on the grounds that a woman of middling appearance can exist.

8.2 (vol. 2: 142–3)

Favorinus tells Gellius ten Greek words of foreign origin, and Aulus Gellius tells Favorinus ten Latin words of foreign origin (only the title of this chapter exists).

8.14 (vol. 2: 148–9)

This chapter included 'A highly entertaining discussion of the philosopher Favorinus with a tiresome person who held forth on the double meaning of certain words' (only the title of this chapter exists).

9.8 (vol. 2: 174–5)

Reflecting on the observation that 'great want arises from great abundance and not from great lack', Gellius recalls that 'Favorinus once, amid loud and general applause, rounded off this thought, putting it into the fewest possible words: "It is not possible for one who wants fifteen thousand cloaks not to want more things; for if I want more than I possess, by taking away from what I have I shall be contented with what remains"' (this is quoted in Greek).

9.13.5 (vol. 2: 194–5)

Gellius recalls Favorinus' response to reading Quintus Claudius' account of Titus Manlius Torquatus' famous defeat of a Gaul in his *Annals*, the philosopher saying 'that his mind was stirred and affected by no less emotion and excitement than if he were himself an eye-witness of their contest'.

10.12.9–10 (vol. 2: 244–5)

Gellius notes that Favorinus (whom he describes as 'a most diligent searcher of ancient records') opined that Archytas the Pythagorean did make a wooden model of a dove which was able to fly. Gellius cites directly from Favorinus, switching from Latin to Greek.

11.5.5 (vol. 2: 310-11)

Gellius notes that Favorinus wrote ('with great keenness and subtlety') ten books entitled *The Pyrronian Principles* (the title is given in Greek).

12.1 (vol. 2: 352-61)

Gellius accompanies Favorinus when he visits the house of a disciple (a noble of senatorial rank) after his wife has given birth to a son. Favorinus controversially opines that the mother should suckle the child herself, rather than the task being entrusted to a wet nurse. He says it is natural for the mother to care for the child, and argues that children are affected by whose milk they drink. He asserts '"What the mischief, then, is the reason for corrupting the nobility of body and mind of a newly born human being, formed from gifted seeds, by the alien and degenerate nourishment of another's milk? Especially if she whom you employ to furnish the milk is either a slave or of servile origin and, as usually happens, of a foreign and barbarous nation, if she is dishonest, ugly, unchaste and a wine-bibber; for as a rule anyone who has milk at the time is employed and no distinction made"' (12.1.17). He also says the affection between the real mother and the child would be destroyed if she did not care for it herself. Gellius remarks that Favorinus gave his speech in Greek, and comments on the inadequacy of Latin to do justice to 'the elegance, copiousness and richness of his words' (12.1.24).

13.25 (vol. 2: 486-501)

When waiting to meet a friend (one of the consuls) in the court of the Forum of Trajan, Favorinus asks what the meaning of the inscription *Ex manubiis* means, which accompanies the gilded horses and images of military standards set up on the roof of the colonnades there. He then launches into a lengthy excursus, in the course of which he comments on his own devotion to Hellenic literature and arts, but amusingly notes that he has not completely neglected the Latin language, 'to which I devote occasional or desultory study', and Gellius remarks on Favorinus' 'marvellous and almost miraculous memory' (13.25.4-5).

14.1 (vol. 3: 2-21)

At Rome, Favorinus discourses in Greek (though Gellius records it in Latin, only citing the occasional Greek term) against the Chaldaeans or astrologers who claim to be able to predict the future from the stars.

14.2 (vol. 3: 20-31)

When Gellius was selected by the praetors to be a judge in charge of private suits he consulted Favorinus ('with whom I associated a great deal at Rome at that time') about a particular case but also about the duties of a judge in general.

16.3 (vol. 3: 134–9)

Favorinus and Gellius visit a sick man, and after conversing in Greek with the doctors there Favorinus commented favourably on the views on hunger and loss of appetite of the physician Erasistratus in his *Distinctions*. At the start of this chapter Gellius records 'I often spent whole days in Rome with Favorinus. His delightful conversation held my mind enthralled, and I attended him wherever he went, as if actually taken prisoner by his eloquence; to such a degree did he constantly delight me with his most agreeable discourse'.

17.10 (vol. 3: 238–45)

Gellius visits Favorinus when during the hot season he is staying at a friend's villa on the coast at Antium (modern Anzio), and Favorinus holds forth on Virgil and compares his description of an eruption of Mount Etna with that of Pindar.

17.12 (vol. 3: 250–3)

Gellius discusses how sophists and philosophers addressed 'ignoble subjects', and notes that Favorinus himself 'took a great deal of pleasure in descending to such subjects', referring to eulogies of Thersites and the quartan fever and quoting (partly in Greek) from the latter.

17.19 (vol. 3: 264–7)

Gellius discusses Epictetus' comments both on professed philosophers and the two supreme faults (lack of endurance and lack of restraint), and notes that Favorinus referred to these.

18.1 (vol. 3: 292–7)

In springtime on the shore at Ostia, where Favorinus was residing, he umpires a discussion on the happy life between two distinguished philosophers, friends of his, one a Peripatetic and the other a Stoic.

18.7 (vol. 3: 318–25)

Favorinus encounters the grammarian Domitius 'The Insane' at the temple of Carmentis and asks him about the meaning and usage of the word *contio*. Domitius rebukes him, complaining that philosophers are concerned with the business of grammarians rather than their own. Later Domitius sent Favorinus a book about the subject of words with multiple meanings. Gellius tracked down for Favorinus, at his request, uses of *contio* in works of Cicero and good early writers.

19.3 (vol. 3: 358–9)

Gellius records Favorinus' view that 'it was more shameful to be praised faintly and coldly than to be censured violently and severely'.

20.1 (vol. 3: 406–27)

While waiting with others at the Palatine to pay respects to the emperor (Antoninus Pius), Favorinus encounters the jurist Sextus Caecilius and they discuss at length the laws of the *Twelve Tables*. Favorinus contends that some of the laws were obscure, or either too cruel or too lenient, or not to be taken as the letter of the law, and Sextus Caecilius responds to these points (taking up the majority of the exchange). Gellius notes that all, including Favorinus, approved of the jurist's responses.

5

Eusebius and His Kind:
Court Eunuchs of the Later Roman Empire

Introduction

It is evident that in the first century AD eunuchs were a regular feature of the Roman imperial court, as slaves and favourites. By the fourth century AD eunuchs continued to be found as slaves and favourites at the imperial court but were said to be powerful both as individuals and as a group, in their role as chamberlains (*cubicularii*) of the emperor and his family. This chapter considers how and why this happened. The Emperor Diocletian (284–305) is often credited with the development, given his supposed orientalization of Roman imperial style, however it seems more likely that it was the result of evolution rather than of a sudden dramatic shift. There are several striking examples of individual apparently powerful court eunuchs in the later Roman empire (fourth to sixth centuries AD), and often these individuals held the office of Grand Chamberlain (*praepositus sacri cubiculi*). The chapter focuses in particular on the career of Eusebius, who was prominent during the reign of Constantius II (337–361), and who was said to be the real power of the emperor's regime, as well as on the career of Eutropius, who served under Theodosius I (379–395) and his son Arcadius (395–408), and who was the only eunuch ever to become a consul. The chapter demonstrates the embedding of eunuchs within the Roman imperial system, which led to the use of court eunuchs by the Byzantine Empire, as well as reflecting the fact that Rome's use of eunuchs continued an eastern tradition, followed for instance by Persia and the Hellenistic kingdoms. The court eunuchs of the later Roman Empire provide a striking and text-rich example of this historical phenomenon.

The emergence of the court eunuch

As noted, the adoption of eunuchs as court officials is usually associated with Diocletian, often credited with saving the Roman Empire after a period of 'crisis' in the third century and giving it its distinct Late Antique character.[1] Diocletian has been perceived, rightly or wrongly, as a great reformer, exerting himself to address the problems confronting the Roman Empire by initiating a series of political, military, economic and religious measures, including the Great Persecution of the Christians, begun in 303.² It appears that part of Diocletian's efforts were aimed at enhancing the status of the office of emperor itself, making it more awe-inspiring and imposing after a period of imperial instability and a high turnover rate in the number of emperors. This entailed, it seems, looking to eastern models of monarchy for inspiration. For instance, the mid-fourth century imperial biographer Sextus Aurelius Victor observes that:

> [Diocletian] was, in fact, the first who really desired a supply of silk, purple and gems for his sandals, together with a gold-brocaded robe. Although these things went beyond good taste and betrayed a vain and haughty disposition, they were nevertheless trivial in comparison with the rest. For he was the first of all after Caligula and Domitian to permit himself to be called 'Lord' in public and to be worshipped and addressed as a god.³

Victor's contemporary Eutropius, in his brief history of Rome, echoes this picture, asserting that Diocletian:

> was first to introduce in the Roman empire a practice more in keeping with royal usage than with Roman liberty, since he gave orders that he should be revered with prostration, although before him all (emperors) were simply greeted. He had his clothing and shoes decorated with gems, whereas previously the emperor's insignia comprised only the purple robe, the rest of his dress was ordinary.⁴

That eunuchs were a key feature of the court of Diocletian (and other emperors associated with him) is well supported by the testimony of the Christian rhetor Lactantius, who taught in Nicomedia (the city where Diocletian primarily resided) during Diocletian's reign until he fled at the time of the Great Persecution.⁵ Recounting in his *On the Deaths of the Persecutors* (written in about 314–315) how palace eunuchs were implicated in setting fire to the palace in Nicomedia (supposedly plotting with the Christians to kill the emperors) and the reaction of Diocletian to this threat, Lactantius asserts that 'Eunuchs who had once enjoyed great power, and on whom Diocletian himself and the whole palace had depended, were killed (Potentissimi quondam eunuchi necati, per quos palatium et ipse ante constabat).'⁶ In his seminal study of the place and power of eunuchs at the later Roman court Keith Hopkins is of the view that Diocletian is associated with the establishment of this characteristic feature of the late empire.⁷ He suggests that 'the consistent use of eunuchs as court chamberlains and their repeated exercise of power were probably connected with the elaboration of court ritual, which can be roughly dated to the end of the third century', and wonders 'whether the capture of the Persian king's harem by Galerius [the Caesar of Diocletian] in AD 298 led to a proliferation of eunuchs in the Roman court'.⁸

The idea that the use of eunuchs at the late Roman court was inspired by the example of Persia is certainly strong in late antique texts. In his first invective against Eutropius the Grand Chamberlain of Arcadius, written in 399 when the eunuch had been honoured as consul, the poet Claudian has the goddess Roma exclaim:

> I admit I have long learned to tolerate this unmanned tribe, ever since the court exalted itself with Arsacid pomp and the example of Parthia corrupted our morals. But till now they were but set to guard jewels and raiment, and to secure silence for the imperial slumber. Never beyond the sleeping-chamber did the eunuch's service pass; not their lives gave guarantee of loyalty (*fidem*) but their dull wits were a sure pledge. Let them guard hidden store of pearls and Tyrian-dyed vestments; they must quit high offices of state.[9]

Likewise, the collection of biographies of emperors from Hadrian (117–138) to Carinus (283–285) known as the *Historia Augusta*, purportedly written by six distinct authors in the reigns of Diocletian and Constantine I (306–337) but it seems actually written by one author in the late-fourth century or perhaps even in the early-fifth century, spells out the Persian exemplar of the use of eunuchs and the associated nature of the ruler.[10] Noting that the Emperor Severus Alexander (222–235) did not employ eunuchs in council or as ministers, it continues:

> these creatures alone cause the downfall of emperors, for they wish them to live in the manner of foreign nations or as the kings of the Persians, and keep them well removed from the people and their friends, and they are go-betweens, often delivering messages other than the emperor's reply, hedging him about, and aiming, above all things, to keep knowledge from him.[11]

There is, however, no need to accept that Rome was deliberately copying the example of Persia.[12] In the cases cited above, the references to Persia were clearly meant to reflect badly on those emperors who did make use of court eunuchs. As has been seen already, the Roman Empire had been utilizing eunuchs since at least the first century BC, and they were a feature of the imperial court from the time of the first Roman imperial dynasty of the Julio-Claudians. In addition, the nature of Roman imperial rule was evolving anyway, from the first-citizen leader model established by Augustus (the emperor as Princeps) to the obvious monarch that he was, reflected for instance in reactions to Nero and Domitian; the Roman Empire in effect became a Hellenistic kingdom, and eunuchs were simply part of this. While the exact progress of this can be hard to track, not least because of a dearth of sources for the history of the Roman Empire in the third century AD, by the time of the fourth century AD, as Hopkins observes, eunuchs had become 'the proper appurtenance of an emperor'.[13]

This is evident from numerous texts in addition to Lactantius. Ammianus Marcellinus in his history which was completed in the late-fourth century AD, and the surviving part of which covers the years 354–378, makes much pointed comment on the role of the Grand Chamberlain Eusebius in the reign of Constantius II (discussed below), but also indicates a general eunuch presence at court, and reveals that other Roman rulers had eunuch chamberlains, such as Eutherius who served both the Emperor Constans (337–350) and the Caesar Julian (355–361), and Gorgonius who served the Caesar Gallus (351–354).[14] A fragment of the history of Eunapius, a contemporary of Ammianus, remarks that the career of the Grand Chamberlain Eutropius (discussed below) encouraged others to become eunuchs and thus swelled their number.[15] In the late-fifth or early-sixth century the historian Zosimus, who drew on the history of Eunapius, remarks on the number of eunuchs in the imperial service under Theodosius I.[16] The sense that eunuchs were a noticeable presence at the imperial court in the fourth century is also conveyed by the cases of those emperors who seem to have tried to control their numbers and their perceived power.[17] Julian, the cousin and heir of Constantius II, was especially known for his measures with regard to the court eunuchs. In his funeral oration for Julian, dating to 365, the Antiochene sophist Libanius records Julian's reduction of court personnel, including eunuchs who were 'more in number than flies around the flocks in spring'.[18] Julian himself in his *Beard-hater* of early 363 remarked in relation to his eunuch tutor Mardonius that 'eunuch' was 'a word which, twenty months ago, was constantly heard and revered, though it is now applied as an insult and a term of abuse'.[19] The fifth-century church historians Socrates and Sozomen both mention Julian's removal of eunuchs from the court.[20] The Emperor Magnus Maximus (383–387) was also noted for his dispensing with eunuchs at court.[21] Whether Julian and Magnus Maximus removed eunuchs completely is however a moot point; notably the bishop of Milan Ambrose met a eunuch Grand Chamberlain when in 387 he went to Trier to visit Magnus Maximus.[22] In any case, the efforts of Julian and Magnus Maximus were short-lived; eunuchs were seen as an important element of the court, and they were here to stay.[23]

The significant place of eunuchs at the late Roman court is also reflected by the fact that they could acquire high social status. Surviving Roman legislation indicates that by 384 the Grand Chamberlain was of the highest senatorial rank of *illustris* (*illustrious*), while a law of 422 concerning Grand Chamberlains asserts that they were to have the same rank as Praetorian Prefects, City Prefects and Masters of Soldiers.[24] In addition to legislation, the *Notitia Dignitatum*, a document dating to the late-fourth or early-fifth century detailing the civil and military offices of both the eastern and western halves of the empire, reveals that in the east the Grand Chamberlain was ranked after Praetorian Prefects, the City Prefect of Constantinople and Masters of Soldiers, and in the west after Praetorian Prefects, the City Prefect of Rome, the Master of Infantry and Masters of Cavalry.[25] This was despite their general origin as slaves of foreign extraction.[26] Court eunuchs of eastern origin are encountered, such as the cases of Eutherius and Eutropius in the fourth century and Narses in the sixth century, all from Armenia.[27] The historian Procopius asserts that in the sixth century most eunuchs at the court in Constantinople hailed from Abasgia, at the eastern end of the Black Sea.[28] Eunuchs could come from the west too, however; Aelius Donatus' commentary on Terence's *The Eunuch* indicates this, identifying Armenia and Gaul as well as east and west in general as places of origin of eunuchs.[29] A Gallic eunuch is met in Ambrose.[30] Imperial legislation indicates the foreign origin of eunuchs too; Constantine I ruled that eunuchs were not to be created within the Roman Empire, and Leo I (457–474) identified the tolerated source of eunuchs, the importation of castrated barbarians.[31]

Given their proximity to Roman rulers and their potential for elevated social status, there developed the notion that court eunuchs could be powerful and wealthy.[32] As noted above, Lactantius asserts that Diolcetian and the palace had come to depend on the eunuchs, who enjoyed great power. Ammianus comments on the growing power of the eunuchs of Constantius II, remarking that 'while performing duties of an intimate nature, by secret whispers [they] supplied fuel for false accusations'.[33] He also states that 'that type of man, after amassing wealth by iniquitous means, usually seeks out secret lurking-places' to retire to.[34] Addressing Julian in 362, Libanius recalls the power of the court eunuchs under Constantius II and the fact that a man would have to 'borrow all the money he could, and purchase from them everything that mattered', to reach the ear of the emperor.[35] In the fifth century, Cyril the Patriarch of Alexandria (412–444), in the context of the Council of Ephesus of 431, paid more in bribes to a chief eunuch at the court of Theodosius II (the Grand Chamberlain Chrysoretus) than he paid to the wife of the Praetorian Prefect of the East, the Master of Offices and the Quaestor, as well as also paying seven other chamberlains.[36] Such was the wealth of leading court eunuchs that they could be significant cultural patrons; Lausus a Grand Chamberlain of Theodosius II (408–450) was the dedicatee of Palladius' *Lausiac History* (dated to 420) and a collector of antique statuary, displayed in his palace in Constantinople.[37] Another Grand Chamberlain of Theodosius II, Antiochus, also had a renowned palace in Constantinople.[38]

Late Roman responses to the status, influence and wealth of court eunuchs echo earlier responses to the position and power of imperial freedmen in the first century AD, especially those of the Emperor Claudius, compounded of course by the fact that the slaves were now also castrated individuals.[39] To better explore the careers of, and responses to, later Roman court eunuchs this chapter turns to a close examination of the cases of Eusebius and Eutropius.

The case of Eusebius

One of the most famous examples of a court eunuch of the later Roman Empire, and one of the earliest documented, is that of Eusebius the Grand Chamberlain of Constantius II.[40] Constantius was one of the sons of Constantine I (the first Christian Roman emperor, often referred to as Constantine the Great) who inherited the eastern territory of his father on his death in 337, including the city of Constantinople.[41] The rest of Constantine's empire was shared between Constantius' brothers Constantine II and Constans, after the elimination of many other male relatives of Constantine I, namely his half-brothers and their sons. These political murders have been called the 'Great Massacre', and Constantius II is understood to have been the leading force in its execution.[42] He went on to become sole emperor himself following the deaths of his brothers, Constantine being killed in 340 and Constans in 350. To assist him rule the empire after 350, Constantius turned to surviving cousins, first Gallus whom he appointed Caesar in 351 before having him executed in 354, and then Julian (Gallus' half-brother by Julius Constantius, Constantine I's own half-brother), whom he elevated to the Caesarship in 355 and was poised to engage in civil war (after Julian was acclaimed Augustus by his troops at Paris in the spring of 360) at the time of his death in late 361. In the sources for Constantius and his reign, the emperor and his regime tend to be drawn in dark hues.[43] He is depicted as a suspicious and cruel ruler, and a heretic to boot. The image of the eunuch Eusebius, who was a prominent official of the emperor (even being portrayed as a dominant force in the regime), is equally alarming.

A major source for the reign is the surviving portion of the history of Ammianus Marcellinus.[44] This was written in Latin, though Ammianus was a Greek (possibly from Antioch in Syria). Ammianus had a military career, one of fairly elite status even though he calls himself simply a soldier.[45] He served in the imperial guard (*protectores domestici*), and saw service under both Constantius II and Julian, the latter of whom is a major focus in his history, in which he is depicted as a heroic figure.[46] Julian himself, renowned as the last pagan Roman emperor, is an important source for the reign of his cousin, for he was a prolific author and several of his works address the character of the regime of Constantius, notably the *Letter to the Athenians*, Julian's justification of his usurpation, written in 361.[47] As an emperor who sought to undermine Christianity and promote paganism, Julian was naturally the target of Christian invective, but so too was his Christian cousin Constantius for he favoured the wrong type of Christianity, Arianism, from the point of view of those who favoured the Nicene creed which was finally established as Orthodoxy in 381.[48] One of the key Christian opponents of Constantius was Athanasius the on-again off-again Patriarch of Alexandria (328–378), who in several of his writings attacks the emperor and his regime.[49] All these authors – Ammianus, Julian and Athanasius – in writing about Constantius II dwell also on the eunuch Eusebius, and together create something of a narrative of his career.[50]

When Eusebius is first encountered in the history of Ammianus, with the Emperor Constantius in Gaul in 353–354, he is holding the office of Grand Chamberlain, so it is likely that he had already provided long service as a chamberlain at the imperial court.[51] The ninth-century summary of the life of the fourth-century bishops of Byzantium Metrophanes and Alexander – by Photius the Byzantine civil servant then twice Patriarch of Constantinople (858–867 and 877–886) – records that Eusebius was *praepositus* in 337, being an accomplice of the Arian priest who had been entrusted by the dying emperor Constantine I with his will; they passed the will on to Constantius II rather than the intended recipient, the eldest son Constantine II.[52] The fifth-century church historian Sozomen also indicates that Eusebius became *praepositus* in 337 after the death of Constantine.[53] Perhaps Eusebius was already attached to Constantius by 337, and was promoted when he became Augustus.

Returning to Ammianus and Gaul in the early 350s, Eusebius is shown fulfilling the role of the emperor's trusted agent, being sent to Cabyllona (modern Châlon-sur-Saône) with gold to distribute to the troops there to appease their discontent at the lack of supply of vital provisions. Ammianus alleges that the explanation for the lack of provisions was concern of the Emperor Constantius about the possible threat from his cousin the Caesar Gallus as the Praetorian Prefect in Gaul, Rufinus, was Gallus' maternal uncle and it was feared that he might encourage the ambitions of his nephew.[54] The intention had been to turn the troops against Rufinus and so bring about his death, but the scheme was put off, hence Eusebius' mission to calm the soldiers. However, the problem of what to do about Gallus remained, and Eusebius was one of the intimates of the emperor who discussed the matter with him at Milan in 354.[55] The plan was to summon Gallus from Antioch to Milan on the pretext of the need to discuss matters of government, and then execute him. Some of the advisers (whom Ammianus designates as flatterers), including Eusebius, also proposed that the Master of Cavalry Ursicinus (upon whom Ammianus attended at this time) should also be recalled on the grounds that in the political vacuum in the east created by the absence of Gallus this general might seize imperial power.⁵⁶ It was further alleged that it was the sons of Ursicinus who were the potential candidates for imperial office, and that Gallus had been deliberately led astray in order to engineer his fall and the rise of Ursicinus' sons.⁵⁷ Ammianus presents the motives for this advice in a negative light, asserting that it was prompted by hostility to Ursicinus. Eusebius is characterized as being prone to doing harm (effusior ad nocendum), and the giving of this advice about Ursicinus is said to have been supported by the other court eunuchs as they were greedy of gain, since they stood to win a share of the property of convicted men. Ursicinus was duly summoned to Milan, as was Gallus. On his journey to Milan Gallus was apprehended at Poetovio in Noricum (modern Ptuj in Slovenia) and then taken to Istria near the town of Pola (modern Pula in Croatia), where he was interrogated by Eusebius as well as the notary Pentadius and the tribune of the guard Mallobaudes.⁵⁸ His execution followed.

Subsequently, in 355 at Aquileia, Eusebius was also one of those (with Arbitio, the Master of Cavalry) entrusted with judging the soldiers from the east accused of being accomplices of Gallus.⁵⁹ Again Ammianus emphasizes the evil character of Eusebius, characterizing him and Arbitio as 'equally unjust and cruel' (iniusti pariter et cruenti). His assessment of their verdicts as judges is grim:

> They, without examining anyone carefully or distinguishing between the innocent and the guilty, scourged and tortured some and condemned them to banishment, others they thrust down to the lowest military rank, the rest they sentenced to suffer death. And after filling the tombs with corpses, they returned as if in triumph and reported their exploits to the emperor, who in regard to these and similar cases was openly inflexible and severe.⁶⁰

As for Urisicinus, he was put on trial for treason but not convicted.⁶¹ Subsequently, he rendered good service to Constantius in 355 by eliminating the usurper Silvanus at Cologne in Gaul, where he remained until 357 when he was returned to the east as Master of Cavalry.⁶² However, at the court in Sirmium in 359 rumours about the ambitions of the general continued to circulate, in which Eusebius was a leading figure. Ammianus reports that the eunuch resented Ursicinus because he would not enrich him and refused to give him his house in Antioch, which the eunuch had demanded of the general.⁶³ Again Eusebius is depicted as harnessing other eunuchs to serve his agenda, the chamberlains denigrating Ursicinus to Constantius in private:

> Eusebius then, like a viper swelling with abundant poison and arousing its multitudinous brood to mischief when they are still barely able to crawl, sent out his chamberlains, already well grown, with directions that, amid the duties of their more private attendance, with the soft utterances of voices always childish and persuasive they should with bitter hatred batter the reputation of that brave man in the too receptive ears of the prince. And they promptly did what they were ordered.⁶⁴

Indeed, the order for Ursicinus' recall was sent out, the intention being to replace him in the east with Sabinianus and for Ursicinus to become Master of Infantry in the west, replacing Barbatio (who had been executed for treason).⁶⁵ Yet when Ursicinus and his men had come as far as Thrace they were ordered to return to Mesopotamia.⁶⁶ Ammianus alleges that this was done for underhand reasons: 'if the Persians were baffled and returned to their own country, the glorious deed would be attributed to the ability of the new leader; but if Fortune proved unfavourable, Ursicinus would be accused as a traitor to his country'.⁶⁷ In the ongoing conflict with Persia, the Romans did indeed suffer a setback, for in 359 the frontier city of Amida (modern Diyarbakir) fell to the enemy. Although Ursicinus subsequently did replace Barbatio as Master of Infantry there was an inquiry in 360 into why Amida had been lost, headed by Arbitio and Florentius the Master of Offices.⁶⁸ This resulted in the sacking and exile of Ursicinus rather than the exposure of the failings of Sabinianus, and again Ammianus emphasizes the role of Eusebius in this outcome. He asserts that Arbitio and Florentius:

> rejected the evident and plausible reasons, and fearing that Eusebius, then head chamberlain (cubiculi tunc praepositus), would take offence if they admitted evidence which clearly showed that what had happened was the result of the persistent inaction of Sabinianus, they turned from the truth and examined into trivial matters far remote from the business in hand.⁶⁹

This prompted an outburst from Ursicinus, which sealed his fate; Ammianus reports that he exclaimed:

> 'Although the emperor despises me, the importance of the present business is such, that it cannot be examined into and punished, except by the judgement of the prince; yet let him know, as if from the words of a seer, that so long as he grieves over what he has learned on no good authority to have happened at Amida, and so long as he is swayed by the will of the eunuchs (ad spadonum arbitrium trahitur), not even he in person with all the flower of his army will be able next spring to prevent the dismemberment of Mesopotamia.'⁷⁰

Eusebius' own fate fast approached, for on 5 October, 361 Constantius died of a fever at Mobsucrenae in Cilicia when journeying west to confront his cousin Julian. Eusebius was with the emperor at the time, and was amongst the leading men of the court who discussed what should be done.⁷¹ Ammianus records that it was reported that Eusebius suggested that Julian should be treated as Constantius' heir (which was indeed done), the eunuch being pricked by his guilty conscience.⁷² However, this did not save Eusebius, for he was one of the agents of Constantius condemned to death at the trials held at Chalcedon which Julian instituted shortly after succeeding his cousin.⁷³ Ammianus was of the view that Eusebius deserved his fate; he relates:

> Eusebius besides, who had been made Constantius' grand chamberlain, a man full of pride and cruelty, was condemned to death by the judges. This man, who had been raised from the lowest station to a position which enabled him almost to give orders like those of the emperor himself, and in consequence had become intolerable, Adrastia, the judge of human acts, had plucked by the ear (as the saying

is) and warned him to live with more restraint; and when he demurred, she threw him headlong, as if from a lofty cliff.⁷⁴

Thus, Ammianus creates a striking picture of Eusebius. He focuses on the eunuch in relation to Ursicinus and Gallus, and the nature of the court and regime of Constantius II, as well as the character of the emperor himself. Seemingly led by his partiality to Ursicinus and Julian, Ammianus depicts Eusebius and Constantius very negatively. He characterizes Eusebius as a trusted and powerful agent of the emperor, always close by his side or undertaking missions for him. The eunuch is portrayed as a major, if not the major, voice at the imperial court, his position recognized by other officials. Ammianus even jokes that the emperor had some influence with the eunuch, an image reinforced at the end of his account of the fate of Eusebius when he says that he had risen to quasi-imperial power.⁷⁵ As already noted, Eusebius is shown harnessing the other eunuch chamberlains in the pursuit of his interests, and his greed of gain is a quality they share. Since Ammianus' narrative only commences in 353 we learn nothing of Eusebius' early career, though the reference to his low station suggests that he had worked his way up through the ranks of chamberlains and had been a slave.

That Eusebius was a slave is in fact stated by Libanius (another supporter of Julian) in his *Funeral Oration for Julian*. Commenting on the three main victims of the trials at Chalcedon, Libanius records Eusebius as the second of these and remarks 'although he had enslaved Constantius he was himself a slave and, what's more terrible, a eunuch', and that Eusebius 'was most responsible for the cruel death of Gallus'.⁷⁶ Indeed, Ammianus' account of Eusebius and his career clearly reflects a more widespread narrative that was already current during the eunuch's lifetime and immediately after his death. Libanius emphasizes the power that Eusebius had over Constantius and his crime of securing the death of Gallus. These aspects are also featured in Julian's *Letter to the Athenians*. Julian asserts:

> it was to gratify a eunuch (ἀνδρογύνου), his chamberlain who was also his chief cook (τοῦ τῶν μαγείρων ἐπιτρόπου), that Constantius gave over to his most inveterate enemies his own cousin, the Caesar, his sister's husband, the father of his niece, the man whose own sister he had himself married in earlier days, and to whom he owed many obligations connected with the gods of the family.⁷⁷

Julian stresses the repugnant nature of the death of Gallus by listing the multiple family ties that connected him to the emperor.⁷⁸ His assertion that Eusebius was also Constantius' chief cook seems rather random, but the noun 'cook' (ὁ μάγειρος) can also be translated as 'butcher', so perhaps Julian is in fact saying that the eunuch was the chief murderer of the regime. The degree of Eusebius' power is also reflected by the following observation of Julian:

> that execrable eunuch (ἀνδρόγυνος), his trusty chamberlain (ὁ πιστὸς αὐτοῦ κατακοιμιστής), unconsciously and involuntarily proved himself my benefactor. For he did not allow me to meet the Emperor often, nor perhaps did the latter desire it; still the eunuch was the chief reason. For what he dreaded was that if we

had any intercourse with one another I might be taken into favour, and when my loyalty (πιστὸς) became evident I might be given some place of trust.⁷⁹

Julian intimates that Eusebius controlled access to the emperor, and thus controlled the emperor himself. Further, Julian indulges in word play again, referring to the quality of trust that Eusebius held (and which was generally ascribed to eunuchs), but then laying claim to it himself, no doubt implying that he was genuinely trustworthy. Finally, as already noted, in his *Beard-hater* Julian indicates something of the important status accorded eunuchs in the regime of Constantius, contrasting this with the situation during his own reign.⁸⁰ Julian was surely thinking in particular of the central place and elevated status that Eusebius held in the government of his cousin.⁸¹

Even in the 'Arian' *Church History* of Philostorgius, Eusebius is associated primarily with the death of Gallus, and in fact it is alleged that he executed the Caesar against the wishes of the emperor.⁸² Describing how Gallus was demoted and confined on an island of Dalmatia⁸³ the summary continues:

> But the eunuch Eusebius ... continued with the others of his party to inflame Constantius' wrath against Gallus, since they feared that respect for his oaths or for his family relationship might cause him to recall the Caesar from exile, and once the latter had escaped the peril he was in, he would bring those evil men to an evil end. And thus their cajolery resulted in men being sent to do away with Gallus. But before the deed had been done, Constantius repented and sent others to prevent the murder. Eusebius' party, though, saw to it secretly that they did not reach the island or show anyone the order rescinding the death sentence until the condemned man had been put to death by the sword. And it happened as they desired. This was why Julian, when afterwards he was invested with empire, exacted retribution from Eusebius and his party for the crime done to his brother.⁸⁴

Philostorgius seems concerned then to defend Constantius by placing the burden of responsibility for the death of Gallus on the shoulders of the eunuch Eusebius.

While some authors are preoccupied with Eusebius' role and influence in the political arena, others record his involvement in religious affairs, though these would have been of concern to Constantius too. Indeed, Eusebius is found as an agent of the emperor here also.⁸⁵ In his *History of the Arians*, composed around 357, Athanasius records that in 356 Constantius despatched the eunuch Eusebius to Rome to win Pope Liberius (352–366) to the Arian cause and secure his opposition to Athanasius.⁸⁶ Athanasius then relates that Eusebius failed in his mission and was angry with Liberius as he was not favourable to the Arians (of whom the eunuch was one) and had rejected the offerings that Eusebius had made at the shrine of St Peter; consequently, when the eunuch returned to Constantius he incited the emperor against Liberius and also stirred up the other court eunuchs, 'for many of those who were about Constantius, or rather the whole number of them, are eunuchs, who engross all the influence with him, and it is impossible to do anything there without them (πολλοὶ δέ, μᾶλλον δὲ τὸ ὅλον εἰσὶν εὐνοῦχοι παρὰ Κωνσταντίῳ καὶ πάντα δύνανται παρ' αὐτῷ, χωρίς τε τούτων οὐδέν ἐστιν ἐκεῖ γενέσθαι)'.⁸⁷ Athanasius asserts that eunuchs were naturally Arians, and thus opponents of Liberius, because of their physical and moral condition: 'It was the eunuchs who instigated these proceedings against all. And the most remarkable circumstance in the matter is this; that the Arian heresy which denies the Son of God, receives its support from eunuchs, who, as both their bodies are fruitless, and their souls barren of virtue, cannot bear even to hear the name of son'.[88]

Following Eusebius' meeting with Liberius in Rome, the pope was subsequently summoned to Milan and interviewed by the emperor to secure his condemnation of Athanasius, as recorded in Theodoret's *Church History*, which is dated to the mid-fifth century.[89] In the dialogue between Constantius and Liberius, Theodoret records Eusebius as interjecting twice, to attack Athanasius and defend the emperor (exclaiming that Liberius was casting Constantius as a Nebuchadnezzar).[90] Having failed to win over Liberius Constantius decided to exile him to Beroea in Thrace. Theodoret also relates that Liberius was offered money three times, first by the emperor, then by the Empress Eusebia and finally by Eusebius, though each time Liberius rejected the gift. Theodoret asserts that Liberius rebuked the eunuch saying 'You have turned all the churches of the world into a desert, and do you bring alms to me, as to a criminal? Begone, and become first a Christian'.[91] Further, Sozomen asserts that Eusebius was a friend of the Arian Eudoxius, the bishop of Antioch, and that he assisted the Arian cause by engineering that two separate church councils met in 359, one in the west at Ariminum and one in the east at Seleucia.[92] Given the prominent role assigned to the court eunuch Eusebius in ecclesiastical affairs it is interesting that he can be confused in later sources with Eusebius the bishop of Nicomedia, a key player in the early years of the reign of Constantius II – or there can even be ambiguity as to which Eusebius is meant, reflecting the fact that they were both perceived as powerful.[93]

The case of Eutropius

Another case of a Grand Chamberlain who is richly documented is that of Eutropius, the *praepositus sacri cubiculi* of the emperor Arcadius, who ruled the eastern empire after the death of his father Theodosius I while his brother Honorius (395–423) ruled the western empire.[94] Like Eusebius, Eutropius is presented by the sources as the leading power at the court of Arcadius (especially for the years 395–399), symbolized by the fact that he gained the honour of becoming one of the consuls for the year 399. Also, like Eusebius, Eutropius attracted intensely virulent comment. Most notorious are the two invectives that the Alexandrian poet Claudian wrote about the eunuch in 399, the first when Eutropius was still a political player and focusing on the fact that he had become consul, the second when Eutropius had fallen from favour and had been exiled to Cyprus.[95] Like Ammianus and the other authors who displayed hostility to Eusebius, Claudian has a particular agenda. His speeches were written for consumption at the western court, which was ostensibly headed by Honorius but in reality controlled by the emperor's father-in-law the half-Vandal general Stilicho; this man had ambitions to unite the entire empire under him, claiming that Theodosius I had left him as regent for both Honorius and Arcadius.[96] In the two invectives Stilicho is depicted as representing the masculine western Roman empire and as the saviour of the corrupted and effeminate eastern empire. The fact that Eutropius was a eunuch was a gift for a writer of invective, and the texts make much play of the gender identity of the consul, treating him both as woman and as neither male nor female.[97] However, they also provide information about Eutropius' life and career which, though put to work in Claudian's hostile purpose, can provide a framework for the study of this eunuch. This framework can be augmented by the wide array of other sources that deal with Eutropius.

Claudian asserts that Eutropius had been a eunuch from an early age, having been castrated (by an Armenian) for the slave trade.[98] He emphasizes that Eutropius had many masters, which reflects badly on the eunuch as his serial owners did not want to keep him. A well-known owner is said to have been the soldier (*miles stabuli*) Ptolemaeus, who kept the eunuch for sexual services until he gave him away to Arinthaeus (Master of Infantry under Emperor Valens, who reigned from 364 to 378).[99] Claudian traces how Eutropius' function altered as he aged. Having ceased to be a sex slave he became a pander and then a 'lady's maid', being part of a bride's dowry for a son-in-law; Claudian visualizes Eutropius combing the hair of his mistress, providing water for ablutions, and fanning her with peacock feathers.[100] Eventually, when Eutropius became repulsive with old age, he was freed, and only then entered imperial service, in which he rose to become master of the court.[101] The status that Eutropius acquired at the court is conveyed by Claudian indicating his close relationship with Arcadius: the eunuch was hailed as the father of the emperor, the emperor in effect being his symbolic son (and heir).[102] A key patron in his promotion at court is said to have been Abundantius (a general under Theodosius I, and consul in 393), who was hoist by his own petard, for Eutropius was responsible for his exile (in 396) and thus acquired his property.[103] Claudian identifies key allies (also men of lowly origin, he impresses upon us) of the eunuch during his government. Hosius, an ex-slave and cook (and the Master of Offices of Arcadius), is said to have been Eutropius' right-hand man, Claudian calling them 'joint rulers of the eastern empire' (2.350: considunt apices gemini dicionis Eoae).[104] Closely associated with Eutropius and Hosius is Leo, an ex-weaver, who led the army to defeat against Tarbigilus and the Greuthungi in 399; he is described as 'Eutropius's Ajax' when he volunteered to take the command against Tarbigilus.[105]

Of Eutropius' roles at the imperial court when established as a leading political figure, Claudian draws attention to two in particular: judge and general.[106] Concerning the latter it is recorded that Eutropius led an expedition against the Getae (the Huns) in the east (in 398), for which he claimed a victory.[107] The eunuch is also depicted as the figure at court who decided what response to make to the revolt of Tarbigilus and his Greuthungi, the event which precipitated Eutropius' fall in 399.[108] Initially, Eutropius ignored the revolt, then tried to buy Tarbigilus off, then (after summoning a council to the palace to discuss the matter) sent a military force against him. Claudian alleges that Tarbigilus was alienated from the regime in Constantinople in the first place as Eutropius refused to give him sufficient remuneration, which again emphasizes the eunuch's apparent power in political decision-making; Eutropius is also said to advise the Senate.[109] Claudian mentions other administrative acts of the eunuch, which are interpreted to reflect his greed: the selling of offices, and the sub-division of provinces.[110] Eutropius' status and roles are further emphasized by Claudian commenting on the number of statues of the eunuch that were erected and the inscriptions which accompanied them.[111] The degree of Eutropius' significance in the eastern empire is conveyed by Claudian when he declares that the eunuch 'is called defender of the laws, father of the emperor, and the court deigns to acknowledge a slave as its overlord'.[112]

The picture of Eutropius and his career provided by Claudian is echoed and expanded by other texts, in particular the *New History* of Zosimus, dating to the late-fifth or early-sixth century but drawing upon the century earlier *History* of Eunapius, of which only fragments survive.[113] It emerges that Eutropius was an agent of Arcadius' father too. Sozomen reports that Theodosius I sent him to Egypt to consult a monk with the gift of prophecy (John, who resided in Thebais) about the outcome of Theodosius' conflict with Eugenius, who had set himself up as emperor in the west in 392.[114] The eunuch received John's prophecy that Eugenius would be defeated but that Theodosius himself would die in Italy after his victory. Claudian alludes to this incident too, observing that when inaugurated as consul Eutropius boasted 'of a prophetic dream he had in Egypt and of the defeat of tyrants which he foretold',[115] but also when he mocks the eunuch as a 'blind Sybil', since he was not able to foresee his own fate.[116] Regarding Eutropius' activities at the court of Arcadius, he is also credited with being instrumental in arranging the emperor's marriage to Aelia Eudoxia (the daughter of Bauto, a Frank) which occurred in April 395.[117] This is placed in the context of court politics in Constantinople, for the Praetorian Prefect Rufinus had wanted the emperor to marry his own daughter and now sought to eliminate Eutropius. Zosimus asserts that the eunuch was party to Stilicho's plan to eliminate Rufinus himself, which was engineered through the general Gainas, a Goth. However, Rufinus was simply replaced as the dominant figure at the eastern court by Eutropius, who was enriched by the greater share of Rufinus' property.[118] The fall of Abundantius at the hands of Eutropius, referred to by Claudian, seems to have been part of a wider story, for Zosimus records that the eunuch also eliminated the general Timasius and commander Bargus in this way, even though Bargus himself had conspired to bring down Timasius.[119] Such activity of Eutropius is presented by Zosimus as the eunuch getting rid of competitors at court and securing wealth and power for himself, and encompasses the case of Abundantius.[120] Eutropius even moved against Stilicho, having him declared a public enemy, and luring Africa away from the west and annexing it to the territory of the eastern empire by winning over the general Gildo (though Gildo was ousted by his brother in 398, and the west regained Africa).[121] Zosimus emphasizes the power that Eutropius had achieved by asserting memorably that 'There was no one at Constantinople who dared look Eutropius in the face' and 'Eutropius ruled Arcadius like a fatted animal (καθάπερ βοσκήματος)'.[122] Eunapius also vividly conjures up the sinister control of the eunuch, remarking that 'The eunuch held power in the palace and, coiling around through the halls, like a true serpent seized everything and dragged it off to his lair'.[123] The political significance of the eunuch (and Stilicho) is also strikingly conveyed by Eunapius when he reflects on the difficulty of acquiring good information about affairs in the West in 'the time of Eutropius'. He observes:

> If any officials or soldiers had access to information on political activity, they related it as they wished, biased by friendship or hostility or a desire to please

someone. And if you brought together three or four of them with conflicting versions as witnesses, there would be a great argument which would proceed from passionate and heated interjections to a pitched battle. They would say, 'Where did you get this from?' 'Where did Stilicho see you?' 'Would you have seen the eunuch?' so that it was quite a task to sort out the tangle.[124]

Another contemporary text which appears to allude to the power of Eutropius (and eunuchs in general) at the eastern court is the philosopher Synesius of Cyrene's treatise *On Kingship*, written at almost exactly the same time as Claudian's invectives.[125] Synesius came on embassy to Arcadius in Constantinople at the end of the fourth century, and seems to have written up his advice to the emperor soon after. Famously, he compares Arcadius to a jellyfish,[126] and complains about the isolation of the emperor within his court. As part of this he seems to point to the power of the court eunuchs over the secluded emperor, especially that of Eutropius.[127] The status of Eutropius is also emphasized in a focused section of the summary of Philostorgius, which notes like Claudian that the eunuch was father of the emperor:

> [Philostorgius] says that Eutropius crept into the imperial residence after Rufinus; he was a eunuch born into slavery who had risen to the rank of *praepositus* but was not satisfied with his situation. Since his castration had kept him from the purple, however, he persuaded the emperor to give him the titles of patrician and consul. And from then on the eunuch was father of the emperor, he who could not engender even an ordinary child.[128]

Regarding the allies of Eutropius, Zosimus mentions the figure of Leo (in negative terms again),[129] but Eunapius also records that Subarmachius the chief of the bodyguards (possibly Count of the Domestics) was 'most loyal of all to Eutropius'.[130]

Of Eutropius' activities at court, the church historians are naturally interested in the eunuch's involvement in ecclesiastical affairs. Philostorgius notes that Eutropius was hostile to Eunomius, ordering the Praetorian Prefect Caesarius to move the heretic from Dacora to Tyana in 396, not allowing him to be buried with his teacher, and issuing edicts for the destruction of his books.[131] Socrates remarks on the role of the eunuch in securing the patriarchate of Constantinople for John Chrysostom (in 398) as the court wished, for Eutropius forestalled the opposition of Theophilus the Patriarch of Alexandria by threatening him with being put on trial.[132] According to Palladius, a contemporary and supporter of John Chrysostom, Eutropius was personally concerned to promote John, having previously met him when on imperial business in the east (perhaps his visit to the monk John in Egypt), and engineered his journey to Constantinople by getting the emperor to write to the governor (τὸν κόμητα) of Antioch.[133] The seemingly special relationship between Eutropius and John Chrysostom also surfaces in Mark the Deacon's *Life* of Porphyry, the bishop of Gaza. Mark says he was sent to Constantinople by Porphyry (in 398) to solicit the emperors to suppress the pagan temples at Gaza.[134] Mark proceeds by taking a letter to John Chrysostom from Porphyry to the patriarch, who then seeks an audience with the chamberlain Eutropius (described as being very powerful with Arcadius), giving him the letter and asking him to acquiesce to the request. Encouraged by Eutropius, John continues to solicit the eunuch, and seven days later there was published an imperial letter ordering the temples of Gaza to be shut and an end put to their ceremonies.[135] While question marks hang over the reliability of this text (Porphyry is not mentioned by any other source, and 'Mark' is writing in the mid-fifth century at the earliest),[136] even if it is fiction it reflects perceptions of Eutropius that existed within his lifetime and persisted beyond it.

The events leading up to the fall of Eutropius are treated at length by Zosimus, and certain church historians are concerned with it too though they give a different explanation for the eunuch's abandonment by the emperor. Zosimus is in line with Claudian, associating Eutropius' disgrace with the revolt of Gothic general Tribigild.[137] He asserts that Gainas was key in the latter event, allying with Tribigild in order to bring down the eunuch whose pre-eminence he resented.[138] Arcadius' reaction to the revolt is to put Eutropius in charge of the empire, and the eunuch deployed Leo and Gainas as generals. On the failure and death of Leo, Gainas brought pressure on Arcadius to eliminate Eutropius on the grounds that he was the cause of the situation with Tribigild.[139] Arcadius duly dismissed Eutropius, who sought sanctuary in church (in Hagia Sophia itself). Removed from there he was exiled to Cyprus, but under pressure from Gainas he was brought to Chalcedon and killed. Zosimus concludes the tale of Eutropius by observing that 'So Fate dealt unexpectedly with Eutropius on both counts, in raising him to heights previously unattained by a eunuch and then in bringing about his death through the hatred of the enemies of the state'.[140] The church historians Philostorgius and Sozomen, however, record that it was Arcadius' wife, the Empress Eudoxia, who was instrumental in bringing down Eutropius.[141] Philostorgius asserts that Eudoxia had been insulted by the eunuch and threatened with removal from the imperial palace, and she responded by reporting the matter to her husband in dramatic fashion. Thus it was that Arcadius finally took action. As for the recall of Eutropius from Cyprus to stand trial, Philostorgius accounts for this by saying that the eunuch was accused by certain individuals (he does not name them) of having misappropriated imperial decorations when he was consul, thus effectively committing treason. He reports that the trial was held at Pantichion and headed by the Prefect Aurelian, and that when found guilty Eutropius was beheaded.[142] It is notable that Photius himself comments that other writers give different reasons for Eutropius' sacking, exile and execution. Socrates and Sozomen seem to be drawn to the story of the fall of Eutropius in particular because of the aspect of the seeking of sanctuary and the role of the Patriarch John Chrysostom in the affair. They note the irony of the fact that Eutropius had been responsible for the law removing the protection of sanctuary, and that while the eunuch sheltered under the altar in the church the patriarch delivered a sermon concerning him (which Socrates claims was an invective against the eunuch, but Sozomen says was focused on pride and fickle fortune).[143] As for his subsequent death, unlike Philostorgius they are not concerned with details. Socrates reports that Eutropius was executed by order of the emperor 'for certain offences' and that his name was removed from the list of consuls, while Socrates just records the fact of his death and notes that the anti-asylum law was repealed.

Interestingly, the oration of John Chrysostom concerning Eutropius has survived.[144] While the oration (titled *On Eutropius the Eunuch, Patrician and Consul*) reveals something of the life of Eutropius it is primarily concerned to make a Christian lesson of the dramatic events of his fall, conveying a moral message about the instability and transience of fortune (indicated by John beginning the oration by quoting from the Bible 'Vanity of vanities, all is vanity': Ecclesiastes 1.2), and about the virtue of mercy. John emphasizes Eutropius' wealth and power. He declares 'who was more exalted than this man? Did he not surpass the whole world in wealth? had he not climbed to the very pinnacle of distinction? did not all tremble and fear before him?' (Τίς γὰρ τούτου γέγονεν ὑψηλότερος; οὐ πᾶσαν τὴν οἰκουμένην παρῆλθε τῷ πλούτῳ; οὐ πρὸς αὐτὰς τῶν ἀξιωμάτων ἀνέβη τὰς κορυφάς; οὐχὶ πάντες αὐτὸν ἔτρεμον, καὶ ἐδεδοίκεισαν;) (2).[145] The status of Eutropius is also reflected by the reference to the large crowds who had come to Hagia Sophia to see what was happening (3). John depicts himself as the friend and compassionate protector of Eutropius, despite the eunuch being an enemy of the church. He refers to the anti-asylum law (3). He claims that the emperor himself felt some mercy for Eutropius, but refers to the insult done to the imperial majesty by the eunuch (ἐκδικίαν τοῦ ὑβρισμένου βασιλέως) (4), perhaps alluding to Eutropius reputedly threatening to remove the Empress Eudoxia from the palace.[146] It is evident that Eutropius was understood as being at risk of execution, the soldiers in particular being incensed with him on behalf of the emperor. Thus, Sozomen's assessment of the oration of John on Eutropius is more accurate: it was not about berating Eutropius but taking lessons from his example and exercising Christian virtue.

In relation to the fall and exile of Eutropius there also survives the law issued in 399 in the names of Arcadius and Honorius to the Praetorian Prefect Aurelian concerning the event. It states:

> All the property of Eutropius, who was once grand chamberlain, We have annexed to the account of Our treasury; he shall be stripped of his splendor, and his consulship shall be vindicated from the foul stain and from the memory of his name and from his low meanness (consulatu a taetra inluvie et a commemoratione nominis eius et caenosis sordibus vindicato). All his acts shall be annulled, that all ages may be mute about him, that a blot may not appear on Our age through the recital of his deeds, and that neither those men who by their courage and their wounds extend the Roman boundaries nor those who guard these territories by preserving the equity of the law may lament the fact that this vile monster defiled the divine gift of the consulship by his contagion (quod divinum praemium consulatus lutulentum prodigium contagione foedavit). He shall know that he has been despoiled also of the dignity of the patriciate and of all the lesser dignities which he has polluted by the perversity of his morals (quas morum polluit scaevitate). All his statues, all his images, in bronze as well as in marble, in pigments, or in whatever material is suitable for portraiture, We order to be destroyed in all cities and towns, both in private and public places, in order that the stigma of our age, so to speak, may not pollute the sight of those who look at such images (ne tamquam nota nostri saeculi obtutus polluat intuentum). And so, in the custody of faithful guards, he shall be conducted to the island of Cyprus, to which Your Sublimity shall know that he has been relegated, and, there surrounded by vigilant guards, he shall not be able to throw all things into confusion by the madness of his own designs.[147]

Of particular interest in the condemnation is the reference to soldiers and lawyers, roles the eunuch himself encroached upon. The mention of the multiplicity of the visual images of Eutropius is notable too, echoing Claudian's mention of the statues of the eunuch. These are also recorded in a fragment of Eunapius, in conjunction with the palaces of Eutropius; it states 'Golden statues of [Eutropius] were set up everywhere, and he built splendid palaces more magnificent than the whole city'.[148] Also striking is the intensely strong and hostile rhetoric, so typical of late Roman imperial legislation. Like the invectives of Claudian, this makes much of Eutropius' identity as a eunuch, depicting him as an immoral monster, a contagion infecting the empire and its people. Nevertheless, the law ultimately reflects the great political significance the eunuch achieved in the Roman Empire.

Reading Eusebius and Eutropius

Concluding his examination of the careers of Eusebius and Eutropius, Dunlap observed that:

> The deceit, the trickery, the rapacity, the cruelty of Eusebius and Eutropius seem to have been characteristic, in some degree, of most eunuchs, and it is easy to understand, after following the careers of these intriguers, the exasperation with which a once famous Chrysaorius exclaimed, 'If you have a eunuch, kill him; if you haven't, buy one and kill him!'[149]

From the vantage point of the early twenty-first century AD Dunlap's remarks of 1924 seem naïve, even shocking. However, he was not alone in such hostile assessments of court eunuchs in history, witness for instance Norman Penzer's verdicts on eunuchs of the Ottoman Empire published in 1936; he asserts 'as a general rule the power of eunuchs has brought in its trail nothing but cruelty, intrigue, corruption, and disaster'.[150] Thankfully in the course of the twentieth century historians did begin to question the stereotypical image of the eunuch and attempt to understand why it was that eunuchs were such a prevalent and important feature of royal and imperial courts in history.[151] In short, the subject of eunuchs began to be treated seriously, and a pioneer in the case of later Roman court eunuchs was Keith Hopkins, who in 1963 published a fundamentally important article on the topic, which was then incorporated as a chapter in his monograph *Conquerors and Slaves*, published in 1978.[152] Hopkins declares that his purpose:

> is to explain why slave eunuchs and particularly ex-slave eunuchs held so much power in the imperial and aristocratic society of Eastern Rome, to put this power in the context of the socio-political developments of the later empire, and to analyse some of the social functions of this power.

Thus, his interest lies particularly in how and why court eunuchs were powerful as individuals and as a group, but as part of his study he considers why the emperors were enthusiastic to employ eunuchs. He identifies various factors. Eunuchs could serve as useful scapegoats, 'soaking up criticisms which might otherwise have fallen upon the emperor'.[153] They also 'fulfilled a vital function' by acting 'as a lubricant preventing too much friction between the emperor and the other forces of the state which threatened his superiority', playing a role in keeping the military and the nobility in their place.[154] This function of eunuchs he places in the social and political transformations that occurred in the Roman Empire between the time of the Principate and the late empire,[155] when under Diocletian and Constantine the equestrian order, the property class below that of the senatorial class which had previously served to balance its power, had become 'assimilated' with it.[156] In addition, the emperor had become a more obviously absolutist ruler, and a more remote figure. Thus eunuchs served the purpose of providing a balance to a 'unified upper order' (taking on the role of the equestrians in the Principate) and also met another 'distinct need, the need of a divine emperor for human information and contact', becoming intermediaries between the ruler and other members of society. He asserts that 'any exercise of power by non-aristocrats limited the power of aristocrats', and that later Roman court eunuchs (like those of the Chinese Empire) worked in the imperial interest and served 'to counteract the power of the nobles'. An advantage of eunuchs, he says, is that the aristocracy would not assimilate such an objectionable group: slaves of barbarian extraction who had been castrated and rendered physically distinct. As such 'They were completely dependent upon the emperor and had no natural allies in society, no other retreat than his protection.' He finally summarizes as follows:

> To recapitulate: the tension between an absolutist monarch and the other powers of the state; the seclusion of a sacred emperor behind a highly formalised court ritual; the need of both parties for intermediaries; the exploitation by eunuchs of this channel for the appropriation to themselves of some of the power of controlling the distribution of favours; the non-assimilability of eunuchs into the aristocracy; the cohesive but non-corporate nature of their corps; and the expertise which resulted from the permanence of their positions as compared with the amateurish, rivalrous and individualistic strivings of aristocrats; all these factors in combination and in interaction can account for the increasing power with which eunuchs were invested, and the continuity with which they, as a body, held it.[157]

The detailed cases of Eusebius and Eutropius serve to demonstrate many of Hopkins' points, and a comparison between them reveals how accounts of court eunuchs could be highly stereotypical and prejudicial. The hostile narratives of the careers of Eusebius and Eutropius clearly originate with authors with distinct agendas. A fragment of the history of Eunapius lays bare his concerns; he declares:

> It was... because of a surfeit of suffering that some compared the eunuch Eutropius to Julian's day and age. Just as the doctors tell us that for survival it is better to have a sick spleen than to suffer with the liver or with that part of the body which extends through the lungs close by the heart, so it happened that, when they were in the grip of the worst misfortunes, people esteemed the mad eunuch in comparison with the evils that were afflicting them.[158]

Anti-eunuch rhetoric pours out of accounts of the careers and characters of Eusebius and Eutropius: they are greedy and corrupt, effeminate and immoral, controlling and tyrannous. It is clear, however, that Eusebius was a trusted agent of the Emperor Constantius II. The accounts of his actions actually reveal him doing a good job, pursuing the interests and security of his master. In fact, he did such a good job that he became synonymous with the regime and paid the ultimate price after the death of Constantius and the succession of Julian. Likewise, Eutropius clearly provided the Theodosian dynasty with valued service, undertaking duties for both Theodosius I and Arcadius. Unlike Eusebius though, Eutropius did not maintain his final master's favour for the length of his reign. Evidently he fell victim to the complex political context and court rivalries that revolved around the youthful brothers Arcadius and Honorius; it is possible that his fall was even engineered by his western rival Stilicho.[159] As with Eusebius also, it is Eutropius who can serve as the focus for criticism of the regime in Constantinople rather than the emperor himself.[160] This rather leaves open the question as to where power actually lay; were the eunuchs truly powerful, or did the emperors in fact control them, and indeed deploy them as useful objects of potential blame?

Conclusion

The later Roman Empire is famous, even infamous, for its use of court eunuchs and for the power they were said to exercise as a group and as individuals, especially in the role of Grand Chamberlain. Certainly, there is rich source material for this phenomenon, and striking case studies exist, such as those of Eusebius and Eutropius. As this book demonstrates, however, eunuchs were part of the history of the Roman Empire long before the advent of Diocletian and the period of Late Antiquity, and not just as devotees of the Great Mother but as slaves and court favourites as well as free individuals. The advantage of taking a longer view of the history of eunuchs in the Roman Empire is that one can track the increasing prominence and significance of eunuchs within it, and appreciate that Rome needs to be situated within a wider Mediterranean world and be seen as sharing Hellenistic court traditions, which in turn were inherited from Persia and Assyria. In its turn, Rome passed on the ancient tradition of court eunuchs to its successor the so-called Byzantine Empire (in actuality the survival of the Roman Empire in the medieval period) which in turn shaped its successor the Ottoman Empire, which maintained the tradition of court eunuchs as late as the early-twentieth century. In this chain of court eunuchs, a vital link is supplied by Rome.

6

'Eunuchs for the Kingdom of Heaven': Self-Castration and Eunuchs in Early Christianity

Introduction

The practice of self-castration within a religious context is probably something most associated with non-Christian religions, such as paganism and Hinduism. It may come as a surprise to many, then, that self-castration as a practice is met in the history of Christianity, notably in the early centuries of the religion, but also more recently, for instance in the figures of the Skoptsy of Russia as late as the early twentieth century.[1] However, such behaviour was not uncontroversial, and steps were taken to outlaw it. Yet, even if they had not castrated themselves, eunuchs could still have a prominent place in early Christianity, being found as converts, martyrs, clergy, monks and saints. The Byzantine Empire continued to be distinguished by eunuchs in prominent Christian roles, including the position of Patriarch of Constantinople, an office held twice in the ninth century by Ignatius the Younger, who was monk, cleric and saint.[2] This chapter explores why self-castration arose as a practice in early Christianity, what the response to this was, and how eunuchs had a conspicuous place in Christianity even if they were not self-castrates. The legacy of these early Christian eunuchs is reflected by those who populate medieval Byzantium but also those encountered in modern times, such as the Skoptsy of Russia. This phenomenon reflects the centrality of physical denial in Christianity.

Eunuchs for the Kingdom of Heaven: self-castration and Christianity

The practice of self-castration in Christianity originates in words ascribed to Jesus Christ in the New Testament, in the Gospel of Matthew. The Gospel relates that when Jesus went from Galilee to Judaea during his ministry he was quizzed by the Pharisees about his views on divorce.[3] His opinions on the matter were hard-line, recalling that God declared that husband and wife were one flesh and should not be put asunder, and asserting that only fornication (*porneia*) was grounds for divorce. On hearing this Jesus's disciples observed to him that it would be better not to marry, whereupon he responded that not all could accept the saying (*logos*), declaring 'For there are eunuchs who have been born so from their mother's womb, and there are eunuchs who have been made eunuchs by men, and there are eunuchs who have made themselves eunuchs for the sake of the kingdom of heaven.'[4] While there are ambiguities in this narrative (for example, what exactly do the disciples mean, and what *logos* is Jesus referring to?), the verse about eunuchs was generally understood by early Christian authors to refer to celibacy.[5] Jesus appears to be saying that while some will follow the path of marriage others will not, but will follow the path of celibacy instead. Thus, he can be thought to be using the term 'eunuch' metaphorically, indicating that celibates are like eunuchs in that they do not marry and eschew sexual relations. However, it is clear that Jesus's words could also be taken literally, for some early Christians understood him to mean that they should castrate themselves in the service of God. Given that at the time self-castration was a practice associated with the service of other deities (notably the Mother of the Gods, as seen in Chapter 1) and interpreted as a sign of religious devotion this was not such a stretch of the imagination.

The most famous example of an early Christian individual who reputedly embraced self-castration is Origen of Alexandria.[6] Origen was born into a Christian family towards the end of the second century AD (probably in 184 or 185) and became a leading intellectual in the Christian community. He was a prolific writer, but only a small percentage of his work has survived as he became a controversial figure, being banished from Alexandria and deposed from his position as priest, though he established himself in about 234 as a teacher at Caesarea in Palestine, where he had been ordained a priest. He died soon after the persecution of Christians conducted under the Emperor Decius (249–251), during which he himself was a target (his father had been martyred *c.* 203, in the reign of Septimius Severus). He was condemned as a heretic at the Council of Constantinople in 533, during the reign of Justinian I (527–565). A key source for the life of Origen is the *Church History* of Eusebius, who was bishop of Caesarea in Palestine in the first half of the fourth century AD, from *c.* 313 to 339.[7] The *Church History* reached its final form in 324/5, after the ending of the persecution of the Christians and the emergence of the Emperor Constantine I as a supporter of the Christian church. Origen, of whom Eusebius was an admirer and promoter, features heavily in Book 6, and there it is related that Origen castrated himself in his youth. Eusebius reports:

> At that time, while Origen was performing the work of instruction at Alexandria, he did a thing which gave abundant proof of an immature and youthful mind, yet withal of faith and self-control (σωφροσύνης). For he took the saying, 'There are eunuchs which made themselves eunuchs for the kingdom of heaven's sake,' in too literal and extreme a sense, and thinking both to fulfil the Saviour's saying, and also that he might prevent all suspicion of shameful slander on the part of unbelievers (for, young as he was, he used to discourse on divine things with women as well as men), he hastened to put into effect the Saviour's saying, taking care to escape the notice of the greater number of his pupils.[8]

Eusebius also notes that despite Origen's care Demetrius the bishop of Alexandria (189–232) learnt what he had done, 'and while he marvelled exceedingly at him for his rash act, he approved the zeal and the sincerity of his faith, bade him be of good cheer, and urged him to attach himself now all the more to the work of instruction'.[9] However, adds Eusebius, later on Demetrius used Origen's self-castration against him, attempting 'to describe the deed as monstrous (ἀτοπωτάτου) to the bishops throughout the world'.[10]

Whether Origen really did castrate himself is a matter of debate. In his own *Commentary on Matthew*, Origen rejected a literal interpretation of the words of Christ (15.1–5).[11] The testimony of Epiphanius the bishop of Salamis in Cyprus (367–403) also muddies the waters.[12] From Palestine like Eusebius, Epiphanius was however no admirer of Origen, considering him as the originator of the heresy of Arianism, that is considering Christ as a lesser being than God.[13] Like Eusebius, Epiphanius touches on the subject of Origen's body. In his *Panarion* (meaning 'Medicine Chest'), a text written in the 370s concerning heresies and how to 'medicate' against them,[14] he reports that:

> [S]ome say that he severed a nerve (νεῦρον ἀποτετμηκέναι) so that he would not be disturbed by sexual pleasure or inflamed and aroused by carnal impulses. Others say no, but that he invented a drug (φάρμακον) to apply to his genitals (τοῖς μορίοις) and dry them up ... And though I put no faith in the exaggerated stories about him, I have not neglected to report what is being said.[15]

Thus, Epiphanius indicates that Origen's 'self-castration' could have been less drastic than one might imagine, if indeed it happened at all. Nevertheless, one has to wonder why an Origen-admirer like Eusebius bothered to mention his self-castration, if indeed there was doubt about its actuality. Given that literal self-castration could be frowned upon by early Christians, Eusebius was risking aligning himself with a questionable hero.[16] As for Origen's own approval of a non-literal interpretation of Matthew 19.12, it is possible that he simply changed his mind later in life, after the enthusiasm of youth had passed.[17]

However, even if doubts surround the case of Origen, it is clear that it is not an isolated example. The Christian apologist Justin Martyr, who lived in the second century AD and was martyred in Rome in about 165, records a projected instance of self-castration in his *First Apology*, written in the mid 150s during the reign of Antoninus Pius, to whom it is addressed together with his two sons.[18] In a chapter dealing with the value Christians attached to continence, and which alludes to the deification of the Emperor Hadrian's boyfriend Antinous soon after his death in 130, he writes:

> And, in order to persuade you that we do not consider licentious sex to be a 'mystery',[19] recently one of ours gave a petition in Alexandria to Felix the governor, praying him to permit a physician to remove his testicles (τοὺς διδύμους), for the physicians there said that they were forbidden to do this without the permission of the governor. But as Felix was in no way willing to subscribe <this petition> the young man remained on his own, being content with his own conscience and that of those who thought like him.[20]

Although the case referred to by Justin is only a projected self-castration, one that did not come to fruition, it is nonetheless revealing. It indicates that some early Christians did contemplate castrating themselves with the purpose of attaining sexual continence. Further, this was to be no ecstatic self-mutilation, but a medical operation (the reluctance of the doctors no doubt an indication that the anti-castration law first introduced by the Emperor Domitian was still in force).[21] Further, this instance predates the supposed self-castration of Origen though it too is located in Alexandria; Walter Stevenson even wonders if the 'intellectual climate' of rejecting the body in second-century AD Alexandria encouraged some to turn to literal castration.[22]

A further instance of self-castration amongst early Christians is met in relation to a group called Valesians (named after Vales), who are discussed by Epiphanius in his *Panarion*.[23] He records that they had been expelled from the church and that some may still exist in Philadelphia over the Jordan. He also asserts that most of them were eunuchs (ἀπόκοποι), embracing castration in order to attain chastity, and that they even enforced castration on those who happened to pass by. Epiphanius associates their behaviour with another declaration of Jesus from the Gospel of Matthew: 'Wherefore if thy hand or thy foot offend thee, cut them off, and cast them from thee: it is better for thee to enter into life halt or maimed, rather than having two hands or two feet to be cast into everlasting fire'.[24] However, he also engages with Matthew 19.12, but observes that the Valesians do not constitute any of the three types of eunuchs identified by Jesus. In addition, he observes 'Because of what has been removed they are no longer men; and they cannot be women because that is against their nature' (58.3.1). Obviously Epiphanius' treatment of the Valesians is hostile and lurid, but in his *On Faith* he also asserts that 'not a few ... dared to make themselves eunuchs'.[25]

A case which brings us into the fourth century AD is that of Leontius, who became the bishop of Antioch in 344 under the Emperor Constantius II.[26] The details of his career are particularly reported by Athanasius the bishop of Alexandria, who was no admirer of Leontius because of their religious differences.[27] Like Origen, Leontius was associated with Arianism, while Athanasius was an advocate of Nicene Christianity, which was finally established as Orthodoxy at the Council of Constantinople in 381 under the Emperor Theodosius I. In his *Apology for his Flight*, dated to the late 350s, Athanasius comments on the sins of the Arians and writes:

> Leontius, for instance, being censured for his intimacy with a certain young woman, named Eustolium, and prohibited from living with her, mutilated himself (ἑαυτὸν ἀπέκοψεν) for her sake, in order that he might be able to associate with her freely. He did not however clear himself from suspicion, but rather on this account he was degraded from his rank as Presbyter, although the heretic Constantius by violence caused him to be named a Bishop.[28]

In his *History of the Arians*, also dated to the late 350s, Athanasius again deals with this case, asserting 'the eunuch (ὁ ἀπόκοπος) Leontius ... ought not to remain in communion even as a layman, because he mutilated himself that he might henceforth be at liberty to sleep with one Eustolium, who is a wife as far as he is concerned, but is called a virgin'.[29]

Thus, when Leontius was a presbyter he castrated himself in order to associate with the Christian woman Eustolium without any suspicion of sexual impropriety, a motive attached to the cases of Origen and the Alexandrian youth in Justin's *First Apology*.[30] Leontius was defrocked for his action according to canon law (see below), but despite this was later installed as bishop of Antioch (344–357/8) according to the wishes of Constantius II.

Locating specific examples of Christian eunuchs is problematized by the possibility of the use of the term 'eunuch' in a metaphorical sense, as already highlighted in relation to the interpretation placed upon Matthew 19.12. Indeed, writing in the early-third century AD Tertullian – the North African father of Latin Christianity – even described Jesus himself as a eunuch, as well as the Apostle Paul.[31] In his *On Monogamy* he declares, 'The Lord himself opened the Kingdom of Heaven to eunuchs (*spadonibus*), as he himself was a eunuch (*spado*). And the Apostle, looking at his example, moreover himself a eunuch (*castratus*), preferred continence (*continentiam*)'.[32] A useful case to consider is that of Melito 'the eunuch', the bishop of Sardis who died around 180. He is met in Eusebius' *Church History*, which includes a letter of Polycrates the bishop of Ephesus to Victor the bishop of Rome, dating to *c.* 194; in the letter he is described as '"Melito the eunuch, who lived entirely in the Holy Spirit, and who lies in Sardis"', and is named as one of the leading Christians in Asia who observed the fourteenth day of the lunar month as the beginning of the Paschal festival.[33] The Latin translation of Eusebius' *Church History* by Rufinus, dating to 402/3, specifies that Melito is a eunuch for the Kingdom of God. As Stevenson notes, in the Penguin translation of the text a footnote has been included observing that 'eunuch' can mean 'celibate'.[34] Stevenson rightly proceeds to ask, why is Melito assumed not to be a real eunuch? Why is Melito singled out to be called a eunuch in the text, and why are not all celibates called eunuchs? This might suggest that Melito was indeed a real eunuch.

That self-castration amongst early Christians was more widespread than would be realized from surviving texts seems to be indicated by one of the canons of the very first church council, held in 325 in Nicaea, a town in Bithynia not far from the city of Chrysopolis where Constantine I had vanquished his rival (and erstwhile brother-in-law) Licinius I (308–324) in the previous year. The Council of Nicaea is a reflection of the changing religious landscape of the Roman Empire, for it was summoned by the Emperor Constantine, who was concerned to support Christianity for the well-being of the empire and probably out of personal commitment to the religion also.[35] The main business of the council was to address the contested nature of Christ in relation to God, but other matters were also dealt with, such as the dating of Easter.[36] However, the very first canon of the council dealt with the issue of self-castrates. The canon runs:

> If a man has been mutilated (ἐχειρουργήθη) by physicians during sickness, or by barbarians, he may remain among the clergy; but if a man in good health has mutilated himself (ἑαυτὸν ἐξέτεμε), he must resign his post after the matter has been proved among the clergy, and in future no one who has thus acted should be ordained. But as it is evident that what has just been said only concerns those who have acted with intention, and have dared to mutilate themselves (ἑαυτοὺς ἐκτέμνειν), those who have been made eunuchs (εὐνουχίσθησαν) by barbarians or

by their masters will be allowed, conformably to the canon, to remain among the clergy, if in other respects they are worthy.[37]

The canon thus addresses self-castration in relation to the holding of clerical office, not amongst the Christian community in general. Clearly the nub of the problem was inflicting castration upon oneself voluntarily and for no good reason: if others castrated you against your own wishes, such as barbarians or masters (indicating that clergy could have been slaves), or on good medical grounds (Justin's doctors come to mind), there was no bar on becoming a cleric. Notably, the canon does not explain why self-castration was a problem, but one explanation is that the purposeful and willing mutilation of one's own body was a crime against the work of the Creator.[38]

The ruling of the canon is also echoed in the *Apostolic Canons*, which despite their attribution to the disciples of Christ were probably written subsequent to the Council of Nicaea, towards the end of the fourth century.[39] A series of canons (21–4) addresses the issue of castration.[40] Canon 21 asserts 'A eunuch (Εὐνοῦχος) if he has been made by the insolence of men, or if his manhood (τὰ ἀνδρῶν) was removed in time of persecution, or if he has been born so (οὕτως ἔφυ), and is worthy, can be a cleric'.[41] Notably this canon includes the category of born eunuch, one of the three types of eunuch identified by Jesus in the Gospel of Matthew. However, it does not mention those who have to be castrated on medical grounds. Canons 22 and 23 deal with self-castration and the holding of clerical office, the first asserting that someone who has castrated himself cannot become a clergyman and the second that a clergyman who castrates himself is to be deposed. Here, unlike in the canon of the Council of Nicaea, an explanation is given: self-castration amounts to self-murder and the perpetrator is an enemy of the work of God. Also of interest is that Canon 24 deals with self-castration among the laity, which had not been addressed by the Council of Nicaea. A layman who mutilates himself is to be excommunicated for three years.

The fact that castration could be a contested issue within Christianity is reflected by the fact that it was associated by some with heretics, as well as paganism as seen in Chapter 1.[42] As already witnessed in this chapter, Epiphanius associates the Valesians with self-castration, and with forcing castration upon others. The affiliation of Origen with self-castration and Arianism is also telling, as is the attack on Leontius the bishop of Antioch. Athanasius even casts the court eunuchs of Constantius II as leading supporters of Arianism because of their inability to have sons of their own; he writes:

> It was the eunuchs who instigated these proceedings against all. And the most remarkable circumstance (τὸ παράδοξον) in the matter is this; that the Arian heresy which denies the Son of God, receives its support from eunuchs, who, as both their bodies are fruitless, and their souls barren of the seeds of virtue, cannot bear even to hear the name of son (ὅιτινες ὡς τῇ φύσει οὕτως καὶ τὴν ψυχὴν ἀρετῆς ἄγονοι τυγχάνοντες οὐ φέρουσιν ἀκούειν ὅλως περὶ υἱοῦ). The Eunuch of Ethiopia indeed, though he understood not what he read, believed the words of Philip, when he taught him concerning our Saviour; but the eunuchs of Constantius cannot endure the confession of Peter, nay, they turn away when the Father manifests the Son, and madly rage against those who say, that the Son of God is His genuine Son, thus

claiming as a heresy of eunuchs (σπαδόντων αἵρεσιν), that there is no genuine and true offspring of the Father. On these grounds it is that the law forbids such persons to be admitted into any ecclesiastical Council; notwithstanding which these have now regarded them as competent judges of ecclesiastical causes, and whatever seems good to them, that Constantius decrees, while men with the name of Bishops dissemble with them. Oh! who shall be their historian? who shall transmit the record of these things to future generations? who indeed would believe it, were he to hear it, that eunuchs who are scarcely entrusted with household services (for theirs is a pleasure-loving race, that has no serious concern but that of hindering in others what nature has taken from them); that these, I say, now exercise authority in ecclesiastical matters, and that Constantius in submission to their will treacherously conspired against all, and banished [the bishop of Rome] Liberius![43]

Further, an imperial law of 389, in the names of the Emperors Valentinian II, Theodosius I and Arcadius and addressed to the Praetorian Prefect Tatianus, deals with Eunomian eunuchs (Eunomiani spadones), that is eunuchs who followed the Eunomian heresy, asserting that they can neither make a will nor inherit by a will.[44]

Opposition to castration within Christianity could also be expressed on the grounds that as a method of securing continence it was effectively cheating, as the individual did not then have to struggle to achieve self-control.[45] For instance, Tertullian in *Against Marcion* observes 'Just as strength is made perfect in weakness, so does abstinence from intercourse become remarkable while intercourse is allowed. Can anyone indeed be called abstinent when deprived of that which he is called to abstain from? Is there any temperance in eating and drinking during famine? Or any putting away of ambition in poverty? Or any bridling of passion in castration (Quae libidinis infrenatio in castratione)?'[46] Clement of Alexandria, a Christian contemporary of Tertullian,[47] in his *Paedagogus* (meaining 'Tutor', and providing education in Christian morality) refers to eunuchs who attend on women in elite households 'because of the belief that they are unable to indulge in lust', and declares 'But a true eunuch (Εὐνοῦχος ... ἀληθής) is not one who is unable, but one who is unwilling, to indulge in pleasure (φιληδεῖν)'.[48] In his attack on the Valesians Epiphanius also reflects this idea, declaring that the self-castrator 'is out of the struggle and runs no more risk of being aroused to the pleasure of lust', and 'will have no further credit for abstaining from sexual relations. With the members which are needed for them removed, he cannot engage in them'.[49] Interestingly, on the category of born eunuchs he asserts they 'certainly have no sin, because they were born that way. On the other hand there is nothing to their credit either, since they cannot do <anything like that> – I mean anything sexual – because they lack the divinely created organs of generation. But neither can they have the kingdom of heaven as a reward for being eunuchs, since they have no experience of the struggle'.[50] Philo of Alexandria, a Jewish philosopher writing in the first half of the first century AD, declared it was better to become a eunuch than to be sex-mad, reflecting again the notion that castration resulted in chastity; tellingly, this passage was used by Origen to justify self-castration.[51]

Conversely, however, there also existed the notion that castration did not guarantee continence anyway, so eunuchs did have to exert themselves to achieve self-control.[52]

Philostratus in his life of the pagan holy man Apollonius of Tyana relates that Apollonius, when at the court of the Parthian king Vardanes, discussed eunuchs with his student Damis, and asserted that eunuchs still feel desire. He says:

> 'Damis, I am pondering within myself why barbarians think eunuchs chaste, and admit them into their women's quarters.' 'Why, a child can see that,' said Damis. 'Castration takes away their ability to have sex, and that is why they have access to harems, even if they want to sleep with the women.' 'What then do you think has been excised from them, erotic feelings or the ability to sleep with women?' 'Both, since if the member which throws the body into frenzy has been done away with, no one can have sexual passion.' After a short pause, Apollonius said, 'You will find out tomorrow, Damis, that eunuchs too have sexual passion,[53] and that their capacity for desire, absorbed through the eyes, does not wither away, but remains hot and glowing... In fact, even if human beings had some supreme skill that was able to expel such things from the mind, I do not think it could lead eunuchs into habits of self-control, making them self-controlled by compulsion, or depriving them of sexual passion by some drastic method. Self-control means that someone in a state of desire and excitement is not overcome by the sexual urge, but instead uses restraint, and shows himself to be master of this madness.'[54]

Epiphanius also notes that self-castrates can feel desire; he comments 'The eunuch in the sage's proverb is not exempt from desire, <but desires> because he cannot gratify his desire, as it says, "The desire of a eunuch to deflower a virgin."'.[55] Such a belief has already been encountered in Terence's *The Eunuch*, when following the rape of Pamphila, the maid Pythias confides in Dorias that she had heard that eunuchs 'were really great lovers of women, but that they couldn't manage it'.[56] Probably the most famous acknowledgement of this idea in a late Roman Christian text comes in Basil of Ancyra's *On Virginity*, where the fourth-century bishop (336–360) warns of the dangers posed to female Christian virgins by eunuchs, especially those castrated after puberty, relating stories he had been told by contemporaries as well as drawing on his physiological understanding.[57] He asserts that although castrated, eunuchs are still men, and like Epiphanius he cites the proverb of Sirach that it is 'The desire of a eunuch to deflower a virgin'.

Nevertheless, the association of castration with chastity was potent, and although deliberate self-castration was frowned upon there developed the idea of 'mystical castration', whereby individuals could become chaste through divine intervention.[58] A case is met in the monk-turned-bishop Palladius' *Lausiac History*.[59] This was written around 420 for the Grand Chamberlain Lausus, a prominent figure at the court of Theodosius II, and probably a eunuch.[60] The text contains stories about holy men and women from early monasticism. One story concerns Elias, an ascetic in Egypt who showed particular concern for female ascetics, building a monastery for them where he sometimes stayed.[61] Tempted by lust, he left the monastery and prayed for God either to kill him or to remove his passion. When he went to sleep in the desert three angels visited him, and he swore to them he would go back to the women's monastery if they took away his passion. Then 'They took hold of him, one by the hands and one by the feet, and the third took a razor and castrated him (ὁ τρίτος λαβὼν ξυρὸν ἐξέτεμεν αὐτοῦ τοὺς διδύμους) – not actually, but in the dream. Then it seemed to him, in this vision, as one might say, that he was cured'. He returned to the monastery and lived on for forty years, no longer affected by passion.

The Ethiopian Eunuch: a place for eunuchs in Christianity

Thus, although self-castration attracted disapprobation in early Christianity, it is evident that eunuchs who had no choice about their castration or condition were acceptable members of the community. Indeed, the New Testament indicates this strongly itself in an episode included in the Acts of the Apostles, which is traditionally attributed to Luke the Evangelist and often dated to the 80s of the first century AD.[62] The episode concerns the baptism of an Ethiopian eunuch by Philip the Evangelist. The story runs as follows:

> Now the angel of the Lord said to Philip, 'Get up and head south on the road that goes down from Jerusalem to Gaza, the desert route.' So he got up and set out. Now there was an Ethiopian eunuch (ἀνὴρ Αἰθίοψ εὐνοῦχος), a court official (δυνάστης) in charge of all the treasury (γάζης) of Candace (that is, the Queen) of the Ethiopians. He had come to Jerusalem to worship, and was returning home. Seated in his carriage, he was reading the prophet Isaiah. The Spirit said to Philip, 'Run and catch up with that carriage.' Philip ran up and heard the man reading Isaiah the prophet. He said to him, 'Do you really understand what you are reading?' He replied. 'How should I be able, unless someone guides me?' So he invited Philip to get in and sit with him. Now this was the passage of Scripture that he was reading:
>
> *He was led like a sheep to the slaughter,*
> *and as a lamb before its shearer is silent,*
> *so he opened not his mouth.*
> *In [his] humiliation justice was denied him.*
> *Who will ever speak of his posterity?*
> *For his life is taken away from this earth.*
>
> Then the eunuch said to Philip, 'Please, sir, about whom does the prophet say this? About himself or about someone else?' Then Philip spoke up, and beginning with that very passage of Scripture, he preached about Jesus to him. As they moved along the road, they came to some water, and the eunuch asked, 'Look, there is some water. What prevents me from being baptized?' [He said to him, 'If you believe with all your heart, it is possible.' He said in reply, 'I believe that Jesus Christ is the son of God.'][63] He ordered the carriage to stop, and both of them, Philip and the eunuch, went down into the water, and he baptized him. When they came up out of the water, the Spirit of the Lord snatched Philip away, and the eunuch saw him no more, but continued on his way quite happy [lit. 'rejoicing'].[64]

Before considering this episode further it is necessary to clarify certain aspects of the story, not least whether the Ethiopian was a real eunuch. First of all, it is commonly observed that the Ethiopia of the Acts of the Apostles (and of antiquity in general) does not equate to present day Ethiopia but is equivalent to countries and regions south of Egypt and modern Sudan, such as Nubia.[65] As for the name Candace, this does not refer to an individual queen but was rather a title signifying the office of queen in Nubia.[66] Regarding the cited passage of Isaiah that the Ethiopian was reading, it is 53.7–8 and Philip interprets it for the eunuch in a Christological sense.[67] However, the key question for the purposes of this chapter is whether the Ethiopian was a castrate. The term eunuch can be understood by some to mean a court title or office with no implications for the physical condition of the individual. Thus, some commentators refer to the episode as 'Philip converts a chamberlain'.[68] However, it can be argued that the Ethiopian is indeed meant to be understood as a castrated person. Given that the Ethiopian is described as a treasurer and a powerful official of the Ethiopian court as well as a eunuch it seems that the use of the latter term has special significance, and is perhaps meant to indicate that the Ethiopian was not just a powerful court official who acted as treasurer but was also a castrated individual.[69] The fact that he is identified as a treasurer may also be significant for this office was particularly associated with eunuchs, as a story recorded by Plutarch about one of Alexander the Great's peers and successors, Lysimachus, demonstrates.[70] One of Lysimachus' rivals, Demetrius, considered himself the real king and cast his competitors as his officials – Seleucus his Master of Elephants, Ptolemy his Admiral, Agathocles his Lord of the Islands, and Lysimachus his Treasurer. Plutarch adds 'When this was reported to these kings, they all laughed at Demetrius, except Lysimachus; he was incensed that Demetrius considered him a eunuch (it was the general practice to have eunuchs for treasurers) (εἰώθεισαν εὐνούχους ἔχειν γαζοφύλακας)'.[71] Although Plutarch was writing in the Roman Empire in the early-second century AD it is likely that he was drawing on contemporary evidence for the early Hellenistic world of the late-third and early-second centuries BC.[72] Ultimately one cannot prove, or disprove, that the Ethiopian was a eunuch in the castrated sense, but perhaps more to the point, even if there is ambiguity readers of the Acts of the Apostles might, and probably did, understand him to be a castrated person.

Further, however, one can suggest that the reading being undertaken by the Ethiopian has import, for the Book of Isaiah had special relevance for the Jewish attitude to eunuchs. In parts of the Old Testament a dim view is taken of eunuchs and their place in the community.[73] In Deuteronomy it is asserted 'No man whose testicles have been crushed or whose organ has been severed shall become a member of the assembly of the LORD',[74] while in Leviticus eunuchs are included in a list of afflicted people who are not allowed to be priests or officiate in the worship of God: 'No one at all who has a blemish shall be qualified: a man who is blind, lame, disfigured, or deformed; a man who has a broken leg or broken arm, or who is a hunchback, or a dwarf, or has a discoloration of the eye, a scar, a lichen, or a crushed testicle'.[75] However, in Isaiah, which is effectively a prophecy concerning final redemption, a much more positive attitude towards eunuchs is evinced, including them in the community:

> The foreigner who adheres to YHVH must not say,
> 'YHVH will surely cut me off from his people';
> and the eunuch must not say,
> 'I am just a withered tree.'
> For this is what YHVH says,
> 'The eunuchs who observe my Sabbaths,
> who choose what is pleasing to me
> and hold fast to my covenant:
> to them I shall give in my house and within my walls
> a memorial and a name
> better than sons and daughters;
> I shall give them a long-lasting name
> that will not be cut off.'[76]

Thus, the Book of Isaiah reveals a contrasting view of eunuchs to Deuteronomy and Leviticus, one that asserts that not only are they acceptable followers of God but they are indeed especially valued by him.[77] In this light the fact that the Ethiopian was reading from Isaiah takes on extra significance, which is further compounded by the importance of the episode itself. Philip's baptism of the eunuch is the first induction of an individual into the 'Christian' community (Philip having previously been preaching in Samaria), an individual who it seems was a Gentile, which also has relevance to the message of Isaiah. Eusebius certainly considered the baptism of the Ethiopian momentous, commenting in his *Church History*:

> While the saving preaching was daily progressing and growing, some providence brought from the land of the Ethiopians an officer (δυνάστην) of the queen of that land, for the nation, following ancestral customs, is still ruled by a woman. Tradition says that he, who was the first of the Gentiles (πρῶτον ἐξ ἐθνῶν) to receive from Philip by revelation the mysteries of the divine word, and was the first-fruits of the faithful throughout the world, was also the first to return to his native land and preach the Gospel of the knowledge of the God of the universe and the sojourn of our Saviour which gives life to men, so that by him was actually fulfilled the prophecy which says, 'Ethiopia shall stretch out her hand to God.'[78]

The significance of the episode had already been emphasized by Irenaeus the bishop of Lyon, in his *Against Heresies*, written in the late-second century AD.[79] Thus, while there is modern debate about whether the Ethiopian was indeed the first of the Gentiles to be converted,[80] it seems clear that early Christians attached great importance to the episode and probably understood the Ethiopian to be a real eunuch. Despite the negative views of eunuchs that could exist in antiquity it is evident that there were positive views too.

It is notable that other Biblical figures could be understood to be real eunuchs, in particular Daniel, famous for interpreting dreams and visions, and his three companions Shadrach, Meshach and Abednego surviving the fiery furnace and himself the lions' den.[81] His story is told in the Book of Daniel.[82] After the capture of Jerusalem by

Nebuchadnezzar Daniel was one of the beautiful, intelligent and elite young Jews taken to Babylon to serve at the court of the king. Entrusted to Ashpenaz the chief of the palace servants (*sārîsîm*), they were trained for three years, Daniel's name being changed to Belteshazzar. Daniel became a trusted advisor to the king, then a chief minister. He survived Nebuchadnezzar, going on to serve the kings Darius the Mede and Cyrus the Persian. Daniel is thus placed into the historical context of the sixth century BC, witnessing the reign of the king of Babylon Nebuchadnezzar (*c*. 605–*c*. 562 BC) and the fall of Babylon to Cyrus the Great, the Achaemenid king of Persia (559– 530 BC). Whether Daniel existed at all is strongly doubted, but the stories about him were potent and developed further, and Christians considered him a prophet. There is also debate about whether he should be understood to be a eunuch. His life and career as described in the Book of Daniel are suggestive of that of a court eunuch. His close relationship with the chief of the palace servants is emphasized, who might have been a eunuch.[83] The Hebrew for palace servants *sārîsîm* is taken from the Assyrian *sa rēsi* which can be read as 'eunuchs'; the Septuagint (the Greek translation of the Old Testament begun in Alexandria in the third century BC) certainly reads it this way, describing Ashpenaz as the 'chief eunuch' (τῷ ἀρχιευνούχῳ).[84] Over time Daniel himself became identified as a eunuch. Particularly interesting is the testimony of the Jewish historian Josephus, who lived under the Roman Empire in the first century AD.[85] Born in Jerusalem in 37 of priestly and royal descent, Josephus played a part in the Jewish revolt against Rome (begun in 66) as commander in Galilee. He was captured by the Romans in 67 but won the favour of the Roman general Vespasian (subsequently emperor from 69 to 79) and became close to his son and eventual successor Titus (78–81). After the fall of Jerusalem to Titus in 70, Josephus was granted Roman citizenship, taking Vespasian's family name Flavius. He was also given a house in Rome, where he settled and lived out the rest of his life. In his *Jewish Antiquities*, dated to 93/94 during the reign of Domitian and providing in Greek a history of the Jews from Adam to AD 66, he raises the possibility that Daniel was a eunuch. He writes:

> Then Nebuchadnezzar, the Babylonian king, took the Jewish youths of noblest birth and the relatives of their king Sacchias who were remarkable for the vigour of their bodies and the comeliness of their features, and gave them over to tutors to be cared for by them, making some of them eunuchs (ἐκτομίας); this same treatment he also gave to those taken in the flower of their age from among the other nations which he had subdued ... among them were four of the family of Sacchias, the first of whom was named Daniel, the second Ananias, the third, Misaëlos and the fourth, Azarias.[86]

The prolific author and ascetic Jerome, writing in the late-fourth century, also asserts that Daniel and the three youths are eunuchs, stating that the Hebrews said and continue to say this themselves, referring to the Book of Daniel as well as the prophecy of Isaiah that some of the male descendants of Hezekiah the king of Judah would be carried off to Babylon and be made eunuchs in the palace of the king.[87] Later in the fifth century, in his *Commentary on Daniel*, Theodoret of Cyrrhus also asserts that the prophecy of Isaiah had been fulfilled by the young Jews being taken from Jerusalem to

Babylon by Nebuchadnezzar.[88] Kathryn Ringrose emphasizes the fact that the Byzantines in the tenth century considered Daniel a eunuch, but as she notes it is evident that this was possible already in the Roman Empire.[89]

Eunuchs as clergy, monks, martyrs and saints

The story of the Ethiopian eunuch and the possible interpretation of the prophet Daniel as a eunuch (incidentally, both court eunuchs) provided positive models for eunuchs in early Christianity, and there are a number of eunuchs met in Christian roles in the later Roman Empire. Eunuchs are discovered as clergy, monks, martyrs and saints, revealing that the disapproval of self-castration is only part of the picture of the story of eunuchs and early Christianity.[90] As the first canon of the Council of Nicaea and the *Apostolic Canons* reveal, eunuchs could fill clerical positions if their physical condition was innate, forced upon them, or the result of vital medical procedure. It must also be acknowledged that the canons created a loophole; even if someone embraced self-castration they could claim that it was inflicted against their wishes or undertaken on the grounds of health. It is noteworthy that of the Christian eunuchs encountered in the later Roman Empire some were greatly admired.

An example of an admired early Christian eunuch is found in the *Church History* of Eusebius. This is the case of Dorotheus, recorded by Eusebius in a section on notable clergy of his own day:

> During Cyril's episcopate [of Antioch] we came to know Dorotheus, a learned man (λόγιον ἄνδρα), who had been deemed worthy of the presbyterate at Antioch. In his zeal for all that is beautiful in divine things, he made so careful a study of the Hebrew tongue that he read with understanding the original Hebrew Scriptures. And he was by no means unacquainted with the most liberal studies and Greek primary education; but withal he was by nature a eunuch (τὴν φύσιν ... εὐνοῦχος), having been so from his very birth (πεφυκὼς ἐξ αὐτῆς γενέσεως), so that even the emperor, accounting this as a sort of miracle (παράδοξον), took him into his friendship and honoured him with the charge of the purple dye-works at Tyre. We heard him giving a measured exposition of the Scriptures in the church.[91]

Like Favorinus then, Dorotheus fell into the category of born eunuch.[92] He was a contemporary of Eusebius, his career spanning the late-third and early-fourth centuries, the church historian encountering him in Antioch when Cyril was bishop of the city.[93] The emperor who appointed him to the dye-works (Dorotheus thus having a secular administrative post as well as being a prominent figure in the Christian community) was perhaps Diocletian (284–305).

In a Christian context, Diocletian is infamous as the initiator of the Great Persecution, begun at his imperial base at Nicomedia in 303. Amongst the victims of the persecution was another Dorotheus, one of the palace servants of the emperor, described by Eusebius as surpassing 'all in his devotion and faithfulness (εὐνούστατός τε καὶ πιστότατος) to [the emperors], and for this reason ... more highly honoured than men who held positions as rulers or governors'.[94] Coupled with this Dorotheus is another palace servant, Gorgonius.[95] Although Eusebius does not spell it out, it seems likely that these celebrated martyrs were in fact eunuchs.[96] Their identification as loyal and esteemed palace personnel would give grounds to suspect it,[97] but their story is indeed associated with a supposed plot on the part of Christians and palace eunuchs to assassinate the emperor and his Caesar Galerius. It is Lactantius who provides the details of the eunuch aspect of this episode; after the issuing of the first edict against the Christians the palace in Nicomedia was set on fire, and it was alleged that the Christians were responsible, having hatched a plot with the palace eunuchs.[98] Investigating the matter, and following a further fire, 'the emperor began to rage not just against the members of his household but against everyone ... Eunuchs who had once enjoyed great power, and on whom Diocletian himself and the whole palace had depended, were killed (Potentissimi quondam eunuchi necati, per quos palatium et ipse ante constabat)'.[99]

Dorotheus and his fellow servants who were victims of the persecution were obviously lionized by fellow Christians. Eusebius declares:

> But among all those whose praises have ever yet been sung as worthy of admiration and famed for courage, whether by Greeks or barbarians, this occasion produced those divine and outstanding martyrs Dorotheus and the imperial servants that were with him. These persons had been deemed worthy of the highest honour by their masters, who loved them no less than their own children; but they accounted the reproaches and sufferings for piety and the many forms of death that were newly devised against them, as truly greater riches than the fair fame and luxury of this life ... Dorotheus and Gorgonius, together with many others of the imperial household, after conflicts of various kinds, departed this life by strangling, and so carried off the prizes of the God-given victory.[100]

Striking also is Eusebius' report that later 'the imperial servants, whose bodies after death had been committed to the ground with fitting honours, their reputed masters, starting afresh, deemed it necessary to exhume them and cast them also[101] into the sea, lest any, regarding them as actually gods (so at least they imagined), should worship them as they lay in their tombs'.[102] It seems rather that the emperors feared that these victims would become the focus of veneration and cult as martyrs, and there can be no doubt, even if the eunuch status of Dorotheus and Gorgonius is disputed, that amongst these Christian heroes were eunuchs. It is evident that for Christians eunuchs could be worthy figures of admiration.

Confirming this last point are the string of accounts of passions and martyrdoms that feature eunuchs, even if they are fictitious, as highlighted by Pascal Boulhol and Isabelle Cochelin.[103] They identify Largus and Smaragdus, eunuchs of the matron widow Lucina in the *Passion of Anthimus* (late-fourth or early-fifth century); the brothers Protus and Hyacinthus, eunuchs of Eugenia, daughter of the Prefect of Egypt; Calocerus and Parthenius, eunuchs of the consul Aemilianus, or rather his daughter Anatolia Calista; John and Paul, eunuchs of Constantina, daughter of Constantine the Great, then servants of the Emperor Julian; the *cubicularii* Domninus of Parma and

Hyacinthus, whose passions seem to date from the sixth century; and Nereus and Achilleus, originally two soldiers who in the version of their passion told around the beginning of the sixth century by a Roman cleric have become transmogrified into eunuchs, cast as *cubicularii* of Flavia Domitilla the niece of Domitian and female martyr of the eponymous Roman catacomb. They also discuss the *Passion* of Indes and Domna, composed about the end of the sixth century. Domna was a young priestess who converted to Christianity under Diocletian, and Indes was her eunuch, 'a barbarian by birth, but civilised and gentle by nature'. They were baptized together by the eunuch deacon Agapios. Denounced as Christians they were thrown in prison, their gaoler a wicked chief eunuch. They were then caught up in the Great Persecution, including the arrest of the Christian eunuchs of the palace, referred to by Eusebius and Lactantius. The *Passion* names Dorotheos and Gorgonius, but also Mardonius, Mygdonius and Peter, and asserts that the six eunuchs (including Indes) were executed. Boulhol and Cochlelin also discuss the *Passion* of the *cubicularius* Eleutherius, which dates to the seventh century at the earliest; they opine that this provides the most complete hagiographic portrait of the perfect Christian eunuch. Asking why such positive views of eunuchs existed in passions and hagiography, so contrasting to other hostile views of eunuchs, they conclude that 'the eunuch of hagiography, the *eunuch saint*, thus appears as the living symbol of perfect self-control'.[104] In effect, it provided a model for monks, ascetics and all Christians, at the time of the expansion of monasticism in the fourth and fifth centuries.

As has been seen, eunuchs were not just fictional idealized role models but real individuals. Some eunuch clergy have already been met (e.g. Dorotheus, Leontius), but others surface too. There is Tigrius, a presbyter in Constantinople who was a supporter of the Patriarch John Chrysostom (398–404); the church historian Sozomen in the 440s records that Tigrius was a barbarian who had been a slave but was freed and was distinguished for his moderation, meekness and charity (τὸ ἦθος ἐπιεικέστατος καὶ πρᾶος καὶ περὶ τοὺς δεομένους καὶ ξένους … δεξιώτατος).[105] Also from the fifth century, the monk-turned-bishop Palladius reports in his *Dialogue on the Life of St John Chrysostom*, written soon after John's fall, that when Heraclides (also a friend of Chrysostom) was deposed as bishop of Ephesus he was replaced by a eunuch.[106] In the mid-fifth century the born eunuch Gabriel became a presbyter in the church of the Ascension in Jerusalem.[107] It seems eunuchs could even become patriarchs; when the Patriarch of Constantinople Macedonius (496–511) was accused of indecent acts with boys it emerged that he had been castrated.[108] From the late-sixth or early-seventh century, the court official Narses who went on to become bishop of Ascalon might have been a eunuch.[109]

Eunuch monks are more readily found.[110] They are encountered in the *Spiritual Meadow* of John Moschus, dating to the early-seventh century. John was a monk and author who lived from the mid-sixth century to the early-seventh century, and in his *Spiritual Meadow* he recorded edifying tales about holy men and women gathered on his travels. Here there are met Cosmas the abbot of the lavra of Pharon in Jerusalem; Theodore the anchorite from the Holy Land who turned sea water into fresh water on a voyage to Constantinople; and John the abbot, whose monastery was at the ninth mile-post from Alexandria.[111] The *Life* of Peter the Iberian, a leading figure in monasticism and church affairs in Palestine in the fifth century, features also the monk John the Eunuch, Peter's stalwart companion and former chamberlain; they fled to the Holy Land from Constantinople in about 437, and when John died he was buried in Peter's monastery between Gaza and Maiuma, where Peter was later buried beside him.[112] The *Sayings of the Fathers*, anecdotes about monks compiled around the late-fifth and early-sixth centuries, records a story about two men who decided to become monks, and then to castrate themselves to become 'Eunuchs for the Kingdom of Heaven'.[113] In the sixth century the monk and prolific hagiographer Cyril of Scythopolis records in his *Life* of Sabas (who was from Cappadocia but founded the Great Lavra in Palestine) that Peter the Patriarch of Jerusalem appointed John the eunuch, the abbot of the monastery of Martyrius, to be the abbot of the New Church.[114] The *Life* of John the Almsgiver, Patriarch of Alexandria (610–619/20), begun by John Moschus and his friend Sophronius the sophist (later Patriarch of Jerusalem 634–38/9),[115] but finished by Leontius the bishop of Neapolis on Cyprus, records a story about a young monk begging alms in Alexandria accompanied by a young woman; impropriety is assumed, and both the monk and girl are beaten, but it is subsequently revealed that the young monk was a eunuch.[116] The existence of eunuch monks is further emphasized by the stories told about the so-called 'transvestite nuns', women who passed themselves off as eunuchs to be able to enter male monasteries; these stories began to appear from the end of the fourth century and were established by the sixth and early seventh centuries, and reveal that it was accepted that eunuchs could be found as monks.[117]

A particularly rich case of a eunuch monk, and one well worth dwelling on, is that of Eutropius, who lived in the first half of the sixth century. He features in a letter of Paul Helladicus, the abbot of the monastery of Elusa in Idumaea, but also in Cyril of Scythopolis' *Life of Sabas*.[118] Paul's letter, described by J.B. Bury as 'one of the most unsavoury documents of Christian monasticism',[119] includes an account of Eutropius' life and experiences in the Holy Land.[120] To begin with it is related that Eutropius renounced the world and became a monk, having been the secretary of Juliana Placidia (νοτάριος Ἰουλιανῆς τῆς κατὰ Πλακιδίαν) the wife of Areobindus the general. This woman is better known as Anicia Juliana, descendant of the Emperor Theodosius I, daughter of the Emperor Olybrius (472), dedicatee of the illuminated manuscript known as the Vienna Dioscurides (c. 512), and builder of the church of St Polyeuctus in Constantinople in the 520s.[121] Having been in the service of this remarkable woman, not only did Eutropius become a monk in the Holy Land but he founded a monastic community specifically for eunuchs, not far from Jericho, in the second tower built by Elias the Patriarch of Jerusalem (494–516). Further, not only was Eutropius the abbot of this monastery he was also a priest. Cyril's *Life* of Sabas adds further details to the picture.[122] He relates that it was a group of Juliana's eunuchs who came to the Holy Land after the death of their mistress (in about 528), and they sought out Sabas as they had admired him when he visited Constantinople.[123] Armed with money they went to him at the Great Lavra and asked to be admitted. Sabas was not won over and would not allow them to enter the lavra or any of his monasteries as it was his rule not to admit beardless youths or eunuchs. However, he did send them on to the coenobium of Theodosius. It is then related that after spending some time there the eunuchs asked the patriarch (Peter, 524–544) for a monastery of their own so that they could live in private together. The patriarch asked Alexander the abbot of the monasteries of the Patriarch Elias of Jerusalem near Jericho to welcome them, and he established a separate monastery for the eunuchs. Cyril concludes this story of the eunuchs of Juliana who turned to the monastic life by observing that 'from then on the separated monastery has received the name of the monastery of the Eunuchs'.[124]

Here, then, is a case of eunuch servants (presumably of slave origin) who turned to the monastic life when their employer died (perhaps they were freed on the death of Anicia Juliana). They appear to have been led by Eutropius, and seem to have maintained a group identity, wanting to reside in a monastery by themselves. Notably the *Life of Sabas* indicates that there was some ambivalence about accepting eunuchs as monks. Sabas would not take them into the lavra under him, though he did send them on to a community monastery; it seems that he considered them not suited for the more rigorous ascetic monastic life in the lavra. Also, in relation to their case it is stated that 'he could not bear to see a feminine face (ὄψιν γυναικείαν) in any of his monasteries'.[125] Anxiety about eunuchs as monks is evident from other aspects and stories relating to Palestinian monasticism. The first regulation in the Sinai monastic rule of Mar Saba was a prohibition against the admittance of a eunuch or a beardless youth into a lavra.[126] In the fifth century, in 428,[127] another abbot (Euthymius, the master of Sabas) did allow the Cappadocian Gabriel, who was a born eunuch (εὐνοῦχον ... ἀπὸ γεννήσεως) and had a feminine face (ὄψιν γυναικείαν),[128] to take a cell in the lavra, though he was forbidden to leave it and indeed did not do so for twenty-five years.[129] It seems that it was feared that the presence of youths and eunuchs would prove sexually tempting to the other monks.[130]

Paul Helladicus' letter in fact dwells on the problem of sexual desire in general. In the course of this it includes a case of desire in relation to Eutropius, though it is the sexual desire that the eunuch experienced himself rather than the sexual desire he inspired in others. The letter reports in Eutropius' own words the lust he felt for his own godson:

> So then this Eutropios after many years made confession with repentance and in affliction said, 'A certain man of Jericho, noble and wealthy, became my friend and brought offerings to my monastery and often ate with me. When a son was born he begged me,' he said, 'to act as his sponsor at holy baptism; and this I did. So the man always brought the child to me, and I used to receive the infant happily with joy and a pure heart in the sincerity of my soul, and I kissed it and embraced it as a child given to me by God through the holy baptism in the Holy Spirit. But when the child had grown and was about ten years old, my thoughts changed for the worse and my state of mind changed to evil. I suffered distress and was driven to loathsome desire and the ferocity of the wicked desire and pleasure was burning me up'... 'So then,' said Eutropios, 'I, having changed my appearance and becoming completely obsessed with my filthy passion (τοῦ πάθους τοῦ ῥυπαροῦ), wished to have intercourse with the child and be united with him to my personal disgrace. But I beseeched God to hinder me and I said, "Lord My God, send instead fire from above and burn me up and do not allow me to carry out this foul deed." God granted that I should come to my senses a little and raise myself from the mud and darkness of my irrational desire.

I said to the father of the child, "Take him and go away to your house and do not bring him to my monastery anymore." So from that moment I never saw the boy. But when the enemy realized that, he attacked me more vigorously and more intensely and more bitterly and impressed on my mind the form of the boy and stuck his likeness and appearance and image on my heart. Under the constraint I did not have the power to tear myself away and cut myself off (χωρισθῆναι) from the utterly foul and serpent-like passion, but even while I was praying and singing and keeping vigil and reading I had the wicked one who binds hand and foot working inside me, the demon of disgraceful desire plundering me and torturing me with passion and subduing me utterly. I fasted, I was austere with my wretched body. I wept, I groaned, I gnashed my teeth as I howled, I struck my head with my fists. I beat my feet with a rod in anger and the evil did not go away, but the part of my body was even more inflamed and rose up (ἐπυροῦτο καὶ ἐπανίστατό) and let fall drops of filth so that my thighs were defiled with impure moisture.'[131]

Thus, we find in Paul's letter a rather explicit account of how a eunuch was tormented by lust, and the impact of the case is heightened by the fact that the eunuch was also a monk and that the object of his desire was his own godson. Paul seems to consider that his readers might be surprised at the revelation that a eunuch could feel desire at all, for in the midst of the narrative of Eutropius he comments:

It is not an amazing thing that a eunuch should feel desire. For Scripture says, 'It is the lust of a eunuch to deflower a virgin' (Sir. 20:4).[132] For not only does a eunuch feel desire but he can also sleep with a woman and have intercourse and produce an emission, except however the eunuch produces weak seed and cannot beget children. Do not be shocked as you hear about the eunuch. For Satan often encourages a woman to desire a woman.[133]

Eutropius' story seems to confirm ancient views that despite their castration eunuchs were indeed lustful beings and not inherently pure. However, the narrative of Eutropius does not end with his inability to control his desire, for he adds:

'Therefore, after a long time had passed like this, when I was in despair and thought I no longer found mercy, against expectation the God of all stooped to have mercy on me. He looked with favour on the humility of my soul and removed from me that dark cloud, and released me from the pernicious temptation. Gaining refreshment in that way, I thanked and [still] thank and until my death will thank Christ our God.'[134]

Thus, eventually Eutropius passes through his trial, relief from which he attributes to the will of God. The eunuch is not irredeemable, and as his narrative makes clear he identified his problem and attempted to resolve it. His case is also significant in that it counters the view that castration was a quick (and cheating) way to celibacy; one is left in no doubt as to the agony and difficulty endured by Eutropius in his attempt to rein in his desires. Eunuchs faced the same struggle as other Christian men.

Conclusion

Eunuchs and castration were live issues in early Christianity in the Roman Empire. Some early Christians thought that they had been enjoined by Christ to embrace castration, whist others understood the words of Matthew 19.12 metaphorically, as an injunction to celibacy. Ultimately the issue of concern was self-castration rather than eunuchs per se, as the ruling of the Council of Nicaea reveals, with those who had been castrated against their will or on health grounds being allowed to be clergy. Within Christianity eunuchs could find a place, as also revealed by the story of the Ethiopian Eunuch and the recognition of eunuchs as martyrs and saints. Further, eunuchs could become monks, and rise to the position of abbot. The discussion of eunuchs and castration within Christianity also brought to the fore issues of sex and gender. The stories of women disguising themselves as eunuch monks speaks to the question of the gender identity of eunuchs, as well as reflecting the fact that they could be monks. The metaphorical meaning of eunuch as celibate was strong, indicated by the development of tales about spiritual castration rather than literal castration. Nonetheless perceptions of eunuchs remained contradictory, with the belief that castration secures chastity co-existing with the view that eunuchs continued to feel desire, so graphically illustrated by the narrative of Eutropius. The legacy of these early Christian eunuchs is shown by those met in the Byzantine Empire but also by those encountered in modern times, such as the Skoptsy of Russia. Their existence demonstrates the centrality of physical denial within Christianity.

7

Military Eunuchs: The Case of Narses

Introduction

When one thinks of the court eunuchs of the later Roman Empire one probably pictures them in their role as chamberlains, attending to the needs of the emperor and his family in the restricted setting of the imperial court. However, court eunuchs could also perform other roles, witness for instance the Grand Chamberlain Eusebius travelling the empire undertaking missions for his master Constantius II.[1] From the sixth century onwards they are even found regularly acting in a military capacity, commanding imperial forces.[2] The most celebrated eunuch general of the later Roman Empire (and the Byzantine Empire as a whole) is Narses, whose campaigns against the Goths in Italy in the sixth century even put the famed general Belisarius in the shade, for it was Narses who managed to defeat the Ostrogoths and restore direct Roman rule in Italy for Justinian I (527–565), the emperor renowned for the reconquest of part of the Roman west, not just Italy but also North Africa and a little of Spain.[3] Narses has been described as 'one of the greatest generals of his era, if not of all time'.[4] His achievements have certainly not been ignored by modern (or ancient) historians of the later Roman Empire: for instance, James Dunlap detailed his career in his study of late Roman and Byzantine Grand Chamberlains; Lawrence Fauber devoted a monograph to him entitled *Narses: Hammer of the Goths*; and the entry for him in the *Prosopography of the Later Roman Empire* runs to sixteen pages.[5] Nevertheless, Narses merits further attention, especially with regard to the fact that he was a *eunuch* general.[6] One should ask how a eunuch came to be appointed as a general, how his status as a eunuch affected how he was written about as a general by contemporary and subsequent authors, and whether he set the precedent for the phenomenon of the late Roman and Byzantine eunuch general. These are the main issues of concern of this chapter, but first it will be established who Narses was, what is known of his career, and what was thought to make him a successful general.

Narses: background and career

Because of his military career, Narses is a major character in the histories of two prominent sixth-century classicizing historians, Procopius and Agathias, both contemporaries of the eunuch.[7] Procopius was from Caesarea in Palestine and became the legal secretary of Belisarius in 527 when he was active on the eastern frontier. He accompanied the general on his campaigns in North Africa and Italy from 533–540, and after that probably remained in Constantinople until his death (possibly in 554 or not long afterwards). He wrote a history of the campaigns of the reign of Justinian in eight books, titled the *Wars*, Books 1–7 completed by 551 and Book 8 by 554.[8] Procopius' narrative was directly continued by Agathias, who was from Myrina in Asia Minor. Agathias was a lawyer too, but unlike Procopius he did not participate in the campaigns in Italy, living and working in Constantinople.[9] His history, which was incomplete when he died (between 579 and 582), consists of five books, covering the period from 552 to 559.[10] Of these two main sources, for Narses, Agathias is much more overtly positive about the eunuch, but it is striking that he is not a target for abuse in another of Procopius' texts, the *Secret History*, a blistering attack on Justinian and his regime; Ernst Stein observed that Narses' omission from the *Secret History* 'is probably all to his credit'.[11] In addition to the histories of Procopius and Agathias, however, Narses features in a range of other texts, both eastern and western. Among the Greek sources are the chronicle of John Malalas and the church history of Evagrius, both written in the sixth century. Those written in Latin in the west include Gregory of Tours' *The History of the Franks*, the *Book of Pontiffs*, and Paul the Deacon's *History of the Lombards*. There is then a richness of material for the study of Narses, befitting his long and significant career which spanned east and west and saw him rise from court eunuch to effective ruler of Italy. Despite this, however, there is much that is not known about his life, and much that is of a legendary quality, as shall be seen.

Narses is an example of a *cubicularius* who rose to great status and fame. In his career he was treasurer and *spatharius*, and he also attained, by 554 at the latest, the ultimate court eunuch post of Grand Chamberlain (*praepositus sacri cubiculi*);[12] his social status increased with his posts, and he ended up holding the distinguished title of *patricius* (derived from the ancient Roman status of patrician).[13] In addition to the usual career path of a distinguished late Roman court eunuch, however, he also acquired a military role. When Procopius first mentions Narses, in the context of events in 530, he records that he was a Persarmenian, that is he was from the part of Armenia under Persian authority.[14] Procopius never reports whether Narses was a deliberate product of the trade in slave eunuchs, but given his origin and function it seems likely that he was. As seen in Chapter 5, Roman legislation took the stance that the only acceptable source of eunuchs was barbarians from outside the empire, and the ethnic origin of other court eunuchs in the later Roman period suggests that Armenia was a usual source.[15] The fact that Narses is first met as a treasurer is also suggestive of his being a typical court eunuch, for this was a function long associated with eunuchs and one that was maintained in the later Roman and Byzantine Empires.[16] Perhaps the very lack of declaration by Procopius that Narses was a product of the slave trade indicates that he was, for it was unusual details that historians tended to comment on; notably Procopius reports that Solomon, another eunuch from the reign of Justinian, was not the product of deliberate castration but had been eunuchized by accident when he was a baby.[17] In his narrative, Procopius does not idly refer to the facts that Narses was a Persarmenian and a treasurer, for both are integral to his story: Narses was receiving deserters from Persarmenia (Aratius and another Narses, together with their mothers), to whom he dispensed a significant amount of money. Interestingly, Malalas reports for the year 531 that when Dorotheus the general of Armenia captured a mountain-top Persian fortress Narses (identified as a *cubicularius*) was sent out by Justinian to take possession of its stores.[18]

Narses is next encountered playing a part in the suppression of the Nika Riot in January 532, though this is not mentioned by the historian Procopius in his extended narrative of the riot but rather by the chronicler Malalas.[19] The Nika Riot is an infamous event in the reign of Justinian, responsible as it was for the destruction of a swathe of the heart of Constantinople (including a previous incarnation of the celebrated church of Hagia Sophia) and ending as it did in the massacre of the rioters.[20] The riot seems to have had its roots in Justinian's crack down on the antisocial activities of members of the Blue and Green factions in Constantinople (though it developed into an attempted coup), and Malalas records that Narses helped to weaken the riot by distributing money to rioters of the Blue faction and thus bribing them to turn against the rioters of the Green faction.[21] Once again, Narses is found associated with the dispensing of money, though Malalas does not designate him specifically as a treasurer but as a *cubicularius* and *spatharius*. Narses thus appears in the usual eunuch guise of a chamberlain, but also as one of the eunuch bodyguard of the emperor.[22] It is possible that in 535 Narses also undertook a mission to Alexandria, for Liberatus records in his *Breviarium* that a Narses who was a *cubicularius* was despatched by the Empress Theodora to restore the deposed Patriarch Theodosius to his see, which entailed having to try to oust its incumbent Gaianus and exile him.[23] The attempt took sixteen months, witnessed violence in the city, and ended in failure, Theodosius having to abandon the scheme in 536.

It was in 538 that Narses (still identified as a treasurer by Procopius) was first despatched to Italy by Justinian, leading major reinforcements to support the commander Belisarius.[24] The two men met at Firmum (modern Fermo) to discuss with the other commanders what action to take. Narses favoured going to Ariminum (modern Rimini), where John the nephew of Vitalian was besieged and in dire straits, and Belisarius agreed to this though it did not accord with his own priorities. Ariminum was thus relieved, but Procopius emphasizes that the relationship between Belisarius and Narses was soured, and they contested for authority over the campaign, the eunuch even asserting that Belisarius was not acting in the interest of the empire.[25] They did both move to besiege Urbinus (modern Urbino), but formed two separate camps. However, convinced by his entourage that Belisarius was wasting his time in a futile siege, Narses and his forces went to Ariminum. When Urbinus unexpectedly surrendered to Belisarius (due to its spring drying up) Procopius records that Narses was 'filled with both astonishment and dejection'.[26] For Narses, John the nephew of Vitalian failed to take Caesena (modern Cesena) but captured Forocornelius (modern Imola) and secured the region of Aemilia itself. Subsequently, when Belisarius commanded John (together with Justinus) to assist his forces in relieving Milan they would not act without the say so of Narses, so Belisarius had to seek the agreement of the eunuch. Narses consented but time had been lost and in 539 Milan fell to the Goths, the city being sacked. Justinian, hearing of the difficulties between Narses and Belisarius, appointed the latter supreme commander of the campaign and recalled the former.[27]

It is usually observed that despite being recalled from Italy, Narses remained in high esteem with Justinian.[28] Certainly at various points in the 540s he is found in the role of the trusted agent of the emperor, and of the empress too. In 541, Theodora sent him and Marcellus the commander of the palace guards with a force of soldiers to the estate of Rufinianae (an Asiatic suburb of Constantinople, near Chalcedon) in order to investigate whether the Praetorian Prefect John the Cappadocian was plotting treason.[29] Around the same time, according to Malalas, Narses was sent by ship to investigate a disturbance near Constantinople's Golden Gate, where a woman had caused panic by predicting that in three days' time the sea was going to rise and flood the city.[30] In 545, Justinian also sent Narses to the Heruli in the Balkans in order to secure their military support for the campaign in Italy.[31] This the eunuch (who had previous contact with the Heruli since they had been among the forces that accompanied him to Italy in 538) managed to do, and he led them into Thrace where they were to overwinter before joining Belisarius. During this mission Narses also exposed the fake Chilbudius.[32] The real Chilbudius had been a general of Thrace for Justinian in the 530s who was killed by the Sclaveni during one of his raids over the Ister.[33] There was, however, another man called Chilbudius (not a Roman but one of the Antae), who became a slave of one of the Sclaveni. He was bought by one of the Antae, who had been told by a Roman captive that this Chilbudius was in fact the Roman Chilbudius. At first Chilbudius denied that he was the Roman general of the same name, but then went along with the deception when the Antae were set on asking Justinian to restore him to his position. It was while the imposter was on his way to the court of Justinian that Narses encountered him and realized that he was not the genuine article. He imprisoned him and then brought him to Constantinople. When Narses is next met again in Procopius' narrative it is when he was appointed supreme commander of the Italian campaign by Justinian, in 551. Thus, our knowledge of Narses' career in the 540s is patchy, as both Dunlap and Fauber recognize. This is largely due to the fact that the major narrative source, Procopius' *Wars*, is focused primarily on the military activities that occurred under Justinian; he is not attempting to produce a comprehensive account of the reign. This should give one pause to think whether Narses really did go unpenalized after his return from Italy. There is simply too little evidence to be definite, and periods of punishment could be brief. On the other hand, it is entirely possible that the eunuch did indeed escape unscathed, as a trusted official of the emperor.

With the advent of the 550s, Narses' career did follow a military path, and was to be conducted in Italy for the rest of his life. Justinian appointed him to head the campaign against the Goths, which Belisarius had been unable to bring to a successful conclusion.[34] In 552, Narses marched into Italy from Salona at the head of a very large force.[35] From Ravenna the Roman army headed south, finally facing the forces of the Ostrogothic king Totila near the village of Taginae (Tadinum) on the Apennines (on the Via Flaminia).[36] Here in June the Ostrogoths were defeated, and Totila died soon after, either from a wound inflicted in the battle which caused him to withdraw or from a wound inflicted as he was fleeing after the defeat.[37] Procopius records that the Romans had to dig up Totila's body in order to confirm the story of a Gothic woman that he was indeed dead,[38] and Malalas reports that Narses sent the king's bloodstained clothes to Constantinople.[39] Following his victory, Narses quickly shed himself of the Lombards in his army (he paid them off and sent them home),[40] then successfully occupied Rome and moved to secure other Italian cities and regions.[41] Valerian was despatched to guard the Po.[42] Narnia in central Italy surrendered to the Romans and a garrison was installed at Spolitium.[43] Perusia (modern Perugia) was also given up.[44] Tarentum was besieged, and the fortresses of Portus, Nepa and Petra Pertusa were all captured.[45] Narses also despatched a force to besiege Cumae in Campania, since it housed most of Totila's treasury, and in addition he gave orders that Centumcellae (modern Civitavecchia) was to be besieged.[46] By this time, the Ostrogoths had appointed a new king, Teias, who mobilized his forces and marched to Campania.[47] Here the two sides faced each other in pitched battle again, at Mons Lactarius (Milk Mountain), probably in October.[48] Once again, Narses was victorious. Procopius asserts that the death of Teias in battle was a crucial moment but notes that even then the Goths did not cease fighting until they recognized the futility of their struggle. The majority of the Goths agreed to leave Italy and not take up arms against the Romans in the future.[49]

Thus, Procopius concludes his monumental history with the successful termination of the Gothic war by Narses, marked by his two victories in pitched battle against the Ostrogoths in 552. Agathias picks up the narrative of Narses' activities in Italy at the very start of his history, in his preface summarizing what Procopius had covered in the *Wars* and beginning Book 1 with the defeat of Teias and the surrender of the Goths.[50] He declares dramatically 'This turn of events led everyone to suppose that the fighting in Italy had been brought to a successful conclusion: in reality it had scarcely begun.'[51] He deals with the threat Narses now faced in the shape of the force of Franks and Alamanni that invaded Italy in 553 (prompted by a Gothic appeal to the Frankish king Theudobald, and led by the Alamanni Butilinus and Leutharis, who were brothers),[52] as well as how Narses attempted to secure Italy, of which he was now effectively ruler. Narses began a siege of Cumae, then targeted other towns in order to impede the invaders. Florentia (modern Florence), Centumcellae, Volaterrae, Luna and Pisa all surrendered.[53] Considerable attention is devoted to Narses' siege of Lucca, which held out against him until late 553.[54] While at Lucca the eunuch received news of the defeats of forces he had sent to Aemilia, the Heruli under their leader Fulcaris being cut down by Butilinus when they attacked Parma, which the Franks had already occupied.[55] This resulted in the Goths in the area siding with the Franks and being unchecked to progress southwards. Forcing Lucca to surrender, Narses then moved north to Ravenna, to winter there (553/4).[56] Here the Goth Aligern came to him and surrendered Cumae, joining forces with the Romans.[57] From Ravenna, Narses moved to Rome and spent the rest of the winter there and readied his troops for battle. The invaders had moved south themselves and divided their forces, Butilinus ending up in the toe of Italy and Leutharis in the heel. Leutharis subsequently decided to head home, but after he crossed the Po and reached the region of Venice he (and his men) fell victim to plague.[58] As for Butilinus, in the autumn he led his army into a pitched battle with Narses in Campania, by the river Casulinus (Volturno).[59] Although Butilinus' forces outnumbered those of the Romans they were routed. Agathias' narrative of Narses' career ends in 555 with the surrender to him of a group of Goths who occupied the fortress of Campsa, following the death of their leader Ragnaris, a Hun; Ragnaris had attempted to shoot Narses with an arrow but missed and was instead shot by Narses' bodyguards and soon died from his wounds.[60]

With Agathias' history being unfinished, historians have to depend largely on a host of western sources for information about the final stages of Narses' career and his death.[61] There are, however, some eastern sources which add to the picture.[62] In terms of the settlement of Italy after Narses' defeat of Totila there exists the Pragmatic Sanction of 13 August 554, which forms part of Justinian's collection of new laws (*Novels*) and deals with legal matters in the wake of the reconquest; it is addressed to Antiochus the 'Magnificent' and Prefect of Italy and Narses the 'Illustrious' and *praepositus sacri cubiculi*.[63] In addition, Malalas reports for 562 that news came that the patrician Narses had captured Verona and Brescia from the Goths and sent the keys and spoils to Constantinople.[64] These events relate to Narses' efforts to secure northern Italy in the wake of further opposition under the leadership of the Frank Amingus and the Goth Widin, which the western sources refer to.[65] It is indeed unfortunate that Agathias did not complete his history, for, despite its shortcomings, it would be preferable to the multitude of western texts which deal with Narses' late career, for they are brief and of dubious quality, having the hallmarks of confusion and legend. These western sources are particularly concerned with Narses' wealth, the reaction against him in Italy, his recall to Byzantium by the new emperor Justin II (565–578) (the nephew of Justinian) and his wife Sophia (the niece of Theodora) after the death of Justinian in 565, his association with the invasion of Italy by the Lombards in 568, and his death. As one follows the texts chronologically it is quite clear that the stories developed with the telling.[66]

Amongst the earliest of the western sources is Gregory of Tours' *The History of the Franks*, which the bishop was still working on in the year of his death, 594.[67] This is notably favourable towards Butilinus, but does record that in the reign of Theudebald (548–555) Narses eventually killed him and so 'Italy was won for the emperor, nor was any afterwards able to recover it'.[68] Gregory also records that the Frank Gundovald defected to Narses in Italy before making his way to the imperial court in Constantinople.[69] Most significantly Gregory touches on the extreme wealth that Narses accrued in Italy, relating a story that the eunuch hid his Italian treasure in the cistern of his house, and that this was only dug up after his death by the Emperor Tiberius (578–582).[70] The *Book of Pontiffs* naturally mentions Narses' relationship with the popes Vigilius (537–555), Pelagius I (556–561) and John III (561–574), and his involvement in ecclesiastical affairs.[71] It was under Narses that Vigilius was restored as pope, though he died when he reached Sicily and was replaced by Pelagius, who was supported by the eunuch. In the biography of John it is conveyed that Narses and this pope had a close relationship, but the biography is especially concerned with Narses' own career and activities. It is reported that Narses had to contend with further military problems: a revolt of the Heruli, who appointed their leader Sindual as king, and then the oppression of Italy led by Amingus, duke of the Franks.[72] Narses was able to defeat both these opponents, which the *Book of Pontiffs* expresses approval of: 'the whole of

Italy was glad'.⁷³ However, it is then related that the Romans 'driven by malice' complained to Justin II and Sophia that Narses treated them like slaves and asked that he be recalled or they would go over to the 'barbarians'.⁷⁴ Discovering what had occurred Narses declared '"If I have maltreated the Romans let me suffer evil"', left Rome for Campania and 'wrote to the Lombard nation to come and occupy Italy'. Then the Pope John went to Naples and begged the eunuch to return to Rome, which they did together. The story concludes abruptly by reporting that much later⁷⁵ Narses died and 'his body was put in a lead coffin and taken back with all his riches to Constantinople'. Thus, the hostility detected in Gregory of Tours is developed here, though it is clear that Narses is depicted as a victim and is perplexed by the action of the Romans.

Writing in the late-sixth century, the bishop Marius of Avenches records in his *Chronicle* under the year 568 the recall of Narses.⁷⁶ He does not link him with the Lombard invasion of Italy, but rather celebrates him as the conqueror of tyrants (the Goths Totila and Teias, the Frank Butilinus, and the Herul Sindbal) and the restorer of Milan and other cities.⁷⁷ Writing in the early-seventh century, the bishop Isidore of Seville in his *Chronicon Maiora* does assert that Narses invited the Lombards into Italy from Pannonia, terrified by threats made by the Empress Sophia, though he does not specify what these were.⁷⁸ Detail is supplied later in the seventh century by the so-called *Fredegar Chronicle*: Sophia had instructed that a golden spindle should be made for Narses 'with which he should spin since he was a eunuch (eo quod eonucus erat); he should rule over slaves, not the peoples' (pensiliariis regerit, non populo); he responded with the remark '"I shall spin a thread of which neither the emperor Justin nor the empress can find the end". Then, summoning the Lombards from Pannonia, he brought them to Italy with their king, Alboin'.⁷⁹

Paul the Deacon's *History of the Lombards*, composed in the eighth century (it was unfinished at the time of his death, most likely in the 790s) deals with many of the same topics of the previous sources, though is notable for expanding the narrative and adding new details too.⁸⁰ Naturally, he records that the Lombards had a part to play in Narses' successful campaign against Totila.⁸¹ Narses' defeat of Butilinus (and the death of Leutharis) is recorded, as well as that of Amingus, who is reported to have been supporting the Goth Widin; Amingus was executed by Narses, but Widin was despatched to Constantinople.⁸² The crushing and execution of Narses' one-time ally Sinduald is recorded, but Paul also details the part that Dagisthaeus played in the securing of Italy.⁸³ Paul touches on Christian affairs too, noting Narses' great piety⁸⁴ and his capture of Vitalis the bishop of Altinum (who had fled to the Franks), whom he then exiled to Sicily.⁸⁵ Then comes the story of Narses' recall and his invitation to the Lombards.⁸⁶ Once again, Narses is the victim of the Romans, who are said to have envied him despite all his labours. The role of Pope John is not featured in this version, but the imperial response is expanded. The emperor is reported to have been very angry with Narses and to have despatched Longinus⁸⁷ to replace him, and the Empress Sophia is said to have sent him a threatening message, addressing the fact that he was a eunuch: she said 'that she would make him portion out to the girls in the women's chamber the daily tasks of wool'.⁸⁸ Narses is reputed to have retorted to this 'that he would begin to weave her such a web as she could not lay down as long as she lived'. As with the chronicles of Isidore and Fredegar, Narses' invitation to the Lombards from his refuge in Naples is the result of fear and hatred of the imperial couple, not of a wish to teach the Romans a lesson. His subsequent return to Rome, death there, and despatch of his body and riches to Constantinople are noted too.[89]

Finally, the deeds of Narses in Italy are also recorded in the *Book of Pontiffs of the Church of Ravenna*, written in the first half of the ninth century by the cleric Agnellus of Ravenna.[90] The tone seems generally positive (there is no mention of why Narses was recalled or of his inviting the Lombards in, though the wealth he acquired from Italy is emphasized again),[91] and there are several chronological indicators concerning the later years of the eunuch's career. It is reported that Justin II recalled Narses in the third year of his reign (so in 568), that Narses had been governor of Italy for sixteen years, and that he died in his ninety-fifth year.[92] This last assertion has been accepted as fact by some, but Stein is surely right to question it on the grounds that neither Procopius nor Agathias mention the age of the eunuch.[93] Since Narses is first encountered working as a court eunuch in 530 perhaps he was born in 510 and initially entered the court in the reign of Justin I (518–527), Justinian's uncle, and went on to become a trusted servant of Justinian. If he had been born in 478 presumably he would have worked at the court of Anastasius I (491–518) and perhaps this would have made him suspect in the eyes of Justin I and his nephew.

Thus, the western sources have a fairly fixed repertoire of Narses' activities in Italy. They focus especially on military activities, but also touch on religious affairs; they emphasize the wealth he acquired from Italy, and how he was betrayed by the Romans; they address his subsequent recall by the emperor and his relations with Justin and Sophia, and the eunuch's invitation to the Lombards; finally, they record his death in Rome and the despatch of his body back to the east. Ultimately, and perhaps surprisingly, Narses emerges as a generally sympathetic character and successful ruler of Italy.[94] He neutralized military threats, retired from public office in 568, and died in Rome in about 573/4. There is an emphasis on the wealth he acquired in Italy, and perhaps this did create some bad feeling.[95] However, there is no reason to believe that he would have invited the Lombards into Italy as an act of revenge.[96] As for his strained relations with Justin and Sophia, it is rather odd that having been recalled he did not return to Constantinople (or was not hunted down) but remained in Italy. A sixth-century eastern text, John of Ephesus' *Church History*, reports that he was buried in his monastery in Bithynia,[97] so there is no sign that Justin and Sophia were displeased with him. The story of Sophia's threats and Narses' response seems just that, a good story which engaged with his status as a eunuch (drawing on established invective: it recalls Claudian's invective against Eutropius where the eunuch is told to busy himself with the female task of spinning rather than the male task of war, and is cast as the forewoman of the spinning girls),[98] and became elaborated over time, and even surfaces in Greek sources. A version of it is found in the tenth-century Byzantine text *On the Governance of the Empire* (*De Administrando Imperio*), compiled under Constantine VII (945–959) for his son Romanos II.[99] In the final analysis Narses is depicted as having a very successful career, both in terms of its longevity and his achievements, as well as in terms of his posthumous reputation.

Narses as a successful general: explanations

The success of Narses as a general seems particularly impressive, especially given Belisarius' inability to defeat the Ostrogoths outright, and it is natural and important to consider why the eunuch was victorious. The major sources Procopius and Agathias certainly indicate several factors that contributed to his achievements:

Good planning

Both Procopius and Agathias remark on Narses' intelligence in planning and strategy. When gathered at Taginae, Narses asks Totila to name the day for battle and the Ostrogothic king says eight days hence, but Narses prepares to fight the next day anyway.[100] Procopius comments that Narses was correct in his response, for Totila turned up the following day. Narses also anticipated that the Goths would try to secure a nearby hill, so had it occupied by his own men.[101] Arranging his forces for the battle Narses placed his barbarian forces on foot at the centre of his phalanx, in order to prevent their flight.[102] When Totila retires to eat and breaks up his formation, Narses suspects a sudden attack so keeps his troops in their ranks and has them eat a small meal while keeping formation.[103] After the victory at Taginae, it is under Narses' direction that Dagisthaeus gained entry to Rome.[104] Interestingly, Procopius had already noted Narses' gift for planning during his time in Italy in the 530s, for he observes that Narses' abandonment of the siege of Urbinus on the grounds that it was impregnable was correct, and that Belisarius only managed to take it as the water supply dried up unexpectedly.[105] Agathias also refers to the eunuch's talent for strategy and planning. Narses uses the 'barbarian' strategy of false flight effectively against the Franks (900 Frankish infantry are killed as a result), and he checks Butilinus by depriving him of supplies, for he 'had very cleverly requisitioned everything in advance'.[106]

Good relationships

In both Procopius and Agathias it is evident that Narses has good relationships with his men as individuals and also as groups. Procopius comments especially on Narses' relationship with his commander John the nephew of Vitalian, which he characterizes as particularly close ('Narses ... loved John above all other men'),[107] even before the eunuch is instrumental in saving his life by relieving the siege of Ariminum in 538 (a debt which John recognized as owing to Narses).[108] When Narses returned to Italy in the 550s, John was still there, and in Procopius he serves as an invaluable source of advice for the eunuch. John informs Narses of how to march along the coast of the Ionian Gulf to Ravenna when the passage was blocked by the Franks, and when the Goths surrendered after the Battle of Mons Lactarius Narses again follows the advice of John regarding the Gothic peace proposals.[109] It is clear that Narses was also close to other men. Procopius refers to his supporters in Italy in the 530s,[110] and Agathias indicates his good relations with other individuals, such as Stephanus (who was sent to tell the other generals off for not keeping up the pressure on Parma) and Bonus (the quaestor of Moesia on the Danube, 'a man of exceptional sagacity with a wide experience of civil as well as military matters').[111] Dagisthaeus seems to have been a trusted and effective agent too, referred to by both Procopius and Paul the Deacon, as already noted.[112] The selection of Paulus as his personal guard on account of his proven valour (he was prominent among the fifty soldiers who occupied the hill by Taginae) also seems to point to Narses' desire to have reliable men around him.[113] The eunuch's close relationship with groups of barbarians is stressed too, particularly his relationship with the Heruli. When Narses was recalled from Italy at the end of the 530s, the Heruli decided to leave as well, even though Belisarius promised to reward them if they remained.[114] It was Narses who was sent to the Heruli in the 540s in order to persuade them to go to Italy again.[115] Agathias also comments on the relationship with the Heruli. He notes Narses' sorrow at the death of the Herul leader Fulcaris, that the Heruli under their leader Sindual (whom the eunuch had appointed to this position over another candidate, Aruth) continued to fight for Narses even though he executed one of their chiefs for killing his servant (an event that perhaps has added significance in the light of the later revolt of the Heruli and the execution of Sindual, as first reported by the *Book of Pontiffs*).[116] The execution of the Herul chief for murder in 554 also demonstrates Narses' firm but fair character, which seems to have earned him respect. Agathias reports that the Herul Fulcaris was more afraid to face Narses and be reprimanded for his folly than to die at the hands of the Franks.[117] Agathias also emphasizes Narses' gift for communication with his troops, even though he had not had training in public speaking.[118] For instance, despite his own sorrow at the death of Fulcaris, Narses knows that he has to encourage his men and keep them motivated.[119]

Generosity

Procopius asserts that part of the reason for Narses' successful relationships was his 'princely generosity' (μεγαλοδωρότατος).[120] This made people eager to serve him, either to repay his kindness or to earn further benefits. Procopius adds that 'the Heruli and the other barbarians were particularly well disposed towards him, having been especially well treated by him'. Narses is depicted offering material incentives to bravery prior to the battle of Taginae.[121] Agathias understands Narses' generosity also in the sense of generosity of spirit. In an episode detailing Narses' relations with Lucca he records how the eunuch released the hostages he had taken. He reports that the hostages then praised Narses: 'They recalled the kind treatment they had received at his hands, and it was whispered in every quarter that he was gentle and affable and that he tempered justice with magnanimity'.[122] This further underlines Narses' 'firm but fair' reputation.

Piety

Both Procopius and Agathias comment on Narses' piety, which is strongly linked to his success. Procopius asserts that Narses attributed his success at Taginae to God (which the historian declares was true).[123] In Agathias, when the inhabitants of Lucca think that Narses has killed his hostages they accuse him of having created a false impression of piety and devotion, indicating that the eunuch was commonly perceived to be pious and devout.[124] Narses justifies executing the Herul chief for murdering his servant on the grounds that it would be 'impious to march into battle without first removing the guilty stain by some act of atonement'.[125] Agathias then comments 'So great was his confidence in the aid of the divinity that he marched out to battle with the conviction of foreordained success'.[126] The piety of Narses is also identified as significant by other sources. The church historian Evagrius notes that the eunuch was devoted to God and to the Virgin, and that it was said that 'she openly commanded him as to the moment when he ought to fight, and that he was not to begin an engagement before he received the sign from her'.[127] Paul the Deacon remarks that Narses 'was a very pious man, a Catholic in religion, generous to the poor, very zealous in restoring churches, and so much devoted to vigils and prayers that he obtained victory more by the supplications which he poured forth to God, than by the arms of war' (Erat autem vir piissimus, in religione catholicus, in pauperes munificus, in recuperandis basilicis satis studiosus, vigiliis et orationibus in tantum studens, ut plus supplicationibus ad Deum profusis quam armis bellicis victoriam obtineret).[128]

Good moral character

Agathias is keen also to emphasize the good moral character of Narses in his assessment of him as an effective general. He notes that despite his successes over the Goths Narses 'did not let victory go to his head or indulge in vulgar bragging ... nor did he give himself over ... to a life of luxury and ease'.[129] Narses realizes too that despite the deaths of Butilinus and Leutharis further campaigns will have to be undertaken against the Franks, and he addresses his men about this in order to prevent them from becoming carried away.[130] The eunuch is also depicted as utterly trustworthy; for example, he kept his word about not killing the Goths at Campsa after they had surrendered to him.[131] This episode led Fauber to declare that Narses' 'plighted word on all occasions was the wonder of a degenerate age'.[132] This reputation for trustworthiness feeds back into the aspect of Narses' good relationships with individuals and groups.

Fortune

Agathias also emphasizes the role that Fortune played in Narses' successes: 'all went well for Narses since fortune lent a hand to his excellent generalship'.[133]

Therefore, there are a range of positive qualities that Procopius and Agathias between them (and supported by remarks in other sources) identify to explain the success of Narses as a general. It must be recognized, however, that Procopius also notes factors which have less to do with the good qualities of the eunuch. He makes clear that the expedition of Narses was strongly supported by Justinian in terms of men and money, so he was already in a stronger position than Belisarius had been.[134] One could argue, though, that this circumstance can be credited to Narses, for Procopius reports that he had demanded such support from the emperor.[135] More overtly negative factors are that the Gothic forces were less numerous, and Procopius also highlights that Totila himself made mistakes and that Fortune was against him.[136] There is the sensation in Procopius, then, that as good as Narses was there were also other factors at play in his success, though, as has been seen, Agathias himself recognizes the role of Fortune.

Thus, there are a range of factors supplied by Procopius and Agathias, both positive and negative, to account for the achievement of Narses. However, it is vital to reflect on the status of this evidence. To what extent do Procopius and Agathias provide adequate explanations for the success of Narses? Certainly, the moral qualities of the eunuch may not strike a modern audience as salient,[137] but the vagueness of the explanations can also be frustrating. For instance, Procopius remarks on the intensely close relationship of Narses and John, but does not explain why this was so. Likewise, Procopius accounts for Narses' good relations with the Heruli in terms of how well the eunuch treated them, but when Belisarius offers to treat them well too, this carries no weight with them, so one is left with the sensation that there must be more to Narses' relationship with the Heruli than has been revealed.[138] Further, the interpretations and facts presented by Procopius and Agathias can be questioned. On Procopius' assertion that Narses placed the barbarians in the centre of the phalanx for the Battle of Taginae so as to prevent them fleeing, the military historian Sir Charles Oman observed that 'this very inadequate reason is evidently not the true one' and fails to do justice to the tactical planning of the eunuch.[139] Agathias' account of Narses' fake execution of the hostages at Lucca is widely doubted.[140] One also has to face the fact that Procopius and Agathias may not have identified other factors that were important, and which can only be guessed at by modern historians. More fundamentally, it needs to be asked to what extent Narses is being presented by Procopius and Agathias as a stereotype of a successful general. Does one learn anything about the reality of the eunuch general?

Narses as eunuch general: characterization and selection

Previous discussions of the career of Narses as a general have certainly failed to do justice to his eunuchood. Procopius and Agathias do touch on it themselves, albeit briefly, and are of the view that a eunuch would not be expected to be a successful general. Procopius observes that Narses was 'keen (ὀξὺς) and more energetic (δραστήριος) than would be expected of a eunuch'.[141] When Agathias comments on Narses' good qualities in relation to him speaking to the troops after the death of the Herul Fulcaris he remarks that:

> These qualities were all the more remarkable in a eunuch and in one who had been brought up in the soft and comfortable atmosphere of the imperial court ... The fact is that the nobility of soul cannot fail to make its mark, no matter what obstacles are put in its path.[142]

Agathias also has Leutharis and Butilinus comment on Narses that 'they were surprised at the Goths being so terrified of a puny little man, a eunuch of the bedchamber, used to a soft and sedentary existence, and with nothing masculine about him'.[143] Procopius asserts that the very appointment of Narses as supreme commander by Justinian was puzzling, and one of the explanations he gives (the other is that the emperor knew that the rest of the commanders would not agree to take orders from John the nephew of Vitalian as they would not consent to be of inferior rank to him) is that a prophecy foretold Narses' success.[144] Procopius reports that he heard this prophecy from a senator in Rome, who related that when Athalaric was king (526–534) a herd of cattle entered Rome through the Forum of Peace and a steer (a castrated bull) mounted a fountain there by which there was a bronze statue of a bull, and the steer stood over this statue. A Tuscan who happened to be passing interpreted this as a sign that 'one day a eunuch would undo the ruler of Rome', which earned him derision at the time; such a scenario was not deemed realistic.

A Byzantinist who has considered the eunuchood of Narses in relation to his generalship is Kathryn Ringrose, dealing with his case in her discussion of Byzantine eunuchs 'as protagonists in the military and political arenas'.[145] She asserts that Procopius and Agathias do not attribute 'Narses' success to traditional, courageous manliness' but 'to the "cleverness" and "deviousness" that they perceived as attributes of eunuchs'.[146] However, while the historians do present Narses as transcending typical expectations of eunuchs, Ringrose does not do justice to their depiction of this eunuch.[147] Agathias asserts explicitly that Narses' 'courage (ἀνδρεῖον) and heroism (μεγαλουργὸν) were absolutely incredible'.[148] Procopius reports that Narses' supporters thought that the eunuch could display bravery (ἀνδρείας) as well as wisdom.[149] In both Procopius and Agathias, Narses is depicted as actively participating in his campaigns; Agathias emphasizes this in particular, noting for instance that Narses rode out from Ariminum against the Franks on a well-trained horse.[150] More significantly, it is clear from military treatises, for example, that being a successful general was not really about bravery anyway, but about intelligence and leadership.[151] The influential treatise of Onasander on the general (*Strategikos*, written in the first century AD and dedicated to Quintus Veranius, consul in 49)[152] asserts for instance that a general should not himself enter battle for 'he can aid his army far less by fighting than he can harm it if he should be killed, since the knowledge of a general is far more important than his physical strength'.[153] He declares that for a general to get involved in fighting is 'not brave (ἀνδρεῖος) but thoughtless and foolhardy', and he observes that 'Even a soldier can perform a great deed by bravery, but no one except the general can by his wisdom plan a greater one,' though he does allow that 'the general must show himself brave[154] before the army, that he may call forth the zeal of his soldiers' but adds that 'he must fight cautiously'.[155] He also notes that a general must do nothing rash: 'everything that is ventured rashly is rather the part of recklessness than of wisdom, and has a greater share of luck than of good judgement'.[156]

It is quite clear that such ideology does affect the way in which Procopius and Agathias depict Narses, but also non-eunuch generals too.[157] For instance, Agathias criticizes Fulcaris on the grounds that he 'did not regard tactical skill and the proper disposition of his forces as the mark of a true general and leader, but prided himself instead on cutting a dash in the field of battle by leading the charge against the enemy in person and by keeping himself in the forefront of the fighting', while he praises the Armenian Chanaranges for combining bravery with good sense.[158] He also observes of Theudebert (who planned to invade Thrace and attack Constantinople) that 'he was capable of equating sheer lunacy with courage'.[159] He has mixed opinions about Germanus the son of Dorotheus, observing that 'despite his extreme youth [he] was an exceptionally able general and possessed qualities of daring and resourcefulness far in excess of his years', but then remarking that his youth meant that he could be immature, for 'he [did not] confine himself to giving orders and encouraging his men like a general but bore the brunt of the fighting like a common soldier'.[160] Interestingly, Agathias also addresses the generalship of Belisarius in the context of his repulse of the Huns and Cotrigurs from Constantinople in 559.[161] Agathias asserts that Belisarius still possessed courage despite his age[162] but emphasizes that intelligence is vital for victory too. He has Belisarius say to his troops 'Brute force without the aid of sound judgement is powerless to defeat an enemy', remark on the distinction between courage and audacity, and observe that taking time to think a problem through is not a sign of cowardice.[163] Ultimately, Agathias declares that the Romans won their victory through Belisarius' 'wisdom and foresight'.[164] Likewise, Procopius praises John the nephew of Vitalian for having wisdom as well as energy, and has Belisarius say to the commanders that advance planning led to the defeat of the Goths, not their lack of courage or lesser numbers.[165] It is also important to appreciate that the ideology found in Onasander is not just reflected in late Roman historiography but in late Roman military manuals too, for Onasander is strongly echoed in the *Strategikon* attributed to the Emperor Maurice (582–602).[166]

The existence of such views may then cast some light on why Justinian felt comfortable appointing Narses to a military post, an appointment historians have struggled to comprehend. Procopius focuses attention on the appointment of Narses to the supreme command of the Gothic war in the 550s, offering just two explanations (one negative, the other supernatural). However, the appointment in 538 deserved comment too, for this was (apparently) Narses' first step on the path of a military career. Of this step Dunlap, for instance, remarks 'It seems strange that a palace eunuch with but little experience, probably, in warfare should be sent on a military expedition'.[167] Some have sought to establish pre-existing military experience for Narses, suggesting for instance that he was actively involved in the suppression of the Nika Riot.[168] Perhaps he also saw action in Alexandria, if indeed he was the Narses sent there in 535.[169] The fact that he was a *spatharius* has been brought into the debate too; some see it as an active military role, though others consider that it was more ceremonial.[170] Strikingly, the writer Robert Graves in his novel *Count Belisarius* depicts Narses as having a yearning for a military career because he 'had been captured in battle when he was eleven years old, and had already at that tender age killed a man with his little sword – for he came of a well-known military family in Armenia'.[171] Despite all these attempts to establish military credentials for Narses it is more important to recognize that military experience was not an essential requirement for being appointed to a military command, witness the case of Liberius, an aged Italian agent of the Ostrogoths with no experience of warfare whom Justinian appointed to lead an expedition to Italy in 550.[172] It has been recognized by some that Narses' apparent military intelligence could have been acquired from studying military manuals; Robert Graves' friend the military historian Basil Liddell Hart thought that Narses had studied the theory of war, and Stein remarks 'strategic theory was at this time an easily-understood science, and the nimble mind of Narses probably made him familiar with it quickly'.[173] Some have suggested also that there were particular reasons for sending Narses to Italy in 538, such as Justinian's desire to keep an eye on Belisarius, or Narses' financial expertise.[174] By the time Justinian put Narses in charge of the campaign in 551, there must have been a host of reasons to do so (not just the fact that the emperor suddenly needed to find a replacement for his relative Germanus who had unexpectedly died in Illyricum while preparing to lead the campaign in Italy – and even then it's telling that Justinian's choice was Narses):[175]

1. Narses already had experience of Italy.
2. He had financial expertise.
3. He had some military experience, having seen conflict in Italy already, and possibly also in 545, for when he was leading the Herul federates through Thrace they encountered the Sclaveni and defeated them.[176]
4. He had a very good relationship with individuals and groups, notably John and the Heruli.
5. He was a proven and trusted agent of the regime.

Thus, Procopius' apparent perplexity about the appointment of Narses seems itself perplexing (he does not even allude to the fact that an advantage of a eunuch is that as a castrated male he could not be a rival for imperial power).[177] This impression is compounded when the military career of Narses is considered in context.

Narses in context

As noted at the start of this chapter, Narses is the most famous case of a eunuch general in Byzantium. One can get the impression that he created the precedent for eunuch generals in the empire. Rodolphe Guilland begins his survey of Byzantine military eunuchs with Narses.[178] Narses became the role model *par excellence*: the Byzantine eunuch John Ionopolites was hailed as a new Narses.[179] Yet, it must be acknowledged that the military career of another eunuch, Solomon, preceded that of his contemporary Narses.[180] Solomon, Procopius tells us, was born near Dara on the eastern frontier and was an accidental eunuch, having suffered some injury when he was still a baby.[181] Thus, he seems not to have been a product of the trade in eunuch slaves. He carved out a military career for himself, being one of the commanders of the federates and manager (*domesticus*) for Belisarius for the expedition to North Africa in 533, before becoming the leading general there after the defeat of the Vandals, as well as Praetorian Prefect (534–536 and 539–544). It is clear from Procopius' account of the career of Solomon in Africa that he was a very celebrated figure,[182] having defeated the Mauri (usually identified by modern historians as Berbers or Moors) several times before succumbing in battle to them in 544.[183] Procopius provides much information about Solomon's activities, and makes clear that he had close personal contact with the eunuch himself. For instance, when there was a mutiny[184] against Solomon by his men in Carthage in 536 Procopius was with him when he escaped in a boat to the ship-yard at Missua.¹⁸⁵ As part of his narrative of Solomon's campaigns against the Mauri, Procopius describes three major victories of the eunuch: at Mammes, at Mount Bourgaon, and then at Babosis by Mount Aurasium.¹⁸⁶ He also comments on the strategy to garrison Mount Aurasium so that the Mauri could not occupy it.¹⁸⁷ Further, Procopius can praise the regime of Solomon, describing it thus after the return of the eunuch to North Africa in 539:

> [Solomon] ruled with moderation and guarded Libya securely, setting the army in order... And he surrounded each city with a wall, and guarding the laws with great strictness, he restored the government completely. And Libya became under his rule powerful as to its revenues and prosperous in other respects.¹⁸⁸

> And as a result of [Solomon's successes in exerting Roman control] all the Libyans who were subjects of the Romans, coming to enjoy secure peace and finding the rule of Solomon wise and very moderate, and having no longer any thought of hostility in their minds, seemed the most fortunate of all men.¹⁸⁹

Thus, Solomon provided a model of a eunuch governor as well as a eunuch general. Concerning his military abilities Procopius testifies that Solomon, like Narses, participated in battle himself and showed great leadership.¹⁹⁰ Before the battle at Mammes, Solomon is depicted addressing his troops to encourage them for the fight.¹⁹¹ He acknowledges that the Mauri have more men but declares that the Romans are more courageous and better organized. In the battle itself a crucial factor in the victorious outcome for the Romans is Solomon leaping down from his horse and leading an attack on part of the circle of camels which the Mauri had formed; the circle collapsed and a rout ensued.¹⁹² Prior to Solomon's victory at Babosis, the Mauri under Iaudas had defeated Solomon's bodyguard Gontharis in battle, but when the eunuch himself approached the Mauri retreated in fear.¹⁹³ Strikingly, Procopius also associates a prophecy with the great success of Solomon (in the context of his victory at Mount Bourgaon), recording that the Mauri 'recalled the saying of their women... that their nation would be destroyed by a beardless man'.¹⁹⁴

It is evident, then, that when Narses was first sent to Italy in 538 there was already an immediate precedent for a eunuch general (and a successful one at that), though oddly Procopius himself does not draw a parallel between Solomon and Narses. Perhaps Procopius felt that the differences between these two eunuchs was significant (one being a court eunuch acquiring a military role and the other being an accidental eunuch who had an established military career), but nevertheless surely the two cases merited some connected comment. Even if Procopius had reason not to associate Narses and Solomon, a further case of a military eunuch in the reign of Justinian might have been expected to generate some reflection: Procopius reports that in 551 the emperor appointed one of the palace eunuchs, Scholasticus, as chief commander of a considerable army against the Sclaveni.¹⁹⁵ Thus, Narses is one of three eunuch commanders that distinguish Justinian's reign, a phenomenon that becomes the norm for Byzantium.¹⁹⁶ There is no doubt that Narses is the most famous of these three; perhaps the fact that he died undefeated and in bed helped him to eclipse the reputation of Solomon. It might be tempting to assert that it was the case of Solomon that set the precedent for the use of eunuch commanders, but it must be remarked (although Guilland did not) that there was at least one earlier late Roman example, for as has been seen the Grand Chamberlain Eutropius commanded an expedition against the Huns in 398.[197] Further, military eunuchs were not unique to the later Roman Empire, for they feature in other cultures, both earlier and subsequent, from ancient Assyria to modern China.[198] Notable examples are Aristonicus in Ptolemaic Egypt under Ptolemy V (204–180 BC); Dionysius a naval officer of Mithridates VI the King of Pontus during the Third Mithridatic War (73–63 BC); Muʾnis al-Muẓaffar ('The Victorious') who was an Abbasid military commander in the tenth century AD; and admiral Zheng He of Ming China, active in the fifteenth century AD.[199] Intriguingly, as late as 2010 the *Hindustan Times* suggested that the Hijras of India could serve in a military capacity.[200]

Conclusion

In the later Roman Empire not only did eunuchs become an institutional feature of the imperial court as chamberlains, they also began to play the role of generals. This is especially evident in the sixth century in the reign of Justinian I, with Narses as the famous case but not the only one. Further, Narses was not the first Roman eunuch general. He was preceded in the sixth century by Solomon, but more significantly by Eutropius in the fourth century. The military role of eunuchs was not unprecedented either, with other examples found in antiquity in different cultures. It did, however, become a particular feature of the continuation of the Roman Empire in the medieval period, the Byzantine Empire.[201] One of the advantages of appointing eunuchs to military commands was that as castrated men they were deemed disqualified from becoming emperors and thus would not usurp power for themselves.[202] As eunuchs they also presented issues of gender identity; since warfare was a male role successful eunuch generals could be cast as masculine, while unsuccessful ones could be presented as effeminate, revealing their 'true' gender identity as feminized men. Within the whole span of the Byzantine Empire, from the fourth to the fifteenth century AD, Narses remained the most famous and most successful of the eunuch generals, a role model for those who came in his wake. Further, however, Narses was not just a chamberlain turned general, he also effectively became the ruler of Roman Italy. This fact makes a dramatic and fitting climax to the story of the eunuchs of the Roman Empire.

Notes

Introduction

1. Shakespeare, *Antony and Cleopatra* 1.5.9–19. See also 2.5.4–9.
2. He accessed it through the English translation of Sir Thomas North, itself a translation of a French translation: Bevington (2005: 2).
3. See for instance Virgil, *Aeneid* 8.685–8, and Horace, *Odes* 1.37. Horace's reference at 1.37.9–10 to Cleopatra's 'contaminated flock of men diseased by vice' (contaminato cum grege turpium/morbo virorum) has been understood as 'an allusion to the eunuchs at the court of the Ptolemies': see West (2008: 54 and 155).
4. Plutarch, *Life of Antony* 60, trans. Scott-Kilvert (1965: 326). For Plutarch see Chapter 4.
5. Lucan, *On the Civil War* 10.127–40, trans. Duff (1928: 599–601).
6. Plutarch, *Life of Pompey* 77, and *Life of Caesar* 48–9.
7. Polybius 28.20–21, and Diodorus of Sicily 30.15 and 17.
8. Polybius 22.22.
9. For Hellenistic eunuchs see Guyot (1980: 92–120) and Strootman (2017: esp. 129–30). See also Rotman (2015a).
10. Renault (1972) and see Tougher (2008b). For Bagoas see Chapter 3.
11. See Grayson (1995).
12. Ammianus Marcellinus 14.6.17, and Claudian, *Against Eutropius* 1.339–42. Notably the classical Greek historian Hellanicus ascribed it to Atossa, a Persian or Assyrian queen: see Gera (1997: esp. 146–8).
13. Tertullian, *Exhortation to Chastity* 12.1. See Shaw (1987: 12) but also Moreschini and Fredouille (1985: 186) who suggest spiritual eunuchs are meant. Tertullian mocks the notion that men need wives to run households by referring to the households of celibates, eunuchs (*res spadonum*), soldiers and travellers.
14. Guyot (1980: 121–76).
15. See Hopkins (1963) (incorporated in Hopkins (1978: 172–96)) and Tougher (2008a: 36–53).
16. Priscus, Fragment 11.1, Blockley (1983: 242–7).
17. They are both treated in Vout (2007: 136–212).
18. The eunuch dimension of the play has been analysed by Dessen (1995).
19. Guyot (1980: 20–4). In Greco-Roman culture, eunuchs were created by damaging or excision of the testicles; there is no evidence that the penis was removed too. Of course, this is not to say that it did not happen, but Liudprand of Cremona, a western ambassador to the court of Constantinople in the tenth century, indicates that in Byzantium penis-less eunuchs were not usual (he had brought some as a gift, created by merchants of Verdun to be sold in Spain), and this seems telling given the Greco-Roman origins of the Byzantine empire: see Liudprand of Cremona, *Antapodosis* 6.6, and Tougher (2008a: 117).
20. Pliny the Elder, *Natural History* 19.28.127.

21 For the Great Mother (also known as Cybele and the Mother of the Gods) and her cult see Vermaseren (1977) and Roller (1999).
22 See Tougher (2008a: 32–4).
23 See Caner (1997).
24 Matthew 19.12. The translation of the Authorized King James Version of the Bible runs 'For there are some eunuchs, which were born so from their mother's womb, and there are some eunuchs, which were made eunuchs of men, and there be eunuchs, which have made themselves eunuchs for the kingdom of heaven's sake.'
25 Council of Nicaea, Canon 1, ed. trans. Hefele (1883: 375–6). See also Caner (1997: 407).
26 For the term *spado* see Guyot (1980: 22 n. 17), Kuefler (2001: 33), and Rotman (2015b: 146–7).
27 See Gleason (1995: 3–20 and 131–58) and Holford-Stevens (2003: 98–130).

Chapter 1

1 Claudian, *Against Eutropius* 1.277–80. His *Against Eutropius* 2.279–303 also focuses on the goddess. For Claudian on Eutropius see Chapter 5.
2 For Hannibal see for instance MacDonald (2015).
3 The other was the sun god Helios. For Julian on the Great Mother see for instance Lancellotti (2002: 125–35), Turcan (1996: 71–3), and Tougher (forthcoming b).
4 See for instance Beard (1994: 173–4) and Bowden (2010: esp. 101).
5 Note, for example, the comments of Roller (1999: 317–18) and Turcan (1996: 35).
6 On the cult of the Great Mother in Rome see for instance Vermaseren (1977: 38–69), Roller (1999: esp. 263–325), Turcan (1996: 28–74 and 342–9), Beard (1994), Rieger (2009), Bowden (2010: 93–104), and Latham (2012).
7 See for instance the comments of Beard (1994: 170 and n. 23). For Christian hostility to the cult see for instance Fear (1996) and Rauhala (2011: 70–81).
8 On Cybele and her cult see especially Roller (1999), Vermaseren (1977), and Borgeaud (2004).
9 Livy 29.10.4–11.8 and 29.14.5–14, trans. Moore (1949: 245–9 and 259–63). For discussion of the introduction of the cult see for instance Beard, North and Price (1998, vol. 1: 96–8) and Bowden (2010: 93–5).
10 For the Megalesia see also Chapter 2.
11 For the role of Scipio Nasica in receiving the goddess see also Valerius Maximus, *Memorable Doings and Sayings* 7.5.2 and 8.15.3.
12 Ovid, *Fasti* 4.265–70. For Ovid's treatment of the Great Mother and her festival see Littlewood (1981). For Ovid see for instance Knox (ed.) (2009).
13 Varro, *On the Latin Language* 6.15.
14 Bowden (2010: 93–4). See however Borgeaud (2004: esp. 74–9).
15 Ovid, *Fasti* 4.249–52, trans. Frazer (1967: 207).
16 For the role of the Magna Mater in the *Aeneid*, and her protection of Aeneas, see for instance Wiseman (1984).
17 See Virgil, *Aeneid* 2.693–7, 2.788, 3.111–14, 6.784–9, 7.138–40, 9.77–122, 10.156–8, 10.219–35, and 10.252–5. Wiseman (1984: 123) comments 'the prominence Virgil gives to the Great Mother in the *Aeneid* is extraordinary. How can we explain it?' He recognizes the Augustus factor, but unnecessarily suggests that he was rehabilitating the Great Mother.
18 *Aeneid* 9.77–122 and 10.219–35.

19 *Aeneid* 10.252–5, trans. West (2003: 218).
20 See Roller (1999: 299–304). She also suggests that the presence of pine cones in the Roman cult of the Magna Mater points to an association with Aeneas and Troy because of the sacred pines of the goddess on Mount Ida (p. 279). One of Martial's epigrams is titled 'Pine cones' and runs 'We are Cybele's fruits; go hence, traveller, [lest] our fall come down upon your luckless head': 13.25, trans. Shackleton Bailey (1993, vol. 3: 183). For Martial see below and Chapter 3.
21 Livy 34.54 and 36.36. Games were also instituted in 194 or 191 BC.
22 Augustus, *Res Gestae* 19, and Ovid, *Fasti* 4.348. The front of the Augustan temple is depicted on a relief in Rome (one of the Valle-Medici reliefs) dated to the mid-first century AD: see Bell (2009). In the image of the temple the two reclining figures flanking the enthroned crown of the Great Mother have usually been identified as Galli (e.g. Vermaseren (1977: 42–3), and Turcan (1996: 43)), an arm of each resting on a tambourine, but Bell argues that they are personifications of Mount Ida and the Palatine Hill, thus emphasizing Augustus' interest in the Trojan origins of the cult and Rome. Roller (1999: 309–11) had identified them as images of Attis but changed her mind and identified them as Galli: Roller (2006).
23 Augustus put priests selected from his freedmen in charge of the cult of the goddess: *CIL* 6.496. See Roller (1999: 315).
24 See Littlewood (1981: 383–5).
25 See Vermaseren (1977: 75) and Turcan (1996: 43). A statue dated to the reign of Claudius (41–54) or the Antonine period (138–193) depicts the goddess with the head of Livia: see Roller (1999: 313).
26 See for instance Cicero, *On the Response of the Haruspices* 13.27 (Claudia is described as 'the woman who was reckoned to be the most chaste of the matrons' (*femina autem, quae matronarum castissima putabatur*), and *In Defence of Caelius* 14.34. He contrasts the chaste Claudia with his notorious contemporary Clodia, sister of his opponent Clodius, who were of the Claudian family. Both these texts date to 56 BC.
27 Ovid, *Fasti* 4.305–44. On the significance of the figure of Claudia Quinta see Burns (2017), who argues that she is mythical, and asserts that 'The miracle of Claudia Quinta and the trapped ship gave the Romans a purely Roman myth about the Magna Mater to celebrate, and anchored her identity as a Roman goddess' (p. 92). Another poet writing under Augustus also mentions the Claudia episode: Propertius, *Elegies* 4.11.51–2. This is an elegy for Cornelia, the stepdaughter of Augustus, who died in 16 BC; for comment see Cairns (2006: 358–61) and Richardson (1977: 481–9).
28 Ovid, *Fasti* 4.326.
29 Herodian 1.11.4–5, trans. Whittaker (1969: 71–3), and see Boin (2013a: 270). In Julian's account of the story of Claudia in his *Hymn to the Mother of the Gods* she is described as a holy virgin (160c), terms also used by Herodian. Roller (1999: 267–8) asserts that Claudia had already become a Vestal by the end of the first century AD, in the epic poem of Silius Italicus about the Second Carthaginian War (*Punica* 17.33–47) and Statius' poem on the wedding of Stella and Violentilla (*Silvae* 1.2.245–6). However, neither Silius Italicus nor Statius specify that Claudia is a Vestal Virgin, just a virgin. Burns (2017: 83 and 96 n. 9) conflates Statius' remarks with those of Herodian and Jerome.
30 See Beard, North and Price (1998, vol. 2: 45–6) and Roller (1999: 312–14). For Claudia and the altar see also Leach (2007).
31 Valerius Maximus, *Memorable Doings and Sayings* 1.8.11. See also Tacitus, *Annals* 4.64.
32 Julian, *Hymn to the Mother of the Gods* 161b.

33 For Attis in general see Lancellotti (2002). For the introduction of Attis by the Greeks into the cult of the Great Mother, probably in the fourth century BC, see for instance Roller (1999: 177–82) who notes that 'there is no indication of a god equivalent to Attis in Phrygian art or cult practice' (p. 178). For the myth of Cybele and Attis see for instance Roller (1999: 237–59) and Vermaseren (1977: 88–92).
34 Ovid, *Fasti* 4.183-6, 221–46, 361–6.
35 Ovid, *Fasti* 4.237–42, trans. Frazer (1967: 207).
36 See for instance the comments of Roller (1999: 241). For other versions see for instance Diodorus Siculus 3.58–59.2, and Pausanias 7.17.9.
37 Pausanias 7.17.10–12, trans. Jones (1966: 269).
38 For Arnobius and his work see Simmons (1995) and Edwards (1999).
39 On Timotheus see for instance Lancellotti (2002: 2 n. 6 with references) and Borgeaud (2004: 44, 46).
40 Arnobius, *Against the Pagans* 5.5–7, trans. Bryce and Campbell (1886: 491–2). For an alternative translation see McCracken (1949, vol. 2: 414–17). I provide the older translation as I find it preserves the explicitness of the original.
41 See for example Vermaseren (1977: 60–2, 94 ('The most celebrated work of art in honour of Attis')), Lambrechts (1952: 154–5), Turcan (1996: 55), Fishwick (1966: 199), Hales (2002: 96–7), and Boin (2013a: 255–8) and (2013b: 183, 189).
42 See for instance Beard, North and Price (1998, vol. 1: 98) and Roller (1999: 274–7). Roller comments that the figurines 'demonstrate that Attis was an essential part of the Mother's cult from its inception in Rome ... Clearly, the Magna Mater's eunuch consort came with her [from Pergamum] to her new home in Rome' (p. 277).
43 See Bell (2009: 76 and n. 39) and Lancellotti (2002: 77–80).
44 See for instance Lancellotti (2002: 80–4).
45 John the Lydian, *On the Months* 4.59.
46 For the calendar see especially Salzman (1990). On the Roman festivals see Vermaseren (1977: 113–24), Graillot (1912: 108–49), Fishwick (1966), Beard (1994: 170–3), and Turcan (1996: 44–7).
47 The calendar also lists for 28 March the Initiation of the Circus of Caligula (*Initium Caiani*). While some consider this part of the festival too (perhaps referring to the initiation of devotees of the goddess) Fishwick argues that it is not connected at all: see Fishwick (1966: 193 and n. 2).
48 See Lambrechts (1952) and Fishwick (1966), though note the reservations in Vermaseren (1977: 113–23).
49 Beard (1994: 164 and 174). On the Galli see for instance Vermaseren (1977: 96–101) and Lancellotti (2002: 96–105).
50 On the Megalensia see for instance Vermaseren (1977: 124–5).
51 Ovid, *Fasti* 4.183–6, trans. Frazer (1967: 203).
52 Ovid, *Fasti* 4.221–2, 361.
53 Ovid, *Fasti* 4.341–2, trans. Frazer (1967: 213).
54 On the servants (*famulos*) of the Mother Goddess being allowed to beg on fixed days see Cicero, *On the Laws* 2.22, and see Beard, North and Price (1998, vol. 2: 353–4). The text concerns Cicero's ideal state but is telling anyway.
55 Dionysius of Halicarnassus, *Roman Antiquities* 2.19.3–5, trans. Cary (1937: 365–7).
56 E.g. translation of 'Gallus' in Martial 5.41.3 by Shackleton Bailey (1993, vol. 1: 365) as '[gelded] priest'.
57 Nock (1925: 32). Pliny the Elder, *Natural History* 35.46.165, refers to the Galli as *sacerdotes* of the Mother of the Gods, but this seems unusual.

58 Bowden (2010: 96–8). Both the second-century BC Greek historian Polybius and Livy refer to the Galli of Pessinus that Romans encountered in Asia Minor in the early-second century BC, but neither specifies that they are eunuchs or priests; in fact the priests go by the name (or rather title, it seems) of Attis and Battaces: Polybius 21.6.7 and 21.37.5, and Livy 38.18.9–10 (and see also 37.9.9). They refer to the Galli wearing ritual dress and images and pectorals. See also Vermaseren (1977: 98) and Gruen (1990: 17). On the priest Battaces coming to Rome from Pessinus at the end of the second century BC see Diodorus of Sicily 36.13.
59 For another example from the first century AD see Pliny the Elder, *Natural History* 11.109.261, and 35.46.165.
60 Valerius Maximus, *Memorable Sayings and Doings* 7.7.6. The episode dates to 77 BC, during the consulship of Mamercus Aemilius Lepidus. Genucius had been left the legacy by Naevius Anus, a freedman of Surdinus. On the story see also Roller (1999: 292) who assumes the Gallus is a priest.
61 Julius Obsequens, *Book of Prodigies* 44a. He was the slave of Servilius Caepio and the episode dates to 101 BC. See also Butler (1998) and Roller (1999: 292). For the *Book of Prodigies*, compiled in the fourth century AD, see also Chapter 4.
62 Pliny the Elder, *Natural History* 35.46.165. Pliny leaves open whether Marcus Caelius can be believed.
63 Juvenal 2.114–16. For Juvenal see below. Writing in the third century AD, Herodian 1.11.2 baldly states that the Galli were eunuchs.
64 Turcan (1996: 45), Vermaseren (1977: 115), and Beard (1994: 172). Writing in the second century AD, Lucian in his *On the Syrian Goddess* 51 says that men who were devotees of Atargatis became Galli by castrating themselves during the spring festival; for commentary see Lightfoot (2003: 507–9). For Lucian see Chapter 4.
65 Roller (1999: 254).
66 Tertullian, *Apology* 15.5. See Borgeaud (2004: 99) and Coleman (1990: 44, 60–1). For further comment on Tertullian see Chapter 6.
67 Vermaseren (1977: 101–7), Turcan (1996: 49–52), McLynn (1996), Beard, North and Price (1998, vol. 1: 384), Lancellotti (2002: 110–15), and Alan Cameron (2011: 159–63). The notion of the initiate being drenched in the blood of the bull while standing in a pit below the sacrifice, conjured up by the Christian poet Prudentius writing in the late-fourth century AD (*Crowns of Martyrdom* 10.1001–50), has been rejected as anti-pagan propaganda: see for example McLynn (1996).
68 See Duthoy (1969), Vermaseren (1977: 45–51), McLynn (1996: 320–9), and Alan Cameron (2011: 142–9). The Phrygianum was close to the Circus of Caligula.
69 Vermaseren (1977: 105) and Lancellotti (2002: 115).
70 See Carcopino (1942: esp. 76–109), Lambrechts (1952: 148–9 and 156–9), Fishwick (1966: 197), Vermaseren (1977: 99), Turcan (1996: 49), Bowden (2010: 97), and Latham (2012: 108). Note however the comments of Beard (1994: 183 n. 53) on the debate about whether Archigalli and Galli are 'different types of priesthood'.
71 Vermaseren (1977: 100) and Hales (2002: 93–5).
72 See Nock (1925) and Lightfoot (2002) and (2003: esp. 62–5). Smith (1996) doubts that the priests of Artemis at Ephesus (the so-called 'Megabyzoi') were eunuchs, but see Roller (1999: 253). One of Smith's reasons for doubting that the 'Megabyzoi' were eunuchs is that Lucian in his *Eunuch* does not mention them (p. 334), but there is no reason that he should have done. For Lucian and his text see Chapter 4.
73 See Engelstein (1999).

74 The parallel is discussed by Roller (1999: 320–5) and Roscoe (1996: 206–13). For the Hijras see Nanda (1999) and Reddy (2005).
75 See Engelstein (1999: 13) and Nanda (1999: xx).
76 See also Roscoe (1996: 203).
77 Ovid, *Fasti* 4.243–4, trans. Frazer (1967: 207).
78 Ovid, *Fasti* 4.363–6, trans. Frazer (1967: 215). For discussion of the name of the Galli see especially Lane (1996). A mainly modern explanation of the name Gallus is that it derives from Galatian, since Gauls from Thrace settled in Phrygia and the territory thus came to be called Galatia: see also Roller (1999: 229). Lane suggests that the river was renamed Gallus after the Galatians and concludes that the Galli were indeed named after the Gauls. Note also that an individual named Gallus (who castrates himself) appears in some versions of the myth of Attis: Lane (1996: 127–9) and Lancellotti (2002: 101). Gallus also means rooster, and images of cockerels can represent the Galli: see Borgeaud (2004: 81) and Hales (2002: 94). Martial 13.64 uses gallus as a pun in an epigram about a castrated cockerel.
79 Nock (1925: esp. 28, 'I would urge that the eunuch has mutilated himself, in the enthusiasm of a great festival, in order that he may be perfectly fitted to serve through his whole life the object of his devotion'). See also the comments of Roller (1999: 253) who remarks 'it may be that the goddess's principal devotees ... were expected to make a permanent commitment to sexual chastity through castration'. For castration in the Christian context see Chapter 6, and the remarks of Borgeaud (2004: 95–7).
80 For Ovid's emphasis on purity see also Littlewood (1981: 386).
81 Lucretius, *On the Nature of Things* 2.614–17, trans. Rouse and Smith (1992: 143). For discussion of Lucretius on the Great Mother (*On the Nature of Things* 2.600–43), see Jope (1985) and Summers (1996).
82 Jope (1985: 254 and 257). Summers (1996: 355–8) also notes Lucretius' lack of mention of Attis, and takes this to support his main argument that Lucretius is describing the Roman festival of the Great Mother.
83 See Jope (1985: esp. 257) and Summers (1996: 341).
84 Varro is included in Augustine, *City of God* 7.24 B, trans. Dyson (1998: 297). See also Turcan (1996: 39–40).
85 Cornutus, *Compendium of Greek Theology* 6.
86 Justin, *First Apology* 27.4, and see the comments of Minns and Parvis (2009: 155 n. 8, and 157 n. 1). For Justin see also Chapter 6. Justin has a religious agenda, but it is possible that the cult did appeal to individuals on the grounds of what today would be termed sexual identity, as is found in the case of the Hijras: see Tougher (2008a: 69). See also Bowden (2010: 104) for other personal reasons for self-mutilation which may have led individuals to the cult.
87 Roller (1999: 254 and 256).
88 Roller (1999: 316) emphasizes the significance of the goddess as the mother of Jupiter.
89 See for instance Latham (2012) (who tracks evolving Roman depictions of the Galli from the late republic to the late empire in relation to evolving Roman identity) and Rauhala (2016).
90 Catullus 63. For discussion of the poem see for instance Beard, North and Price (1998, vol. 1: 164–6), Roller (1999: 304–7), Takács (1996), Latham (2012: 98–100), and Rauhala (2016: 245–6).
91 For comment see especially Skinner (1993); at 114 she remarks 'Through Attis' rash act the conceptual category of the masculine is destabilized. Its weakening is signalled

most conspicuously on the lexical level, where syntactical gender distinctions merge into the epicene'. Oddly, neither Takács nor Roller make use of Skinner's article.
92 Catullus 63.4–11, trans. Cornish (1962: 91).
93 Catullus 63.21–4, trans. Cornish (1962: 93).
94 Catullus 63.58–68, trans. Cornish (1962: 95).
95 Catullus 63.27 and 69, trans. Cornish (1962: 93 and 97).
96 Valerius Maximus, *Memorable Sayings and Doings* 7.7.6, trans. Shackleton Bailey (2000, vol. 2: 177–9).
97 Trans. Shackleton Bailey (2000, vol. 2: 179).
98 See Rauhala (2016: 250). For the idea of eunuchs as ill-omened and polluting see also discussion in Chapter 4 and Chapter 5.
99 For Juvenal see Braund (2004: 18–24). Martial is discussed further in Chapter 3. For their discussion of Galli see also Latham (2012: 111–13), and for Juvenal on the Galli see Richard (1966).
100 Juvenal 6.518–19, trans. Braund (2004: 283).
101 Juvenal 6.511–16, trans. Braund (2004: 283).
102 For the association of the Galli with cymbals and drums see also Juvenal 8.176 and 9.62. He can also refer to eunuchs in general, not just Galli. In his first satire one of the things he lists that makes it hard not to write satire is 'When a womanly eunuch takes a wife!' (cum tener uxorem ducat spado): 1.22, trans. Braund (2004: 133). In 6.366–78 he addresses the sexual appeal for women of post-pubertal eunuchs as opposed to prepubertal ones.
103 Like Juvenal he also deals with eunuchs in general. He can refer to eunuchs as slaves, e.g. 3.38.32 (a eunuch working at Faustinus' Baian villa), 3.82.15–17 (a eunuch in the household of Zoilus, who helps his master urinate while he drinks at a dinner party), and 10.91 (eunuchs in Almo's household).
104 Celaenae was a city in Phrygia
105 Martial 5.41.1–3, trans. Shackleton Bailey (1993, vol. 1: 365). Note that there is a typographical error in Shackleton Bailey's translation, for it reads 'gilded' rather than 'gelded'.
106 Softness (*mollitia*) is associated with effeminacy: see for example Williams (2010: 139–53).
107 Martial 8.46.4, trans. Shackleton Bailey (1993, vol. 2: 195–7). The identification of eunuchs with women is emphasized again in the short epigram which declares that 'Numa saw Thelys the eunuch (*spadonem*) in a gown (*toga*) and said he was a convicted adulteress (*moecham*)': 10.52, trans. Shackleton Bailey (1993, vol. 2: 375). The eunuch (whose name Thelys means 'Female' in Greek) is being equated with women, for women convicted of adultery had to dress in a toga, just as prostitutes did. In another epigram, Martial depicts a eunuch (named as Dindymus) as a very unsatisfactory sexual partner for a woman, since he is not a man: 11.81.
108 Martial 14.204.
109 Martial 3.91. Martial also says that women like to have eunuchs so they can have sex and not get pregnant: 6.67.
110 See for example Rauhala (2016: 240–1) and Latham (2012: 88–9).
111 Martial 3.81. This is the arresting translation of Simon Price from Beard (1994: 175). The translation of Shackleton Bailey (1993, vol 1: 245) runs: 'What concern have you, eunuch Baeticus (*Baetice galle*), with the feminine abyss? This tongue of yours should be licking male middles (*medios . . . viros*). Why was your cock cut off with a Samian shard if you were so fond of a cunt, Baeticus? Your head should be castrated.

You may be a eunuch (*gallus*) loinwise, but you cheat Cybele's rites. With your mouth you're a man'.
112 Beard, North and Price (1998, vol. 2: 211).
113 Bowden (2010: 99–100). For the issue of images of Galli and gender ambiguity through dress see also Hales (2002: 91–3) and Roller (2006). Salzman (1990: 86–91 and Fig. 34) argues that the image of April in the fourth-century illustrated Calendar of Philocalus (surviving only in copies of a Carolingian copy) can be 'identified either as a Gallus . . . or as a theatrical performer participating in the Megalesia' (p. 88). The figure depicts a bald/shaven-headed heavy-set beardless old man dressed in a short tunic, playing castanets and a percussion instrument with his foot and dancing in front of a cult statue, which Salzman identifies as a statue of Attis (p. 89). The image of April 'thus represents the popular festival of the Magna Mater' (p. 90). He looks very different to the tomb portrait.
114 See Beard (1994), Roller (1999: 293–6), and Latham (2012: 87).

Chapter 2

1   Dessen (1995: 125).
2   *The Eunuch* 30–3. The Greek title of Menander's play is *Kolax*. On the addition of Thraso and Gnatho and how this serves the theme of the play see Goldberg (1986: 105–22). For Greek comedy in Rome see for instance Brown (2016), and for Terence and Greek New Comedy specifically see Brown (2013). For Roman Republican theatre see Manuwald (2011), especially pp. 244–57 for Terence.
3   Goldberg (1999). On the rape see for instance Christenson (2013: 263–9).
4   Eds Augoustakis and Traill (2013). For scholarship on Terence see for example Augoustakis and Traill (2013: 7–9).
5   Barsby (1999) and (2001).
6   Brothers (2000).
7   Brown (2006). Other recent translations are those by Frederick Clayton (in rhyming couplets) and David Christenson: Clayton and Leigh (2006: 103–52) and Christenson (2010: 273–334), which also includes discussion of the play at pp. 31–6. Earlier work on Terence is of interest too, such as Thomas Cooke's three volume edition and translation of the plays published in 1734. A second edition appeared in 1748 in two volumes; the first volume was dedicated to the Duke of Somerset (the Chancellor of Cambridge University 1689-1748), and the second (which contained *The Eunuch*) to the Duke of Newcastle upon Tyne Thomas Pelham-Holles, who succeeded the Duke of Somerset as Chancellor of Cambridge (1748-68), and was Prime Minister in 1754-6 and again in 1757-62. For Thomas Pelham-Holles see Browning (1975)
8   Brown (2006: ix). It would be fascinating to see a production of *The Eunuch*. Radice (1976: 160) records that 'Robert Graves has even suggested that *The Eunuch* could be "recast as a modern musical with great success"', though she does not supply a reference; see Graves (1963: xi).
9   In his commentary Brothers (2000: 191) observes that 'Dorus makes his only appearance in the play, and his character is hardly developed at all', but does not discuss what his character is.
10 Dessen (1995: 123). Guyot (1980: 53 and 60 n. 76) touches on Terence's *The Eunuch* when dealing with the subjects of eunuchs as slaves in private houses and as catamites. Notably neither Barsby nor Brothers use Guyot.

11 Dessen (1995: 124).
12 Dessen (1995: 128). For instance, from the starting point of the service role of the eunuch, she points out that '*All* the social relationships between the characters rest … on an exchange of services.'
13 Barsby (1999: 114–15). He observes 'Dessen interestingly sees the eunuch not simply as a plot element but as central to an interpretation of the play in terms of sexual ambivalence, gender strife, and role reversal'. More recently David Christenson's chapter devoted to the play in the 2013 Wiley-Blackwell *Companion to Terence* owes a clearer debt to Dessen's work, concluding 'In the figure of the eunuch, variously seen by audience members as disgusting, decadent, ambiguous, or alluring, Terence found fertile ground to reevaluate norms of sexuality and gender': Christenson (2013: 279). Oddly, however, Sharon L. James's chapter on 'Gender and sexuality in Terence' in the same volume does not mention Dessen or eunuchs at all. On Dessen's importance in relation to the study of the prologues of the plays of Terence see Boyle (2004: 8).
14 In the main I am persuaded by Dessen, though I do not agree with all her observations.
15 For Aelius Donatus' commentary and its composite nature see for instance Barsby (2000), Victor (2013: 353–8), and Demetriou (2014). Victor (2013: 356) advises that the commentary 'is best read not as the expression of an individual or even of a milieu and a time, but of a tradition', and Grant (1986: 60–1) notes that the 'commentary which has been transmitted to us is not the work as Donatus originally composed it but a late compilation'. The text of the commentary (with French translation and notes) is available at http://hyperdonat.huma-num.fr/editions/html/commentaires.html (accessed 14 February 2019); this site Hyperdonat is hosted by Jean Moulin University Lyon 3. On Terence in Late Antiquity generally see Cain (2013).
16 The plays are, in chronological order: *The Girl from Andros* (166 BC), *The Mother-in-Law* (165 BC), *The Self-Tormentor* (163 BC), *The Eunuch* (161 BC), *Phormio* (161 BC), and *The Brothers* (160 BC). The dates are calculated from the production notices attached to the plays: Barsby (1999: 3 and n. 10).
17 On the popularity of Terence see for instance Parker (1996).
18 On the problems of Terence's biography see for instance Barsby (1999: 1–6) and Brothers (2000: 11–16).
19 Suetonius also draws on Varro, Gaius Memmius, the grammarian Santra, Julius Caesar and Cicero.
20 Barsby (1999: 2).
21 See for instance Radice (1976: 12).
22 *The Self-Tormentor* 22–6; *The Brothers* 15–21.
23 On the idea of the 'Scipionic Circle' see for instance Hanchey (2013).
24 *The Eunuch* 397–415. See for instance the comments of Barsby (1999: 161) and also Starks (2013: 137–8).
25 *The Eunuch* 167–8, trans. Brothers (2000: 67). Barsby (1999: 115) notes, however, that '*reginae*' could just mean 'wealthy women'.
26 This is the scene shown on the cover of this book (though note that Chaerea and Antipho were labelled the wrong way round). The image is from the Vatican Terence (Codex Vaticanus Latinus 3868), an illustrated Carolingian manuscript of the plays of Terence produced in the early ninth century but copied from a lost late antique manuscript, thought to have been produced in Rome *c.* 400 AD: see Wright (2006: esp. 34–64 for *The Eunuch* material). Dorus is depicted at folio 27v (Dorus reveals the substitution scheme; note that Phaedria and Dorus are labelled the wrong way round).

The manuscript can be viewed online at https://digi.vatlib.it/view/MSS_Vat.lat.3868 (accessed 13 September 2019).
27 *The Eunuch* 613–14, trans. Brothers (2000: 107).
28 *The Eunuch* 811–12, trans. Brothers (2000: 129).
29 See Barsby (1999: 262) and Brothers (2000: 202).
30 *The Eunuch* 1023, trans. Brothers (2000: 147).
31 *The Eunuch* 1038–40, trans. Brothers (2000: 149).
32 Barsby (1999: 172).
33 *The Eunuch* 169, trans. Brothers (2000: 67).
34 *The Eunuch* 984.
35 Expensive: Barsby (1999: 115). Cheap: Brothers (2000: 168). Thraso dismisses the Ethiopian as worth only three minae: *The Eunuch* 471.
36 See n. 25 above. It seems rather odd that Brothers (2000) does not comment on the reference to '*reginae*'.
37 *The Eunuch* 366–8, trans. Brothers (2000: 85).
38 *The Eunuch* 373–4, trans. Brothers (2000: 87).
39 *The Eunuch* 576–96.
40 *The Eunuch* 578–9, trans. Brothers (2000: 105).
41 See Collins (2009, esp. 15–16), and Euripides, *Orestes* 1426–30. See also Llewellyn-Jones (2002: 34) and Hall (1989: 158).
42 *The Eunuch* 476–8, trans. Brothers (2000: 97).
43 *The Eunuch* 606.
44 *The Eunuch* 657, trans. Brothers (2000: 111).
45 *The Eunuch* 665–6, trans. Brothers (2000: 113).
46 Barsby (1999: 212). He draws on the testimony of Juvenal and Martial, discussed in Chapter 1. On the question of the sexual ability of eunuchs see also Chapter 6.
47 *The Eunuch* 474 and 479. Barsby (1999: 174) comments that 'This is the only suggestion in the play that Thraso shares the lechery of the typical *miles gloriosus*', but there are other sexual elements in the play relating to Thraso, as Dessen (1995: 131) argues. She is surely right to detect allusions to a sexual relationship between Thraso and the king (*The Eunuch* 403–8), observing that Thraso himself is presented as being like a court eunuch of the king and that 'the sexual innuendos hint at gender ambiguity and the eunuch's contribution to that ambiguity'. There is also the suggestion that Thraso was sexually interested in a young male Rhodian (*The Eunuch* 426), and Dessen characterizes Thraso as 'a sexually insatiate "switch hitter"'. See also the comments of Brothers (2000: 180).
48 On the Roman view of eunuchs as physically beautiful see also Tougher (2013).
49 *The Eunuch* 375, trans. Brown (2006: 169).
50 Brothers (2000: 87).
51 *The Eunuch* 231, trans. Brothers (2000: 71).
52 *The Eunuch* 356–7, trans. Brothers (2000: 85).
53 *The Eunuch* 661–2, trans. Brothers (2000: 111).
54 *The Eunuch* 681–9, trans. Brothers (2000: 115).
55 See for instance Brothers (2000: 191) and Barsby (1999: 215). As Barsby notes, Donatus also records the view (of Edesionus) that Terence changed the text to indicate the pale colour of eunuchs.
56 Claudian, *Against Eutropius* 1.38–41, 61–77, and 110–31. For Claudian on Eutropius see Chapter 5.
57 Something of the assumptions about how eunuchs looked facially is perhaps suggested by the depiction of a mask of a eunuch (identified by an accompanying inscription

'EVNVCV') on a lintel stone of a theatre door at Thubursicum Numidarum (Khamissa) in Africa, dated to the second or possibly third century AD: see Boissier (1901) (with photograph), Gsell (1922: 131, number 1330), and Dessen (1995: 125). Unfortunately, the image depicting the masks for *The Eunuch* in the illustrated late antique manuscript of Terence's plays had been lost by the time the Carolingian copy was made in the ninth century (Codex Vaticanus Latinus 3868): see Wright (2006: 3).
58 Barsby (1999: 214–15), commenting on line 683.
59 *The Eunuch* 370. On Chaerea's costume as a eunuch see also the comments of Christenson (2013: 262–3).
60 *The Eunuch* 683–4, trans. Brothers (2000: 115).
61 Barsby (1999: 214–15), and see Jones and Morey (1931), Plates 227–32. On Eugraphius' commentary see for instance Demetriou (2014: 794–7) and Laborie (2012).
62 Wright (2006: 218) opines 'There can be no reason to suppose eunuchs wore such a costume in actuality ... but there must have been a traditional costume like this for eunuchs on stage in mime or other entertainments'. The potential for the comic effect of the costume of the eunuch is well-reflected in an advertising poster for a Spanish adaptation of the play by Jordi Sánchez and Pep Anton Gómez, *El eunuco*, staged for instance in the Auditorium of Galicia, Santiago de Compostela, on 10 May 2015: 'Chaerea' (called Lindus in the adaptation, and played by actor Alejo Sauras) is shown dressed as the eunuch wearing tight white shorts, a highly decorative headdress of feathers and pendants, and golden bangles on his wrists and ankles (https://www.pousadasdecompostela.com/en/informar/el-eunuco-de-terencio-auditorio-de-galicia, accessed 13 September 2019).
63 *The Eunuch* 601–2.
64 *The Eunuch* 610 and 906–7.
65 *The Eunuch* 907–8.
66 *The Eunuch* 1015–16.
67 See for example Tougher (2008a: 32).
68 *The Eunuch* 579–80, trans. Brothers (2000: 105).
69 Barsby (1999: 194).
70 Barsby (1999: 245).
71 *The Eunuch* 865.
72 Barsby (1999: 201) on *The Eunuch* 606, citing Adams (1984: 52–3). See also Brothers (2000: 169) and Martin (1995: 148).
73 Dessen (1995: 132–3). She also notes that 'In one short scene ... Chaerea moves between male and female, divine and mortal'.
74 Adams (1984: 53).
75 *The Eunuch* 357, trans. Brothers (2000: 85). Barsby (1999: 152) translates this as 'that old woman of a man', while Brown (2006: 169) renders it as 'that old man who's really a woman'.
76 *The Eunuch* 688, Barsby (1999: 215). Donatus says that eunuchs suffer from hydropsy in their old age (veternosus morbo vetere confectus ac diuturno, quales sunt qui hydropem patiuntur. Ei recte, nam saepe eunuchi in senecta veternosi sunt et cito hoc laborant morbo).
77 On eunuchs as monsters see also Chapter 4.
78 *The Eunuch* 696. Brothers (2000: 115) translates this as 'You horror'.
79 Barsby (1999: 216). Dorias does refer to the rape of Pamphila by the 'eunuch' as 'a monstrous thing': *The Eunuch* 656, trans. Brothers (2000: 111).

80 Aelius Donatus himself emphasizes the fact that it refers to the condition of Dorus as a eunuch.
81 *The Eunuch* 643, 645 and 648.
82 *The Eunuch* 661. The reference to the theft has elicited next to no remarks in the commentaries. Brothers (2000: 190) observes in relation to Pythias' description of the state of Pamphila after the rape 'It is tempting to see Pythias' remark as one exaggerated or distorted by her state of extreme agitation (cf. her suspicion that Chaerea may have stolen something from the house as he fled (660–1), about which nothing further is heard)'. Dessen (1995: 137) remarks on the accusation of theft in the prologue (line 23, Terence stealing the characters of the soldier and sponger) and links it to rape and contamination, but perhaps it links to the reference to theft within the play itself, acting as an in-joke.
83 Dessen (1995: 128). She continues 'by having the attractive freeborn Roman [*sic*] youth confront the "other" in himself in the cross-dressing scene and learn "difference" from Thais, Terence skilfully eases audience anxiety while allowing these anxieties expression through the negative comments about Dorus and the posturing of Thraso'.
84 For the use of castration as a punishment in Rome see Dessen (1995: 125 and n. 11).
85 Plautus, *The Braggart Soldier* 1394–1437. On castration as the punishment for adultery in comedy see Barsby (1999: 262) and Brothers (2000: 202).
86 *The Eunuch* 957–8, trans. Brothers (2000: 141).
87 Guyot (1980: 53).
88 Dessen (1995: 126). See also Christenson (2010: 31).
89 Dessen (1995: 126). See also Barsby (1999: 6) and Christenson (2013: 262). Lowe (2008: 93) notes that the new festival of the Great Mother was 'Terence's regular festival for the first five years of his career'. On the Megalensian Games and theatre see also Leigh (2004: 2–3).
90 Livy 42.6, and see Gruen (1984: 651).
91 Gruen (1984: 646, 664).
92 Gruen (1984: 651–2).
93 Gruen (1984: 690), and pp. 693–4 for another Ptolemaic embassy in Rome in 168.
94 Polybius 28.20, 21, and see Gruen (1984: 649–52). For Eulaeus see Guyot (1980: 195–8).
95 Barsby (1999: 114–15).
96 Roller (1999: 319 and n. 116).
97 Barby (1999: 3–6). The context is also noted by Dessen (1995: 126). For detailed discussion of the period see Gruen (1984) and Eckstein (2008), though the latter only tracks as far as 170 BC. See also the comments of Erskine (1994: esp. 49–50).
98 Leigh (2004: 1).
99 Starks (2013).
100 Starks (2013: 137–8, 146–50).
101 Starks (2013: 150), citing Leigh (2004: 170–1).
102 Barsby (1999: 3). See also Gruen (1984: 295–9).

Chapter 3

1 For Sporus see for instance Guyot (1980: 227), Champlin (2003: esp. 145–50), and Vout (2007: 136–66) and (2002). For Earinus see for instance Guyot (1980: 203), Henriksén (1997), and Vout (2007: 167–212).

2   Suetonius, *Life of Domitian* 7, and Martial 2.60, 6.2 and 9.5, 7. On Domitian's law see for instance the comments of Bosworth (2002: 352–3).
3   Suetonius, *Life of Nero* 28.
4   Trans. Edwards (2000: 209).
5   In the subsequent chapter Suetonius observes that Nero himself also played the part of the bride, to his freedman Doryphorus, 'even imitating the shouts and wails of a virgin being deflowered'. It seems that Suetonius has misidentified the freedman, for it should be Pythagoras (as Tacitus and Cassius Dio assert): see Warmington (1977: 85) and Woods (2006/7: 50–1).
6   On the Sigillaria ('the fair where goods were offered for sale as gifts for Saturnalia') see Champlin (2003: 149).
7   Suetonius, *Life of Nero* 46.2.
8   Suetonius, *Life of Nero* 48. Suetonius indicates this included Phaon himself and Nero's secretary Epaphroditus. The fourth is named by the late antique text *Epitome de Caesaribus* as Neophytus, another freedman: see Champlin (2003: 272 n. 8).
9   Suetonius, *Life of Nero* 49.3.
10 Plutarch, *Life of Galba* 9. On Plutarch's biographies see for instance Desideri (2017).
11 Murison (1999: 57) comments that 'Dio seems to have a slightly morbid interest in the eunuch Sporus ... since even in his epitome he has more references to him than any other source'. Champlin (2003: 145) remarks that compared to the account of Suetonius about Nero's relationship with Sporus 'For once, Dio's narrative is superior'.
12 For Cassius Dio and his history see for instance Millar (1964) and Kemezis (2014: esp. 17–18, 90–149).
13 Cassius Dio 62.28.
14 Cassius Dio 62.13.
15 Trans. Cary (1925: 159).
16 It is also noted again that Nero had a 'husband' (his freedman Pythagoras), and again the story alludes to other sexual activities of the emperor. See also Cassius Dio 63.22.4, where a speech of Vindex the Gaul attacking Nero refers to the emperor's marriages to Sporus and Pythagoras.
17 Cassius Dio 62.12.3–4.
18 Cassius Dio 63.27.3–28.1.
19 Cassius Dio 63.29.2. See Cary (1925: 192–3 notes 2 and 3). Of these Byzantine sources John of Antioch says that Sporus fled from the emperor when he threatened to kill him.
20 Cassius Dio 63.8.3. For comment see Murison (1999: 57–8), who notes that Tacitus relates that Otho had been a lover of Poppaea and restored her statues.
21 Cassius Dio 64.10.1, trans. Cary (1925: 237). Champlin (2003: 147 and 309 n. 5) argues that the specific case of the rape of Persephone/Prosperina is meant.
22 Aurelius Victor 5.16, trans. Bird (1994: 8). Oddly Dufraigne (2003: 83 n. 25) does not name Sporus in his commentary on the passage.
23 Dio, *Oration* 21.6–9. For Dio see for instance Jones (1978), Swain (ed.) (2000), and Jackson (2017).
24 Dio, *Oration* 21.10.
25 Dio, *Oration* 21.4.
26 Trans. Cohoon (1939: 277–9).
27 On this point see Champlin (2003: 146 and 309 n. 3).
28 For the obscurity of Dio here see Champlin (2003: 147 and 309 n. 6).

29 For Statius see for instance Newlands (2002). For Martial see for example Sullivan (1991).
30 See for instance Henriksén (1997: esp. 291–4). He argues that Martial wrote his poems on Earinus before Statius wrote his. On the poems on Earinus see also Williams (2010: 35).
31 See for instance the remarks of Henriksén (1997: 282) who notes that 'Martial does not make any substantial addition to our knowledge of Earinus'.
32 For discussion of the poem see Newlands (2002: 105–17) and Garthwaite (1984).
33 For Pollius Felix see for instance Newlands (2002: 154–5) who describes him as 'a successful example of the wealthy and socially mobile entrepreneur'. Pollius lived in a villa with a view of the Bay of Naples, and Statius wrote two poems on his Campanian estate.
34 Trans. Shackleton Bailey (2003: 175).
35 Trans. Shackelton Bailey (2003: 217–25).
36 Domitian and Domitia Longina had married in AD 70.
37 Note that none of the Earinus epigrams are included in the selection published by Penguin.
38 Trans. Shackleton Bailey (1993: 241–3).
39 See for instance the comments of Henriksén (1997: 292 n. 29).
40 On this see for instance Vout (2007: 175–7), who argues that the now common order of 12 and 13 should be reversed, so that the question posed at the end of 13 should then be picked up at the start of 12.
41 Trans. Shackleton Bailey (1993: 243).
42 Trans. Shackleton Bailey (1993: 245).
43 Trans. Shackleton Bailey (1993: 245).
44 Trans. Shackleton Bailey (1993: 247).
45 Henriksén (1997: 281) argues that this poem was written later than the other five, 'which were presumably written at the time of the offering'.
46 Trans. Shackleton Bailey (1993: 263).
47 Cassius Dio 67.2.3.
48 On this passage see the comments of Murison (1999: 210–11).
49 Alexander Pope, *An Epistle to Dr Arbuthnot*, lines 305–8, featuring his famous phrase 'Who breaks a butterfly upon a wheel?' The poem was published in 1735. See Walker (1985: esp. 35–6) and Lounsbury (1991: 3748–9).
50 Sporus: L.J. Trafford, *The History Girls* (https://the-history-girls.blogspot.com/2018/05/the-eunuch-that-would-be-empress-by-lj.html, accessed 13 September 2019). Earinus: Cheryl Morgan, *History Matters* (http://www.historymatters.group.shef.ac.uk/earinus-roman-civil-rights-activist/, accessed 13 September 2019).
51 Vout (2007). See also Vout (2002) on the case of Sporus.
52 Vout (2007: xiii).
53 Vout (2007: 5). She notes that not just 'bad' emperors have sex stories told about them, remarking 'Even the best emperors have sex.'
54 Vout (2007: 11).
55 Sporus in Chapter 3, Earinus in Chapter 4: Vout (2007: 136–66, 167–212). On the marriage of Sporus and Nero see also Williams (2010: 284–6).
56 Vout (2007: 14).
57 Vout (2007: 163 n. 36). For Tacitus see for example Woodman (ed.) (2009).
58 She asks, for instance, does Suetonius' 'resentment of Hadrian find a voice in Nero?' (Suetonius having been dismissed by Hadrian in 120): Vout (2007: 139).

59 Vout (2007: 152). On the significance of Sporus in Suetonius' crafting of his life of Nero see also Lounsbury (1991).
60 Vout (2007: 158, and in general 157–60).
61 Vout (2007: 160).
62 She remarks that 'there is negligible evidence as to [Earinus'] existence beyond Martial and Statius' text': Vout (2007: 173). She notes that funerary inscriptions do feature the name of Earinus, though these could refer to other individuals, and that there may be portraits of Earinus but they have not been identified as such, and anyway 'what would distinguish him from other pretty boys?' On the problems of identifying visual images of eunuchs see for instance Tougher (2008a: 23–4).
63 Vout (2007: 170).
64 Vout (2007: 15).
65 Callimachus was a Hellenistic poet writing in the third century BC. His poem on the lock of Berenice concerns the dedication of a lock of her hair by the Ptolemaic queen Berenice II, wife of Ptolemy III Euergetes (246–221 BC), at the temple of Arsinoe Aphrodite at Zephyrium, fulfilling a vow to do so on the safe return of her husband from war. Catullus, the Roman Republican poet of the first century BC, translated the poem into Latin: Catullus 66. See also the comments of Newlands (2002: 106–7).
66 She argues that Statius is drawing on Catullus 63: Vout (2007: 191–5).
67 Vout (2007: 172, 203).
68 Vout (2007: 194). See also Newlands (2002: 110, 112, 113–14).
69 Vout (2007: 167). She also considers the role of Earinus as mediator between the emperor and his subjects (a function ascribed to court eunuchs of the later Roman Empire: see Chapter 5): Vout (2007: 184). On power through proximity see also Vout (2007: 21).
70 Vout (2007: 172–3).
71 Vout (2007: 198).
72 Though Vout (2007: 180) observes that epigram 9.11 'plays throughout with castration'.
73 Vout (2007: 179). See Garthwaite (1984).
74 Vout (2007: 183). Martial also mentions the mirror.
75 Vout (2007: 193).
76 Vout (2007: 190). Martial, however, suggests that Earinus is maturing, through Ganymede's frustration at not being able to do so.
77 Vout (2007: 189).
78 Vout (2007: 242).
79 Vout (2007: 205 n. 8). This is Henriksén (1997).
80 Henriksén (1997: 284). On the methods of compression and excision see for instance Tougher (2008a: 30–1).
81 Henriksén (1997: 294).
82 Henriksén (1997: 287).
83 Henriksén (1997: 288).
84 Henriksén (1997: 289).
85 Henriksén (1997: 289).
86 Henriksén (1997: 291).
87 Henriksén (1997: 284 and 288 n. 17) and Sullivan (1991: 39).
88 Henriksén (1997: 291).
89 Champlin (2003: esp. 145–50) and Woods (2009).

90 For his discussion of the sources for the reign of Nero see Champlin (2003: 36–52). He notes that the main sources Tacitus, Suetonius and Cassius Dio drew on narratives of the reign written by contemporaries of Nero (Pliny the Elder, Fabius Rusticus and Cluvius Rufus) and he concludes that regarding the 'facts' they report 'we should not only weigh them for accuracy and probability' we should also be alert to, and question, how they interpret them. He asserts finally 'we should never, ever accept without questioning their explanations of Nero's motives'.
91 Champlin (2003: 145).
92 Champlin (2003: 147).
93 Champlin (2003: 147).
94 Champlin (2003: 147).
95 Champlin (2003: 149).
96 Champlin (2003: 149–50).
97 Woods (2009: 79).
98 See for instance the comments of Newlands (2002: 107–8, 112).
99 For Jupiter and Ganymede see for instance Williams (2010: 59–64).
100 Vout (2007: 152).
101 Champlin (2003: 37).
102 Tacitus, *Histories* 2.71. Vout (2007: 152) remarks that Sporus associated with Otho, Galba and Vitellius after Nero's death, but Galba is not mentioned in connection with the eunuch: it is Nymphidius who acquires Sporus.
103 Garthwaite (1984: 112).
104 Vout (2007: 21).
105 Garthwaite (1984: 115–16 and 121–2).
106 Vout (2007: 211 n. 104).
107 Vout (2007: 198).
108 For Curtius and his history of Alexander see for instance Baynham (1998). For Alexander in the Roman world generally see especially Spencer (2002).
109 Curtius 10.1.22-38.
110 Curtius 10.1.26, trans. Yardley (2004: 240).
111 Curtius 10.1.37, trans. Yardley (2004: 240). Renault (1975: 197) notes the ridiculousness of this remark given recent Persian history, for another eunuch, also called Bagoas, had held sway, so it seems that the comment is meant for Roman consumption.
112 Curtius 10.1.42, trans. Yardley (2004: 241).
113 Curtius 6.5.23, trans. Yardley (2004: 127).
114 Curtius 10.1.29.
115 Plutarch, *Life of Alexander* 67.3–4. Hamilton (1999: xliii).
116 Bagoas also surfaces in Plutarch's *How to Tell a Flatterer from a Friend* 24, where the influence of Bagoas with Alexander is asserted.
117 Quintilian, *Training in Oratory* 5.12.21, trans. Butler (1921: 309). Quintilian alludes to the Galli by referring to the timbrels so associated with them. Smith (1996: 325) suggests that Megabyzus refers to some famous eunuch (like Bagoas) rather than to a eunuch priest of Artemis in Ephesus. The Doryphorus (Spear-Bearer) is a famous Greek sculpture of a male youth.
118 Vout (2007: 198). Note also the rather odd statement of Richlin (2017: 125) that 'Eunuchs hover around the edges of the Second Sophistic, freakish figures'.
119 See also Tougher (2013).
120 Martial 3.81 and 11.81.

121 Dio, *Oration* 21.11.
122 Champlin (2003: 42–4); at p. 44 he asserts that the histories of Pliny the Elder and Cluvius Rufus were probably 'exceptionally accurate', and at p. 49 he argues that the account of the death of Nero is probably drawn from the history of Cluvius Rufus.
123 Hamilton (1999: xix n. 3). Plutarch refers to remembering a discussion which took place at the time of Nero's visit: *On the E at Delphi* 385b and 391e. See also Jones (1967).
124 Suetonius, *Life of Otho* 10.1.
125 See now also Drinkwater (2019: 311–12).
126 Vout (2007: 15, 'from an unspecified but obviously Greek part of the empire').
127 Champlin (2003: 147).
128 One is put in mind of the fairy Mustardseed in Shakespeare's *A Midsummer Night's Dream*. For slave names in Rome see for instance Bruun (2013). The anonymous reader for this book suggested that 'another positive way of reading Sporus' name might be that as a eunuch he was preserving his seed (and, according to Roman medical theories, his life essence by not being able to rid himself of it)'.
129 On child exposure and abandonment in the Roman world see for instance Corbier (2001) and Harris (1994). Harris (1994: 19) observes 'We know not only that most foundlings became slaves, but that very many Roman slaves came from regions in Asia Minor where child-exposure is likely to have been common'.
130 Newlands (2002: 105, 112).
131 Williams (2010: 286) remarks that 'Nero feminized Sporos to an extreme, even shocking degree'.
132 Statius, *Silvae* 3.4.74. Shackleton Bailey's 'mollify sex' seems rather too weak. Vout (2007: 188) translates it as 'to crush someone's sex'.
133 Suetonius, *Life of Domitian* 7. It is thought that Domitian introduced the law early in his reign (possibly in 82), and then re-issued it in 92 or 93: Vout (2007: 172–4). See also Henriksén (1997: 284 n. 5).
134 Ammianus Marcellinus 18.4.5, trans. Rolfe (1940–52, vol. 1: 425). The law (in conjunction with that banning the planting of new vines) is also referred to in Philostratus, *Life of Apollonius of Tyana* 6.42. This was written in the third century AD although Apollonius lived in the first century AD.
135 Martial 2.60, 6.2, 9.5, 9.7.
136 Trans. Shackleton Bailey (1993: 241).
137 Guyot (1980: 121–9). See also Murison (2004: 349–50) and Rotman (2015a: 149–51).
138 Suetonius, *Life of Titus* 7.
139 Tacitus, *Histories* 2.71.
140 Tacitus, *Annals* 14.59, trans. Jackson (1937, vol. 4: 203).
141 Tacitus, *Annals* 12.66, Suetonius, *Life of Claudius* 44, and *Life of Galba* 15.
142 Suetonius, *Life of Claudius* 28. For Posides see also Pliny, *Natural History* 31.2; a body of hot water in the Bay of Baiae took its name from him. Posides is also referred to in a satire of Juvenal, in relation to extravagant building: 14.91.
143 Tacitus, *Annals* 4.8, 10, trans. Jackson (1937, vol. 3: 21).
144 It is notable that Tacitus discusses the nature of his evidence for the episode, distinguishing between reputable sources and rumour. As Lygdus was tortured to provide testimony presumably Tacitus' sources included legal evidence.
145 Pliny, *Natural History* 7.39. For Pliny and his *Natural History* see for instance Murphy (2004).
146 Pliny, *Natural History* 12.5. He mentions this eunuch in relation to a plane tree he introduced to his suburban estate in Italy.

147 Plutarch, *How to Profit by One's Enemies* 11.
148 Quintilian, *Training in Oratory* 5.12.17–21, trans. Butler (1921: 309).
149 Petronius, *Satyricon* 27. For Petronius see for instance Prag and Repath (eds) (2009).
150 Seneca, *Letter* 114.6, trans. Gummere (1925, vol. 3: 305). See also the comments of Williams (2010: 147). For Seneca see Griffin (1976).
151 See Chapter 5. On Earinus Vout (2007: 211 n. 106) comments 'he is a prototype for the eunuchs who inhabit later courts in Rome and Byzantium'.
152 Claudian, *Against Eutropius* 1.440–1. On imperial freedmen in the early Roman Empire see Duff (1928: 143–86), Weaver (1967), and now MacLean (2018: 104–30). On freedmen in the late Republic see Treggiari (1969), with discussion of Chrysogonus at pp. 181–4. Cicero's *In Defence of Sextus Roscius of Ameria* of 80 BC is a key (hostile) source for Chrysogonus. See also Plutarch, *Life of Cicero* 3.
153 Prudentius, *Against Symmachus* 1.271–7, as noted by Vout (2007: 139).

Chapter 4

1 This episode is discussed further in Chapter 6.
2 On intersex see for instance Harper (2007) and Preves (2005). A modern case which has generated much comment is that of the South African athlete Caster Semenya: see for instance 'What is an intersex athlete? Explaining the case of Caster Semenya', https://www.theguardian.com/sport/2016/jul/29/what-is-an-intersex-athlete-explaining-the-case-of-caster-semenya (accessed 5 March 2019), and 'Caster Semenya unquestionably a woman, say her lawyers before court case against IAAF', https://www.bbc.co.uk/sport/athletics/47244017 (accessed 5 March 2019). Semenya has the condition hyperandrogenism. She identifies as a woman. Another case of an intersex athlete is that of Erika/Erik Schinegger. Erika Schinegger was a member of the Austrian ski team and in 1966 won the downhill run at the World Alpine Ski Championships. Prior to the 1968 Olympics she had a gender test and it was found that she had male chromosomes; she was a biological male whose genitalia had developed internally. She subsequently transitioned to Erik and married in 1975. Schinegger wrote a book about his experiences, published in 1988, and in 2005 a documentrary entited *Erik(A)* was released. See https://www.skiinghistory.org/news/erik-schinegger-forgotten-world-champion (accessed 8 March 2019).
3 For Favorinus see especially the introduction in Amato and Julien (2005: 1–317), Holford-Strevens (1997) and (2017: 233–8) (as well as Holford-Strevens (2003: 98–130), the revised version of Holford-Strevens (1988: 72–92)), Gleason (1995: esp. 3–20 and 131–58), and Barigazzi (1966: 3–84) and (1993). For a suggested chronology of Favorinus' life see Amato and Julien (2005: 33–7).
4 Beall (2001: 101).
5 Stevenson (1995: 509 and n. 43).
6 Gleason (1995: 158).
7 Polemo is discussed further below.
8 Philostratus, *Lives of the Sophists* 1.8.
9 For Philostratus and his *Lives of the Sophists* see for instance Kemezis (2014: esp. 18–20, 196–226), Bowie and Elsner (eds) (2009), and Miles (2017). The text is dedicated to a Gordian: either the Gordian who became Emperor Gordian I in 238, his son who became Gordian II in the same year, or his grandson Emperor Gordian III,

who reigned from 238 to 244. For the identity of Gordian see Kemezis (2014: 294–7), who doubts the more recent suggestion that it is Gordian III.

10 For Herodes Atticus see for instance Tobin (1997: esp. 13–67) and Holford-Strevens (2017: 238–42). See also Keulen (2009: 130) who notes the 'erotic nature of the delightful company of admired sophists'. It is useful to consider the observation of Masterson (2014: 2) that in the later Roman period 'same-sex desire was a conspicuous vehicle for expressing friendship, patronage, solidarity, and other important relationships between elite men'. See also n. 38 below.
11 On the name Autolecythus see Keulen (2009: 119–20) who sees in it references to Favorinus as avaricious, a flatterer, and also sexually passive as it can signify 'well-hung'. See also Holford-Strevens (2005: 438).
12 This should be *On Pointless Talk*: see for instance Holford-Strevens (1997: 200).
13 Pyrrho of Elis lived *c.* 365–275 BC and is considered the founder of scepticism.
14 Trans. Wright (1921: 23–9).
15 For the sources for Favorinus see Amato and Julien (2005: 319–84).
16 See also Keulen (2009: 119, stating 'Favorinus probably came from a very wealthy family').
17 In his *Corinthian Oration* 25 Favorinus comments on his own facility for Greek and his Hellenism although he was a Roman (and of equestrian rank to boot). Bowie (1997: 7) notes that there is 'no secure attestation of Dio as Favorinus' teacher' and observes that Plutarch seems to have had a greater influence upon him.
18 For this appointment to 'the flaminate of the Narbonensian *concilium*' see for instance Bowersock (1969: 35).
19 On Favorinus' status as a philosopher see for example Amato and Julien (2005: 155–92), Beall (2002: 88–92), and Gleason (1995: esp. 131–45), and on his philosophical position see for instance Ioppolo (1993) and Holford-Strevens (1997: 203–17).
20 On the rhythm of Favorinus' speech see for instance Goggin (1951), Gleason (1995: 19), Beall (2001: 96–100), and Amato and Julien (2005: 89–93). Gleason (1995: xxviii) also observes 'Favorinus undoubtedly appealed to popular taste. It must have added to his appeal ... that he somehow managed to combine the charm of a certain feminine softness with the articulate dignity of a man'. See also the remarks of Whitmarsh (2005: 36).
21 *Corinthian Oration* 8. Favorinus says the statue was made at the time of his second visit to Corinth and was set up in front of the library. He also says that he first visited Corinth almost ten years before the time of writing the oration: *Corinthian Oration* 1.
22 Noted by Baldwin (1975: 21) who then lists and summarizes these episodes. For Aulus Gellius and his work see also Holford-Strevens (2003) (the revised version of Holford-Strevens (1988)), Keulen (2009), and now Howley (2018) who emphasizes the literary nature of the text and its fictionality.
23 Beall (2001: 87). On Favorinus in the *Attic Nights* see also Gleason (1995: 138–45) and Howley (2018: 235–50). Beall (2001: 100–1) argues that Favorinus 'was the logical hero of this work. First, Gellius required an authority for his excursion into miscellaneous erudition, and one who credibly bridged the gap between minute or "frigid" studies and more serious intellectual pursuits. Favorinus, as a philosophical orator known for his polymathy, was the ideal choice. Second, Gellius wished to promote a renewal of interest in early Latin literature and Roman antiquities, but within the context of a unified, bilingual culture. Favorinus, as a Gallic convert to Hellenism who retained a sense of his Roman roots, could be portrayed as exemplifying a "balanced" approach

to Greek and Latin studies. Third, Gellius noticed that Favorinus' style had a certain affinity with early Latin prose and that it showed how the latter could be adapted to contemporary tastes'.
24 Baldwin (1975: 21).
25 Beall (2001: 104).
26 For a list and summary of the episodes see also Baldwin (1973: 21–8).
27 Howley (2018: 207, 241). For Favorinus as Aulus Gellius' 'personal Socrates' see also Holford-Strevens (2003: 105).
28 Keulen (2009: esp. 97–189) and Holford-Strevens (2009). See also the criticisms of Howley (2018: 242) and Binder (2010), who states 'the main reason for my scepticism [is Keulen's] construction of implied readership'; one 'has to presuppose a prodigiously erudite reader'.
29 *Life of Hadrian* 16.10–11.
30 Philostratus, *Lives of the Sophists* 2.6, trans. Wright (1921: 205). On Quadratus see for instance Syme (1983b: 280–2).
31 For details of Favorinus' known writings see for instance Amato and Julien (2005: 37–71 (p. 43: in addition to the three surviving texts ascribed to him 'il ne reste que le titre d'une vingtaine d'écrits et environ 160 fragments au total')), Holford-Strevens (1997: 200–1), and Barigazzi (1966: 12–21). On the authorship of the *Corinthian Oration* and *On Fortune* see for instance Goggin (1951). For discussion and analysis of the *Corinthian Oration* see for instance Barigazzi (1966: 298–302), Gleason (1995: 8–20), Whitmarsh (2001: 119–21), König (2001: esp. 160–7), and Amato and Julien (2005: 53–8, 413–72). Favorinus wrote the speech in response to the Corinthians taking down the statue which they had set up to him. For editions and French translations of the speeches see Amato and Julien (2005: 392–412 (*Corinthian Oration*), and 478–92 (*On Fortune*)); these editions supersede those of Barigazzi (1966: 302–13 and 254–61). For English translations of the speeches see Lamar Crosby (1946: 5–47 (*Corinthian Oration*)) and (1951: 45–71 (*On Fortune*)). For the fragments of Favorinus' writings see Amato (2010), and Barigazzi (1966: 139–242).
32 For discussion and analysis of the speech *On Exile* see for instance Gleason (1995: 145–58), Whitmarsh (2001: 168–78) (who also provides a translation at pp. 302–24), and Amato and Marganne (eds) (2015). Volume 2 of the Belles Lettres edition of the works of Favorinus will be devoted to the speech on exile: see Amato and Marganne (eds) (2015: 8). For an edition (with Italian translation) see Tepedino Guerra (2007), as well as Barigazzi (1966: 375–409).
33 'Favorinus', Suda On Line, tr. Malcom Heath, 26 March 1999, accessed 16 February 2019, http://www.stoa.org/sol-entries/phi/4.
34 *Attic Nights* 11.5.5. On Favorinus and the Pyrrhonians see for instance Ioppolo (1993, esp. 184) and Holford-Strevens (1997: 212–17).
35 For Plutarch and Favorinus see for instance Bowie (1997: 2–3) and Amato and Julien (2005: 15–16, 18). For Plutarch and Fronto and Favorinus see for instance Holford-Strevens (1997: 190 and 199). On Plutarch see for instance Brenk (2017). On Fronto and Favorinus see also Howley (2018: 247) who notes the 'erotic charge' in Favorinus' response to Fronto's speech in Aulus Gellius, *Attic Nights* 2.26.20. On Fronto see Champlin (1980) and Fleury (2017).
36 Philostratus, *Lives of the Sophists* 2.5, trans. Wright (1921: 203).
37 Other pupils: 3.1, 12.1. The visit to Fronto: 2.26. The consular friend: 13.25. Further, one of Favorinus' friends had a villa at Antium and the eunuch was a guest there: 17.10.

38 Amato and Julien (2005: 30 n. 89, 36). Howley (2018: 247–8) comments on Gellius being captivated by Favorinus' speech, noting the 'erotic language' characterizing their relationship at *Attic Nights* 16.3.1. As noted above, the view of Keulen (2009) of the more ambiguous relationship of Aulus Gellius with Favorinus has not met with acceptance.
39 Aulus Gellius, *Attic Nights* 4.1 and 20.1. See also Baldwin (1975: 102). Favorinus dedicated to (a) Hadrian the first book of his treatise *On the Cataleptic Phantasy*: Bowie (1997: 3) and Holford-Strevens (1997: 198). It has been suggested that Favorinus' *Alcibiades* was dedicated to Hadrian's chamberlain the freedman P. Aelius Alcibiades of Nysa: see Bowie (1997: 4, 13 n. 13).
40 On Favorinus' difficulties with Hadrian see for instance Swain (1989), Gleason (1995: 146–7), Bowie (1997: 4–11), and Amato and Julien (2005: 19–29).
41 Epitome of Cassius Dio 69.3.3–4, trans. Cary (1925: 429).
42 *Life of Hadrian* 15.12–13, trans. Magie (1922: 49). See also Birley (1976: 74).
43 Epitome of Cassius Dio 69.3.6, trans. Cary (1925: 431).
44 See the remarks of Swain (1989: 154).
45 Swain (1989: 157) asserts 'I am inclined to dismiss the exile … The speech is a fine example of characterization and impersonation'. On the question of the exile see also Holford-Strevens (2015) and (1997: 196–8), Amato and Julien (2005: 19–29), Bowie (1997: 5), Gleason (1995: 145–58), Barton (1994: 183), and Bowersock (1969: 36 and 51–2). Interestingly, the oration refers to the speaker's parents and beloved sister, who are reported to be deceased (Whitmarsh (2001: 311)), but there is no reference to a wife (just his 'remaining household'), which might support the identity of the speaker as a eunuch. However, the speaker also anticipates his 'future descendants' (Whitmarsh (2001: 309)), which does not fit with him being a eunuch unless one assumes that adopted children are meant. For discussion see Holford-Strevens (2015).
46 *Corinthian Oration* 33–5. See the remarks of Swain (1989: 154), Gleason (1995: 17), Bowie (1997: 6), and Holford-Strevens (1997: 192–6).
47 Swain (1989: 157–8).
48 Amato and Julien (2005: 23, 35).
49 Holford-Strevens (2015: 131).
50 Gleason (1995: 147).
51 Lucian, *Demonax* 12–13.
52 Galen, *On the Best Form of Education* 40, trans. Holford-Strevens (1997: 208). For Galen and Favorinus see for instance Ioppolo (1993), Barton (1994: 148 and 222 n. 70), Gleason (1995: 144), Holford-Strevens (1997: 208–12), Opsomer (1997: 18–24), and Amato and Julien (2005: 36, 179–92) who believe Favorinus was dead by this time (the text is dated to 161–166), though others do not agree. On Galen see also Mattern (2017).
53 See Opsomer (1997), and Keulen (2009: 106–8).
54 For Polemo see for instance Gleason (1995: esp. 21–54). For Polemo and Favorinus see also Bowersock (1969: 90–1). On competition between sophists in Philostratus' *Lives of the Sophists* see König (2011: 283–93).
55 Swain (1989: 150) and Amato and Julien (2005: 28–9). For Philostratus' life of Polemo see *Lives of the Sophists* 1.25.
56 Philostratus, *Lives of the Sophists* 1.25, trans. Wright (1921: 119).
57 See Hoyland (2007: 329–463, esp. 376–9).
58 See the comments of Baldwin (1975: 29–31). Keulen (2009: esp. 113–34) detects allusions to the more controversial aspects of Favorinus' life in the *Attic Nights*,

arguing that Aulus Gellius expects his readers to have these details in mind when reading the text. Keulen makes much of Favorinus' reputation for avarice, despite admitting himself that there is 'no specific testimony that speaks explicitly of Favorinus' avarice' (p. 118); Keulen finds it in the episode of Favorinus trying to evade the priesthood, but this reading is rather forced.

59 Howley (2018: 242 and n. 99), rejecting Keulen (2009: 113–34). He adds 'if we consider the Gellian evidence for Favorinus on its own terms, we may find a corrective to, rather than collusion with, the invective to which Favorinus was subjected' (and see also Holford-Strevens (2009)). In fact, Howley finds 'Favorinus' problematic queerness' illuminating of the 'very program of Gellius' work'. Certainly, Aulus Gellius can situate Favorinus in relation to issues of sex and gender, and at least Keulen recognizes this even if one does not agree with the conclusions he draws.

60 Philostratus, *Lives of the Sophists* 1.25, trans. Wright (1921: 131).

61 Polemo, *Physiognomy* 1 (A20), trans. Hoyland (2007: 377–9). See also the translation in Gleason (1995: 7), Barton (1994: 118), and Mason (1979: 4).

62 See Repath (2007a: 549–50).

63 Anonymus Latinus, *Book of Physiognomy* 40, trans. Repath (2007a: 583).

64 For Lucian see for instance Baldwin (1973) and Richter (2017).

65 On the work and its association with Favorinus see also Gleason (1995: 132–5).

66 Lucian, *Eunuch* 4, trans. Harmon (1936: 335). On the significance of the name Bagoas see also Gleason (1995: 133) who observes the 'very name connotes the luxury and effeminacy of Persian slaves'.

67 Lucian, *Eunuch* 6, trans. Harmon (1936: 337).

68 Lucian, *Eunuch* 7, trans. Harmon (1936: 339).

69 Lucian, *Eunuch* 7, trans. Harmon (1936: 339).

70 For Hermias see Guyot (1980: 207–9). The niece of Hermias, whom he adopted, married Aristotle.

71 Lucian, *Eunuch* 10, trans. Harmon (1936: 341–3). On the inspiration of the real case of Favorinus see also Gleason (1995: 134).

72 Lucian, *Eunuch* 11, trans. Harmon (1936: 343).

73 Lucian, *Eunuch* 12, trans. Harmon (1936: 343–5). Interestingly, eunuchs themselves could be associated with old men and trustworthiness.

74 Lucian, *Eunuch* 13, trans. Harmon (1936: 345). I.e. having his genitals intact.

75 This notion seems to have been commonplace: see for instance Aulus Gellius, *Attic Nights* 9.2, where Herodes Atticus rebukes a man (with a very long beard) who claims to be a philosopher by saying '"I see a beard and a cloak, but I do not yet see a philosopher"'. On the beard as a symbol of the philosopher see for instance Zanker (1995: esp. 108–13).

76 Goggin (1951: 200–1) thinks Lucian 'had in mind actual singing delivery in certain parts of the speech'.

77 Lucian, *Demonax* 12–13, trans. adapted from Harmon (1913: 151–3) (Harmon coyly translates 'Balls' as 'Those you lack'). On these exchanges see also Gleason (1995: 135–7).

78 Mason (1979). See also Retief and Cilliers (2003). Amato and Julien (2005: 13–14 n. 39) comment only briefly on Favorinus' condition as a 'eunuch'.

79 Mason (1979: 8). Bettini (1991: 84) comments 'disparity of breast size marks the hermaphrodite'.

80 Mason (1979: 9).

81 Retief and Cilliers (2003: 76).

82 As noted by Mason (1979: 9).
83 Noted by Barton (1994: 118).
84 Brisson (2002: 14).
85 Brisson (2002: 24–31). On the 'androgyne expiations' see also MacBain (1982: 127–35).
86 Livy 27.11.4. See also 31.12.6–10 (200 BC; cases among the Sabines of a birth and a sixteen-year-old) and 39.22.5 (186 BC; a case of a twelve-year-old in Umbria).
87 Livy 27.37.6, trans. Moore (1943: 359). MacBain (1982: 65–71 and 132) notes the context of the anxiety felt at the time of the invasion of Italy by Hasdrubal.
88 Brisson (2003: 31–8).
89 Diodorus Siculus 32.10.2 and 32.11.
90 Diodorus Siculus 32.12, trans. Walton (1957: 455).
91 Diodorus Siculus 32.12, trans. Walton (1957: 455–7).
92 Brisson (2003: 38), though he notes that 'abnormal children continued to be committed to the waters to drown', citing Tibullus 2.5.80, where Apollo is beseeched to be propitious. Tibullus was a Roman poet writing at the end of the first century BC: see for instance Cairns (1979).
93 Pliny the Elder, *Natural History* 7.3.34, trans. Rackham (1942: 529). Note that *in deliciis* can have the connotation of delight and pleasure; Rolfe (1927, vol. 2: 169) translates this part of the Pliny passage quoted in Aulus Gellius as 'instruments of pleasure'. See also the remarks of Holford-Strevens (2003: 103 n. 30) and Keulen (2009: 130 and 201), who says that Gellius represents Favorinus 'as a source of sexual pleasure'.
94 Aulus Gellius, *Attic Nights* 9.4.16. This chapter in Gellius is about marvels among barbarians, awful and deadly spells, and on sudden changes of women into men. He records that he draws the information on sex changes from Pliny the Elder; they are at *Natural History* 7.4.36, and Pliny asserts that he had seen such a case himself in Africa, that of Lucius Constitius a citizen of Thysdritum changing into a man on his wedding day. The remark about hermaphrodites is appended to these stories by Aulus Gellius, but in Pliny it precedes them.
95 Baldwin (1975: 11, and 25 ('maliciously')), thus anticipating the view of Keulen 2009 that Aulus Gellius' presentation of Favorinus is double-edged, as discussed above; Keulen at p. 201 also notes Gellius' use of this Pliny passage, to humiliate Favorinus he argues. See the comments of Holford-Strevens (2003: 103), and his assertion that Gellius' relationship with Favorinus was 'the warmest friendship of his life' (p. 107). On Aulus Gellius' affection for Favorinus see also Howley (2018: 242 and n. 99).
96 Augustine, *City of God* 16.8.
97 Trans. Matthews Sanford and McAllen Green (1965: 47). For the chapter Augustine depends mainly on Pliny the Elder, *Natural History* 7.2.10–30.
98 Gleason (1995: 3).
99 On Dura-Europos see for instance Brody and Hoffman (eds) (2011), Chi and Heath (eds) (2011), and Dirven (1999). The fresco no longer survives.
100 Elsner (1998: 213 with Fig. 139). See also Dirven (1999: 295–302) and (2011: 214), and Cumont (1926: 122–34, 364–6).
101 See the discussion in Dirven (1999: 296–7). Guyot (1980: 101, 217) suggests Otes was a Parthian court eunuch or functionary.
102 Guyot (1980: 217) suggests Gorsak is Otes' slave or adopted son.
103 Eusebius, *Church History* 7.32.3, trans. Oulton (1932: 229). See also *PLRE* 1, Dorotheus 1, 269, and Guyot (1980: 195). Gleason (1995: 6 n. 23) also notes the case of Dorotheus.

104 Procopius, *Wars* 3.11.6 and 9.
105 For Solomon see *PLRE* 3B, Solomon 1, 1167–77, and Chapter 7 below.
106 Pliny, *Natural History* 11.110, trans. Rackham (1940: 599).
107 Gleason (1995: 4).
108 Amato and Julien (2005: 12).
109 Lucian, *The Mistaken Critic* 17, trans. Harmon (1936: 393).
110 Artemidorus, *Interpretation of Dreams* 2.69, trans. White (1975: 134). See also 4.37 which records 'Someone dreamt that he saw eunuchs. His penis became diseased' (p. 201).
111 Claudian, *Against Eutropius* 1.1–8, 21, trans. Platnauer (1922: 139–41). See also *Against Eutropius* 2.40–9, and the comments of Long (1996: 109–12).
112 Adamantius, *Physiognomy* 2 B3, trans. Repath (2007b: 519). For Adamantius and his text see for instance Repath (2007b: 487–92).
113 Quintilian, *Training in Oratory* 5.12.17, trans. Butler (1921: 307).
114 Quintilian, *Training in Oratory* 5.12.17–18, trans. Butler (1921: 307–9).
115 Quintilian, *Training in Oratory* 5.12.19, trans. Butler (1921: 309).
116 Howley (2018: 241) remarks 'The grammarian's bawling of *penus* at the famous "eunuch" Favorinus is an obvious sort of insult, which Favorinus seems to ignore. Instead, in asking "what IS *penus*," he lends philosophical gravitas to grammatical conversation, directing his audience's attention upwards from trivia to the essence and truth of language'. See the further discussion in Howley (2018: 243), and also in Keulen (2009: 87–94 and 126–30).

Chapter 5

1 For Diocletian and interpretations of his reign see for instance Rees (2004) and Harries (2012: 1–101). On the third century see for instance Hekster (2008).
2 On the Great Persecution see further discussion in Chapter 6.
3 Sextus Aurelius Victor, *The Caesars* 39, trans. Bird (1994: 41). For Victor see also Bird (1984).
4 Eutropius, *Breviarium* 9.26, trans. Bird (1994: 63).
5 For Lactantius see for instance Creed (1984: xxv–xxix) and Christensen (1980). Lactantius went on to become tutor of Crispus, son of the first Christian emperor Constantine I 'the Great' (306–337).
6 Lactantius, *On the Deaths of the Persecutors* 14.2–15.2, trans. Creed (1984: 21–3). Lactantius also refers to a 'worthless eunuch' (vilis eunuchus) at the court of Constantine in Gaul, a victim in the alleged attempted murder of Constantine by his father-in-law Maximian in 310: *On the Deaths of the Persecutors* 30.1–5.
7 Hopkins (1963) and (1978: 172–96).
8 Hopkins (1978: 192–3). For the latter suggestion Hopkins cites the ninth-century Byzantine chronicler Theophanes (AM 5793), but later Roman writers note the episode too: see Mango and Scott (1997: 13 n. 4). Lactantius does remark that Galerius imitated Persian royal domination: *On the Deaths of the Persecutors* 21.
9 Claudian, *Against Eutropius* 1.414–23, trans. Platnauer (1922: 169–71). For Claudian see further below.
10 On eunuchs in the *Historia Augusta* see Alan Cameron (1965) and Guyot (1980: 157–64). On the *Historia Augusta* generally see Syme (1983a) and Alan Cameron (2011: 743–82).

11 *Historia Augusta* 18.66.3–4, trans. Magie (1924: 311).
12 See Tougher (2008a: 51–2).
13 Hopkins (1978: 193).
14 Ammianus Marcellinus 15.2.10 (Gorgonius), and 16.7.2–8 (Eutherius). For eunuchs in the history of Ammianus see Tougher (1999).
15 Eunapius 65.7; see Blockley (1983: 98–9). For Eunapius in general see Blockley (1981: 1–26) and Penella (1990: esp. 1–38).
16 Zosimus 4.28.2.
17 See Hopkins (1978: 180).
18 Libanius, *Oration* 18.130, trans. Norman (1969: 363). For Libanius see Cribiore (2007). Libanius also refers to eunuchs at the court of Constantius II, and the power they had, in *Oration* 14.3 (dating to autumn 362 and addressed to Julian) and *Oration* 62.9 (dating to about 382): see Norman (1969: 100–3) and (2000: 91–2).
19 Julian, *Beard-hater* 352a–b, trans. Wright (1913–23, vol. 2: 461). Claudius Mamertinus in his *Speech of Thanks* to Julian of New Year 362 comments on the influence of eunuchs at the court prior to Julian: *Speech of Thanks* 19.4.
20 Socrates 3.1.48–50, and Sozomen 5.5.8.
21 Zosimus 4.37.2.
22 Ambrose, *Letter* 24.2. See also Guyot (1980: 233).
23 Tougher (2008a: 39–42).
24 *Theodosian Code* 7.8.3, and 6.8.1. On the late Roman ranking system see for instance Jones (1964, vol. 1: 528–30). The law of 422 was inspired by the case of Macrobius, a Grand Chamberlain of Theodosius II: *PLRE* 2, Macrobius 2, 698–9. On the social status of court eunuchs see also Rotman (2015b).
25 *Notitia Dignitatum* Or. 1 and Oc. 1.
26 On eunuch slaves see for instance de Wet (2015: 256–70) and Rotman (2015a: 149–51).
27 Eutherius: Ammianus Marcellinus 16.7.5; Eutropius: Claudian, *Against Eutropius* 1.44–51; Narses: Procopius, *Wars* 1.15.31. Note also the case of the Armenian eunuchs Calocerus and Parthenius, who were brothers: see for example de Gaiffier (1957: 30) and Chapter 6 below.
28 Procopius, *Wars* 8.3.17.
29 Aelius Donatus, *Commentary on Terence's* The Eunuch, on line 689. The text of the commentary (with French translation and notes) is available at http://hyperdonat.huma-num.fr/editions/html/commentaires.html (accessed 14 February 2019). See also Guyot (1980: 31), Scholten (1995: 28 and n. 124), and Barsby (1999: 215).
30 See Wiedemann (1986).
31 Justinian, *Code* 4.42, ed. Frier (2016, vol. 2: 992–4). On Roman legislation on eunuchs and castration see Rotman (2015b).
32 See for instance Hopkins (1978: 177–8).
33 Ammianus Marcellinus 14.11.3, trans. Rolfe (1940–52, vol. 1: 91); see also 20.2.4 and 21.16.16.
34 Ammianus Marcellinus 16.7.7, trans. Rolfe (1940–52, vol. 1: 229). See also 18.5.4 on the eunuchs' love of wealth. The church historian Socrates associates Eusebius and the eunuchs of Constantius II in general with rapacity and extortion: 3.1.46 and 48.
35 Libanius, *Oration* 14.3, trans. Norman (1969: 103).
36 Epiphanius, *Letter to Maximian Patriarch of Constantinople*, ed. Schwartz (1922–3: 293 (pp. 222–4) and 294 (pp. 224–5)). See Elton (2009: 139–40), Hopkins (1978: 178), Bury (1923, vol. 1: 354 and n. 2), Batiffol (1919), Nau (1910: 367–9), and Hefele (1908: 398–9). Two of the chamberlains are female: Marcella and Droseria.

37 For Lausus see *PLRE* 2, Lausus 1, 660, and Scholten (1995: 230–1). For his palace and statue collection see Mango, Vickers and Francis (1992), and Bardill (1997). For Palladius and the *Lausiac History* see Chapter 6. Lausus 3 (*PLRE* 2, 661) may also be Lausus 1: a letter to him from Firmus the bishop of Caesarea refers to his generosity and distinguished house in Constantinople, where Firmus met Lausus following the Council of Ephesus (Firmus, *Letters* 9, ed. and French trans. Calvet-Sebasti and Gatier (1989: 88–91); *Letters* 20 is also addressed to Lausus). For Firmus and his letters see Calvet-Sebasti and Gatier (1989).
38 For Antiochus see *PLRE* 2, Antiochus 5, 101–2, Scholten (1995: 228–30), and Greatrex and Bardill (1996). See also the remarks of Elton (2009: 135).
39 On imperial freedmen see Chapter 3.
40 For Eusebius see *PLRE* 1, Eusebius 11, 302–3, Dunlap (1924: 260–70), Mudd (1989: 26–33), Guyot (1980: 199–201), Scholten (1995: esp. 212–13), and Schlinkert (1996: 251–61).
41 On Constantius II and his brothers see for instance Maraval (2013) and Harries (2012: 185–207).
42 See Burgess (2008).
43 See for instance Michael Whitby (1999) and Teitler (1992).
44 For Ammianus and his history see Kelly (2008), Drijvers and Hunt (1999), Barnes (1998), Matthews (1989), and Thompson (1947).
45 Ammianus Marcellinus 31.16.9.
46 See Ross (2016).
47 See Humphries (2012).
48 For the theological disputes of the fourth century see Hanson (1988), and further discussion in Chapter 6.
49 See Barnes (1993).
50 Supplemented by several others, as will be seen.
51 Ammianus Marcellinus 14.10.5.
52 Photius, *Bibliotheca* 256: Henry (1974: 225). The fifth-century church historians Rufinus, Socrates and Sozomen also say that the will was entrusted to an Arian presbyter: Rufinus 10.12, Socrates 1.39.3–4, and Sozomen 2.34. The 'Arian' fifth-century church historian Philostorgius 2.16 asserts rather that the will was entrusted to Eusebius the bishop of Nicomedia, perhaps reflecting some confusion with the eunuch Eusebius.
53 Sozomen 3.1.4. See also Socrates 2.2.5–6.
54 For Rufinus see *PLRE* 1, Vulcacius Rufinus 25, 782–3.
55 Ammianus Marcellinus 14.11.1–2. For Eusebius' role in the fall of Gallus see also Dunlap (1924: 264–6).
56 For Ursicinus see *PLRE* 1, Ursicinus 2, 985–6. For Eusebius' part in the fall of Ursicinus see also Dunlap (1924: 266–9).
57 Ammianus Marcellinus 14.11.3.
58 Ammianus Marcellinus 14.11.19–21.
59 Ammianus Marcellinus 15.3.2.
60 Trans. Rolfe (1940–52, vol. 1: 119).
61 Ammianus Marcellinus 15.2.1–6.
62 Ammianus Marcellinus 15.5.18–31 and 16.10.21. Ammianus reports however that the emperor stated that Ursicinus had embezzled funds from the Gallic treasury: 15.5.36.
63 Ammianus Marcellinus 18.4.3. See also 16.8.13 where Eusebius appears in a list of leading men under Constantius who 'had a boundless eagerness for riches, without consideration for justice or right': trans. Rolfe (1940–52, vol. 1: 239).

64 Ammianus Marcellinus 18.4.4, trans. Rolfe (1940–52, vol. 1: 425).
65 Ammianus Marcellinus 18.5.5. For the fall of Barbatio see 18.3; Ammianus relates that Barbatio and his wife Assyria had anticipated the death of Constantius.
66 Ammianus Marcellinus 18.6.5–6.
67 Trans. Rolfe (1940–52, vol. 1: 437–9).
68 Ammianus Marcellinus 20.2.
69 Ammianus Marcellinus 20.2.3, trans. Rolfe (1940–52, vol. 2: 7).
70 Ammianus Marcellinus 20.2.4, trans. Rolfe (1940–52, vol. 2: 7).
71 Ammianus Marcellinus 21.15.4.
72 For Eusebius' attitude to Julian see also Dunlap (1924: 269–70). Note, however, that Ammianus does not mention a specific eunuch opposition to Julian in his narrative: see Tougher (1999: 69 and 73 n. 24).
73 For the trials see Ammianus Marcellinus 22.3. For comment see Tougher (2007: 44–6).
74 Ammianus Marcellinus 22.3.12, trans. Rolfe (1940–52, vol. 2: 197).
75 Ammianus Marcellinus 18.4.3, and 22.3.12.
76 Libanius, *Oration* 18.152, trans. Norman (1969: 379). The other named victims are the notary Paul 'the Chain' and Ursulus the Count of the Sacred Largesses.
77 Julian, *Letter to the Athenians* 272d, trans. Wright (1913–23, vol. 2: 253–5).
78 See also Tougher (2012: 183).
79 Julian, *Letter to the Athenians* 274a–b, trans. Wright (1913–23, vol. 2: 257).
80 Julian, *Beard-hater* 352a–b.
81 Julian also seems to refer to Eusebius disparagingly in a letter to his friend and doctor Oribasius written when he was Caesar in Gaul: *Letter* 4 384d, Wright (1913–23, vol. 3: 11), 'As for that abominable eunuch (τοῦ μιαροῦ ἀνδρογύνου), I should be glad to learn when he said these things about me, whether it was before he met me, or since. So tell me whatever you can about this'.
82 It is notable, however, that the pagan historian Zosimus does not name Eusebius as a key figure in the plot against Gallus; he merely says that some of the court eunuchs were involved in a wider plot: Zosimus 2.55.2.
83 On the question of the Istrian island see Bidez and Des Places (2013: 311 n. 6).
84 Philostorgius 4.1, trans. Amidon (2007: 63–4). For the association of Eusebius' execution with the death of Gallus see also Socrates 3.1.49, and Sozomen 5.5.8.
85 For Eusebius' role in ecclesiastical affairs see also Dunlap (1924: 261–4).
86 Athanasius, *History of the Arians* 35.
87 Athanasius, *History of the Arians* 37, trans. in Robertson (1892: 283). See also Hanson (1988: 340) and Barnes (1993: 118 and 130).
88 Athanasius, *History of the Arians* 38, trans. in Robertson (1892: 283). For further discussion of eunuchs and heresy see Chapter 6. On Eusebius and Arianism see also Socrates 2.2.5–6 and Sozomen 3.1.4. A petition of Arians to the Emperor Jovian (363) indicates the important role court eunuchs played in facilitating influence in religious affairs, naming Eusebius and Bardio (also a eunuch of Constantius II), and referring to Jovian's own eunuch Probatius (probably his Grand Chamberlain): Athanasius, *Letter* 56, *To Jovian*, Appendix, trans. in Robertson (1892: 569). See *PLRE* 1, Bardio, 147–8, and Probatius 2, 733, and Guyot (1980: 191–2 and 224) though he confuses the bishop Euzoius for a court eunuch (p. 202).
89 Theodoret, *Church History* 2.16. The summoning and exile of Liberius is also recorded by Ammiamus Marcellinus 15.7.6–10, though Eusebius is not mentioned.
90 Theodoret, *Church History* 2.16.9 and 15.

91 Theodoret, *Church History* 2.16.29, trans. Jackson (1892: 79). Note that the chapter divisions in Jackson are not the same as those in the edition in Martin and Canivet (2006).
92 Sozomen 4.16.22–3.
93 See for example Hunt (1989: 87 n. 6). Interestingly the Eusebius mentioned in Palladius, *Lausiac History* 63, as working with the Arians against Athanasius has been identified as both the eunuch and the bishop: *PLRE* 1, Eusebius 11, 302, and Meyer (1964: 216). On Eusebius of Nicomedia see also Gwynn (1999).
94 For Eutropius see *PLRE* 2, Eutropius 1, 440–4, Dunlap (1924: 272–84), Scholten (1995: 223–37), Schlinkert (1996: 266–70), Liebeschuetz (1991: 92–108), and now Sidéris (2018).
95 On the invectives see especially Long (1996) and Schweckendiek (1992). See also Guyot (1980: 167–70) and the comments of Dunlap (1924: 272). For Claudian see especially Cameron (1970) and Ware (2012). On Claudian on the fall of Eutropius see the comments of Dewar (1990).
96 For Stilicho see for instance *PLRE* 1, Flavius Stilicho, 853–8, McEvoy (2013: esp. 153–86), and Kampen (2009: 123–38).
97 In addition to Long (1996) see Tougher (2005: esp. 64–6) and (2015a: esp. 150–4). Note also Eunapius' remark that 'though [Eutropius] was an eunuch, he strove to be a man': Eunapius, *History*, Fragment 65.1, trans. Blockley (1983: 97).
98 Claudian, *Against Eutropius* 1.44–57.
99 Claudian, *Against Eutropius* 1.33–44 and 58–77. *PLRE* 1, Ptolemaeus 2, 753, suggesting he was 'a high-ranking officer, perhaps *tribunus stabuli*'. *PLRE* 1, Flavius Arinthaeus, 102–3. Arinthaeus is also mentioned as a former master at 1.478–80.
100 Claudian, *Against Eutropius* 1.77–109. *PLRE* 2, Eutropius 1, 440, thinks the bridal dowry mentioned by Claudian was that of Arinthaeus' daughter (as does Dunlap (1924: 272)), but this seems to be over-interpreting the text.
101 Claudian, *Against Eutropius* 1.110–70.
102 Claudian, *Against Eutropius* 2.68–9 (and also Praef. 49–50).
103 *PLRE* 1, Flavius Abundantius, 4–5.
104 Claudian, *Against Eutropius* 2.345–53, and see also 2.558–9. *PLRE* 1, Hosius, 445.
105 Claudian, *Against Eutropius* 2.376–461, and see also 2.558–9. *PLRE* 2, Leo 2, 66–2.
106 Claudian, *Against Eutropius* 1.284–6.
107 Claudian, *Against Eutropius* 1.234–71. On this campaign see also the comments of Dunlap (1924: 276). For eunuchs as military commanders in the later Roman Empire see Chapter 7.
108 Claudian, *Against Eutropius* 2.304–408. On this military situation see also Dunlap (1924: 280–1).
109 Claudian, *Against Eutropius* 2.177–80, and Praef. 57–8.
110 Claudian, *Against Eutropius* 1.190–209, and 2.585–90.
111 Claudian, *Against Eutropius* 2.70–83. For references to visual images of Eutropius see below.
112 Claudian, *Against Eutropius* 2.68–9, trans. Platnauer (1922: 189).
113 For Zosimus see Paschoud (2000: vii–cxxvi) and Ridley (1982: xi–xv).
114 Sozomen 7.22.7–8.
115 Claudian, *Against Eutropius* 1.311–13, trans. Platnauer (1922: 163).
116 Claudian, *Against Eutropius* 2, Praef. 37–8.

117 Zosimus 5.3. See also Eunapius, *History*, Fragment 64.1 (Blockley (1983: 92–5)). For Eudoxia see *PLRE* 2, Aelia Eudoxia 1, 410, and Holum (1982: esp. 48–78). On Eutropius' role in arranging the marriage see also Dunlap (1924: 273–4).
118 Zosimus 5.8.1–2.
119 Zosimus 5.9–10.3. On Eutropius and Timasius see also Eunapius, *History*, Fragment 65.3 (Blockley (1983: 96–7)), and Sozomen 8.7.2. On Eutropius and Bargus see also Eunapius, *History*, Fragment 65.4 (Blockley (1983: 96–9)). *PLRE* 1, Flavius Timasius, 914–15. *PLRE* 2, Bargus, 210–11.
120 Zosimus 5.10.4–5. Zosimus also comments generally on Eutropius' greed and use of informers: 5.12.2. Eunapius, *History*, Fragment 65.5 (Blockley (1983: 98–9)), remarks on Eutropius' knowledge of what was happening within families, while Fragment 65.6 refers to the eunuch's 'prying ears', trans. Blockley (1983: 99).
121 Zosimus 5.11. *PLRE* 1, Gildo, 395–6. On Eutropius turning against Stilicho after the fall of Abundantius see also Eunapius, *History*, Fragment 65.8 (Blockley (1983: 100–1)).
122 Zosimus 5.11.1 and 5.12.1, trans. Ridley (1982: 104).
123 Eunapius, *History*, Fragment 65.2, trans. Blockley (1983: 97).
124 Eunapius, *History*, Fragment 66.2, trans. Blockley (1983: 103).
125 For Synesius and his *On Kingship*, see Petkas (2018), Cameron and Long (1993: esp. 103–42), Liebeschuetz (1991: 105–7), and Barnes (1986: esp. 104–9). For Synesius in general see Bregman (1982) and Seng and Hoffman (2012). Synesius became bishop of Ptolemais (410–414).
126 Synesius, *On Kingship* 14.3, ed. and French trans. Lamoureux and Aujoulat (2008: 109), trans. Fitzgerald (1930: 124).
127 Synesius, *On Kingship* 14.4, ed. and French trans. Lamoureux and Aujoulat (2008: 110), trans. Fitzgerald (1930: 125). See Petkas (2018: 126–7), Cameron and Long (1997: 107–9), and also Liebeschuetz (1991: 106–7) who notes the targets of 'courtiers (presumably freedmen-eunuchs) and German mercenaries' and that the speech dates to 'a time when Eutropius was at the height of his power and dangerous'.
128 Philostorgius 11.4, trans. Amidon (2007: 147).
129 Zosimus 5.14.1–2, and Eunapius, *History*, Fragment 67.5 (Blockley (1983: 104–5)).
130 Eunapius, *History*, Fragment 67.8, trans. Blockley (1983: 105–7). Eunapius says he was always drunk, was from Colchis and was of royal birth. *PLRE* 2, Subarmachius, 1037.
131 Philostorgius 11.5. For the order for the destruction of Eunomian and Montanist books see also *Theodosian Code* 16.5.34, issued to the Praetorian Prefect Eutychianus in Constantinople in 398.
132 Socrates 6.2.10, and also Sozomen 8.2.19. For John Chrysostom see for instance Mayer and Allen (2000), Kelly (1995), and Liebeschuetz (2011: 97–247).
133 Palladius, *Dialogue on the Life of St John Chrysostom* 5, ed. Coleman-Norton (1928: 29.24–30.8), trans. Meyer (1985: 36).
134 Mark the Deacon, *Life of Porphyry* 26, ed. and French trans. Lampadaridi (2016: 104–5) and Grégoire and Kugener (1930: 22–3). For a partial English translation see Rapp (2001: 59–74).
135 Hilarius, a functionary under the Master of Offices, was to carry out the order.
136 Lampadaridi (2016: 12–19 and 23–5), Rapp (2001: 55–6), and Kelly (1995: 142, 168–70). The text also refers to another court eunuch, Amantius the chamberlain and *castrensis* of the Empress Eudoxia, with whom he is said to be very powerful, and who is praised for his piety, and who also helped with securing the closure of pagan temples in Gaza: see for instance *Life of Porphyry* 36, 37, 52. See also *PLRE* 2,

Amantius 1, 66, Lampadaridi (2016: 205–6 n. 72, and 206 n. 73), and Scholten (1995: 236–7). For the post of *castrensis sacri palatii* (Steward of the Sacred Palace) see Guyot (1980: 140–1) and Costa (1972).
137 Zosimus 5.13–18. *PLRE* 2, Tribigildus, 1125–26.
138 This scenario was clearly drawn from Eunapius: see Eunapius, *History*, Fragment 67.10 (Blockley (1983: 106–7)). Eunapius calls Tribigild Argibild. *PLRE* 1, Gainas, 379–80.
139 Zosimus 5.17.5.
140 Zosimus 5.18.3, trans. Ridley (1982: 107).
141 Philostorgius 11.6, and Sozomen 8.7.3 Eudoxia is also associated with the fall of John Chrysostom (he was exiled in 403 and then again in 404); see for instance Palladius, *Dialogue on the Life of St John Chrysostom* 6, and Holum (1982: 57–8, 72–8).
142 *PLRE* 1, Aurelianus 3, 128–9.
143 Socrates 6.5.2–7, and Sozomen 8.7.4. See also Liebeschuetz (2011: 225).
144 *PG* 52, 391–396. Another homily by John Chrysostom was thought to be about Eutropius too, concerning his arrest after leaving Hagia Sophia (*PG* 52, 396–414). However, Alan Cameron (1988) (and see also (1993: 241)) has convincingly argued that it has been misidentified and in fact refers to the case of the *comes* John in 400. Kelly (1995: 154–6) accepts this, while Liebeschuetz (1991: 104 n. 4) remains open-minded. The orations are translated by Stephens (1889: 249–52 and 252–65). There is also a translation of the first oration by Mayer and Allen (2000: 132–9). For comment see Kelly (1995: 147–50).
145 Trans. Stephens (1889: 250).
146 Philostorgius 11.6. See Alan Cameron (1988: 40 n. 21).
147 *Theodosian Code* 9.40.17, eds Mommsen and Meyer (1954: 505), trans. Pharr (1952: 257–8).
148 Eunapius, *History*, Fragment 65.7, trans. Blockley (1983: 99).
149 Dunlap (1924: 284). The saying ascribed to Chrysaorius is found in a Byzantine world history, that of George Cedrenus (which dates to the late-eleventh or early-twelfth century): ed. Bekker (1839: 29.8–11).
150 Penzer (1936: 138). See Tougher (2008a: 15–16).
151 Mudd (1989: 26–33) provides a very useful contrast with Dunlap on Eusebius.
152 Hopkins (1963) and (1978: 172–96).
153 Hopkins (1978: 174).
154 Hopkins (1978: 180).
155 For what follows see Hopkins (1978: 181–91).
156 For the equestrian order see Davenport (2019).
157 Hopkins (1978: 191). For further discussion and refinement of the views of Hopkins see for instance Patterson (1982: 314–31), Tougher (2008a: 48–9), and Rotman (2015b).
158 Eutropius, *History*, Fragment 67.9, trans. Blockley (1983: 107).
159 See for instance Ridley (1982: 211 n. 48).
160 For the use of eunuchs in general by Ammianus to criticize Constantius II see for instance Thompson (1947: 54, 55), Blockley (1975: 142–3), and Tougher (1999: 70–1).

Chapter 6

1 For self-castration and eunuchs in early Christianity see especially Caner (1997), Stevenson (2002), Kuefler (2018) and (2001: esp. 260–73), Moxnes (2003: 72–90), and Collins (2013). For the Skoptsy see for instance Engelstein (1999).

2   For Ignatius see Smithies and Duffy (2013) and Tougher (2004: 98–102).
3   Matthew 19.1–12. For commentary on this section of Matthew's Gospel see for instance Davies and Allison (1997: 4–30). See also Beare (1981: 384–92) and McNeile (1915: 271–6).
4   Matthew 19.12. Davies and Allen (1997: 22) note that rabbis also identified two types of eunuchs, born and man-made.
5   See for instance Justin, *First Apology* 15.4, and Epiphanius, *Panarion* 58.4.5–9. See also Collins (2013: esp. 74–8) who places Jesus's words within the Jewish context and the value placed on reproduction, saying Jesus 'opens the possibility of celibacy as a legitimate, even preferable path for the righteous, something unthinkable within mainstream Judaism' (p. 78).
6   For Origen see for instance Trigg (1998).
7   For Eusebius see for instance Barnes (1981).
8   Eusebius, *Church History* 6.8.1–2, trans. Oulton (1932: 29).
9   Eusebius, *Church History* 6.8.3, trans. Oulton (1932: 29).
10 Eusebius, *Church History* 6.8.4, trans. Oulton (1932: 31).
11 For discussion of his argument see for instance Stevenson (2002: 134–6).
12 For Epiphanius see Jacobs (2016) and Kim (2015).
13 See Lyman (1997). For Arius and Arianism in general see Hanson (1988) and Williams (2001).
14 On Epiphanius' use of medical metaphors in the *Panarion* see Flower (2018).
15 Epiphanius, *Panarion* 64.3.11–13, ed. Holl (1980: 409), trans. Williams (1994: 134).
16 For Eusebius on Origen see also Burrus (2000: 25–8).
17 Caner (1997: 401 n. 26) and Stevenson (2002: 127–30) are of the view that Origen did castrate himself. See also Hanson (1966).
18 For Justin see for instance Parvis and Foster (eds) (2007), and Minns and Parvis (2009: esp. 32–46).
19 As Minns and Parvis (2009: 161 n. 3) observe, 'Justin uses the technical term for a religious rite reserved for the initiated'.
20 Justin, *First Apology* 29.2–3, trans. Minns and Parvis (2009: 161).
21 On the law of Domitian see Chapter 3.
22 Stevenson (2002: 129).
23 Epiphanius, *Panarion* 58, ed. Holl (1980: 358–63), trans. Williams (1994: 98–102). On the Valesians see also Stevenson (2002: 129); he says they are monks. Kuefler (2001: 272 and 388 n. 124) notes that Augustine, *On Heresies* 37, copies what Epiphanius records about the Valesians.
24 Matthew 18.8, Authorized King James Version. See also Matthew 5.29–30.
25 Epiphanius, *On Faith* 7.13.5, trans. Williams (1994: 654).
26 Barnes (1993: 125).
27 For Athanasius see for instance Barnes (1993).
28 Athanasius, *Apology for his Flight* 26.3, trans. in Robertson (1892: 264), ed. Opitz (1935–41: 85–6).
29 Athanasius, *History of the Arians* 28, trans. in Robertson (1892: 279), ed. Opitz (1935–41: 198). This indicates that Eustolium belonged to the group of women known as *subintroductae*, female Christian ascetics who could live with male Christian ascetics in 'spiritual marriages', adhering to Christian ideals of continence. Like self-castration, the practice was controversial; see for instance Clark (1977) and de Wet (2017), who has proposed that these relationships could signify an alternative form of domestic slavery. See also de Wet (2015: 266–7). It has been suggested that the

reference to the sister/wife of the Grand Chamberlain Eutropius in Claudian, *Against Eutropius* 1.263, 2 Praef. 41, 2.88–90, is one such woman: see Long (1996: 133–4) and Tougher (2008a: 46).
30 The case of Leontius is also reported by the fifth-century church historians Theodoret of Cyrrhus and Socrates: Theodoret, *Church History* 2.24.1–2, and Socrates 2.26.9–10.
31 For Tertullian see for instance Barnes (1971) and Dunn (2004).
32 *On Monogamy* 3.1, ed. trans. Stevenson (2002: 125–6). See also Kuefler (2001: 265–7), Moxnes (2003: 84–6), and Davies and Allison (1997: 24).
33 Eusebius, *Church History* 5.24.5, trans. Lake (1926: 507).
34 Stevenson (2002: 123); the Penguin translation is Williamson (1964: 231). Interestingly, the Latin translation of Eusebius' *Church History* by Rufinus, dating to 402/3, specifies that Melito is a eunuch for the Kingdom of God: Rufinus, *Church History* 5.24.5, ed. Mommsen in Schwartz and Mommsen (1903: 493). This might suggest that Rufinus thought he was a metaphorical eunuch but does not preclude the possibility that he thought he was a castrate.
35 For Constantine see for instance Barnes (1981) and (2011), Drake (2000), Lenski (ed.) (2012), and Bardill (2012).
36 On the Council of Nicaea see for instance Barnes (1981: 214–19) and (2011: 120–26), Hanson (1988: 152–72), and Drake (2000: 250–7).
37 Council of Nicaea, Canon 1, ed. trans. Hefele (1883: 375–6). See also Caner (1997: 407).
38 The anonymous reader of this book suggests another – 'given the strength of Roman gender roles, could it be the motivation that clerics were repudiating their masculinity if they castrated themselves and thus (given the assumption about clerical status and male identity) forfeiting their right to be clerics?'
39 See for instance Caner (1997: 407), and Hefele (1883: 449–92).
40 See Hefele (1883: 466–7).
41 Ed. Hefele (1883: 466).
42 On castration and heresy see for instance Caner (1997: 406–7) and Stevenson (2002: 130).
43 *History of the Arians* 38.3–5, trans. in Robertson (1892: 283), ed. Opitz (1935–41: 204). Athanasius also dwells on the role of Constantius II's Grand Chamberlain in the pursuit of the emperor's religious policy, as discussed in Chapter 5.
44 *Theodosian Code* 16.5.17, ed. Mommsen and Meyer (1954: 861). For Eunomius see Vaggione (2000). For the Eunomians – 'neo-Arians' – and Theodosius I's attitude to them see Escribiano Paño (2009: 53–7). The church historian Philostorgius (10.6) says Theodosius expelled from the palace some of his chamberlains (and thus possibly eunuchs) for their Eunomian views; see also Vaggione (2000: 354–5).
45 See for instance Kuefler (2001: 266) and Ringrose (1999: 123–30) and (2003b: 111–16).
46 *Against Marcion* 1.29, ed. trans. Evans (1972: 82–5).
47 For Clement see Osborn (2005).
48 *Paedagogus* 3.4.26, trans. Wilson (1867: 292), ed. Marcovich (2002: 164). See also Collins (2013: 80). For Clement on eunuchs see also Horstmanshoff (2000).
49 *Panarion* 38.1.4 and 4.12, trans. Williams (1994: 101–2).
50 *Panarion* 38.3.3–4, trans. Williams (1994: 100).
51 Philo, *That the Worse Attacks the Better* 176. See Davies and Allison (1997: 23 n. 112), Abusch (2002: 111), and Stevenson (2002: 130).
52 See for instance Caner (1997: 412–13).
53 Sure enough, the following day a eunuch is found in bed with one of the king's wives: *Life of Apollonius* 1.37.

54 *Life of Apollonius* 1.34, ed. trans. Jones (2012: 112–15).
55 *Panarion* 38.4.14, trans. Williams (1994: 102). The proverb referred to is the Biblical Ecclesiasticus (also called Wisdom of Sirach) 20.4, dating to the second century BC.
56 *The Eunuch* 665–6, trans. Brothers (2000: 113).
57 Basil of Ancyra, *On Virginity* 61–4, ed. *PG* 30, 793–801, and for Old Slavic text and French translation see Vaillant (1943: 37–83). For comment see Sidéris (2017: 176–93), Harper (2011: 338–9), Caner (1997: 412–13), Elm (1994: 122–4), and Rouselle (1988: 123). See also Shaw (1997).
58 See for instance Kuefler (2018: 182–3) and more generally Murray (1999).
59 For Palladius see Katos (2011).
60 For Lausus see Chapter 5.
61 Palladius, *Lausiac History* 29, trans. Meyer (1964: 88–90), ed. Bartelink (1974: 144–6). See also Elm (1994: 322–4) and Caner (1997: 411).
62 For the Acts of the Apostles see for instance Fitzmyer (2010), as well as Haenchen (1971) and Bruce (1952).
63 Omitted by the 'Western text': see Fitzmyer (2010: 69–70).
64 Acts of the Apostles 8.26–39, trans. Fitzmyer (2010: 409). The King James version begins 'And the angel of the Lord spoke unto Philip, saying, "Arise, and go toward the south unto the way that goeth down from Jerusalem unto Gaza, which is desert". And he arose and went: and behold, a man of Ethiopia, a eunuch of great authority under Candace queen of the Ethiopians, who had the charge of all her treasure, and had come to Jerusalem for to worship, was returning, and sitting in his chariot, read Esaias the prophet'. For commentary on the episode see especially Fitzmyer (2010: 409–17), but also Barrett (1994: 419–35), Haenchen (1971: 309–17), and Bruce (1952: 189–95). See too the interesting comments of Spencer (1997: 90–4), who stresses the 'multi-faceted liminal location' of the episode. On the episode of the Ethiopian eunuch see also Spencer (1992) and Solevåg (2016).
65 Fitzmyer (2010: 412). Barrett (1994: 424) asserts it is the Sudan and the capital was Meroe.
66 Fitzmyer (2010: 412).
67 Fitzmyer (2010: 413–14). See also the comments of Barrett (1994: 429–30) and Blenkinsopp (2002: 91). On the Isaiah passage see Blenkinsopp (2002: 344–57).
68 For instance, Haenchen (1971: 309).
69 See the comments of Marshall (1980: 162) and Spencer (1997: 93).
70 Plutarch, *Life of Demetrius* 25.
71 Trans. Perrin (1920: 61). For Lysimachus see Lund (1992). An interesting case of a Hellenistic eunuch treasurer is Philetaerus the Attalid: see Guyot (1980: 219–20) and Tougher (2008a: 21–2).
72 For example, the history of Hieronymus of Cardia; for Hieronymus see Roisman (2012: 9–30) and Hornblower (1981). Lund (1992: 16) suggests another contemporary (Duris of Samos) is the source.
73 For the Old Testament view of eunuchs see for instance Stevenson (2002: 132–3). For the Bible on eunuchs see also Boulhol and Cochelin (1992: 59–62).
74 Deuteronomy 23.1, trans. in Phillips (1973: 153), with commentary at p. 154. The exclusion is also applied to descendants of irregular unions, Ammonites and Moabites: Deuteronomy 23.2–3.
75 Leviticus 21.18–20, trans. Milgrom (2000: 1302), with commentary at pp. 1828 and 1841–3. It is of note that Leviticus 22.24 also takes a dim view of sacrificial animals that are impaired: 'You shall not offer to YHWH (an animal) with bruised, crushed, torn, or cut-off (testicles)', trans. Milgrom (2000: 1303).

76 Isaiah 56.3–5, trans. Blenkinsopp (2003: 3), with comment at pp. 130–43. Blenkinsopp asserts (p. 137) 'Apart from the book of Esther and possibly Daniel, this is one of the few places where we can be sure that *sārîs* refers to a sexually-mutilated male rather than a court official'. For Isaiah 56.3–5 see also Goldingay (2014: 71–80). The Book of Wisdom 3.14 also speaks positively of eunuchs, evidently referencing Isaiah 56.3–5; it states '[T]he eunuch who has not acted unlawfully or meditated wickedness against the Lord will receive the exquisite gift of grace in return for his steadfastness and a portion in the temple of the Lord to delight his heart the more' (trans. Winston (1979: 130), with comment at pp. 131–2). The Book of Wisdom was written in Greek by a Hellenized Jew in Alexandria after the establishment of Roman rule at the end of the first century BC.

77 See for instance the comments of Barrett (1994: 424–5), Spencer (1997: 93–4), and Kuefler (1996: 283) and (2001: 259). See also the interesting discussion of Wright and Chan (2012).

78 Eusebius, *Church History* 2.1.13, trans. Lake (1926: 109–11). The prophecy is Psalms 68.31.

79 Irenaeus, *Against Heresies* 4.23.2. Irenaeus was from Smyrna but became bishop of Lyon. For Irenaeus see Foster and Parvis (eds) (2012), and Grant (1997). For the significance of the Ethiopian eunuch see also Boulhol and Cochelin (1992: 61–2).

80 Fitzmyer (2010: 410), asks 'Is he a Gentile? Or a disaspora Jew?', and favours seeing him 'as a Jew, or possibly a Jewish proselyte'. See also the remarks of Barrett (1994: 421) who considers the eunuch neither a born Jew nor a proselyte but a Gentile. Barrett also accepts that the Ethiopian is a real eunuch. Haenchen (1971: 314) argues that the story is deliberately vague about whether the Ethiopian is a Gentile or a Jew.

81 Other potential model eunuchs are John the Baptist and the prophet Elijah: see Kuefler (2001: 270) and (2018: 180).

82 For commentary on the Book of Daniel see Hartman and Di Lella (1978), Heaton (1956), and Montgomery (1927). See also Ginsberg (1990).

83 See for instance Hartman and Di Lella (1978: 129) and Montgomery (1927: 119, 124–5). Ginsberg (1990: 505) uses the term 'grand vizier'.

84 For discussion of the meaning of the term *ša rēši* see Grayson (1995: 91–3). For the use of 'eunuch' in the Septuagint see Cornelius (2009). For eunuchs in the Bible see also Retief and Cilliers (2005).

85 For Josephus see Rajak (1983).

86 Josephus, *Jewish Antiquities* 10.186–8, trans. Marcus (1937: 261–3). Josephus also identifies the person entrusted with the care of the Jewish youths as a eunuch: *Jewish Antiquities* 10.190. For the tradition that Daniel was a eunuch see Davies and Allison (1997: 24) and Kuefler (1996: 281 and 295 notes 25 and 26).

87 Jerome, *Against Jovinian* 1.25, and see also his *Commentary on Daniel* 1.1.3. Isaiah 39.7, and 2 Kings 20.18. For Jerome see Rebenich (2002). For Isaiah 39 see Blenkinsopp (2000: 486–9). See also Ringrose (2003a: 104 n. 38) and (2003b: 235 n. 6). Neither Ringrose nor Kuefler (1996) refer to the Josephus passage in relation to the idea that Daniel was a eunuch.

88 Theodoret, *Commentary on Daniel* 1.3–4, ed. trans. Hill (2006: 22–3). The passage is noted by Ringrose (2003a: 86) and (2003b: 89). For Theodoret see Urbainczyk (2002).

89 Ringrose (2003a) and (2003b: 87–100). Ringrose is particularly concerned with the construction of a positive image of court eunuchs in the Byzantine Empire. She makes much of the fact that Symeon Metaphrastes in the tenth century uses the term ἐκτομίας to refer to Daniel ((2003a: 90) and (2003b: 92)), but as has been seen Josephus used this term himself to refer to the Jewish youths who became eunuchs.

90 See also Tougher (2008a: 71–4).

91 Eusebius, *Church History* 7.32.2–4, trans. Oulton (1932: 229).
92 As noted in Chapter 4.
93 Guyot (1980: 195) dates Cyril's bishopric to 280–302.
94 Eusebius, *Church History* 8.1.4, ed. trans. Oulton (1932: 252–3). For this Dorotheus see also *PLRE* 1, Dorotheus 2, 270, and Guyot (1980: 194–5).
95 For Gorgonius see *PLRE* 1, Gorgonius 1, 398, and Guyot (1980: 206). As seen in Chapter 5, a Gorgonius was the Grand Chamberlain of the Caesar Gallus (351–4).
96 See for instance Boulhol and Cochelin (1992: 63), and de Gaiffier (1957: 26, 34).
97 And perhaps their names too.
98 Lactantius, *On the Deaths of the Persecutors* 14.2.
99 Lactantius, *On the Deaths of the Persecutors* 15.1–2, trans. Creed (1984: 23).
100 Eusebius, *Church History* 8.6.1–5, ed. trans. Oulton (1932: 264–7).
101 As they had done with the bodies of other victims of the persecution.
102 Eusebius, *Church History* 8.6.7, trans. Oulton (1932: 267–9).
103 Boulhol and Cochelin (1992: esp. 63–9). See also de Gaiffier (1957), Guyot (1980: 134 n. 20), Kuefler (2001: 264 and 386 n. 86), and Messis (2014: 78–9). Kuefler lists Nereus and Achilleus, Calocerus and Parthenius, Prothus and Hyacinthus, Indes, Tigrius, Boethazat and Azat, and Melito of Sardis.
104 Boulhol and Cochelin (1992: 73, 'l'eunuque de l'hagiographie, le *saint eunuque*, apparaît donc comme le symbole vivant de la parfaite *enkratéia*').
105 Sozomen 8.24.8–9. See also Socrates 6.15.15.
106 Palladius, *Dialogue on the Life of St John Chrysostom* 15 and 20, ed. Coleman-Norton (1928: 92.6 and 125.30), trans. Meyer (1985: 98 and 132). See also Boulhol and Cochelin (1992: 58). For Palladius see Katos (2011).
107 Cyril of Scythopolis, *Life of Euthymius* 30, 37. For Gabriel see further below.
108 Evagrius 3.32. See also Scholten (1998: 67 n. 109). For Evagrius see Allen (1981) and Whitby (2000).
109 *PLRE* 3, Narses 11, 935–6; he might have been *praepositus sacri cubiculi*.
110 See for instance Boulhol and Cochelin (1992: 72) who remark that eunuch monks were numerous from the fifth and sixth centuries. Kuefler (2001: 275) observes 'It is entirely possible that some of the earliest monks in the East were self-made eunuchs; they were known for their feats of asceticism and their disregard for the body'.
111 John Moschus, *Spiritual Meadow* 40, 173, and 184.
112 John Rufus, *Life of Peter the Iberian* 31, 48, 59–61, 65, 105, 118–19, 171, 188. See Horn and Phenix (2008), and Horn (2006: esp. 65, 68–73).
113 *Sayings of the Desert Fathers* 15.11, ed. Guy (2003: 352–6), trans. Wortley (2012: 273–4). See also Jacobs (2016: 61–2). The two monks were excommunicated for castrating themselves. Once the monks accepted that they had done wrong they were received again by the Patriarch of Alexandria.
114 Cyril of Scythopolis, *Life of Sabas* 86. For Sabas, and Palestinian monasticism, see Patrich (1995) and Binns (1994). For Cyril of Scythopolis see Stallman-Pacitti (1991) and Binns (1994: 23–40).
115 On Moschus and Sophronius see Chadwick (1974).
116 Leontius of Neapolis, *Life of John the Almsgiver* 23. For Leontius see Festugière and Rydén (1974).
117 Noted by Boulhol and Cochelin (1992: 72). See also Caner (1997: 14), Talbot (1996: xii–xiii, xiv, 1–5, 13), Patlagean (1976), and Anson (1974).
118 The monastery of Elusa also features in John Moschus, *Spiritual Meadow* 164. The note in Wortley (1992: 252) states 'Eleousa (El-Khalasa today) was in the Desert of

Beersheba. There was both a lavra and a bishop there, a suffragan of Petra'. On Idumaea and Elusa see also di Segni (2004: 54–5) and Hirschfeld (2004: 62, 64–6).
119 Bury (1923, vol. 2: 412 n. 5).
120 Paul Helladicus, *Letter*, ed. Lundström (1902: 20.22–23.7). The text of this late antique letter was incorporated into a twelfth-century rule (*typikon*) for the Byzantine monastery of St John the Forerunner of Phoberos, in a section about 'whether boys are to be accepted into the monastery or not': see Thomas and Hero (eds) (2000: 941–2). See also Jordan (2000).
121 For Anicia Juliana see Harrison (1989), Kiilerich (2001), and Nathan (2011). See also Patrich (1995: 282).
122 Cyril of Scythopolis, *Life of Sabas* 69, ed. Schwartz (1939: 171).
123 Sabas' meetings with Juliana, and the Empress Ariadne, are recorded by Cyril of Scythopolis, *Life of Sabas* 53.
124 Trans. Price (1991: 181). For Byzantine monasteries for eunuchs see for instance Tougher (2006) and Messis (2014: 111–15).
125 Cyril of Scythopolis, *Life of Sabas* 69, ed. Schwartz (1939: 171.13), trans. Price (1991: 180). See also Patrich (1995: 263).
126 See Patrich (1995: 274 and 263).
127 Patrich (1995: 46–7).
128 Cyril of Scythopolis, *Life of Euthymius* 16, trans. Price (1991: 21), ed. Schwartz (1939: 25.23, 26.3).
129 Cyril of Scythopolis, *Life of Euthymius* 28, 37. However, Gabriel through the patronage of the Empress Eudocia, estranged wife of Theodosius II, went on to become in Jerusalem a priest of the church of the Resurrection and abbot of the monastery of St Stephen the Protomartyr, and built for himself a hermitage on the hill of the Ascension; he lived until he was eighty, and was buried in the hermitage: Cyril of Scythopolis, *Life of Euthymius* 30, 37. For the patronage of Eudocia in Jerusalem see Klein (2012) and Hunt (1982: 237–43); it was Eudocia who founded the church of St Stephen.
130 See for instance Chitty (1966: 66–7) and Patrich (1995: 263 n. 78).
131 Paul Helladicus, *Letter*, ed. Lundström (1902: 20.27–22.23), trans. Robert Jordan in Thomas and Hero (eds) (2000: 941–2).
132 As seen above, Basil of Ancyra in his *On Virginity* and Epiphanius in his *Panarion* also cite this Biblical verse.
133 Paul Helladicus, *Letter*, ed. Lundström (1902: 21.13–19), trans. Robert Jordan in Thomas and Hero (eds) (2000: 941–2).
134 Paul Helladicus, *Letter*, ed. Lundström (1902: 22.23–23.3), trans. Robert Jordan in Thomas and Hero (eds) (2000: 942).

Chapter 7

1 As seen in Chapter 5.
2 See for example Guilland (1943: 205–14), and Ringrose (2003b: esp. 128–41).
3 For the famed Belisarius see for instance the eighteenth-century life of the general by Lord Mahon and Robert Graves' novel *Count Belisarius*: Coulston (2006) and Graves (1938). Both heroize Belisarius at the expense of Narses; Lord Mahon is particularly hostile to the eunuch. For the Ostrogoths and Ostrogothic Italy see for instance

Heather (1996: 216–76), Arnold (2014), and Arnold, Bjornlie and Sessa (eds) (2016). For Justinian see for instance Moorhead (1994) and Maas (ed.) (2005).
4 Fauber (1990: 135), though note the reservations of Rance (2005).
5 Dunlap (1924: 284–99); Fauber (1990); *PLRE* 3B, Narses 1, 912–28. See also Martyn (2007).
6 For a preliminary version of this chapter see Tougher (forthcoming a), written for a conference in 2013. Recently Narses has also been the subject of study by Michael Stewart (Stewart (2015); and see also Stewart (2017: 44–9)); we conducted our research independently but reached similar conclusions, though our work has different emphases. For Narses see now also Brodka (2018), which I was not able to consult before completing this chapter.
7 For Procopius see for instance Averil Cameron (1985) and Lillington-Martin and Turquois (eds) (2018). For Agathias see especially Averil Cameron (1970).
8 Procopius also wrote the *Secret History* (an invective on the regime of Justinian which focused on the pair of married couples, Justinian and his wife Theodora and Belisarius and his wife Antonina) and, contrastingly, the *Buildings* (a panegyrical account of the empire-wide building work undertaken by Justinian, though it omits Italy).
9 On Agathias' lack of personal knowledge see for instance Averil Cameron (1970: 31).
10 Averil Cameron (1970: 37) memorably observes that 'Agathias' is a political history which is very short on politics, a classical history which had to accommodate Christian motivation, a military history written by a lawyer'. Agathias was also a poet, writing the *Daphniaca* (which has not survived) and many epigrams, one hundred of which are included in the collection called the *Cycle*, which he himself compiled: see Frendo (1975: ix).
11 Stein (1949: 357), 'est probablement tout à son honneur'. See also Fauber (1990: 11) who remarks that Narses was 'one of the very few public men of the reign at whom [Procopius] threw no mud'. Rance (2005: 469) suggests that there may be 'veiled hostility' toward Narses in Procopius' *Wars*, but I am not convinced by this.
12 Several western sources also identify him as a *chartularius* (e.g. Paul the Deacon 2.1), but so does an eastern source, John of Ephesus (*Church History* 3.1.39).
13 On the title of *patricius* see for instance Jones (1964, vol. 1: 528).
14 *Wars* 1.15.31. Armenia had been split between Rome and Persia in AD 387: see for instance Greatrex (2000).
15 See also Tougher (2002: 144). Procopius reports elsewhere that during the reign of Justinian most eunuchs in the Roman Empire came from Abasgia, at the eastern end of the Black Sea: *Wars* 8.3.12–17.
16 See Chapter 6, in relation to the 'Ethiopian Eunuch'.
17 *Wars* 3.11.6
18 Malalas 18.66. *PLRE* 3A, Dorotheus 2, 420–1.
19 Malalas 18.71. Procopius' narrative: *Wars* 1.24. Karlin-Kayter (1973: 87–8 n. 2) and (1981b: 10) suggests that the *cubicularius* and *spatharius* Calopodius mentioned as a source of grievance for the Green faction in the so-called *Akta dia Kalopodion* (an exchange between the Greens and a herald of Justinian, and associated with the Nika Riot) should be identified as Narses, but there no grounds to support this: see also Whitby and Whitby (1989: 114 n. 345).
20 For the Nika Riot see for example Greatrex (1997).
21 For the circus factions see Alan Cameron (1976).
22 For the position of *spatharius* see for instance Jones (1964: 567–8). Chrysaphius – a chief eunuch of Theodosius II, famous for devising a plot to assassinate Attila the

Hun in 449 – was a *spatharius*: see *PLRE* 2, Chrysaphius, 295–7, and Scholten (1995: 248–9).
23 Liberatus 20, ed. Schwartz (1936: 135). *PLRE* accepts that this Narses is our Narses. Liberatus was a deacon of Carthage during the reign of Justinian who wrote an account of the Christological debates in the Roman Empire from 428 to 544. Theodora was motivated by her 'Monophysite' (more accurately 'Miaphysite') agenda, that is supporting Christians who adhered to the single nature view of the nature of Christ rather than the Orthodox ('Chalcedonian') position of the dual nature of Christ: for the Christological disputes in the reign of Justinian and Theodora's position within these see for instance Lee (2013: 279–85). It is possible that Narses was a 'Monophysite'.
24 *Wars* 6.13.16–18. See also Malalas 18.88. For Procopius' narrative of Narses' activities in Italy at this time see *Wars* 6.16–22.
25 *Wars* 6.18.29. On the relationship between Narses and Belisarius see also Parnell (2017: 108–12).
26 *Wars* 6.19.18, trans. Dewing (1914–28, vol. 4: 33).
27 *Wars* 6.22.4–5.
28 Dunlap (1924: 287) ('It would be natural to suppose that Narses was punished in some manner for his marked insubordination, but this was not the case. He seems to have lost none of his favour at court, but to have remained the most trusted servant and minster of the Emperor and his consort'), and Fauber (1990: 50 and 53) ('recalled, but not in disgrace'; 'It is clear that the events in Italy had done little, or nothing, to impair the regal trust in the ability and loyalty of Narses').
29 *Wars* 1.25.24–30. Marcellus was killed by John's bodyguard. According to Procopius Theodora hated John and with the assistance of Antonina planned to orchestrate his downfall by coaxing him to make an attempt to seize power.
30 Malalas 18.90.
31 *Wars* 7.13.21–6. For the Heruli see for instance Sarantis (2016: 253–65) and (2010), and Steinacher (2010).
32 *Wars* 7.14.
33 For the Sclaveni see Sarantis (2016: 65–88, 247–53, 278–88) and (2013: 767–9).
34 *Wars* 8.21.6. See also Malalas 18.110
35 *Wars* 8.26.5.
36 *Wars* 8.29.4–6. Procopius alleges that this was on the site where the Roman general Camillus had defeated the Gauls (in the fourth century BC), called Busta Gallorum (meaning 'Tombs of the Gauls'). It seems that these assertions are incorrect, though many textbooks still refer to the battle in which Narses defeated Totila as the Battle of Busta Gallorum. On Procopius' account of the battle see Whately (2016: 203–10).
37 *Wars* 8.32.22–8 and 33–6.
38 *Wars* 8.32.31–2.
39 Malalas 18.116.
40 *Wars* 8.33.2.
41 *Wars* 8.33.13–27.
42 *Wars* 8.33.8.
43 *Wars* 8.33.9.
44 *Wars* 8.33.10–12.
45 *Wars* 8.34.16.
46 *Wars* 8.34.19–20.
47 *Wars* 8.34.21–3.
48 Procopius' narrative of the battle: *Wars* 8.35.20–35.

49 *Wars* 8.35.36–8.
50 Agathias, Preface 22–32.
51 Agathias 1.1.1, trans. Frendo (1975: 9).
52 Agathias 1.5–7.
53 Agathias 1.11.6.
54 Agathias 1.12–13.
55 Agathias 1.14–15.5.
56 Agathias 1.19.1.
57 Agathias 1.20.3–6.
58 Agathias 2.3.3–8. Agathias reports with satisfaction that this was a punishment for their impiety, for their wicked behaviour.
59 Agathias 2.4–9.
60 Agathias 2.14.3–7.
61 Material evidence can also contribute to knowledge of Narses. For instance, an inscription on the bridge over the Anio on the Via Salaria not far from Rome dated 565 records that Narses (referred to as *patricius* and former *praepositus sacri cubiculi* and former consul) rebuilt it after it had been destroyed by the Goths: *CIL* 6.1199, and see Bury (1923, vol. 2: 283 n. 5) and Fauber (1990: 147–8 and Plate 7). The bridge was severely damaged in 1798 and 1867 but is immortalized in a print of 1754 by Piransesi: Ficacci (2006: 297, no. 365). Some argue that Narses is included in the mosaic depicting Justinian and his court in the sanctuary of the church of San Vitale in Ravenna, but this is unlikely as the mosaic was completed in the 540s, before Narses was such a prominent figure in Italy: see for instance Manara (1983: 16–17), Fauber (1990: 16 and 198 n. 39), Andreescu-Treadgold and Treadgold (1997) (they argue that John the nephew of Vitalian was added to the mosaic in the late 540s: p. 721), and Deliyannis (2010: 241–2 and 382 n. 174). Both or one of the male figures in the companion mosaic of Theodora and her female entourage have been thought by some to be eunuchs/a eunuch: see for instance Andreescu-Treadgold and Treadgold (1997: 714), Ringrose (2003b: 166 Fig. 8), and Deliyannis (2010: 240).
62 Narses is also mentioned very briefly in the *Chronicle* of Marcellinus, written in Constantinople during the reign of Justinian but in Latin. The chronicle covered up to the year 534 and is followed by an anonymous continuation which breaks off in the year 548: see the entries 538.5, 538.7, and 539.1 (Croke (1995: 48)).
63 Justinian, *Novels*, Appendix 7, trans. Miller and Sarris (2018: 1116–30).
64 Malalas 18.140.
65 For these events see for instance Stein (1949: 610–11). A surviving fragment (3.1) of Menander Protector's *History* (a late-sixth-century eastern text written as a continuation of Agathias' *History*) deals with Narses' conflict with Amingus: see Blockley (1985: 44–5).
66 Dunlap (1924: 294) observes of the story of Narses' betrayal of Italy that 'Its picturesqueness grew as it was told'.
67 For Gregory (bishop of Tours 573–594) and his history see for instance Heinzelmann (2001), Goffart (1988: 112–234), and Dalton (1927, vol. 1).
68 *History of the Franks* 4.9, trans. Dalton (1927, vol. 2: 122).
69 *History of the Franks* 6.24.
70 *History of the Franks* 5.19. The location of the house is unclear: see Dalton (1927, vol. 2: 543).
71 For the *Book of Pontiffs*, lives of the popes first compiled in the sixth century then kept up to date down to the ninth century, see for instance Davis (1989: i–xxxviii).

72 The *Book of Pontiffs* associates Butilinus with Amingus, a sign of confusion.
73 Trans. Davis (1989: 60).
74 Another sign of confusion is that the emperor named is Justinian, not Justin.
75 Though before and in proximity to the death of John himself, who died in July 574.
76 Favrod (1993: 80–1). For Marius and his *Chronicle* see Favrod (1993). The *Chronicle* covers the years 455–581. See also Goffart (1988: 389 n. 184).
77 See also the entries for the years 553 and 554, recording the defeats of Totila and Teias: Favrod (1993: 76–7).
78 Isidore of Seville, *Chronicon Maiora*, First Redaction, 402: Koon and Wood (2008) (see also Isidore of Seville, *Chronicon* 116: Wolf (2008)). Isidore calls Narses *patricius* and refers to his defeat of Totila. For Isidore see for instance Wood (2012). See also Goffart (1988: 389 n. 184).
79 *Fredegar Chronicle* 3.65, trans. Woodruff (1988: 72). The chronicle covers from Creation to 642 and has been dated to the 660s. The name of the author is first attested in the late-sixteenth century. For the *Fredegar Chronicle* see for instance Collins (2007) and Fischer (2014).
80 For Paul and his history see for instance Goffart (1988: 329–431). For the Lombards see for instance Christie (1995).
81 Paul the Deacon 2.1.
82 Paul the Deacon 2.2.
83 For Dagisthaeus see below.
84 Paul the Deacon 2.3. Narses is also identified as *patricius*.
85 Paul the Deacon 2.4.
86 Paul the Deacon 2.5.
87 *PLRE* 3B, Longinus 5, 797.
88 Trans. Foulke in Peters (2003: 59).
89 Paul the Deacon 2.11.
90 For Agnellus and his text see Deliyannis (2004) and Pizarro (1995).
91 Agnellus 90 and 95.
92 Agnellus 90 and 95.
93 Stein (1949: 356 n. 1). On the question of Narses' age see also Fauber (1990: 13) who asserts that the year usually given for the eunuch's birth is 478, as proposed by Hodgkin.
94 See also Goffart (1988: 388–9 and n. 184).
95 Fauber (1990: 169) questions how much weight can be put on the evidence for the tax burden placed on Italy by Narses, but see Christie (1991: 88–9).
96 Fauber (1990: 181) observes that 'this legendary tale itself has been put on trial'. However, it is possible that the Lombards were officially invited to settle in Italy as federates: see for instance Christie (1991) and (1995: 60–3). As Christie (1991: 108) observes, it remains an open question whether the Lombards were formally invited in as federates or simply invaded.
97 John of Ephesus, *Church History* 3.1.39.
98 Claudian, *Against Eutropius* 1.273–6 and 2.370–5. See also Fauber (1990: 179–80) and Tougher (2005: 65). For Claudian on Eutropius see Chapter 5.
99 Constantine VII, *On the Governance of the Empire* 27.14–37. In this garbled version the empress is named as Eirene and there is no emperor. The dispute arose when Narses asked the empress for money to conduct his campaigns, on which he had spent the tribute she expected to receive. For commentary see Jenkins (ed.) (1962: 89).

Notes to pp. 127–130

100 *Wars* 8.29.8–10.
101 *Wars* 8.29.11–15.
102 *Wars* 8.31.5.
103 *Wars* 8.32.1–4.
104 *Wars* 8.33.21–3.
105 *Wars* 6.19.8–17.
106 Agathias 1.22.1–6, and 2.4.3 (trans. Frendo (1975: 35)).
107 *Wars* 6.16.5, trans. Dewing (1914–28, vol. 4: 5).
108 *Wars* 6.18.2–3. For John see *PLRE* 3A, Ioannes 46, 652–61. For his uncle Vitalian see *PLRE* 2, Fl. Vitalianus 2, 1171–6. John was the son-in-law of Germanus, Justinian's relative (from 545, when he was back in Constantinople: *Wars* 7.12.11). For the close relationship between Narses and John, and on Narses' network in Italy in the period 538–539, see also Parnell (2017: 114–18).
109 *Wars* 8.26.24–25 and 8.35.34–36.
110 *Wars* 6.18.3.
111 Agathias 1.17.3, and 1.19.1 (trans. Frendo (1975: 27)).
112 For Dagisthaeus see *PLRE* 3A, Dagisthaeus 2, 380–3.
113 *Wars* 8.29.22–8.
114 *Wars* 6.22.5.
115 *Wars* 7.13.21.
116 Agathias 1.15.10–11, 1.20.8, and 2.7.2–7.
117 Agathias 1.15.2.
118 Agathias 1.16.1.
119 Agathias 1.15.11.
120 *Wars* 8.26.14, trans. Dewing (1914–28, vol. 5: 333).
121 *Wars* 8.31.9.
122 Agathias 1.13.7, trans. Frendo (1975: 21); 'great munificence' is more accurate.
123 *Wars* 8.33.1.
124 Agathias 1.12.9.
125 Agathias 2.7.2, trans. Frendo (1975: 39).
126 Agathias 2.7.5, trans. Frendo (1975: 39).
127 Evagrius 4.24, trans. Michael Whitby (2000: 222).
128 Paul the Deacon 2.3, trans. Foulke in Peters (2003: 56).
129 Agathias 1.8.2, trans. Frendo (1975: 16).
130 Agathias 2.11.3–5.
131 Agathias 2.14.6–7.
132 Fauber 1990, 131.
133 Agathias 2.9.1, trans. Frendo (1975: 40).
134 Note the comments of Whately (2016: 209).
135 *Wars* 8.26.8–9.
136 *Wars* 8.30.17, 8.32.8 and 28–9.
137 Though they were vital for the ancients: see for example Smith (1998: 151).
138 The Heruli had a role to play in the suppression of the Nika Riot, so perhaps Narses formed close bonds with them then. There is also the question of why Narses' relationship with the Heruli soured, leading to the defeat and death of Sindual. There is simply not enough information to understand why this occurred, though as noted above Narses had created some tension in 554 when he executed the Herul chief for murdering his servant.
139 Oman (1898: 34). See also the comments of Rance (2005: esp. 459–62).

140 See for example Averil Cameron (1970: 38). A dim view can be taken of Agathias' knowledge about the campaigns he describes but see Colvin (2013) who suggests that both Agathias and Procopius, in relation to the war in Lazica specifically, used documentary sources in the production of their narratives.
141 *Wars* 6.13.16, trans. Dewing (1914–28, vol. 3: 403).
142 Agathias 1.16.1-2, trans. Frendo (1975: 24).
143 Agathias 1.7.8, trans. Frendo (1975: 16).
144 *Wars* 8.21.6-19, trans. Dewing (1914–28, vol. 5: 273–7).
145 Ringrose (2003b: 128 and esp. 132–3).
146 Ringrose (2003b: 133).
147 See also Stewart (2015: 6-7) and Martyn (2007: 53).
148 Agathias 1.16.2, trans. Frendo (1975: 24). On *andreia* in general see Rosen and Sluiter (eds) (2003).
149 *Wars* 6.18.7.
150 Agathias 1.21.5. See also Dunlap (1924: 290). For Narses on horseback again see Agathias 2.7.2.
151 See also Stewart (2015: 7).
152 On Onasander and his treatise see for instance Smith (1998).
153 Onasander 33, trans. Illinois Greek Club (1923: 481).
154 Literally 'danger-loving'.
155 Onasander 33, trans. Illinois Greek Club (1923: 483).
156 Onasander 32, trans. Illinois Greek Club (1923: 475). Also revealing are Onasander's comments about the other qualities a general requires. He notes that a general should be chosen not on the grounds of birth or wealth 'but because he is temperate, self-restrained, vigilant, frugal, hardened to labour, alert, free from avarice, neither too young nor too old, indeed a father of children if possible, a ready speaker, and a man with a good reputation' (1, trans. Illinois Greek Club (1923: 375)). He also asserts that a good general 'must be trustworthy, affable, prompt, calm, not so lenient as to be despised, nor so severe as to be hated' (2, trans. Illinois Greek Club (1923: 387)).
157 Onasander also refers to the need for generosity to the troops (2); the need to take advice (3); the need for piety (5); the need to drill the army in winter (9); the need to feed the army (12); the need to keep up morale (13); the need to allow feasts after successes to encourage the troops to endure hardship (35); the need to treat surrendered cities well to encourage others to surrender (38); the need for the general not to be 'overweening in his good fortune, but gracious' (42).
158 Agathias 1.14.3 (trans. Frendo (1975: 22)) and 2.6.4. He also opines that Fulcaris would not have died 'had but his wisdom been proportionate to his valour': 1.15.10, trans. Frendo (1975: 23).
159 Agathias 1.4.4, trans. Frendo (1975: 12).
160 Agathias 5.21.2 and 5.23.3, trans. Frendo (1975: 157 and 159).
161 Agathias 5.15.7–20.4.
162 Agathias 5.16.1.
163 Agathias 5.17.5 (trans. Frendo (1975: 152)), and 5.18.2–3.
164 Agathias 5.20.3, trans. Frendo (1975: 156).
165 *Wars* 6.10.7 and 6.18.12–14.
166 See for instance Dennis (1984).
167 Dunlap (1924: 285). See also the analysis of Fauber (1990: 46).
168 Fauber (1990: 40) cites Browning for this: see Browning (1971: 112). The ninth-century Byzantine chronicler Theophanes seems to be the source for this: AM 6024,

trans. Mango and Scott (1997: 280). On the question of Narses' military experience see also Stein (1949: 357–8).
169 As noted above, *PLRE* 3B does include it as part of our Narses' career.
170 See Rotman (20015b: 140–2).
171 Graves (1938: Chapter 8). For Graves' *Count Belisarius* see for instance Tougher (2015b).
172 *Wars* 7.39.6–7. However, Liberius was quickly recalled as he proved unsuitable. For Liberius see O'Donnell (1981) and see also the comments of Rance (2005: 470).
173 Liddell Hart (1941: 64) (noted by Fauber (1990: 71)) and Stein (1949: 358, 'La stratégie théorique était à cette époque une science facile à apprendre, et l'esprit agile de Narsès eut probablement vite fait de se familiariser avec elle'). For Liddell Hart see Reid (2008). It is notable that Liddell Hart did not include the chapter on 'Byzantine Wars – Belisarius and Narses' in his *The Decisive Wars of History: A Study in Strategy*, published in 1929, but only in the revised version *The Strategy of Indirect Approach*, first published in 1941 (later published in 1954 as just *Strategy*) (though he does mention Belisarius in 1929: 39). In the Preface to the revised version he states that the chapter on the Byzantine wars had been included at the urging of T.E. Lawrence (better known as 'Lawrence of Arabia'): Liddell Hart (1941: ix). It was Lawrence who also inspired Graves' novel *Count Belisarius*, published in 1938: see Tougher (2015b: 80–1). Perhaps Liddell Hart was also influenced to add the chapter by the publication of Graves' novel, though he certainly already knew Lord Mahon's biography of Belisarius, as Graves borrowed it from him when writing the novel: see Tougher (2015b: 82).
174 See for example Hodgkin (1880–99, vol. 4: 275) and Stein (1949: 357).
175 See also the analysis of Fauber (1990: 69–70). For the sudden death of Germanus (either Justinian's cousin or nephew) see *Wars* 7.40.9. John the nephew of Vitalian was Germanus' son-in-law.
176 *Wars* 7.13.24–5.
177 As alluded to by Philostorgius 11.4 in relation to the career of Eutropius, as noted in Chapter 5.
178 Guilland (1943: 205). On Procopius not mentioning that eunuchs could not become emperor see also Stewart (2015: 8).
179 See for instance Tougher (2008a: 121). John was a *parakoimomenos* (akin to the post of *praepositus sacri cubiculi* in the later Roman Empire) active under Alexios III Angleos (1195–1203).
180 For Solomon see *PLRE* 3B, Solomon 1, 1167–77, Stewart (2017: 40–3), and Pringle (2001: esp. 22–31). The late-sixth-century *Church History* of Pseudo-Zachariah records that Solomon was from the fortress of Idriphthon (9.2), and the early-seventh-century Byzantine historian Theophylact Simocatta reports that Solomon was from the district of Solachon (*History* 2.3.12–13), both near Dara. See Greatrex (ed.) (2011: 318–19 n. 36).
181 *Wars* 3.11.6 and 9.
182 One of the explanations Procopius gives for would-be assassins not killing Solomon in 536 is his fame: *Wars* 4.14.25. Solomon is also mentioned very briefly in the *Chronicle* of Marcellinus: see the entries 535.1, 536.2, 539.5, 540.4, and 541.3 (Croke (1995: 45, 46, 48, and 49)). For inscriptions featuring Solomon see for instance Pringle (2001: 319–27).
183 On the issue of terminology and modern study of the Berbers see Merrills (2004: 5, 14–16).
184 Procopius asserts that there were multiple causes for this: ownership of land, religion, and Vandals who had returned to Africa: *Wars* 4.14.7–21 (and he later mentions pay

185 *Wars* 4.14.38–40. One would like to know whether the abuse the mutineers directed at Solomon in the hippodrome touched on his eunuchood, but Procopius gives no details of what they said: *Wars* 4.14.31. After this mutiny Solomon went back to Constantinople but was subsequently restored to North Africa by Justinian, after Germanus had suppressed the mutiny: *Wars* 4.19.1–4.

as a factor: *Wars* 4.15.55). He also stresses that Justinian is the real target of the mutiny: *Wars* 4.14.42.

186 *Wars* 4.11.5, 4.12.3 and 4.19.17.
187 *Wars* 4.20.22.
188 *Wars* 4.19.3–4.
189 *Wars* 4.20.33. However, Procopius then details how this ideal situation soured, blaming in particular the behaviour of Solomon's nephew Sergius, who was governor of Tripolis and took over the government of Libya after the death of his uncle: *Wars* 4.21.1 and 22.1–2.
190 Kaldellis (2004: 189) asserts that 'Solomon is the most highly praised person in the *Vandal War*', but it is notable that Procopius himself does not praise Solomon directly.
191 *Wars* 4.11.23–36. Procopius also gives the commanders of the Mauri a speech: *Wars* 4.11.37–46. Interestingly this does not touch on the eunuchood of Solomon: one might have expected it to attack Solomon on these grounds, as Agathias makes Leutharis and Butilinus do in the case of Narses.
192 *Wars* 4.11.50–6.
193 *Wars* 4.19.5–16.
194 *Wars* 4.12.28, trans. Dewing (1914–28, vol. 2: 313).
195 *Wars* 7.40.35. For Scholasticus see *PLRE* 3B, Scholasticus 1, 1117. Fauber (1990: 72) notes his existence too. Stein (1949: 524–5) suggests that Scholasticus was chief of the *spatharo-cubiculi* and thus a military figure.
196 Guilland (1943: 205).
197 See Chapter 5.
198 As noted for instance in Grayson (1995).
199 Aristonicus: Polybius 22.22, and see Guyot (1980: 182–3). Dionysius: Appian, *Mithridatic Wars* 76–7, and see Guyot (1980: 194). Mu'nis: see Kennedy (2018). Zheng He: see for instance Tsai (1996: 153–64).
200 *Hindustan Times*, 20 June 2010.
201 A prominent case is that of Peter 'Phokas' in the tenth century AD; his notable military achievements are recorded in the history of Leo the Deacon: see Tougher (2018: 237).
202 Though they could of course assist others to attempt to usurp power.

References

Abusch, R. (2002), 'Eunuchs and gender transformation: Philo's exegesis of the Joseph narrative', in S. Tougher (ed.), *Eunuchs in Antiquity and Beyond*, 103–21, London: The Classical Press of Wales and Duckworth.
Adams, J.N. (1984), 'Female speech in Latin comedy', *Antichthon* 18: 43–77.
Allen, P. (1981), *Evagrius Scholasticus the Church Historian*, Leuven: Peeters.
Amador, J.D.H. (2005), 'Queers on account of the kingdom of heaven: rhetorical constructions of the eunuch body', *Scriptura* 90: 809–23.
Amato, E. (2010), *Favorinos d'Arles, Oeuvres*, vol. 3, *Fragments*, Paris: Les Belles Lettres.
Amato, E. and Y. Julien (2005), *Favorinos d'Arles, Oeuvres*, vol. 1, *Introduction générale – Témoignages – Discours aux Corinthiens – Sur la Fortune*, Paris: Les Belles Lettres.
Amato, E. and M.-H. Marganne (eds) (2015), *Le traité* Sur l'exil *de Favorinos d'Arles. Papyrologie, philologie et littérature*, Rennes: Presses Universitaires de Rennes.
Amidon, P.R. (1997), *The Church History of Rufinus of Aquileia, Books 10 and 11*, New York and Oxford: Oxford University Press.
Amidon, P.R. (2007), *Philostorgius*, Church History, Atlanta: Society of Biblical Literature.
Andreescu-Treadgold, I. and W. Treadgold (1997), 'Procopius and the imperial panels of S. Vitale', *The Art Bulletin* 79: 708–23.
Androutsos, G. (2006), 'Hermaphroditism in Greek and Roman antiquity', *Hormones* 5: 214–17.
Anson, J. (1974), 'The female transvestite in early monasticism: the origin and development of a motif', *Viator* 5, 1–32.
Arnold, J.J. (2014), *Theoderic and the Roman Imperial Restoration*, Cambridge: Cambridge University Press.
Arnold, J.J., M.S. Bjornlie and K. Sessa (eds) (2016), *A Companion to Ostrogothic Italy*, Leiden and Boston: Brill.
Arnott, W.G. (1975), *Menander, Plautus, Terence*, Oxford: Oxford University Press.
Ashmore, S.G. (1908), *The Comedies of Terence*, New York: Oxford University Press.
Augoustakis, A. and A. Traill (2013), 'Introduction', in A. Augoustakis and A. Traill (eds), *A Companion to Terence*, 1–14, Chichester: Wiley-Blackwell.
Augoustakis, A. and A. Traill (eds) (2013), *A Companion to Terence*, Chichester: Wiley-Blackwell.
Baldwin, B. (1973), *Studies in Lucian*, Toronto: Hakkert.
Baldwin, B. (1975), *Studies in Aulus Gellius*, Lawrence, KS: Coronado Press.
Bardill, J. (1997), 'The palace of Lausus and nearby monuments in Constantinople: a topographical study', *American Journal of Archaeology* 101: 67–95.
Bardill, J. (2012), *Constantine, Divine Emperor of the Christian Golden Age*, New York: Cambridge University Press.
Barigazzi, A. (1966), *Favorino de Arelate, Opere*, Florence: Felice Le Monnier.
Barigazzi, A. (1993), 'Favorino di Arelate', *ANRW* II.34.1: 556–81.
Barnes, T.D. (1971), *Tertullian: A Historical and Literary Study*, Oxford: Oxford University Press (repr. 1985, with a Postscript).

Barnes, T.D. (1981), *Constantine and Eusebius*, Cambridge, MA and London: Harvard University Press.
Barnes, T.D. (1986), 'Synesius in Constantinople', *Greek, Roman and Byzantine Studies* 27: 93-112.
Barnes, T.D. (1993), *Athanasius and Constantius: Theology and Politics in the Constantinian Empire*, Cambridge, MA and London: Harvard University Press.
Barnes, T.D. (1998), *Ammianus Marcellinus and the Representation of Historical Reality*, Ithaca and London: Cornell University Press.
Barnes T.D. (2011), *Constantine: Dynasty, Religion and Power in the Later Roman Empire*, Chichester: Wiley Blackwell.
Barrett, C.K. (1994), *A Critical and Exegetical Commentary on The Acts of the Apostles*, vol. 1, Edinburgh: T&T Clark.
Barsby, J. (1991), *Terence, The Eunuch, Phormio, The Brothers: A Companion to the Penguin Translation*, Bristol: Bristol Classical Press.
Barsby, J. (ed.) (1999), *Terence, Eunuchus*, Cambridge: Cambridge University Press.
Barsby, J. (2000), 'Donatus on Terence: the *Eunuchus* commentary', in E. Stärk and G. Vogt-Spira (eds), *Dramatische Wäldchen: Festschrift für Eckard Lefèvre zum 65. Geburtstag (Spudasmata* 80), 491-513, Hildesheim: Georg Olms.
Barsby, J. (2001), *Terence*, vol. 1, Cambridge, MA and London: Harvard University Press.
Bartelink, G.J.M. (1974), *Palladio*, La Storia Lausiaca, Rome and Milan: Fondazione Lorenzo Valla and Arnoldo Mondadori.
Barton, T.S. (1994), *Power and Knowledge: Astrology, Physiognomics, and Medicine under the Roman Empire*, Ann Arbor: The University of Michigan Press.
Batiffol, P. (1919), 'Les présents de saint Cyrille à la cour de Constantinople', in his *Études de liturgie et d'archéologie chrétienne*, 154-79, Paris: J. Gabalda and Auguste Picard.
Baynham, E. (1998), *Alexander the Great: The Unique History of Quintus Curtius*, Ann Arbor: The University of Michigan Press.
Beall, S.M. (2001), '*Homo Fandi Dulcissimus*: the role of Favorinus in the *Attic Nights* of Aulus Gellius', *AJP* 122: 87-106.
Beard, M. (1994), 'The Roman and the foreign: the cult of the "Great Mother" in imperial Rome', in N. Thomas and C. Humphrey (eds), *Shamanism, History, and the State*, 164-90, Ann Arbor: University of Michigan Press.
Beard, M., J. North and S. Price (1998), *Religions of Rome*, 2 vols (vol. 1, *A History*, vol. 2, *A Sourcebook*), Cambridge: Cambridge University Press.
Beare, F.W. (1981), *The Gospel according to Matthew: A Commentary*, Oxford: Basil Blackwell.
Bekker, I. (1839), *Georgius Cedrenus*, vol. 2, Bonn: E. Weber.
Bell, R. (2009), 'Revisiting the pediment of the Palatine metroön: a Vergilian interpretation', *PBSR* 77: 65-99.
Bettini, M. (1991), *Anthropology and Roman Culture: Kinship, Time, Images of the Soul*, trans. J. Van Sickle, Baltimore, MD: John Hopkins University Press.
Bevington, D. (2005), *Antony and Cleopatra*, Cambridge: Cambridge University Press.
Bidez, J. and É. Des Places (2013), *Philostorge*, Histoire ecclésiastique, Paris: Éditions du Cerf.
Bidez, J. and F. Winkelmann (1981), *Philostorgius*, Kirchengeschichte, Berlin: De Gruyter.
Binder, V. (2010), 'Wytse Keulen, *Gellius the Satirist: Roman Cultural Authority in* Attic Nights', *Journal of Roman Studies* 100: 308-10.
Binns, J. (1994), *Ascetics and Ambassadors of Christ: The Monasteries of Palestine 314-631*, Oxford: Clarendon Press.

Bird, H.W. (1984), *Sextus Aurelius Victor: A Historiographical Study*, Liverpool: Francis Cairns.
Bird, H.W. (1994), *Aurelius Victor: De Caesaribus. Translated with an Introduction and Commentary*, Liverpool: Liverpool University Press.
Birley, A. (1976), *Lives of the Later Caesars. The First Part of the* Augustan History, *with Newly Compiled Lives of Nerva and Trajan*, Harmondsworth: Penguin Books.
Bitton-Ashkelony, B. and A. Kofsky (eds) (2004), *Christian Gaza in Late Antiquity*, Leiden and Boston: Brill.
Blenkinsopp, J. (2000), *Isaiah 1–39: A New Translation with Introduction and Commentary*, New York: Doubleday.
Blenkinsopp, J. (2002), *Isaiah 40–55: A New Translation with Introduction and Commentary*, New York: Doubleday.
Blenkinsopp, J. (2003), *Isaiah 56–66: A New Translation with Introduction and Commentary*, New York: Doubleday.
Blockley, R.C. (1975), *Ammianus Marcellinus: A Study of his Historiography and Political Thought*, Brussels: Latomus.
Blockley, R.C. (1981), *The Fragmentary Classicising Historians of the Later Roman Empire: Eunapius, Olympiodorus, Priscus and Malchus*, vol. 1, Liverpool: Francis Cairns.
Blockley, R.C. (1983), *The Fragmentary Classicising Historians of the Later Roman Empire: Eunapius, Olympiodorus, Priscus and Malchus*, vol. 2, *Text, Translation and Historiographical Notes*, Liverpool: Francis Cairns.
Blockley, R.C. (1985), *The* History *of Menander the Guardsman: Introductory Essay, Text, Translation, and Historiographical Notes*, Liverpool: Francis Cairns.
Boin, D. (2013a), 'A late antique statuary collection at Ostia's sanctuary of Magna Mater: a case-study in late Roman religion and tradition', *PBSR* 81: 247–77.
Boin, D. (2013b), *Ostia in Late Antiquity*, Cambridge: Cambridge University Press.
Boissier, M. (1901), 'Claveau d'une des portes de la façade du théâtre de Khamissa (Afrique)', *Comptes rendus des séances de l'Académie des Inscriptions et Belles-Lettres* 1–2: 344.
Borgeaud, P. (2004), *Mother of the Gods: From Cybele to the Virgin Mary*, trans. L. Hochroth, Baltimore and London: The John Hopkins University Press.
Bosworth, A.B. (2002), 'Vespasian and the slave trade', *CQ* 52: 350–7.
Boulhol, P. and I. Cochelin (1992), 'La réhabilitation de l'eunuque dans l'hagiographie antique (IVe–VIe siècles)', *Studi di antichità cristiana* 48: 49–76.
Bowden, H. (2010), *Mystery Cults in the Ancient World*, London: Thames & Hudson.
Bowersock, G.W. (1969), *Greek Sophists in the Roman Empire*, Oxford: Clarendon Press.
Bowie, E. (1997), 'Hadrian, Favorinus, and Plutarch', in J. Mossman (ed.), *Plutarch and his Intellectual World: Essays on Plutarch*, 1–15, London and Swansea: Duckworth in association with The Classical Press of Wales.
Bowie, E. and J. Elsner (eds) (2009), *Philostratus*, Cambridge: Cambridge University Press.
Boyle, A.J. (2004), 'Introduction: Terence's mirror stage', in A.J. Boyle (ed.), *Rethinking Terence, Ramus* 33, 1–9.
Boyle, A.J. (ed.) (2004), *Rethinking Terence, Ramus* 33.
Braund, S.M. (2004), *Juvenal and Persius*, Cambridge, MA and London: Harvard University Press.
Bregman, J. (1982), *Synesius of Cyrene: Philosopher-Bishop*, Berkeley/Los Angeles/London: University of California Press.

Brenk, F.E. (2017), 'Plutarch: philosophy, religion, and ethics', in D.S. Richter and W.A. Johnson (eds), *The Oxford Handbook of the Second Sophistic*, 291–309, Oxford and New York: Oxford University Press.

Brisson, L. (2002), *Sexual Ambivalence: Androgyny and Hermaphroditism in Graeco-Roman Antiquity*, trans. J. Lloyd, Berkeley/Los Angeles/London: University of California Press.

Brodka, D. (2018), *Narses. Politik, Krieg und Historiographie*, Berlin: Peter Lang.

Brody, L.R. and G.L. Hoffman (eds) (2011), *Dura-Europos: Crossroads of Antiquity*, Chestnut Hill, MA: McMullen Museum of Art, Boston College.

Brothers, A.J. (2000), *Terence, The Eunuch: Edited with Translation and Commentary*, Warminster: Aris & Phillips Ltd.

Brown, P. (2006), *Terence: The Comedies. Translated with Introduction and Explanatory Notes*, Oxford: Oxford University Press.

Brown, P. (2013), 'Terence and Greek New Comedy', in A. Augoustakis and A. Traill (eds), *A Companion to Terence*, 17–32, Chichester: Wiley-Blackwell.

Brown, P. (2016), 'Greek comedy at Rome', in B. van Zyl Smit (ed.), *A Handbook to the Reception of Greek Drama*, 63–77, New York: Wiley-Blackwell.

Browning, R. (1971), *Justinian and Theodora*, London: Weidenfeld and Nicolson.

Browning, R. (1975), *The Duke of Newcastle*, New Haven and London: Yale University Press.

Bruce, F.F. (1952), *The Acts of the Apostles. The Greek Text with Introduction and Commentary*, 2nd edn, London: The Tyndale Press.

Bruun, C. (2013), 'Greek or Latin? The owner's choice of names for *vernae* in Rome', in M. George (ed.), *Roman Slavery and Roman Material Culture*, 19–42, Toronto: University of Toronto Press.

Bryce, H. and H. Campbell (1886), 'Arnobius, *Against the Heathen*', in *Ante-Nicene Fathers*, vol. 6, 413–539, Buffalo, NY: Christian Literature Publishing Company.

Burgess, R.W. (2008), 'The summer of blood: the "great massacre" of 337 and the promotion of the sons of Constantine', *DOP* 62: 5–51.

Burns, K. (2017), 'Constructing a new woman for the body politic: the creation of Claudia Quinta', *Helios* 44: 81–98.

Burrus, V. (2000), *'Begotten, Not Made': Conceiving Manhood in Late Antiquity*, Stanford, CA: Stanford University Press.

Bury, J.B. (1923), *History of the Later Roman Empire from the Death of Theodosius I to the Death of Justinian (A.D. 395 to A.D. 565)*, 2 vols, London: Macmillan.

Butler, H.E. (1921), *The Institutio Oratoria of Quintilian*, vol. 2, London and New York: W. Heinemann and G.P. Putnam's Sons.

Butler, S. (1998), 'Notes on a *membrum disiectum*', in S.R. Joshel and S. Murnaghan (eds), *Women and Slaves in Greco-Roman Culture: Differential Equations*, 236–55, London and New York: Routledge.

Cain, A. (2013), 'Terence in Late Antiquity', in A. Augoustakis and A. Traill (eds), *A Companion to Terence*, 380–96, Chichester: Wiley-Blackwell.

Cairns, F. (1979), *Tibullus: A Hellenistic Poet at Rome*, Cambridge: Cambridge University Press.

Cairns, F. (2006), *Sextus Propertius: The Augustan Elegist*, Cambridge: Cambridge University Press.

Calvet-Sebasti, M.-A. and P.-L. Gatier (1989), *Firmus de Césarée*, Lettres, Paris: Éditons du Cerf.

Cameron, Alan (1965), 'Eunuchs in the "Historia Augusta"', *Latomus* 24: 155–8.

Cameron, Alan (1970), *Claudian: Poetry and Propaganda at the Court of Honorius*, Oxford: Oxford University Press.
Cameron, Alan (1976), *Circus Factions: Blues and Greens at Rome and Byzantium*, Oxford: Clarendon Press.
Cameron, Alan (1988), 'A misidentified homily of Chrysostom', *Nottingham Medieval Studies* 32: 34–48.
Cameron, Alan (2011), *The Last Pagans of Rome*, Oxford and New York: Oxford University Press.
Cameron, Alan and J. Long (1993), *Barbarians and Politics at the Court of Arcadius*, Berkeley/Los Angeles/Oxford: University of California Press.
Cameron, Averil (1970), *Agathias*, Oxford: Clarendon Press.
Cameron, Averil (1985), *Procopius and the Sixth Century*, London: Duckworth.
Caner, D.F. (1997), 'The practice and prohibition of self-castration in early Christianity', *Vigiliae Christianae* 51: 396–415.
Carcopino, J. (1942), 'La Réforme romaine du culte de Cybèle et d'Attis', in his *Aspects mystiques de la Rome païenne*, 49–171, Paris: L'Artisan du Livre.
Cary, E. (1925), *Dio's Roman History*, vol. 8, *Books 61–70*, London and New York: William Heinemann and G.P. Putnam's Sons.
Cary, E. (1937), *The Roman Antiquities of Dionysius of Halicarnassus*, vol. 1, London and Cambridge, MA: William Heinemann Ltd and Harvard University Press.
Chadwick, H. (1974), 'John Moschus and his friend Sophronius the sophist', *The Journal of Theological Studies* 25: 41–74.
Champlin, E. (1980), *Fronto and Antonine Rome*, Cambridge, MA and London: Harvard University Press.
Champlin, E. (2003), *Nero*, Cambridge, MA and London: Belknap.
Chew, K. (2006), 'Virgins and eunuchs: Pulcheria, politics and the death of emperor Theodosius II', *Historia* 55: 207–27.
Chi, J.Y. and S. Heath (eds) (2011), *Edge of Empires: Pagans, Jews, and Christians at Roman Dura-Europos*, New York: Princeton University Press.
Chitty, D.J. (1966), *The Desert a City: An Introduction to the Study of Egyptian and Palestinian Monasticism under the Christian Empire*, Oxford: Blackwell.
Christensen, A.S. (1980), *Lactantius the Historian*, Copenhagen: Museum Tusculanum.
Christenson, D. (2010), *Roman Comedy: Five Plays by Plautus and Terence*, Indianapolis, IN: Focus.
Christenson, D. (2013), '*Eunuchus*', in A. Augoustakis and A. Traill (eds), *A Companion to Terence*, 262–80, Chichester: Wiley-Blackwell.
Christie, N. (1991), 'Invasion or invitation? The Longobard occupation of northern Italy, A.D. 568–569', *Romanobarbarica* 11: 79–108.
Christie, N. (1995), *The Lombards*, Oxford: Basil Blackwell Ltd.
Clark, E.A. (1977), 'John Chrysostom and the *subintroducate*', *Church History* 46: 171–85.
Clayton, F.W. and M. Leigh (2006), *The Comedies of Terence*, Exeter: University of Exeter Press.
Cohoon, J.W. (1939), *Dio Chrysostom, with an English Translation*, vol. 2, London and Cambridge, MA: Heinemann and Harvard University Press.
Coleman, K.M. (1990), 'Fatal charades: Roman executions staged as mythological enactments', *JRS* 80: 44–73.
Coleman-Norton, P.R. (1928), *Palladii Dialogus de vita S. Joannis Chrysostomi*, Cambridge: Cambridge University Press.

Collins, J. (2013), 'Appropriation and development of castration and practice in early Christianity', in L. Tracy (ed.) (2013), *Castration and Culture in the Middle Ages*, 73–86, Cambridge: D.S. Brewer.

Collins, P. (2009), 'An ivory fan handle from Nimrud', *Metropolitan Museum Journal* 44: 9–20.

Collins, R. (2007), *Die Fredegar-Chroniken*, Hanover: Hahnsche Buchhandlung.

Colvin, I. (2013), 'Reporting battles and understanding campaigns in Procopius and Agathias: classicising historians' use of archived documents as sources', in A. Sarantis and N. Christie (eds), *War and Warfare in Late Antiquity*, vol. 2, 571–97, Leiden and Boston: Brill.

Cooley, A.E. (2009), Res Gestae Divi Augusti: *Text, Translation, and Commentary*, Cambridge: Cambridge University Press.

Corbier, M. (2001), 'Child exposure and abandonment', in S. Dixon (ed.), *Childhood, Class and Kin in the Roman World*, 52–73, London and New York: Routledge.

Cornelius, S. (2009), '"Eunuchs"? The ancient background of *eunouchos* in the Septuagint', in J. Cook (ed.), *Septuagint and Reception: Essays Prepared for the Association for the Study of the Septuagint in South Africa*, 321–33, Leiden and Boston: Brill (= *Supplements to the Vetus Testamentum*, vol. 127).

Cornish, F.W. (1962), *Catullus*, London and Cambridge, MA: William Heinemann Ltd. and Harvard University Press.

Costa, E.A., Jr. (1972), 'The office of the "castrensis sacri palatii" in the fourth century', *Byz* 42: 358–87.

Coulston, J. (2006), *Lord Mahon, The Life of Belisarius the Last Great General of Rome*, Yardley, PA: Westholme.

Creed, J.L. (1984), *Lactantius, De Mortibus Persecutorum*, Oxford: Clarendon Press.

Cribiore, R. (2007), *The School of Libanius in Late Antique Antioch*, Princeton, NJ: Princeton University Press.

Croke, B. (1995), *The Chronicle of Marcellinus: A Translation and Commentary*, Sydney: Australian Association for Byzantine Studies.

Cumont, F. (1926), *Fouilles de Doura-Europos (1922–1923)*, Paris: Paul Geuthner.

Curta, F. (ed.) (2010), *Neglected Barbarians*, Turnout: Brepols.

Dalton, O.M. (1927), *Gregory of Tours, The History of the Franks, Translated with an Introduction*, 2 vols, Oxford: Clarendon Press.

Davenport, C. (2019), *A History of the Roman Equestrian Order*, Cambridge: Cambridge University Press.

Davies, W.D. and D.C. Allison (1997), *A Critical and Exegetical Commentary on the Gospel According to Saint Matthew*, vol. 3, Edinburgh: T&T Clark.

Davis, R. (1989), The Book of Pontiffs (Liber Pontificalis). *The Ancient Biographies of the First Ninety Roman Bishops to AD 715. Translated with an Introduction*, Liverpool: Liverpool University Press.

De Gaiffier, B. (1957), 'Palatins et eunuques dans quelques documents hagiographiques', *AnBoll* 75: 17–46.

De Wet, C.L. (2015), *Preaching Bondage: John Chrysostom and the Discourse of Slavery in Early Christianity*, Oakland, CA: University of California Press.

De Wet, C.L. (2017), 'Revisiting the *subintroductae*: slavery, asceticism and "syneisaktism" in the exegesis of John Chrysostom', *Biblical Interpretation* 25: 58–80.

Deliyannis, D.M. (2004), *Agnellus of Ravenna*, The Book of Pontiffs of the Church of Ravenna. *Translated with an Introduction and Notes*, Washington, DC: The Catholic University of America Press.

Deliyannis, D.M. (2010), *Ravenna in Late Antiquity*, New York: Cambridge University Press.
Demetriou, C. (2014), 'Aelius Donatus and his commentary on Terence's comedies', in M. Fontaine and A.C. Scafuro (eds), *The Oxford Handbook of Greek and Roman Comedy*, 782–99, New York: Oxford University Press.
Demetriou, C. (2015), 'Donatus' commentary: the reception of Terence's performance', in A.J. Turner and G. Torello-Hill (eds), *Terence between Late Antiquity and the Age of Printing: Illustration, Commentary and Performance*, 181–99, Leiden and Boston: Brill.
Dennis, G.T. (1984), *Maurice's* Strategikon. *Handbook of Byzantine Military Strategy*, Philadelphia: University of Pennsylvania Press.
Desideri, P. (2017), 'Plutarch's *Lives*', in D.S. Richter and W.A. Johnson (eds), *The Oxford Handbook of the Second Sophistic*, 311–26, Oxford and New York: Oxford University Press.
Dessen, C.S. (1995), 'The figure of the eunuch in Terence's *Eunuchus*', *Helios* 22: 123–39.
Dewar, M. (1990), 'The fall of Eutropius', *CQ* 40: 582–4.
Dewing, H.B. (1914–28), *Procopius*, History of the Wars, 5 vols (vol. 1, Books 1–2; vol. 2, Books 3–4; vol. 3, Books 5–6.15; vol. 4, Books 6.16–7.35; vol. 5, Books 7.36–8), London and New York: William Heinemann and the Macmillan Co.
Di Segni, L. (2004), 'The territory of Gaza: notes on historical geography', in B. Bitton-Ashkelony and A. Kofsky (eds), *Christian Gaza in Late Antiquity*, 41–59, Leiden and Boston: Brill.
Dirven, L. (1999), *The Palmyrenes of Dura-Europos. A Study of Religious Interaction in Roman Syria*, Leiden/Boston/Köln: Brill.
Dirven, L. (2011), 'Strangers and sojourners: the religious behaviour of Palmyrenes and other foreigners in Dura-Europos', in L.R. Brody and G.L. Hoffman (eds), *Dura-Europos: Crossroads of Antiquity*, 201–20, Chestnut Hill, MA: McMullen Museum of Art, Boston College.
Dodwell, C.R. (2000), *Anglo-Saxon Gestures and the Roman Stage*, Cambridge: Cambridge University Press.
Drake, H.A. (2000), *Constantine and the Bishops: The Politics of Intolerance*, Baltimore and London: The John Hopkins University Press.
Drijvers, J.W. and D. Hunt (eds) (1999), *The Late Roman World and its Historian: Interpreting Ammianus Marcellinus*, London and New York: Routledge.
Drinkwater, J.F. (2019), *Nero: Emperor and Court*, Cambridge: Cambridge University Press.
Duff, A.M. (1928), *Freedmen in the Early Roman Empire*, Oxford: Clarendon Press.
Duff, J.D. (1927–34), *Silius Italicus*, Punica, 2 vols, London and New York: William Heinemann and G.P. Putnam's Sons.
Duff, J.D. (1928), *Lucan*, London and New York: William Heinemann and G.P. Putnam's Sons.
Dufraigne, P. (2003), *Aurélius Victor*, Livre des Césars, 2nd edn, Paris: Les Belles Lettres.
Dunlap, J.E. (1924), 'The office of the grand chamberlain in the later Roman and Byzantine empires', in A.E.R. Boak and J.E. Dunlap, *Two Studies in Later Roman and Byzantine Administration*, 161–301, New York and London: Macmillan.
Dunn, G.D. (2004), *Tertullian*, London: Routledge.
Duthoy, R. (1969), *The Taurobolium: Its Evolution and Terminology*, Leiden: Brill.
Dyson, R.W. (1998), *Augustine*, The City of God against the Pagans, Cambridge: Cambridge University Press.
Earl, D.C. (1962), 'Terence and Roman politics', *Historia* 11: 469–85.

Eckstein, A.M. (2008), *Rome Enters the Greek East: From Anarchy to Hierarchy in the Hellenistic Mediterranean, 230–170 BC*, Malden, MA/Oxford/Victoria: Blackwell Publishing.

Edwards, C. (2000), *Suetonius*, Lives of the Caesars. *Translated with an Introduction and Notes*, Oxford: Oxford University Press.

Edwards, M. (1999), 'The flowering of Latin apologetic: Lactantius and Arnobius', in M. Edwards, M. Goodman and S. Price (eds), *Apologetics in the Roman Empire: Pagans, Jews, and Christians*, 197–221, Oxford: Oxford University Press.

Elm, S. (1994), *'Virgins of God': The Making of Asceticism in Late Antiquity*, Oxford: Clarendon Press.

Elsner, J. (1998), *Imperial Rome and Christian Triumph: The Art of the Roman Empire AD 100–450*, Oxford and New York: Oxford University Press.

Elton, H. (2009), 'Imperial politics at the court of Theodosius II', in A. Cain and N. Lenski (eds), *The Power of Religion in Late Antiquity*, 133–43, Farnham and Burlington, VT: Ashgate.

Engelstein, L. (1999), *Castration and the Heavenly Kingdom: A Russian Folktale*, Ithaca and London: Cornell University Press.

Erskine, A. (1994), 'Greek embassies and the city of Rome', *Classics Ireland* 1: 47–53.

Escribiano Paño, M.V. (2009), 'The social exclusion of heretics in *Codex Theodosianus* XVI', in J.-J. Aubert and P. Blanchard (eds), *Droit, religion et société dans le* Code Théodosien, 39–66, Geneva: Université de Neuchâtel.

Evans, E. (1972), *Tertullian*, Adversus Marcionem. *Books 1 to 3*, Oxford: Clarendon Press.

Fauber, L.H. (1990), *Narses: Hammer of the Goths*, Gloucester and New York: Alan Sutton and St Martin's Press.

Favrod, J. (1993), *La* Chronique *de Marius d'Avenches (455–581). Texte, traduction et commentaire*, 2nd edn, Lausanne: University of Lausanne.

Fear, A.T. (1996), 'Cybele and Christ', in E.N. Lane (ed.), *Cybele, Attis and Related Cults: Essays in Memory of M.J. Vermaseren*, 37–50, Leiden: Brill.

Festugière, A.J. and L. Rydén (1974), *Léontios de Néapolis*, Vie de Syméon le Fou *et* Vie de Jean de Chypre, Paris: Librairie Orientaliste Paul Geuthner.

Ficacci, L. (2006), *Piranesi: The Etchings*, Köln: Taschen.

Fischer, A. (2014), 'Reflecting Romanness in the Fredegar Chronicle', *Early Medieval Europe* 22: 433–45.

Fishwick, D. (1966), 'The *cannophoroi* and the March festival of Magna Mater', *Transactions and Proceedings of the American Philological Associaton* 97: 193–202.

Fitzgerald, A. (1930), *The Essays and Hymns of Synesius of Cyrene*, vol. 1, London: Oxford University Press.

Fitzmyer, J.A. (2010), *The Acts of the Apostles. A New Translation with Introduction and Commentary*, New Haven and London: Yale University Press (orig. pub. 1998, Doubleday).

Flower, R. (2018), 'Medicalizing heresy: doctors and patients in Epiphanius of Salamis', *JLA* 11: 251–73.

Fleury, P. (2017), 'Fronto and his circle', in D.S. Richter and W.A. Johnson (eds), *The Oxford Handbook of the Second Sophistic*, 245–54, Oxford and New York: Oxford University Press.

Fontaine, M. and A.C. Scafuro (eds) (2014), *The Oxford Handbook of Greek and Roman Comedy*, New York: Oxford University Press.

Forehand, W.E. (1985), *Terence*, Boston: Twayne Publishers.

Foster, P. and S. Parvis (eds) (2012), *Irenaeus: Life, Scripture, Legacy*, Minneapolis: Fortress Press.

Frazer, J.G. (1967), *Ovid's* Fasti, London and Cambridge, MA: William Heinemann Ltd and Harvard University Press.
Frendo, J.D. (1975), *Agathias*, The Histories. *Translated with an Introduction and Short Explanatory Notes*, Berlin and New York: De Gruyter.
Frier, B.W. (2016), *The* Codex *of Justinian: A New Annotated Translation with Parallel Latin and Greek Text*, 3 vols, Cambridge: Cambridge University Press.
Garthwaite, J. (1984), 'Statius, *Silvae* 3.4: on the fate of Earinus', *ANRW* II.32.1: 111–24.
Gera, D. (1997), *Warrior Women: The Anonymous* Tractatus de Mulieribus, Leiden: Brill.
Ginsberg, H.L. (1990), 'The Book of Daniel', in W.D. Davies and L. Finkelstein (eds), *The Cambridge History of Judaism*, vol. 2, *The Hellenistic Age*, 504–23, Cambridge: Cambridge University Press.
Gleason, M.W. (1995), *Making Men: Sophists and Self-Presentation in Ancient Rome*, Princeton, NJ: Princeton University Press.
Goffart, W. (1988), *The Narrators of Barbarian History (*A.D. *550–800): Jordanes, Gregory of Tours, Bede, and Paul the Deacon*, Princeton, NJ: Princeton University Press.
Goggin, M.G. (1951), 'Rhythm in the prose of Favorinus', *YCS* 12: 149–201.
Goldberg, S.M. (1986), *Understanding Terence*, Princeton, NJ: Princeton University Press.
Goldberg, S. (1999), 'John Barsby (ed.), *Terence*, Eunuchus', *BMCR* 1999.06.23, http://bmcr.brynmawr.edu/1999/1999-06-23.html (accessed 22 March 2019).
Goldingay, J. (2014), *A Critical and Exegetical Commentary on Isaiah 56–66*, London and New York: Bloomsbury Publishing.
Graillot, H. (1912), *Le culte de Cybèle, Mère des dieux, à Rome et dans l'Empire romain*, Paris: Fontemoing.
Grant, J.N. (1986), *Studies in the Textual Tradition of Terence*, Toronto and London: University of Toronto Press.
Grant, R.M. (1997), *Irenaeus of Lyons*, London and New York: Routledge.
Graves, R. (1938), *Count Belisarius*, London: Cassell.
Graves, R. (1963), *The Comedies of Terence*, London: Cassell.
Grayson, A.K. (1995), 'Eunuchs in power: their role in the Assyrian bureaucracy', *Alter Orient und Altes Testament* 240: 85–98.
Greatrex, G. (1997), 'The Nika riot: a reappraisal', *JHS* 117: 60–86.
Greatrex, G. (2000), 'The background and aftermath of the partition of Armenia in AD 387', *Ancient History Bulletin* 14: 35–48.
Greatrex, G. (ed.) (2011), *The* Chronicle *of Pseudo-Zachariah Rhetor: Church and War in Late Antiquity*, Liverpool: Liverpool University Press.
Greatrex, G. and J. Bardill (1996), 'Antiochus the *praepositus*: a Persian eunuch at the court of Theodosius II', *DOP* 50: 171–97.
Grégoire, H. and M.-A. Kugener (1930), *Marc le diacre*, Vie de Porphyre évêque de Gaza, Paris: Les Belles Lettres.
Griffin, M.T. (1976), *Seneca: A Philosopher in Politics*, Oxford: Clarendon Press.
Gruen, E.S. (1984), *The Hellenistic World and the Coming of Rome*, Berkeley/Los Angeles/London: University of California Press.
Gruen, E.S. (1990), 'The advent of the Magna Mater', in his *Studies in Greek Culture and Roman Policy*, 5–33, Leiden: Brill.
Gsell, S. (1922), *Inscriptions latines de l'Algérie*, vol. 1, Paris: Édouard Champion.
Guilland, R. (1943), 'Les eunuques dans l'empire byzantin. Etude de titulature et de prosopographie byzantines', *REB* 1: 197–238.
Gummere, R.M. (1925), *Seneca*, Epistles, vol. 3, London and New York: Heinemann and G.P. Putnam's Sons.

Guy, J.-C. (2003), Les Apophtegmes des Pères: collection systématique, chapitres X–XVI, Paris: Éditions du Cerf.
Guyot, P. (1980), *Eunuchen als Sklaven und Freigelassene in der griechisch-römischen Antike*, Stuttgart: Klett-Cotta.
Gwynn, D.M. (1999) 'Constantine and the other Eusebius', *Prudentia* 31: 94–124.
Habicht, C. (1969), *Die Inschriften des Asklepieions*, Berlin: De Gruyter.
Haenchen, E. (1971), *The Acts of the Apostles: A Commentary*, Oxford: Basil Blackwell.
Hales, S. (2002), 'Looking for eunuchs: the *galli* and Attis in Roman art', in S. Tougher (ed.), *Eunuchs in Antiquity and Beyond*, 87–102, London: The Classical Press of Wales and Duckworth.
Hall, E. (1989), *Inventing the Barbarian: Greek Self-Definition through Tragedy*, Oxford: Clarendon Press.
Hamilton, J.R. (1999), *Plutarch: Alexander*, 2nd edn, London: Bristol Classical Press.
Hamilton, W. (1986), *Ammianus Marcellinus, The Later Roman Empire (A.D. 354–378), with an Introduction and Notes by A. Wallace-Hadrill*. Harmondsworth: Penguin Books.
Hanchey, D.P. (2013), 'Terence and the Scipionic *grex*', in A. Augoustakis and A. Traill (eds), *A Companion to Terence*, 113–31, Chichester: Wiley-Blackwell.
Hanson, R.P.C. (1966), 'A note on Origen's self-mutilation', *Vigiliae Christianae* 20: 81–2.
Hanson, R.P.C. (1988), *The Search for the Christian Doctrine of God: The Arian Controversy 318–381*, Edinburgh: T&T Clark.
Harmon, A.M. (1913), *Lucian*, vol. 1, London and New York: William Heinemann and Macmillan.
Harmon, A.M. (1936), *Lucian*, vol. 5, Cambridge, MA and London: Harvard University Press and William Heinemann Ltd.
Harper, C. (2007), *Intersex*, Oxford and New York: Berg.
Harper, K. (2011), *Slavery in the Late Roman World, AD 275–425*, Cambridge: Cambridge University Press.
Harries, J. (2012), *Imperial Rome AD 284 to 363: The New Empire*, Edinburgh: Edinburgh University Press.
Harris, W.V. (1994), 'Child-exposure in the Roman empire', *JRS* 84: 1–22.
Harrison, M. (1989), *A Temple for Byzantium: The Discovery and Excavation of Anicia Juliana's Palace-Church in Istanbul*, Austin: University of Texas Press.
Hartman, L.F. and A.A. Di Lella (1978), *The Book of Daniel: A New Translation with Notes and Commentary*, New York: Doubleday.
Heather, P. (1996), *The Goths*, Oxford: Blackwell Publishers Ltd.
Heaton E.W. (1956), *The Book of Daniel: Introduction and Commentary*, London: SCM Press Ltd.
Hefele, C.J. (1883), *A History of the Christian Councils, from the Original Documents, to the Close of the Council of Nicaea, A.D. 325*, 2nd edn (revised), Edinburgh: T&T Clark.
Hefele, C.J. (1908), *Histoire des conciles d'aprés les documents originaux*, vol. 2.1, Paris: Letouzey et Ané.
Heinzelmann, M. (2001), *Gregory of Tours: History and Society in the Sixth Century*, Cambridge: Cambridge University Press.
Hekster, O. (2008), *Rome and Its Empire, AD 193–284*, Edinburgh: Edinburgh University Press.
Henriksén, C. (1997), 'Earinus: an imperial eunuch in the light of the poems of Martial and Statius', *Mnemosyne* 50: 281–94.
Henry, R. (1974), *Photius*, Bibliothèque, vol. 7, Paris: Les Belles Lettres.

Hill, R.C. (2006), *Theodoret of Cyrus:* Commentary on Daniel, Atlanta: Society of Biblical Literature.
Hirschfeld, Y. (2004), 'The monasteries of Gaza: an archaeological review', in B. Bitton-Ashkelony and A. Kofsky (eds), *Christian Gaza in Late Antiquity*, 61–88, Leiden and Boston: Brill.
Hodgkin, T. (1880–99), *Italy and Her Invaders*, 8 vols (vol. 4, 1896; vol. 5, 1895), Oxford: Clarendon Press.
Höfert, A., M. Mesley and S. Tolino (eds) (2018), *Celibate and Childless Men in Power: Ruling Eunuchs and Bishops in the Pre-Modern World*, London and New York: Routledge.
Holford-Strevens, L. (1988), *Aulus Gellius*, London: Duckworth.
Holford-Strevens, L. (1997), 'Favorinus: the man of paradoxes', in J. Barnes and M. Griffin (ed.), *Philosophia Togata II: Plato and Aristotle at Rome*, 188–217, Oxford: Clarendon Press.
Holford-Strevens, L. (2003), *Aulus Gellius. An Antonine Scholar and His Achievement*, Oxford and New York: Oxford University Press.
Holford-Strevens, L. (2005), *Aulus Gellius. An Antonine Scholar and His Achievement*, paperback edn with Addenda, Oxford and New York: Oxford University Press.
Holford-Strevens, L. (2009), 'Wytse Keulen, *Gellius the Satirist: Roman Cultural Authority in Attic Nights*', *BMCR* 2009.05.13, http://bmcr.brynmawr.edu/2009/2009-05-13.html (accessed 22 March 2019).
Holford-Strevens, L. (2015), 'L'exil de Favorinos eut-il réellement lieu?' in E. Amato and M.-H. Marganne (eds), *Le traité Sur l'exil de Favorinos d'Arles. Papyrologie, philologie et littérature*, 123–32, Rennes: Presses Universitaires de Rennes.
Holford-Strevens, L. (2017), 'Favorinus and Herodes Atticus', in D.S. Richter and W.A. Johnson (eds), *The Oxford Handbook of the Second Sophistic*, 233–44, Oxford and New York: Oxford University Press.
Holford-Strevens, L. and A. Vardi (eds) (2004), *The Worlds of Aulus Gellius*, Oxford: Oxford University Press.
Holl, K. (1980), *Epiphanius II. Panarion haer. 34–64*, Berlin: Akademie-Verlag.
Holum, K.G. (1982), *Theodosian Empresses: Women and Imperial Dominion in Late Antiquity*, Berkeley/Los Angeles/London: University of California Press.
Hopkins, K. (1963), 'Eunuchs in politics in the later Roman empire', *PCPS* 189: 62–80.
Hopkins, K. (1978), *Conquerors and Slaves*, Cambridge: Cambridge University Press.
Horn, C.B. (2006), *Asceticism and Christological Controversy in Fifth-century Palestine: The Career of Peter the Iberian*, Oxford: Oxford University Press.
Horn, C.B. and R.R. Phenix, Jr (2008), *John Rufus: The Lives of Peter the Iberian, Theodosius of Jerusalem, and the Monk Romanus*, Atlanta: Society of Biblical Literature.
Hornblower, J. (1981), *Hieronymus of Cardia*, Oxford: Oxford University Press.
Horstmanshoff, M. (2000), 'Who is the true eunuch? Medical and religious ideas about eunuchs and castration in the works of Clement of Alexandria', in S. Kottek and M. Horstmanshoff (eds), *From Athens to Jerusalem: Medicine in Hellenized Jewish Lore and in Early Christian Literature*, 101–18, Rotterdam: Erasmus Publishing.
Howley, J.A. (2018), *Aulus Gellius and Roman Reading Culture: Text, Presence, and Imperial Knowledge in the* Noctes Atticae, Cambridge and New York: Cambridge University Press.
Hoyland, R. (2007), 'A new edition and translation of the Leiden Polemon', in S. Swain (ed.), *Seeing the Face, Seeing the Soul. Polemon's Physiognomy from Classical Antiquity to Medieval Islam*, 329–463, Oxford: Oxford University Press.

Humphries, M. (2012), 'The tyrant's mask? Images of good and bad rule in Julian's *Letter to the Athenians*', in N. Baker-Brian and S. Tougher (eds), *Emperor and Author: The Writings of Julian the Apostate*, 75–90, Swansea: The Classical Press of Wales.

Hunt, E.D. (1982), *Holy Land Pilgrimage in the Later Roman Empire* AD 312–460, Oxford: Clarendon Press.

Hunt, D. (1989), 'Did Constantius II have "court bishops"?', in E.A. Livingstone (ed.), *Studia Patristica* 19: 86–90.

Illinois Greek Club (1923), *Aeneas Tacticus, Asclepiodotus, Onasander*, London and New York: Heinemann and G.P. Putnam's Sons.

Ioppolo, A.M. (1993), 'The Academic position of Favorinus of Arelate', *Phronesis* 38: 182–213.

Jachmann, G. (1929), *Terentius: Codex vaticanus latinus 3868 picturis insignis*, Leipzig: Otto Harrassowitz.

Jackson, B. (1892), *The Ecclesiastical History, Dialogues, and Letters of Theodoret*, in *Nicene and Post-Nicene Fathers*, vol. 3, Second Series, Buffalo, NY: Christian Literature Co.

Jackson, C.R. (2017), 'Dio Chrysostom', in D.S. Richter and W.A. Johnson (eds), *The Oxford Handbook of the Second Sophistic*, 217–32, Oxford and New York: Oxford University Press.

Jackson, J. (1937), *Tacitus*, Annals, vols 3 and 4, Cambridge, MA and London: Harvard University Press and William Heinemann Ltd.

Jacobs, A.S. (2016), *Epiphanius of Cyprus: A Cultural Biography of Late Antiquity*, Oakland, CA: University of California Press.

James, S.L. (1998), 'From boys to men: rape and developing masculinity in Terence's *Hecyra* and *Eunuchus*', *Helios* 25: 31–47.

Jenkins, R.J.H. (ed.) (1962), *Constantine Porphyrogenitus*, De Administrando Imperio: *A Commentary*, London: Athlone Press.

Jones, A.H.M. (1964), *The Later Roman Empire 284–602: A Social, Economic, and Administrative Survey*, 3 vols, Oxford: Basil Blackwell Ltd.

Jones, C.P. (1967), 'The teacher of Plutarch', *Harvard Studies in Classical Philology* 71: 205–13.

Jones, C.P. (1978), *The Roman World of Dio Chrysostom*, Cambridge, MA and London: Harvard University Press.

Jones, C.P. (2012), *Philostratus*, The Life of Apollonius of Tyana, *Books I–IV*, revised edn, Cambridge, MA and London: Harvard University Press.

Jones, L.W. and C.R. Morey (1931), *The Miniatures of the Manuscripts of Terence Prior to the Thirteenth Century*, 2 vols, Princeton: Princeton University Press.

Jones, W.H.S. (1966), *Pausanias*, Description of Greece, vol. 3, London and Cambridge, MA: William Heinemann Ltd and Harvard University Press.

Jope, J. (1985), 'Lucretius, Cybele, and religion', *Phoenix* 39: 250–62.

Jordan, R.H. (2000), 'John of Phoberou: a voice crying in the wilderness', in D. Smythe (ed.), *Strangers to Themselves: The Byzantine Outsider*, 61–73, Aldershot: Ashgate.

Kaldellis, A. (2004), *Procopius of Caesarea: Tyranny, History, and Philosophy at the End of Antiquity*, Philadelphia: University of Pennsylvania Press.

Kampen, N. (2009), *Family Fictions in Roman Art*, Cambridge: Cambridge University Press.

Karlin-Hayter (1973), 'Les Ἄκτα διὰ Καλαπόδιον. Le contexte religieux et politique', *Byz* 43: 84–107, repr. Karlin-Hayter 1981a, II.

Karlin-Hayter, P. (1981a), *Studies in Byzantine Political History: Sources and Controversies*, London: Variorum Reprints.

Karlin-Hayter, P. (1981b), 'La forme primitive des Ἄκτα διὰ Καλαπόδιον', in P. Karlin-Hayter, *Studies in Byzantine Political History: Sources and Controversies*, I, 1–13, London: Variorum Reprints.

Katos, D.S. (2011), *Palladius of Helenopolis: The Origenist Advocate*, Oxford: Oxford University Press.

Keil, C.F. (1884), *Biblical Commentary on the Old Testament. The Book of the Prophet Daniel*, Edinburgh: T&T Clark.

Kelly, G. (2008), *Ammianus Marcellinus, The Allusive Historian*, Cambridge: Cambridge University Press.

Kelly, J.N.D. (1995), *Golden Mouth: The Story of John Chrysostom – Ascetic, Preacher, Bishop*, London: Duckworth.

Kemezis, A.M. (2014), *Greek Narratives of the Roman Empire under the Severans: Cassius Dio, Philostratus and Herodian*, Cambridge: Cambridge University Press.

Kennedy, H. (2018), 'Mu'nis al-Muẓaffar: an exceptional eunuch', in A. Höfert, M. Mesley and S. Tolino (eds), *Celibate and Childless Men in Power: Ruling Eunuchs and Bishops in the Pre-Modern World*, 79–91, London and New York: Routledge.

Keulen, W. (2009), *Gellius the Satirist: Roman Cultural Authority in* Attic Nights, Leiden and Boston: Brill.

Keydell, R. (1967), *Agathiae Myrinaei Historiarum Libri Quinque*, Berlin: De Gruyter.

Kiilerich, B. (2001), 'The image of Anicia Juliana in the Vienna Dioscurides: flattery or appropriation of imperial imagery?', *Symbolae Osloenses* 76: 169–90.

Kim, Y.R. (2015), *Epiphanius of Salamis: Imagining an Orthodox World*, Ann Arbor: University of Michigan Press.

Klein, K.M. (2012), 'Do good in thy good pleasure unto Zion: the patronage of Aelia Eudokia in Jerusalem', *Wiener Jahrbuch für Kunstgeschichte* 60: 85–96.

Knox, P.E. (ed.) (2009), *A Companion to Ovid*, Malden MA and Chichester: Wiley-Blackwell.

König, J. (2001), 'Favorinus' *Corinthian Oration* in its Corinthian context', *PCPS* 47, 141–71.

König, J. (2011), 'Competitiveness and anti-competitiveness in Philostratus' *Lives of the Sophists*', in N. Fisher and H. van Wees (eds), *Competition in the Ancient World*, 279–300, Swansea: The Classical Press of Wales.

Konstan, D. (1983), *Roman Comedy*, Ithaca and London: Cornell University Press.

Konstan, D. (1986), 'Love in Terence's *Eunuch*: the origins of erotic subjectivity', *AJP* 107, 369–93.

Konstan, D. (1995), *Greek Comedy and Ideology*, New York and Oxford: Oxford University Press.

Koon, S. and J. Wood (2008), 'The *Chronica Maiora* of Isidore of Seville', *e-Spania* [En ligne], 6 décembre 2008, mis en ligne le 13 décembre 2008, URL: http://journals.openedition.org/e-spania/15552; DOI: 10.4000/e-spania.15552 (accessed 23 July 2019).

Kottek, S. and Horstmanshoff, M. (eds) (2000), *From Athens to Jerusalem: Medicine in Hellenized Jewish Lore and in Early Christian Literature*, Rotterdam: Erasmus Publishing.

Kuefler, M. (1996), 'Castration and eunuchism in the middle ages', in V.L. Bullough and J.A. Brundage (eds), *Handbook of Medieval Sexuality*, 279–306, New York and London: Garland Publishing Inc.

Kuefler, M. (2001), *The Manly Eunuch: Masculinity, Gender Ambiguity, and Christian Ideology in Late Antiquity*, Chicago and London: The University of Chicago Press.

Kuefler, M. (2018), 'Physical and symbolic castration and the Holy Eunuch in late antiquity, third to sixth centuries CE', in A. Höfert, M. Mesley and S. Tolino (eds), *Celibate and Childless Men in Power: Ruling Eunuchs and Bishops in the Pre-Modern World*, 177–91, London and New York: Routledge.

Laborie, S.A. (2012), 'Le commentaire d'Eugraphius aux comédies de Térence', *Études littéraires* 43: 29–54.

Lake, K. (1926), *Eusebius, The Ecclesiastical History*, vol. 1, London and New York: William Heinemann and G.P. Putnam's Sons.

Lamar Crosby, H. (1946), *Dio Chrysostom*, vol. 4, London and Cambridge, MA: Heinemann and Harvard University Press.

Lamar Crosby, H. (1951), *Dio Chrysostom*, vol. 5, London and Cambridge, MA: Heinemann and Harvard University Press.

Lambrechts, P. (1952), 'Les fêtes "phrygiennes" de Cybèle et d'Attis', *Bulletin de l'Institut historique belge de Rome* 27: 141–70.

Lamoureux, J. and N. Aujoulat (2008), *Synésios de Cyrène*, vol. V.II, Paris: Les Belles Lettres.

Lampadaridi, A. (2016), *La conversion de Gaza au christianisme. La Vie de S. Porphyre de Gaza par Marc le Diacre (BHG 1570)*, Brussels: Société des Bollandistes.

Lancellotti, M.G. (2002), *Attis between Myth and History: King, Priest and God*, Leiden: Brill.

Lane, E.N. (1996), 'The name of Cybele's priests the "Galloi"', in E.N. Lane (ed.), *Cybele, Attis and Related Cults: Essays in Memory of M.J. Vermaseren*, 117–33, Leiden: Brill.

Lane, E. N. (ed.) (1996), *Cybele, Attis and Related Cults: Essays in Memory of M.J. Vermaseren*, Leiden: Brill.

Latham, J. (2012), '"Fabulous clap-trap": Roman masculinity, the cult of the Magna Mater, and literary constructions of the galli at Rome from the late Republic to late antiquity', *Journal of Religion* 92: 84–122.

Leach, E.W. (2007), 'Claudia Quinta (*Pro Caelio* 34) and an altar to Magna Mater', *Dictynna* [En ligne], 4, mis en ligne le 29 novembre 2010. URL: http://dictynna.revues.org/157 (accessed 7 August 2019).

Lee, A.D. (2013), *From Rome to Byzantium AD 363 to 565: The Transformation of Ancient Rome*, Edinburgh: Edinburgh University Press.

Leigh, M. (2004), *Comedy and the Rise of Rome*, Oxford: Oxford University Press.

Lenski, N. (ed.) (2012), *The Cambridge Companion to the Age of Constantine*, revised edn (orig. pub. 2006), New York: Cambridge University Press.

Levinson, J. (2000), 'Cultural androgyny in Rabbinic literature', in S. Kottek and M. Horstmanshoff (eds), *From Athens to Jerusalem: Medicine in Hellenized Jewish Lore and in Early Christian Literature*, 119–40, Rotterdam: Erasmus Publishing.

Liddell Hart, B. (1929), *The Decisive Wars of History: A Study in Strategy*, London: G. Bell and Sons Ltd.

Liddell Hart, B. (1941), *The Strategy of Indirect Approach*, London: Faber & Faber Ltd.

Liebeschuetz, J.H.W.G. (1991), *Barbarians and Bishops: Army, Church, and State in the Age of Arcadius and Chrysostom*, Oxford: Oxford University Press.

Liebeschuetz, J.H.W.G. (2011), *Ambrose and John Chrysostom: Clerics between Desert and Empire*, Oxford: Oxford University Press.

Lightfoot, J.L. (2002), 'Sacred eunuchism in the cult of the Syrian goddess', in S. Tougher (ed.), *Eunuchs in Antiquity and Beyond*, 71–86, London: The Classical Press of Wales and Duckworth.

Lightfoot, J.L. (2003), *Lucian on the Syrian Goddess*, Oxford: Oxford University Press.

Lillington-Martin, C. and E. Turquois (eds) (2018), *Procopius of Caesarea: Literary and Historical Interpretations*, London and New York: Routledge.

Littlewood, R.J. (1981), 'Poetic artistry and dynastic politics: Ovid at the Ludi Megalenses (*Fasti* 4.179–372)', *CQ* 31: 381–95.

Llewellyn-Jones, L. (2002), 'Eunuchs and the royal harem in Achaemenid Persia (559–331 BC)', in S. Tougher (ed.), *Eunuchs in Antiquity and Beyond*, 19–49, London: The Classical Press of Wales.

Long, J. (1996), *Claudian's* In Eutropium: *Or, How, When, and Why to Slander a Eunuch*, Chapel Hill and London: The University of North Carolina Press.

Lounsbury, R.C. (1991), '*Interquos et Sporus erat*: the making of Suetonius' "Nero"', *ANRW* II.33.5: 3748–79.

Lowe, J.C.B. (1983), 'The *Eunuchus*: Terence and Menander', *CQ* 33: 428–44.

Lowe, N.J. (2008), *Comedy*, Cambridge: Cambridge University Press.

Lund, H.S. (1992), *Lysimachus: A Study in Early Hellenistic Kingship*, London and New York: Routledge.

Lundström, V. (1902), *Anecdota Byzantina e codicibus Upsaliensibus cum aliis collatis*, Uppsala and Leipzig: In Libraria Lundequistiana and Otto Harrassowitz.

Lyman, J.R. (1997), 'The making of a heretic: the life of Origen in Epiphanius *Panarion* 64', in *Studia Patristica* 31: 445–51.

Maas, M. (ed.) (2005), *The Cambridge Companion to the Age of Justinian*, New York: Cambridge University Press.

MacBain, B. (1982), *Prodigy and Expiation: A Study in Religion and Politics in Republican Rome*, Brussels: Latomus.

MacDonald, E. (2015), *Hannibal: A Hellenistic Life*, New Haven and London: Yale University Press.

MacLean, R. (2018), *Freed Slaves and Roman Imperial Culture: Social Integration and the Transformation of Values*, Cambridge: Cambridge University Press.

Magie, D. (1922), *The* Scriptores Historiae Augustae, vol. 1, London and New York: William Heinemann and G.P. Putnam's Sons.

Magie, D. (1924), *The* Scriptores Historiae Augustae, vol. 2, London and New York: William Heinemann and G.P. Putnam's Sons.

Manara, E. (1983), 'Di un'ipotesi per l'individuazione dei personaggi nei pannelli del S. Vitale a Ravenna e per la loro interpretazione', *Felix Ravenna* 125–126: 13–37.

Mango, C. and R. Scott (1997), *The Chronicle of Theophanes Confessor: Byzantine and Near Eastern History AD 284–813*, Oxford: Clarendon Press.

Mango, C., M. Vickers and E.D. Francis (1992), 'The palace of Lausus at Constantinople and its collection of ancient statues', *Journal of the History of Collections* 4: 89–98.

Manuwald, G. (2011), *Roman Republican Theatre*, Cambridge: Cambridge University Press.

Maraval, P. (2013), *Les Fils de Constantin*, Paris: CNRS.

Marcovich, M. (2002), *Clementis Alexandrini* Paedagogus, Leiden and Boston: Brill.

Marcus, R. (1937), *Josephus,* Jewish Antiquities, vol. 6, London: Heinemann.

Marmon, S. (1995), *Eunuchs and Sacred Boundaries in Islamic Society*, New York and Oxford: Oxford University Press.

Marouzeau, J. (1947), *Térence. Texte établi et traduit*, vol. 1, Andrienne – Eunuque, Paris: Les Belles Lettres.

Marshall, I.H. (1980), *The Acts of the Apostles: An Introduction and Commentary*, Leicester and Grand Rapids, MI: Inter-Varsity Press and William B. Eerdmans Publishing Company.

Martin, A. and P. Canivet (2006), *Théodoret de Cyr,* Histoire ecclésiastique, vol. 1 *(livres I–II)*, Paris: Éditons du Cerf.

Martin, R.H. (1995), 'A not-so-minor character in Terence's *Eunuchus*', *CP* 90: 139–51.

Martyn, J. (2007), 'The eunuch Narses', in C. Bishop (ed.), *Text and Transmission in Medieval Europe*, 46–57, Newcastle: Cambridge Scholars Publishing.

Mason, H.J. (1979), 'Favorinus' disorder: Reifenstein's syndrome in antiquity?' *Janus* 66: 1–13.

Masterson, M. (2014), *Man to Man: Desire, Homosociality, and Authority in Late-Roman Manhood*, Columbus: The Ohio State University Press.

Mattern, S.P. (2017), 'Galen', in D.S. Richter and W.A. Johnson (eds), *The Oxford Handbook of the Second Sophistic*, 371–88, Oxford and New York: Oxford University Press.

Matthews, J. (1989), *The Roman Empire of Ammianus*, London: Duckworth.

Matthews Sanford, E. and W. McAllen Green (1965), *St Augustine,* City of God, vol. 5, Cambridge, MA: Harvard University Press.

Mayer, W. and P. Allen (2000), *John Chrysostom*, London and New York: Routledge.

McCracken, G.E. (1949), *Arnobius of Sicca,* The Case against the Pagans, 2 vols, Cork: The Mercier Press Ltd.

McEvoy, M.A. (2013), *Child Emperor Rule in the Late Roman West,* AD *367–455*, Oxford: Oxford University Press.

McLynn, N. (1996), 'The fourth-century "taurobolium"', *Phoenix* 50: 312–30.

McNeile, A.H. (1915), *The Gospel According to St. Matthew. The Greek Text with Introduction, Notes, and Indices*, London: Macmillan.

Merrills, A. (2004), 'Vandals, Romans and Berbers: understanding late antique North Africa', in A. Merrills (ed.), *Vandals, Romans and Berbers: New Perspectives on Late Antique North Africa*, 3–28, Aldershot and Burlington, VT: Ashgate.

Messis, C. (2014), *Les eunuques à Byzance, entre réalité et imaginaire*, Centre d'études byzantines, néo-helleniques et sud-est européenes: Paris.

Meyer, R.T. (1964), *Palladius,* The Lausiac History, Mahwah NJ: Paulist Press.

Meyer, R.T. (1985), *Palladius,* Dialogue on the Life of St John Chrysostom, New York and Mahwah, NJ: Newman Press.

Miles, G. (2017), 'Philostratus', in D.S. Richter and Johnson (eds), *The Oxford Handbook of the Second Sophistic*, 273–89, Oxford and New York: Oxford University Press.

Milgrom, J. (2000), *Leviticus 17-22: A New Translation with Introduction and Commentary*, New York: Doubleday.

Millar, F. (1964), *A Study of Cassius Dio*, Oxford: Oxford University Press.

Miller, D.J.D. and P. Sarris (2018), *The Novels of Justinian: A Complete Annotated English Translation*, 2 vols, Cambridge: Cambridge University Press.

Minns, D. and P. Parvis (2009), *Justin, Philosopher and Martyr:* Apologies, Oxford: Oxford University Press.

Mommsen, Th. and P.M. Meyer (1954), *Theodosiani Libri XVI*, I.2, Berlin: Weidmann.

Montgomery, J.A. (1927), *A Critical and Exegetical Commentary on The Book of Daniel*, Edinburgh: T&T Clark.

Moore, F.G. (1943), *Livy*, vol. 7, *Books 26–27*, London and Cambridge, MA: William Heinemann Ltd and Harvard University Press.

Moore, F.G. (1949) *Livy*, vol. 8, *Books 28–30*, London and Cambridge, MA: William Heinemann Ltd and Harvard University Press.

Moorhead, J. (1994), *Justinian*, London and New York: Longman.

Moravcsik, Gy. and R.J.H. Jenkins (1967), *Constantine Porphyrogenitus,* De Administrando Imperio, Washington DC: Dumbarton Oaks.

Moreschini, C. and J.-C. Fredouille (1985), *Tertullien, Exhortation à la chasteté*, Paris: Éditions du Cerf.
Morey, C.M. (1931), 'The Vatican Terence', *CP* 26: 374–85.
Moxnes, H. (2003), *Putting Jesus in His Place: A Radical Vision of Household and Kingdom*, Louisville and London: Westminster John Knox Press.
Mudd, M.M. (1989), *Studies in the Reign of Constantius II*, New York: Carlton Press.
Murison, C.L. (1999), *Rebellion and Reconstruction: Galba to Domitian. An Historical Commentary on Cassius Dio's Roman History Books 64-67 (A.D. 68-96)*, Atlanta, GA: Scholars Press.
Murison, C.L. (2004), 'Cassius Dio on Nervan legislation (68.2.4): nieces and eunuchs', *Historia* 53: 343–55.
Murphy, T. (2004), *Pliny the Elder's Natural History: The Empire in the Encyclopedia*, Oxford: Oxford University Press.
Murray, J. (1999), 'Mystical castration: some reflections on Peter Abelard, Hugh of Lincoln and sexual control', in J. Murray (ed.), *Conflicted Identities and Multiple Masculinities: Men in the Medieval West*, 73–91, New York and London: Garland Publishing Inc.
Nanda, S. (1999), *Neither Man nor Woman: The Hijras of India*, 2nd edn, Belmont, CA: Wadsworth.
Nathan, G. (2011), 'The *Vienna Dioscorides*' *dedicatio* to Anicia Juliana: a usurpation of imperial patronage?' in L. Garland and G. Nathan (eds), *Basileia: Essays on Imperium and Culture in Honour of E. M. and M. J. Jeffreys*, 95–102, Brisbane: Australian Association for Byzantine Studies.
Nau, F. (1910), *Nestorius, Le livre d'Héraclide de Damas*, Paris: Letouzey et Ané.
Newlands, C.E. (2002), *Statius' Silvae and the Poetics of Empire*, Cambridge: Cambridge University Press.
Nock, A.D. (1925), 'Eunuchs in ancient religion', *Archiv für Religionswissenschaft* 23: 25–33, repr. in A.D. Nock, *Essays on Religion and the Ancient World*, vol. 1, 7–15, Oxford: Clarendon Press.
Nock, A.D. (1972), *Essays on Religion and the Ancient World*, 2 vols, Oxford: Clarendon Press.
Norman, A.F. (1969), *Libanius, Selected Works*, vol. 1, *The Julianic Orations*, Cambridge, MA and London: Harvard University Press and William Heinemann Ltd.
Norman, A.F. (2000), *Antioch as a Centre of Hellenic Culture as Observed by Libanius*, Liverpool: Liverpool University Press.
Norwood, G. (1923), *The Art of Terence*, Oxford: Basil Blackwell.
O'Donnell, J.J. (1981), 'Liberius the patrician', *Traditio* 37: 31–72.
Oman, C. (1898), *A History of the Art of War. The Middle Ages from the Fourth Century to the Fourteenth Century*, London: Methuen.
Opitz, H.-G. (1935–41), *Athanasius Werke* 2.1, *Die Apologien*, Berlin and Leipzig: De Gruyter.
Opsomer, J. (1997), 'Favorinus versus Epictetus on the philosophical heritage of Plutarch. A debate on epistemology', in J. Mossman (ed.), *Plutarch and his Intellectual World: Essays on Plutarch*, 17–39, London and Swansea: Duckworth in association with The Classical Press of Wales.
Osborn, E. (2005), *Clement of Alexandria*, Cambridge: Cambridge University Press.
Oulton, J.E.L. (1932), *Eusebius*, The Ecclesiastical History, vol. 2, London and New York: William Heinemann and G.P. Putnam's Sons.
Pack, R.A. (1963), *Artemidori Daldiani Onirocriticon Libri V*, Leipzig: Teubner.
Parker, H.N. (1996), 'Plautus vs. Terence: audience and popularity re-examined', *AJP* 117: 585–617.

Parnell, D.A. (2017), *Justinian's Men: Careers and Relationships of Byzantine Army Officers, 518–610*, London: Palgrave Macmillan.

Parvis, S. and P. Foster (eds) (2007), *Justin Martyr and His Worlds*, Minneapolis: Fortress Press.

Paschoud, P. (2000), *Zosime,* Histoire nouvelle, vol. 1, *livres I–II*, Paris: Les Belles Lettres.

Patlagean, E. (1976), 'L'histoire de la femme déguisée en moine et l'évolution de la sainteté féminine à Byzance', *Studi Medievali* 17: 597–623.

Patrich, J. (1995), *Sabas, Leader of Palestinian Monasticism: A Comparative Study in Eastern Monasticism, Fourth to Seventh Centuries*, Washington, DC: Dumbarton Oaks.

Patterson, O. (1982), *Slavery and Social Death: A Comparative Study*, Cambridge, MA and London: Harvard University Press.

Penella, R.J. (1990), *Greek Philosophers and Sophists in the Fourth Century AD: Studies in Eunapius of Sardis*, Leeds: Francis Cairns.

Penzer, N.M. (1936), *The Harem: An Account of the Institution as it Existed in the Palace of the Turkish Sultans with a History of the Grand Seraglio from its Foundation to Modern Times*, London: George G. Harrap & Co.

Perrin, B. (1920), *Plutarch's* Lives, vol. 9, London and New York: William Heinemann and G.P. Putnam's Sons.

Peters, E. (2003), *Paul the Deacon,* History of the Lombards. *Translated by William Dudley Foulke*, Philadelphia: University of Pennsylvania Press.

Petkas, A. (2018), 'The king in words: performance and fiction in Synesius' *De Regno*', *AJP* 139: 123–51.

Pharr, C. (1952), *The Theodosian Code and Novels and the Sirmondian Constitutions*, New York: Greenwood Press.

Philips, J.E. (2000), 'The persistence of slave officials in the Sokoto caliphate', in M. Toru and J.E. Philips (eds), *Slave Elites in the Middle East and Africa: A Comparative Study*, 215–34, London and New York: Kegan Paul International.

Phillips, A. (1973), *Deuteronomy: Commentary*, Cambridge: Cambridge University Press.

Pizarro, J.M. (1995), *Writing Ravenna: The* Liber Pontificalis *of Andreas Agnellus*, Ann Arbor: The University of Michigan Press.

Platnauer, M. (1922), *Claudian*, vol. 1, London and New York: William Heinemann Ltd and G.P. Putnam's Sons.

Prag, J. and I. Repath (eds) (2009), *Petronius: A Handbook*, Chichester and Malden, MA: Wiley-Blackwell.

Preves, S.E. (2005), *Intersex and Identity: The Contested Self*, New Brunswick, NJ: Rutgers University Press.

Price, R.M. (1991), *Cyril of Scythopolis: The Lives of the Monks of Palestine*, Kalamazoo, MI: Cistercian Publications.

Pringle, D. (2001), *The Defence of Byzantine Africa from Justinian to the Arab Conquest*, Oxford: Hadrian Books Ltd.

Rackham, H. (1940), *Pliny,* Natural History, vol. 3, Cambridge, MA and London: Harvard University Press and William Heinemann Ltd.

Rackham, H. (1942), *Pliny,* Natural History, vol. 2, Cambridge, MA and London: Harvard University Press and William Heinemann Ltd.

Radice, B. (1976), *Terence, The Comedies. Translated with an Introduction*, Harmondsworth: Penguin Books.

Rajak, T. (1983), *Josephus: The Historian and his Society*, London: Duckworth.

Rance, P. (2005), 'Narses and the battle of Taginae (Busta Gallorum) 552: Procopius and sixth-century warfare', *Historia* 54: 424–72.

Rapp, C. (2001), 'Mark the Deacon, *Life of St Porphyry of Gaza*', in T. Head (ed.), *Medieval Hagiography: An Anthology*, 53–75, New York and London: Routledge.
Rauhala, M. (2011), 'Devotion and deviance: the cult of Cybele and the others within', in M. Kahlos (ed.), *The Faces of the Other: Religious Rivalry and Ethnic Encounters in the Later Roman World*, 51–82, Turnhout: Brepols.
Rauhala, M. (2016), '*Obscena galli praesentia*: dehumanizing Cybele's eunuch-priests through disgust', in D. Lateiner and D. Spatharas (eds), *The Ancient Emotion of Disgust*, 235–52, New York: Oxford University Press.
Rebenich, S. (2002), *Jerome*, London and New York: Routledge.
Reddy, G. (2005), *With Respect to Sex: Negotiating Hijra Identity in South India*, Chicago, IL and London: The University of Chicago Press.
Rees, R. (2004), *Diocletian and the Tetrarchy*, Edinburgh: Edinburgh University Press.
Reid, B.H. (2008), 'Hart, Sir Basil Henry Liddell (1895–1970)', *Oxford Dictionary of National Biography*, https://doi.org/10.1093/ref:odnb/33737 (accessed 29 July 2019).
Renault, M. (1972), *The Persian Boy*, London: Longman.
Renault, M. (1975), *The Nature of Alexander*, London: Allen Lane.
Repath, I. (2007a), 'Anonymus Latinus, *Book of Physiognomy*', in S. Swain (ed.), *Seeing the Face, Seeing the Soul. Polemon's Physiognomy from Classical Antiquity to Medieval Islam*, 549–635, Oxford: Oxford University Press.
Repath, I. (2007b), 'The *Physiognomy* of Adamantius the Sophist', in S. Swain (ed.), *Seeing the Face, Seeing the Soul. Polemon's Physiognomy from Classical Antiquity to Medieval Islam*, 487–547, Oxford: Oxford University Press.
Retief, F.P. and J.F.G. Cilliers, (2003), 'Congenital eunuchism and Favorinus', *South African Medical Journal* 93: 73–6.
Retief, F. P. and L. Cilliers (2005), 'Eunuchs in the Bible', *Acta Theologica Supplementum* 7: 247–58.
Richard, L. (1966), 'Juvénal et les galles de Cybèle', *Revue de l'histoire des religions* 169: 51–67.
Richardson, L., Jr. (1977), *Propertius Elegies I–IV*, Norman, OK: University of Oklahoma Press.
Richlin, A. (2017), 'Retrosexuality: sex in the second sophistic', in D.S. Richter and W.A. Johnson (eds), *The Oxford Handbook of the Second Sophistic*, 115–35, Oxford and New York: Oxford University Press.
Richter, D.S. (2017), 'Lucian of Samosata', in D.S. Richter and W.A. Johnson (eds), *The Oxford Handbook of the Second Sophistic*, 327–44, Oxford and New York: Oxford University Press.
Richter, D. S. and W.A. Johnson (eds) (2017), *The Oxford Handbook of the Second Sophistic*, Oxford and New York: Oxford University Press.
Ridley, R.T. (1982), *Zosimus, New History*, Canberra: Australian Association for Byzantine Studies.
Rieger, A.-K. (2009), 'Tradition locale contre unité supra-régionale: le culte de Magna Mater', *Trivium* 4: 1–34.
Ringrose, K. M. (1996), 'Eunuchs as cultural mediators', *BF* 23: 75–93.
Ringrose, K.M. (1999), 'Passing the test of sanctity: denial of sexuality and involuntary castration', in L. James (ed.), *Desire and Denial in Byzantium*, 123–37, Aldershot: Ashgate.
Ringrose, K.M. (2003a), 'Reconfiguring the prophet Daniel: gender, sanctity, and castration in Byzantium', in S. Farmer and C.B. Pasternack (eds), *Gender and Difference in the Middle Ages*, 73–106, Minneapolis and London: University of Minnesota Press.

Ringrose, K.M. (2003b), *The Perfect Servant: Eunuchs and the Social Construction of Gender in Byzantium*, Chicago and London: The University of Chicago Press.

Robertson, A. (1892), *Select Writings and Letters of Athanasaius, Bishop of Alexandria*, in *Nicene and Post-Nicene Fathers*, vol. 4, Second Series, Buffalo, NY: Christian Literature Co.

Roisman, J. (2012), *Alexander's Veterans and the Early Wars of the Successors*, Austin: University of Texas Press.

Rolfe, J.C. (1927), *Aulus Gellius,* Attic Nights, 3 vols, Cambridge, MA and London: Harvard University Press and William Heinemann.

Rolfe, J.C. (1940–52), *Ammianus Marcellinus*, 3 vols, Cambridge, MA and London: Harvard University Press and William Heinemann Ltd.

Roller, L.E. (1999), *In Search of God the Mother: The Cult of Anatolian Cybele*, Berkeley, Los Angeles, London: University of California Press.

Roller, L.E. (2006), 'The priests of the Mother – gender and place', in C.C. Mattusch, A.A. Donohue and A. Brauer (eds), *Common Ground: Archaeology, Art, Science and Humanities*, 52–5, Oxford: Oxbow Books.

Roscoe, W. (2006), 'Priests of the goddess: gender transgression in ancient religion', *History of Religions* 35: 195–230.

Rosen, R.M. and I. Sluiter (eds) (2003), *Andreia: Studies in Manliness and Courage in Classical Antiquity*, Leiden and Boston: Brill.

Ross, A.J. (2016), *Ammianus' Julian: Narrative and Genre in the* Res Gestae, Oxford: Oxford University Press.

Rotman, Y. (2015a), 'The imperial eunuch: traces of Hellenistic institution in Roman epigraphy', *Dike* 18: 143–57.

Rotman, Y. (2015b), 'The paradox of Roman eunuchism: a juridical-historical approach', *Scripta Classica Israelica* 34: 129–50.

Rouse, W.H.D. and M.F. Smith (1992), *Lucretius,* De Rerum Natura, Cambridge MA and London: Harvard University Press.

Rouselle, A. (1988), *Porneia: On Desire and the Body in Antiquity*, trans. F. Pheasant, New York: Basil Blackwell.

Rouselle, A. (2004), *La contamination spirituelle. Science, droit et religion dans l'Antiquité*, 2nd edn, Paris: Les Belles Lettres.

Rushton Fairclough, H. (1916–18), *Virgil*, 2 vols, London and New York: William Heinemann and G.P. Putnam's Sons.

Sarantis, A. (2010), 'The Justinianic Herules: from allied barbarians to Roman provincials', in F. Curta (ed.), *Neglected Barbarians*, 361–402, Turnout: Brepols.

Sarantis, A. (2013), 'Military encounters and diplomatic affairs in the north Balkans during the reigns of Anastasius and Justinian', in A. Sarantis and N. Christie (eds), *War and Warfare in Late Antiquity*, vol. 2, 759–808, Leiden and Boston: Brill.

Sarantis, A. (2016), *Justinian's Balkan Wars: Campaigning, Diplomacy and Development in Illyricum, Thrace and the Northern World* A.D. *527–65*, Prenton: Francis Cairns.

Sarantis, A. and Christie, N. (eds) (2013), *War and Warfare in Late Antiquity*, 2 vols, Leiden and Boston: Brill.

Schlinkert, D. (1994), 'Der Hofeunuch in der Spätantike: Ein gefährlicher Außenseiter?' *Hermes* 122: 342–59.

Schlinkert, D. (1996), Ordo senatorius *und nobilitas: Die Konstitution des Senatsadels in der Spätantike. Mit einem Appendix über den* praepositus sacri cubiculi*, den 'allmächtigen' Eunuchen am kaiserlichen Hof*, Stuttgart: Franz Steiner.

Scholten, H. (1995), *Der Eunuch in Kaisernähe: zur politischen und sozialen Bedeutung des* praepositus sacri cubiculi *im. 4. und 5. Jahrhundert n. Chr*, Frankfurt: Peter Lang.

Scholten, H. (1998), 'Der oberste Hofeunuch. Die politische Effizienz eines gesellschaftlich Diskriminierten', in A. Winterling (ed.), *Comitatus: Beiträge zur Erforschung des spätantiken Kaiserhofes*, 51–73, Berlin: De Gruyter.
Schwartz, E. and Mommsen, T. (1903), *Eusebius Werke*, vol. 2.1, Leipzig: J.C. Hinrichs.
Schwartz, E. (1922–3), *Acta conciliorum oecumenicorum*, 1.4, Berlin and Leipzig: De Gruyter.
Schwartz, E. (1936), *Acta conciliorum oecumenicorum*, 2.5, Berlin and Leipzig: De Gruyter.
Schwartz, E. (1939), *Kyrillos von Skythopolis*, Leipzig: J.C. Hinrichs Verlag.
Schweckendiek, H. (1992), *Claudians Invektive gegen Eutrop* (In Eutropium). *Ein Kommentar*, Hildesheim: Olms-Weidmann.
Scott-Kilvert, I. (1965), *Makers of Rome: Nine Lives by Plutarch*, London: Penguin Books.
Seeck, O. (1962), *Notitia Dignitatum*, Frankurt: Minerva (orig. pub. 1876).
Segal, E. (ed.) (2001), *Oxford Readings in Menander, Plautus, and Terence*, Oxford: Oxford University Press.
Seng, H. and L.M. Hoffmann (eds) (2012), *Synesios von Kyrene: Politik – Literatur – Philosophie*, Turnhout: Brepols.
Shackleton Bailey, D.R. (1993), *Martial,* Epigrams, 3 vols, Cambridge MA and London: Harvard University Press.
Shackleton Bailey, D.R. (2000), *Valerius Maximus,* Memorable Doings and Sayings, 2 vols, Cambridge, MA and London: Harvard University Press.
Shackleton Bailey, D.R. (2003), *Statius,* Silvae, Cambridge, MA and London: Harvard University Press.
Shaw, B. (1987), 'The family in late antiquity: the experience of Augustine', *P&P* 115: 3–51.
Shaw, T.M. (1997), 'Creation, virginity and diet in fourth-century Christianity: Basil of Ancyra's *On the True Purity of Virginity*', *Gender & History* 9: 579–96.
Sidéris, G. (2017), 'Les débats sur l'eunucité et la nature physiologique des eunuques à Byzance (IVe–XIIe siècle)', in E. Pibiri and F. Abbot (eds), *Féminité et masculinité altérées: transgression et inversion des genres au Moyen Âge*, 145–206, Florence: SISMEL Edizioni del Galluzzo.
Sidéris, G. (2018), 'The rise and fall of the High Chamberlain Eutropius: eunuch identity, the third sex and power in fourth-century Byzantium', in C. Fletcher et al. (eds), *The Palgrave Handbook of Masculinity and Political Culture in Europe*, 63–84, London: Palgrave Macmillan.
Simmons, M.B. (1995), *Arnobius of Sicca: Religious Conflict and Competition in the Age of Diocletian*, Oxford: Clarendon Press.
Skinner, M.B. (1993), '*Ego mulier*: the construction of male sexuality in Catullus', *Helios* 20: 107–31.
Smith, C.J. (1998), 'Onasander on how to be a general', in M. Austin, J. Harries and C. Smith (eds), *Modus Operandi: Essays in Honour of Geoffrey Rickman*, 151–66, London: Institute of Classical Studies.
Smith, J.O. (1996), 'The high priests of the temple of Artemis at Ephesus', in E.N. Lane (ed.), *Cybele, Attis and Related Cults: Essays in Memory of M.J. Vermaseren*, 323–35, Leiden: Brill.
Smithies, A. and J.M. Duffy (2013), *Nicetas David,* The Life of Patriarch Ignatius, Washington, DC: Dumbarton Oaks.
Solevåg, A.R. (2016), 'No nuts? No problem! Disability, stigma, and the baptized eunuch in Acts 8:26–40', *Biblical Interpretation* 24: 81–99.
Spencer, D. (2002), *The Roman Alexander: Reading a Cultural Myth*, Exeter: University of Exeter Press.
Spencer, F.S. (1992), 'The Ethiopian eunuch and his Bible: a social-science analysis', *Biblical Theology Bulletin* 22: 155–65.

Spencer, F.S. (1997), *Acts*, Sheffield: Sheffield Academic Press.
Stallman-Pacitti, C.J. (1991), *Cyril of Scythopolis: A Study in Hagiography as Apology*, Brookline, MA: Hellenic College Press.
Starks, J.H., Jr. (2013), 'opera in bello, in otio, in negotio: Terence and Rome in the 160s BCE', in A. Augoustakis and A. Traill (eds), *A Companion to Terence*, 132–55, Chichester: Wiley-Blackwell.
Stein, E. (1949), *Histoire du Bas-Empire*, vol. 2, *De la disparition de l'Empire d'Occident à la mort de Justinien (476–565)*, Paris/Brussels/Amsterdam: Desclée de Brouwer.
Steinacher, R. (2010), 'The Herules: fragments of a history', in F. Curta (ed.), *Neglected Barbarians*, 319–60, Turnout: Brepols.
Stephens, W.R.W. (1889), *Saint Chrysostom: On the Priesthood, Ascetic Treatises, Select Homilies and Letters, Homilies on the Statues*, in *Nicene and Post-Nicene Fathers*, vol. 9, First Series, Buffalo, NY: Christian Literature Co.
Stevenson, W. (1995), 'The rise of eunuchs in Greco-Roman antiquity', *Journal of the History of Sexuality* 5: 495–511.
Stevenson, W. (2002), 'Eunuchs and early Christianity', in S. Tougher (ed.), *Eunuchs in Antiquity and Beyond*, 123–42, London: The Classical Press of Wales and Duckworth.
Stewart, M.E. (2015), 'The *andreios* eunuch-commander Narses: sign of a decoupling of martial virtues and masculinity in the early Byzantine empire?', *Cerae* 2: 1–25.
Stewart, M.E. (2017), 'Breaking down barriers: eunuchs in Italy and North Africa, 400–620', in A. Brown and B. Neil (eds), *Byzantine Culture in Translation*, 33–54, Leiden and Boston: Brill.
Strootman, R. (2017), 'Eunuchs, renegades and concubines: the "paradox of power" and the promotion of favourites in the Hellenistic empires', in A. Erskine, L. Llewellyn-Jones and S. Wallace (eds), *The Hellenistic Court: Monarchic Power and Elite Society from Alexander to Cleopatra*, 121–43, Swansea: The Classical Press of Wales.
Sullivan, J.P. (1991), *Martial: The Unexpected Classic. A Literary and Historical Study*, Cambridge: Cambridge University Press.
Summers, K. (1996), 'Lucretius' Roman Cybele', in E.N. Lane (ed.), *Cybele, Attis and Related Cults: Essays in Memory of M.J. Vermaseren*, 337–65, Leiden: Brill.
Swain, S. (1989), 'Favorinus and Hadrian', *ZPE* 79: 150–8.
Swain, S. (ed.) (2000), *Dio Chrysostom: Politics, Letters and Philosophy*, Oxford and New York: Oxford University Press.
Swain, S. (ed.) (2007), *Seeing the Face, Seeing the Soul. Polemon's* Physiognomy *from Classical Antiquity to Medieval Islam*, Oxford: Oxford University Press.
Syme, R. (1983a), *Historia Augusta Papers*, Oxford: Clarendon Press.
Syme, R. (1983b), 'The proconsuls of Asia under Antoninus Pius', *ZPE* 51: 271–90.
Takács, S.A. (1996), 'Magna Deum Mater Idaea, Cybele, and Catullus' *Attis*', in E.N. Lane (ed.), *Cybele, Attis and Related Cults: Essays in Memory of M.J. Vermaseren*, 367–86, Leiden: Brill.
Talbot, A.-M. (1996), *Holy Women of Byzantium: Ten Saints' Lives in English Translation*, Washington, DC: Dumbarton Oaks.
Teitler, H.C. (1992), 'Ammianus and Constantius. Image and reality', in J. den Boeft, D. den Hengst and H.C. Teitler (eds), *Cognitio Gestorum: The Historiographic Art of Ammianus Marcellinus*, 117–22, Amsterdam: Royal Netherlands Academy of Arts and Sciences.
Tenney, F. (1933), 'On Suetonius' life of Terence', *AJP* 54: 269–73.
Teppedino Guerra, A. (2007), *Favorino di Arelate. L'esilio (Pap. Vat. Gr. 11 verso)*, Rome: Edizioni dell'Ateneo.

Thomas, G.S.R. (1971), 'Flavius Antonius Eustochius (*CIL* VI, 508) n'était pas un archigalle', *Revue belge de philologie et d'histoire* 49: 55–65.

Thomas, J. and A.C. Hero (2000), *Byzantine Monastic Foundation Documents: A Complete Translation of the Surviving Founders'* Typika *and Testaments*, vol. 3, Washington, DC: Dumbarton Oaks.

Thompson, E.A. (1947), *The Historical Work of Ammianus Marcellinus*, Cambridge: Cambridge University Press.

Tobin, J. (1997), *Herodes Attikos and the City of Athens: Patronage and Conflict under the Antonines*, Amsterdam: J.C. Gieben.

Tougher, S. (1997), 'Byzantine eunuchs: an overview, with special reference to their creation and origin', in L. James (ed.), *Women, Men and Eunuchs: Gender in Byzantium*, 168–84, London and New York: Routledge.

Tougher, S. (1999), 'Ammianus and the eunuchs', in J.W. Drijvers and D. Hunt (eds), *The Late Roman World and its Historian: Interpreting Ammianus Marcellinus*, 64–73, London and New York: Routledge.

Tougher, S. (2002), 'In or out? Origins of court eunuchs', in S. Tougher (ed.), *Eunuchs in Antiquity and Beyond*, 143–59, London: The Classical Press of Wales and Duckworth.

Tougher, S. (ed.) (2002), *Eunuchs in Antiquity and Beyond*, London: The Classical Press of Wales and Duckworth.

Tougher, S. (2004), 'Holy eunuchs! Masculinity and eunuch saints in Byzantium', in P.H. Cullum and K.J. Lewis (eds), *Holiness and Masculinity in the Middle Ages*, 93–108, Cardiff: University of Wales Press.

Tougher, S. (2005), 'Two views on the gender identity of Byzantine eunuchs', in A. Shaw and S. Ardener (eds), *Changing Sex and Bending Gender*, 60–73, New York and Oxford: Berghahn Books.

Tougher, S. (2006), '"The angelic life": monasteries for eunuchs', in E.M. Jeffreys (ed.), *Byzantine Style, Religion and Civilization: In Honour of Sir Steven Runciman*, 238–52, Cambridge: Cambridge University Press.

Tougher, S. (2007), *Julian the Apostate*, Edinburgh: Edinburgh University Press.

Tougher, S. (2008a), *The Eunuch in Byzantine History and Society*, London and New York: Routledge.

Tougher, S. (2008b), 'The Renault Bagoas: the treatment of Alexander the Great's eunuch in Mary Renault's *The Persian Boy*', *New Voices in Classical Reception Studies* 3: 77–89.

Tougher, S. (2012), 'Imperial blood: family relationships in the dynasty of Constantine the Great', in M. Harlow and L. Larsson Lovén (eds), *Families in the Roman and Late Antique World*, 181–98, London: Continuum.

Tougher, S. (2013), 'The aesthetics of castration: the beauty of Roman eunuchs', in L. Tracy (ed.), *Castration and Culture in the Middle Ages*, 48–72, Cambridge: D.S. Brewer.

Tougher, S. (2015a), 'Eunuchs in the east, men in the west? Dis/unity, gender and orientalism in the fourth century', in R. Dijkstra, S. van Poppel and D. Slootjes (eds), *East and West in the Roman Empire of the Fourth Century: An End to Unity?*, 147–63, Leiden and Boston: Brill.

Tougher, S. (2015b), 'Robert Graves as historical novelist: *Count Belisarius* – genesis, gender, and truth', in A.G.G. Gibson (ed.), *Robert Graves and the Classical Tradition*, 77–97, Oxford: Oxford University Press.

Tougher, S. (2018), 'Byzantine court eunuchs and the Macedonian dynasty (867–1056): family, power and gender', in A. Höfert, M. Mesley and S. Tolino (eds), *Celibate and Childless Men in Power: Ruling Eunuchs and Bishops in the Pre-Modern World*, 229–45, London and New York: Routledge.

Tougher, S. (forthcoming a), 'Byzantine eunuchs as generals: the case of Narses', in M. Grünbart (ed.), *Verflechtungen zwischen Byzanz und dem Orient*.
Tougher, S. (forthcoming b), 'Julian the apologist: Christians and pagans on the Mother of the Gods', in R. Flower and M. Ludlow (eds), *Rhetoric and Religious Identity in Late Antiquity*.
Tracy, L. (ed.) (2013), *Castration and Culture in the Middle Ages*, Cambridge: D.S. Brewer.
Treggiari, S. (1969), *Roman Freedmen During the Late Republic*, Oxford: Clarendon Press.
Trigg, J.W. (1998), *Origen*, London and New York: Routledge.
Tsai, S.-s.H. (1996), *The Eunuchs in the Ming Dynasty*, Albany, NY: State University of New York Press.
Turcan, R. (1996), *The Cults of the Roman Empire*, trans. Antonia Nevill, Oxford and Cambridge, MA: Blackwell.
Turner, A.J. and G. Torello-Hill (eds) (2015), *Terence between Late Antiquity and the Age of Printing: Illustration, Commentary and Performance*, Leiden and Boston: Brill.
Urbainczyk, T. (2002), *Theodoret of Cyrrhus: The Bishop and the Holy Man*, Ann Arbor: The University of Michigan Press.
Vaggione, R.P. (2000), *Eunomius of Cyzicus and the Nicene Revolution*, Oxford: Oxford University Press.
Vaillant, V. (1943), De Virginitate *de Saint Basile*, Paris: Institut d'Études Slaves.
Vermaseren, M.J. (1966), *The Legend of Attis in Greek and Roman Art*, Leiden: Brill.
Vermaseren, M.J. (1977), *Cybele and Attis, the Myth and the Cult*, London: Thames & Hudson.
Victor, B. (2013), 'History of the text and scholia', in A. Augoustakis and A. Traill (eds), *A Companion to Terence*, 343–62, Chichester: Wiley-Blackwell.
Victor, B. (2014), 'The transmission of Terence', in M. Fontaine and A.C. Scafuro (eds), *The Oxford Handbook of Greek and Roman Comedy*, 699–716, New York: Oxford University Press.
Vout, C. (2002), 'Nero and Sporus', in J.-M. Croisille and Y. Perrin (eds), *Neronia VI: Rome à l'époque néronienne*, 493–502, Brussels: Latomus.
Vout, C. (2007), *Power and Eroticism in Imperial Rome*, Cambridge: Cambridge University Press.
Walker, J.D. (1985), 'Circles of contingency: Alexander Pope's *Epistle to Arbuthnot*', *South Central Review* 2: 31–43.
Walton, F.R. (1957), *Diodorus Siculus*, Library of History, vol. 11, Cambridge, MA and London: Harvard University Press and William Heinemann.
Ware, C. (2012), *Claudian and the Roman Epic Tradition*, Cambridge: Cambridge University Press.
Warmington, B.H. (1977), *Suetonius, Nero: Text with Introduction and Notes*, Bristol: Bristol Classical Press.
Weaver, P.R.C. (1967), 'Social mobility in the early Roman empire: the evidence of the imperial freemen and slaves', *P&P* 37: 3–20.
West, D. (2003), *Virgil, The Aeneid*, London: Penguin Books.
West, D. (2008), *Horace, The Complete Odes and Epodes*, Oxford: Oxford University Press.
Whately, C. (2016), *Battles and Generals: Combat, Culture, and Didacticism in Procopius' Wars*, Leiden and Boston: Brill.
Whitby, Michael (1999), 'Images of Constantius', in J.W. Drijvers and D. Hunt (eds), *The Late Roman World and its Historian: Interpreting Ammianus Marcellinus*, 77–88, London and New York: Routledge.

Whitby, Michael (2000), *The* Ecclesiastical History *of Evagrius Scholasticus*, Liverpool: Liverpool University Press.
Whitby, Michael and Mary Whitby (1986), *The* History *of Theophylact Simocatta: An English Translation with Introduction and Notes*, Oxford: Clarendon Press.
Whitby, Michael and Mary Whitby (1989), Chronicon Paschale *284–628 AD. Translated with Notes and Introduction*, Liverpool: Liverpool University Press.
White, R.J. (1975), *The Interpretation of Dreams.* Oneirocritica *by Artemidorus. Translation and Commentary*, Park Ridge, NJ: Noyes Press.
Whitmarsh, T. (2001), *Greek Literature and the Roman Empire: The Politics of Imitation*, Oxford: Oxford University Press.
Whitmarsh, T. (2005), *The Second Sophistic*, Oxford: Oxford University Press.
Whittaker, C.R. (1969), *Herodian*, vol. 1, Cambridge, MA and London: Harvard University Press and William Heinemann Ltd.
Wiedemann, T. (1986), 'An early Irish eunuch?', *Liverpool Classical Monthly* 11: 139–40.
Williams, C.A. (2010), *Roman Homosexuality*, 2nd edn, Oxford and New York: Oxford University Press.
Williams, F. (1994), *The* Panarion *of Epiphanius of Salamis, Books II and III (Sects 47–80, De Fide)*, Leiden/New York/Köln: Brill.
Williams, R. (2001), *Arius: Heresy and Tradition*, revised edn, London: SCM Press.
Williamson, G.A. (1964), *Eusebius,* The History of the Church, Harmondsworth: Penguin Books Ltd.
Wilson, W. (1867), *The Writings of Clement of Alexandria*, Edinburgh: T&T Clark.
Winston, D. (1979), *The Wisdom of Solomon: A New Translation with Introduction and Commentary*, New York: Doubleday.
Wiseman, T.P. (1984), 'Cybele, Virgil and Augustus', in T. Woodman and D. West (eds), *Poetry and Politics in the Age of Augustus*, 117–28 and 225–9, Cambridge: Cambridge University Press.
Wittfogel, K.A. (1957), *Oriental Despotism: A Comparative Study of Total Power*, New Haven: Yale University Press.
Wolf, K.B. (2008), '*Chronicon*, Isidore of Seville, *c.* 616', *Medieval Texts in Translation*, online 22 May 2009, https://scholarship.claremont.edu/cgi/viewcontent.cgi?article=1044&context=pomona_fac_pub (accessed 23 July, 2019).
Wood, J. (2012), *The Politics of Identity in Visigothic Spain: Religion and Power in the Histories of Isidore of Seville*, Leiden: Brill.
Woodman, A.J. (ed.) (2009), *The Cambridge Companion to Tacitus*, Cambridge: Cambridge University Press.
Woodruff, J.E. (1988), *The* Historia Epitomata *(Third Book) of the* Chronicle *of Fredegar: An Annotated Translation and Historical Analysis of Interpolated Material*, PhD Dissertation: The University of Nebraska-Lincoln.
Woods, D. (2006/07), 'Nero, "Doryphorus", and the Christians', *Eranos* 104: 49–59.
Woods, D. (2009), 'Nero and Sporus', *Latomus* 68: 73–82.
Wortley, J. (1992), *John Moschos,* The Spiritual Meadow (Pratum Spirituale*)*, Kalamazoo, MI: Cistercian Publications.
Wortley, J. (2012), *The Book of the Elders: Sayings of the Desert Fathers: The Systematic Collection*, Collegeville, MN: Liturgical Press.
Wright, D.H. (2006), *The Lost Late Antique Illustrated Terence*, Vatican City: Biblioteca Apostolica Vaticana.
Wright, J.L. and M.J. Chan (2012), 'King and eunuch: Isaiah 56:1–8 in light of honorific royal burial practices', *Journal of Biblical Literature* 131: 99–119.

Wright, W.C. (1913–23), *The Works of the Emperor Julian*, 3 vols, London and New York: Heinemann and Macmillan.
Wright, W.C. (1921), *Philostratus,* Lives of the Sophists; *Eunapius,* Lives of the Philosophers, Cambridge, MA: Harvard University Press.
Yardley, J. (2004), *Quintus Curtius Rufus,* The History of Alexander, *with an Introduction and Notes by W. Heckel*, London: Penguin.
Zanker, P. (1995), *The Mask of Socrates: The Image of the Intellectual in Antiquity*, trans. A. Shapiro, Berkeley/Los Angeles/Oxford: University of California Press.

Index

Abasgia 82, 173 n.15
Abundantius 90, 91
Achilles 38, 47
Adamantius the Sophist, *Physiognomy* 70
Aelius Donatus, Commentary on Terence 22, 27–8, 29, 82, 145 n.15, 147 n.76, 161 n.29
Aemilius Paullus 23, 31
Aeneas 9, 139 n.20
Agapios, eunuch deacon 113
Agathias 119–20, 123–4, 126, 127–32, 178 n.140
Agathocles, king of Sicily 108
Agdistis 10–11, 11–13
Agnellus of Ravenna, *Book of Pontiffs of the Church of Ravenna* 126
Akta dia Kalopodion 173 n.19
Alamanni 123
Alboin, king of Lombards 125
Alcibiades, P. Aelius, freedman of Hadrian 157 n.39
Alexander, abbot of monasteries of Elias 115
Alexander the Cilician 59
Alexander the Great 2, 24, 47–8, 108
Aligern, Goth 123
Almo, river 13
Amantius, chamberlain of Eudoxia 165–6 n.136
Ambrose, bishop of Milan 82
Amida 86
Amingus, Frank 124, 125, 175 n.65, 176 n.72
Ammianus Marcellinus 6, 51, 81, 84–7, 89
Anastasius I 126
Anicia Juliana 114, 115, 172 n.123
Antae 122
Antinous, lover of Hadrian 53, 101
Antioch 69, 84, 85, 92, 102
　governor of 92

Antiochus, Grand Chamberlain of Theodosius II 83
Antiochus, Prefect of Italy 124
Antiochus IV Epiphanes 30
Antoninus Pius 13, 59, 73, 77, 101
Antony, Mark 1–2, 9
Apollonius, minister of Antiochus IV Epiphanes 30
Apollonius of Tyana 106
Apostolic Canons 104, 111
Arbitio, Master of Cavalry 85
Arcadius 53, 79, 80, 89–95, 97, 105
Areobindus, general 114
Arinthaeus, Master of Infantry 90, 164 n.99 and n.100
Aristonicus, eunuch of Ptolemy V 2, 135
Aristotle 64, 65
Arles 56, 58
Armenia 82, 120, 132, 173 n.14
Armenian 90, 161 n.27
Arnobius of Sicca, *Against the Pagans* 11–13
Arsacids 81
Artemidorus, *Interpretation of Dreams* 70, 160 n.110
Aruth, Herul 128
Asclepius 36, 37, 39, 40, 43, 45, 50, 51
　temple of at Pergamum 36, 37, 38, 43, 50
Ashpenaz, chief of palace servants in Babylon 100
Assyria 2, 27, 97, 110
　Neo-Assyrian reliefs 27
Athalaric, king of Ostrogoths 131
Athanasius, Patriarch of Alexandria 84, 88, 89, 102, 104–5
　Apology for his Flight 102
　History of the Arians 88–9, 104–5
Athens 3, 6, 24, 30, 58, 61, 63
　statue of Favorinus at 57, 58, 60
Athenians 57

Attalus, king of Pergamum 8, 19
Attila the Hun 3, 173–4 n.22
Attis 4, 5, 7–20, 37, 39, 47, 50, 144 n.113
   March festival of 13, 15
   statue of at Ostia 13
Attis, Gallus, in poem of Catullus 6, 18
Augustine, *City of God* 68
Augustus/Octavian 1–2, 8, 9, 14, 33, 35, 52, 53
Aulus Gellius, *Attic Nights* 6, 56, 58, 59, 61, 68, 71–7
Aurelian, Praetorian Prefect 93, 94
Aurelius Victor, *De Caesaribus* 35, 80
Autolecythus, Indian slave of Favorinus 57
   name 155 n.11

Babylon 110–11
Baeticus, Gallus 19–20, 48, 143–4 n.111
Bagoas, eunuch 152 n.111
Bagoas, eunuch of Alexander the Great 2, 47–8
Bagoas, eunuch philosopher in Lucian's *Eunuch* 63–5, 67, 158 n.66
Bagoas, referred to by Quintilian 48
Barbatio 86
Bardio, eunuch of Constantius II 163 n.88
Bargus, commander 91
Basil of Ancyra, *On Virginity* 106
Bauto, Frank 91
beards 4, 42, 50, 56, 58, 61, 64, 65, 66, 70, 114, 115, 134, 158 n.75
Belisarius 6, 69, 119, 120, 121–2, 122, 127, 128, 129, 130, 132, 133, 172 n.3, 179 n.173
Berenice, sister-wife of Ptolemy III 42
Bible
   Acts of the Apostles 5, 107–8
   Daniel 109–10, 170 n.76
   Deuteronomy 108, 109
   Esther 170 n.76
   Isaiah 107–9, 170 n.76
   Leviticus 108, 109
   Matthew 4, 16, 55, 99–100, 101, 102, 103, 104, 117
   Psalms 170 n.78
   Wisdom 170 n.76
   Wisdom of Sirach (Ecclesiasticus) 106, 116, 169 n.55
bodies changing sex 67–8, 159 n.94

Bonus, quaestor of Moesia 127–8
Book of Physiognomy 62
Book of Pontiffs 120, 124–5, 128
Butilinus 123–4, 124, 125, 127, 129, 130, 176 n.72, 180 n.191

Caesarius, Praetorian Prefect 92
Caligula 80
   circus of 140 n.47, 141 n.68
Callimachus, *Lock of Berenice* 41, 42
Callo/Callon 68
Calopodius, *cubicularius* and *spatharius* 173 n.19
Calvia Crispinilla 34
camels 134
Candace, queen of the Ethiopians 107, 108, 109
Carinus 81
Carthage 22, 133–4
Cassius Dio 34, 43, 44, 46, 49, 60, 60–1
   Roman History 34–5, 40, 41, 59–60, 60
castration 10, 11, 15, 17, 19, 34, 35, 38, 41, 42, 43, 44, 45, 46, 49, 50, 51, 52, 55, 63, 66, 70, 70–1, 82, 90, 92, 100, 101, 104, 105, 106, 107, 108, 110, 113, 116, 117, 120, 133, 135, 170 n.76
   castrates not allowed to be emperor 92, 133, 135
   by compression and excision 42, 45, 50
   effects of 4
   law of Domitian banning 33, 37, 42, 43, 51, 102
   legislation on, late Roman 82, 105, 120
   on medical grounds 4, 102, 103, 104, 111, 117
   mystical/spiritual 106–7, 117
   as punishment 5, 15, 16, 17, 22, 25, 30
   steer (castrated bull) 131
   voluntary 3–4, 5, 7, 10, 11, 12, 13, 14, 15, 15–17, 18, 19, 20, 30, 48, 55, 69, 99–107, 114, 117
castrensis sacri palatii (Steward of the Sacred Palace) 165–6 n.136
Catullus 6, 17–18, 41
   on Gallus Attis 6, 17–18
Chaerea, posing as a eunuch 21, 24, 25, 26, 27, 28, 28–9, 30
Chalcedon, trials at 86–7, 87

Chanaranges, Armenian commander 131
Chilbudius, general 122
China 135
Chios 60
Christianity 4, 5–6, 16, 80, 84, 88–9, 92–3, 94, 99–117, 124, 125, 126, 128–9, 174 n.23
  'Arianism' 101, 102, 104–5
  canon law 103, 103–4, 105, 111
  eunuch clergy 99, 102–5, 111–13
  eunuch monks 111–17
  Great Persecution 80, 100, 111–12, 113
  heresy and castration 104–5
  monasticism 106–7, 113
Chrysaorius, on eunuchs 95
Chrysaphius, eunuch of Theodosius II 3, 173–4 n.22
Chrysogonus, freedman of Sulla 53, 154 n.152
Chrysoretus, Grand Chamberlain of Theodosius II 83
Claudia Quinta 8, 9, 9–10, 16, 139 n.26 and n.27
  chastity of 10
  as vestal virgin 10
Claudia Synthyche, dedicates altar to Claudia Quinta 10
Claudian, invectives on Eutropius 6, 7, 28, 53, 70, 80–1, 89–91, 92, 93, 126
Claudians 9, 139 n.26
Claudius 13, 47, 52, 53, 83
  and festival of Attis 13
  freedmen of 83
Claudius Mamertinus 161 n.19
Clement of Alexandria, *Paedagogus* 105
Cleopatra I 31
Cleopatra VII 1–2, 6, 9, 41
Cluvius Rufus 45, 49
cockerels 142 n.78
Constans I 81, 83
Constantine I 81, 82, 83, 84, 96, 100, 103, 112, 160 n.5 and n.6
Constantine II 83, 84
Constantine VII, *On the Governance of the Empire* (*De Administrando Imperio*) 126
Constantius II 6, 35, 79, 81, 82, 83, 83–9, 97, 102, 103, 104–5, 119, 161 n.18, 163 n.88

Corinth 56, 58, 59, 60
  statue of Favorinus at 56, 58, 59, 60, 155 n.21
Cornelius Scipio 23
Cornutus, Stoic philosopher 17
Cotrigurs 132
Council of Nicaea 4, 103–4, 117
  Canon 1 103–4, 111, 117
Cronus 17
Cupid 50
Cyprus 89, 93, 94
Cyril, bishop of Antioch 111
Cyril, Patriarch of Alexandria 83
Cyril of Scythopolis 114, 115
  Life of Sabas 114, 115
Cyrus the Great, Persian king 47, 110

Dagisthaeus 125, 127, 128
Damis, student of Apollonius of Tyana 106
Daniel, prophet 109–11
  as eunuch 110–11, 170 n.86
Dara 69, 133, 179 n.180
Darius III, Persian king 2, 47
Darius the Mede 110
Dean, James 47
Decius 100
Demetrius, bishop of Alexandria 100–1
Demetrius, Hellenistic king 108
Demetrius, nephew of Antiochus IV Epiphanes 30–1
Demonax of Cyprus, Cynic 60, 65–6
Dindymus, eunuch 9, 48, 143 n.107
Dindymus, Mount 9, 10
Dio Chrysostom 35, 43, 44, 45, 46, 49, 52, 56, 56–7, 58, 59
  On Beauty 35, 49
Diocletian 3, 79–80, 81, 82, 96, 97, 111–12, 113
Diodorus Siculus 67, 68
  Historical Library 67–8
Dionysius, eunuch naval commander 135
Dionysius of Halicarnassus 14
Doctor Johnson 6, 58
Domitian 3, 33, 35, 35–40, 41, 42, 43, 44–5, 46, 48, 49, 50, 51, 80, 81, 110, 113
Dorotheus, eunuch presbyter of Antioch 69, 111, 113

Dorotheus, general of Armenia 121
Dorotheus, palace servant of Diocletian 111–12, 113
Dorus, eunuch 22, 24, 25, 26, 27, 28, 29, 30, 48
Drusus, son of Tiberius 52
Dura-Europos 69
  'temple of Bel' in 69

Earinus, eunuch of Domitian 3, 5, 6, 33, 35–51, 53
  name of 39, 42, 49
  visual image of 151 n.62
elephants 24, 31, 108
Eleutherius *cubicularius*, *Passion* of 113
Elias, ascetic in Egypt 106–7
Elias, Patriarch of Jerusalem 114, 115
Elijah, prophet 170 n.81
empire
  Byzantine 97
  Chinese 96
  Ottoman 95, 97
empress 34, 40, 42, 43, 51
  Aelia Eudoxia 91, 93, 94, 165–6 n.136, 166 n.141
  Ariadne 172 n.123
  Constantina, daughter of Constantine I 112
  Domitia Longina 36
  Eudocia 172 n.129
  Flavia Domitilla, niece of Domitian 113
  Livia 9, 139 n.25
  Poppaea (Sabina) 34, 41, 43, 44, 46, 49
  Sophia 124, 125, 125–6, 126
  Theodora 121, 122, 124, 174 n.23, 175 n.61
Endymion 37, 47, 50
Epaphroditus, freedman of Nero 35
Ephesus 57, 58
  eunuch bishop of 113
  priests of Artemis ('Megabyzoi') at 141 n.72, 152 n.117
Epictetus 60, 76
Epiphanius, bishop of Salamis in Cyprus 101, 102, 104, 105, 106
  On Faith 102
  Panarion 101, 102
Ethiopia 108

Ethiopian Eunuch 5, 104, 107–9, 111, 117
Eudoxius, bishop of Antioch 89
Eugenius 91
Eugraphius, Commentary on Terence 28
Eulaeus, eunuch of Ptolemy VI 2, 31
Eunapius 81–2, 91, 92, 96
  History 81–2, 91, 91–2, 96
Eunomians 105, 168 n.44
Eunomius 92, 168 n.44
eunuch
  chief, wicked 113
  Gallic 82
  Grand Chamberlain of Magnus Maximus 82
  Thessalian freedman of Marcus Aeserninus 52
eunuchs
  Abbasid 135
  accidental 69, 120, 133, 134
  and age 29, 46–7, 49, 50, 90, 147 n.76, 158 n.73
  Assyrian 97
  and beauty 27, 30, 35, 40, 42, 45, 47, 48, 49, 50, 52, 53, 70–1
  as bodyguard (*spatharius*) 120, 121, 132, 173 n.19, 173–4 n.22
  born eunuchs 4, 5, 55, 61, 62, 63, 66–71, 100, 104, 105, 111, 113, 115
  Byzantine 97, 99, 117, 119, 133, 134, 135
  as chamberlains (*cubicularii*) 3, 5, 79–97, 108, 112–13, 114, 120, 121, 135, 173 n.19
  childless 89, 92, 104–5, 116, 157 n.45
  Chinese 96, 135
  at court 3, 5, 6, 42, 49, 51, 53, 79–97, 104–5, 107–11, 111–13, 119–26, 134–5
  and desire 3, 4, 6, 16, 19–20, 27, 29, 30, 33–5, 42, 44, 47–8, 51, 52, 56, 57, 60, 61, 62, 64–5, 67, 90, 101, 103, 105–6, 113, 114–17, 155 n.10, 159 n.93, 168 n.53
  dress 5, 14, 19, 20, 22, 24, 25, 26, 28, 34, 35, 37, 44, 48, 49, 50, 56, 69, 147 n.62
  ethnic identity 6, 14, 20, 41, 82, 96, 113, 120, 161 n.27
  as free individuals 5, 6, 55, 68–9, 71, 97, 133

and gender identity 4, 5, 6, 7, 14, 15, 16, 18–20, 27, 28, 29–30, 34, 35, 38, 39, 40, 41, 42, 47, 48, 49, 50, 52, 56, 61, 62, 62–3, 63–6, 67, 67–9, 70, 70–1, 90, 97, 102, 114, 115, 117, 125, 126, 130–1, 135, 143 n.106, 158 n.59, 164 n.97, 168 n.38
as generals 6, 69, 90, 95, 119, 135
and greed 30, 61, 62, 85, 87, 95, 97, 157–8 n.58, 161 n.34
as guardians of women 3, 24, 26–7, 90, 105, 106, 112–13, 175 n.61
Hellenistic 97, 135
ill-omened/polluting 63, 66, 70, 94, 95, 159 n.92, 160 n.110
as loyal/trustworthy 81, 88, 97, 111–12, 158 n.73
as martyrs and saints 111–13
metaphorical 4, 55, 100, 103, 117
as monsters 29, 63, 66, 67–8, 70, 71, 94, 95
monastic rules on 114, 115
Ottoman 95, 97
Parthian 159 n.101
as patrons 5, 36, 47, 50, 83
Persian 80–1, 97, 152 n.111
post-pubertal 27, 48, 66, 106, 143 n.102
power/influence 2, 3, 5, 6, 43, 47–8, 50–1, 53, 79–97, 112, 135
and religion 3–4, 5–6, 6, 7–20, 55, 69, 88–9, 99–117, 124, 125, 126, 128–9
roles of 5, 22, 26, 33, 42, 45, 50, 52, 90, 96, 105, 119
as slaves 3, 4, 5, 6, 24, 26, 31, 33–53, 66, 69, 70, 79–97, 104, 110, 113, 115, 120, 133, 143 n.103
as teachers 27, 64, 65, 82, 100–1
term eunuch as title/office 108, 110, 170 n.76
term *eunuchus* 3, 21, 55
term *spado* 4
theatre masks 146–7 n.57
as treasurers 107, 108, 120, 120–1, 133, 169 n.71
visual images of 4, 20, 27, 56, 57, 58, 59, 60, 69, 91, 94, 95, 139 n.22, 144 n.113, 146–7 n.57, 151 n.62, 155 n.21, 175 n.61

voice 4, 5, 18, 22, 28–9, 55, 56, 57, 58, 61, 62, 64, 65, 85
wealthy 43, 52, 58, 82, 83, 91, 94, 124, 125, 126
and wills 15, 105
and wives 102, 157 n.45, 167–8 n.29
eunuchs in *Passions*
  Calocerus and Parthenius 112, 161 n.27
  Domninus and Hyacinthus *cubicularii* 112–13
  Eleutherius *cubicularius* 113
  Indes 113
  John and Paul 112
  Largus and Smaragdus 112
  Nereus and Achilleus 113
  Protus and Hyacinthus 112
Euripides, *Orestes* 27
  Phrygian slave in, possible eunuch 27
Eusebius, bishop of Nicomedia 89, 164 n.93
Eusebius, Grand Chamberlain of Constantius II 5, 79, 81, 83–9, 95–7, 119, 163 n.81
Eusebius of Caesarea 69, 100–1, 103, 109, 111, 112, 113
  Church History 69, 100–1, 103, 109, 111, 112
Eustolium 102–3, 167 n.29
Eutherius, eunuch 81, 82
Euthymius, abbot 115
Eutropius, *Breviarium* 80
Eutropius, eunuch abbot of monastery of Elusa 6, 114–16, 117
  godson of 115–16
Eutropius, Grand Chamberlain of Arcadius 5, 6, 7, 28, 53, 70, 79, 80, 81–2, 82, 89–97, 126, 135, 167–8 n.29
  anti-asylum law 93–4
  as 'father' of Arcadius 92
  as 'son' of Arcadius 90
  visual images of 91, 94, 95
Evagrius 120, 129
  Church History 120

fans/fanning, eunuchs and 27, 28, 90
Favorinus of Arles 4, 5, 6, 55–77, 111
  as priest 56, 58, 59, 60

statues of 4, 56, 57, 58, 59, 60, 155 n.21
    writings of 57, 59
Felix, governor of Alexandria 101
Firmus, bishop of Caesarea 162 n.37
    Letters 162 n.37
Florentius 86
Franks 123, 125, 127, 128, 129, 131
Fredegar Chronicle 125, 126
Fronto 59, 73
Fulcaris, Herul leader 123, 128, 130, 131, 178 n.158

Gabriel, eunuch monk and presbyter 113, 115, 172 n.129
Gaianus, Patriarch of Alexandria 121
Gainas, Goth 91, 93
Galatia/Galatians 142 n.78
Galba 46, 49, 52
Galen 60
    On the Best Form of Education 60
Galerius, Caesar of Diocletian 80, 112, 160 n.8
Galli 3–4, 5, 7–20, 30, 48, 70
    Archigalli 15, 141 n.70
    'cut priest' 64, 70
    devotees of Cybele 66
    of Pessinus 141 n.58
    as term 14–15, 16, 142 n.78
    visual images of 20, 139 n.22, 144 n.113
Gallus, Caesar of Constantius II 81, 83, 84–5, 87, 88
Gallus, father of Ia 12
Gallus, river 13, 16, 142 n.78
Ganymede 36, 39, 40, 45, 49, 50
Gaza 92–3, 107, 114
generalship 127–35, 178 n.156 and n.157
Genucius, eunuch 15, 18
Germanus, cousin/nephew of Justinian I 133, 177 n.108, 179 n.175, 180 n.185
Germanus, son of Dorotheus 132
Getae 90
Gildo, general 91
Gontharis, bodyguard of Solomon 134
Gorgonius, eunuch of Gallus 81, 171 n.95
Gorgonius, palace servant of Diocletian 112, 113
Gorsak, servant/adopted son of Otes 69, 159 n.102

Grand Chamberlain (*praepositus sacri cubiculi*) 5, 79, 81, 82, 83, 83–97, 120, 124
Graves, Robert 132, 144 n.8, 172 n.3, 179 n.173
    Count Belisarius 132, 172 n.3, 179 n.173
Great Mother (Magna Mater/Mother of the Gods/Cybele/Idaean Goddess) 3–4, 5, 6, 7–20, 21, 30, 39, 48, 66, 97, 100
    Megalesia (April festive of) 8, 9, 13, 14, 16, 17, 20, 30, 144 n.113
    Megalesian games 3, 8, 14, 16, 24, 30
    temple of in Rome 3, 9, 10, 13, 30, 139 n.22
Gregory of Tours 120, 124
    The History of the Franks 120, 124
Greuthungi 90
Gundovald, Frank 124

Hadrian 4, 13, 33, 41, 46, 53, 55, 56–7, 58, 59, 59–60, 60–1, 81, 101, 157 n.39
Hagia Sophia 93, 94, 121
hair 6, 35, 36–40, 42, 43, 45, 50, 62, 90
Halotus, eunuch of Claudius 52
Hannibal 7
harem
    Parthian 106
    Persian 80
Helen of Troy 27
Hellenistic kingdoms 2, 3, 6, 30–1, 79, 81, 97, 108, 135, 169 n.71
    Ptolemies 2, 31
    Rome as 81
    Seleucids 24, 30–1
Heraclides, bishop of Ephesus 113
Herais/Diophantus 67
hermaphrodites 56, 61, 67, 68, 69, 159 n.94
    pseudo-hermaphroditism 66–7
Hermias, tyrant of Atarneus, eunuch 64, 65, 158 n.70
Herodes Atticus 57, 59, 61, 155 n.10
Herodian 10
Heruli 122, 123, 124, 128, 129, 130, 133, 177 n.138
Hezekiah, king of Judah 110
Hijras 16, 135, 142 n.86

Historia Augusta 59, 60, 81
Honorius 89, 94, 97
Hopkins, Keith 80, 81, 95–6
Hosius, Master of Offices 90
Huns 90, 132, 135
Hylas 37, 47, 50

Iaudas, leader of Mauri 134
Ida, Mount 9, 36, 139 n.20 and n.22
Ignatius the Younger, Patriarch of Constantinople, eunuch 99
Indes, barbarian eunuch 113
Intersex 4, 55, 68, 71, 154 n.2
Irenaeus, bishop of Lyon 109, 170 n.79
  Against Heresies 109
Isaiah, prophet 107, 108, 109, 110
Isidore of Seville, *Chronicon Maiora* 125, 126

Jackson, Michael 56
Jerome 110
Jesus 4, 55, 99–100, 101, 102, 103, 104, 107, 108, 109, 116, 117
  as eunuch 103
Jews 110–11
  Jewish attitudes to eunuchs 108–9
John, *comes* under Arcadius 166 n.144
John, monk in Egypt 91, 92
John, nephew of Vitalian 121, 127, 130, 131, 132, 133, 175 n.61, 177 n.108, 179 n.175
John III, Pope 124, 124–5, 125
John the Almsgiver 114
  Life of 114
John the Baptist 170 n.81
John the Cappadocian, Praetorian Prefect 122
John of Ephesus, *Church History* 126
John the eunuch, abbot of New Church 114
John the Eunuch, companion of Peter the Iberian 114
John the Lydian, *On the Months* 13
John Chrysostom, Patriarch of Constantinople 92–3, 93–4, 113, 166 n.141
  On Eutropius the Eunuch, Patrician and Consul 93–4
John Ionopolites, as new Narses 133

John Moschus 113, 114
  Spiritual Meadow 113
Josephus 110, 170 n.89
  Jewish Antiquities 110
Jovian 163 n.88
Julian 7, 10, 81, 82, 83, 84, 86, 87, 87–8, 88, 96, 97, 112, 163 n.81
  hymn on the Great Mother 7, 10
Julius Caesar 2
Julius Constantius 83
Julius Obsequens, *Book of Prodigies* 67
Jupiter 9, 11, 12, 24, 36, 39, 40, 45, 49, 50, 142 n.88
Justin I 126
Justin II 124, 125, 126
Justin Martyr 17, 101–2, 103, 104
  First Apology 101, 103
Justinian I 6, 69, 100, 119, 120, 121, 122, 124, 126, 129, 130–1, 132, 133, 134, 135, 174 n.23, 175 n.61, 177 n.108, 180 n.184 and n.185
  mosaic of in San Vitale 175 n.61
  Novels of 124
Juvenal 15, 19

Lactantius 80, 81, 82, 112, 113
  On the Deaths of the Persecutors 80
Laelius, Gaius 22, 23
Lausus, Grand Chamberlain of Theodosius II 83, 106, 162 n.37
Lawrence, T.E. 179 n.173
Leo I 82
Leo, general 90, 92, 93
Leontius, bishop of Antioch 102–3, 104, 113
Leontius, bishop of Neapolis 114
lettuce, eunuch's 3
Leutharis 123, 125, 129, 130, 180 n.191
Libanius 82, 83, 87
Liberatus 121, 174 n.23
  Breviarium 121
Liberius, commander 132, 179 n.172
Liberius, Pope 88–9, 105
Licinius I 103
Liddell Hart, Basil 132, 179 n.173
Livy 8, 9, 10, 13, 14, 67
Lombards 123, 124, 125, 126, 176 n.96
Longinus 125
Lord Hervey, as Sporus 40

Lord Mahon 172 n.3, 179 n.173
Lucan 2
Lucca, siege of 123, 128, 128–9, 130
Lucian 6, 60, 63–6, 67
  Eunuch 6, 61, 63–6, 67
  Life of Demonax 60, 65–6
  On the Syrian Goddess 141 n.64
  The Mistaken Critic 70
Lucius Constitius, citizen of Thysdritum 159 n.194
Lucretius, *On the Nature of Things* 17
Luke the Evangelist 107
Lygdus, eunuch of Drusus 52
Lysimachus, Hellenistic king 108

Macedon 3, 31
Macedonius, Patriarch of Constantinople, eunuch 113
Macrobius, Grand Chamberlain of Theodosius II 161 n.24
Maecenas 52
Magnus Maximus 82
  eunuch Grand Chamberlain of 82
Malalas, John 120, 121, 122, 123, 124
  Chronicle 120
Mallobaudes, tribune of the guard 85
Marcellinus, *Chronicle* of 175 n.62, 179 n.182
Marcellus, commander of palace guards 122
Marcus Aeserninus 52
Marcus Aurelius 63
Mardian, eunuch of Cleopatra VII 1, 2
Mardonius, eunuch tutor 82
Mardonius, palace eunuch 113
Marius of Avenches 125
  Chronicle 125
Mark the Deacon 92–3
  Life of Porphyry 92–3
Martial 19–20, 35, 36, 39–40, 41, 42, 43, 45, 48, 50, 51
  epigrams 36, 39–40, 42, 43, 45, 48, 50, 51
Mauri 133–4
Maurice, *Strategikon* 132
Megabyzus 48, 152 n.117
'Megabyzoi' 141 n.72, 152 n.117
Melito the eunuch, bishop of Sardis 103, 168 n.34

Menander Protector, *History* of 175 n.65
Meroe 169 n.65
Midas, king of Pessinus 12
Mithridates VI, king of Pontus 135
monastery of Elusa 171–2 n.118
monastery of eunuchs 115
Mu'nis al Muẓaffar ('The Victorious'), Abbasid eunuch military commander 135
Mygdonius, palace eunuch 113

Nana, daughter of Sangarius 12
Narcissus 37, 47, 50
Narcissus, freedman of Claudius 53
Narses, bishop of Ascalon 113
Narses, *cubicularius* 121, 132, 174 n.23
Narses, eunuch general 5, 6, 119–35
  chartularius 173 n.12
  devotion to Virgin 129
  horse of 131
  image of? 175 n.61
  inscription on bridge near Rome 175 n.61
  monastery in Bithynia 126
  spatharius 132
Nebuchadnezzar, king of Babylon 89, 110, 111
Nero 3, 33–5, 41, 43–4, 45–6, 48, 49–50, 52, 81
Nicomedia 80, 111–12
Nika Riot 121, 132, 173 n.19, 177 n.138
Nisus 38, 47
Notitia Dignitatum 82
Nubia 108
Nymphidius, Praetorian Prefect of Nero 34, 35, 43, 44, 46, 51

Olybrius 114
Onasander, *Strategikos* 131, 132, 178 n.156 and n.157
Origen of Alexandria 100–1, 102, 103, 104, 105
  Commentary on Matthew 101
Ostia 8, 13, 76
Ostrogoths 6, 119, 121, 122–3, 123, 124, 127, 129, 130, 132, 175 n.61
Otes the eunuch 69
  fresco of 69

Otho 35, 43, 44, 46, 49, 51
Ovid, *Fasti* 8, 9, 9–10, 10, 14, 16

Paezon, eunuch of Sejanus 52
Palatine Hill 3, 8, 9, 13, 20, 30, 139 n.22
   temple of Great Mother on 2, 9, 10, 13, 30, 139 n.22
Palladius 83, 92, 106, 113
   Dialogue on the Life of St John Chrysostom 113
   Lausiac History 83, 106–7, 164 n.93
Parthia 69, 81, 106
Passion
   of Anthimus 112
   of Eleutherius the *cubicularius* 113
   of Indes and Domna 113
   of Nereus and Achilleus 113
Paul, apostle, as eunuch 103
Paul the Deacon 120, 125, 128, 129
   History of the Lombards 120, 125–6
Paul Helladicus 114, 116
   Letter 114, 115–16
Paulus, personal guard of Narses 128
Pausanias, *Description of Greece* 10–11
Pelagius I, Pope 124
Pelago, eunuch of Nero 52
Pelham-Holles, Thomas, Duke of Newcastle 144 n.7
Pentadius, notary 85
Pergamum 8, 9, 36, 38, 39, 42, 43, 45, 50, 51, 60
   temple of Asclepius at 36, 38, 45, 50
Persarmenia 120, 120–1
Persia 2, 79, 80–1, 86, 97, 110, 120, 158 n.66, 160 n.8
Persians 35, 37, 86
Pessinus 8, 9, 11, 12, 13, 141 n.58
Peter, palace eunuch 113
Peter, Patriarch of Jerusalem 114, 114–15
Peter the Iberian 113–14
   Life of 113–14
Peter Phokas, Byzantine eunuch general 180 n.201
Petronius 52
   Satyricon 52
Phaon, freedman of Nero 34, 35
Philetaerus, eunuch treasurer 169 n.71
Philip, evangelist 104, 107–9
Philip V, king of Macedon 9

Philo of Alexandria 105
Philocalus, Calendar of 13, 144 n.113
Philostorgius, *Church History* 88, 92, 93
Philostratus 56, 58, 59, 60, 61, 67, 106
   Life of Apollonius of Tyana 106, 153 n.134
   Lives of the Sophists 56–8, 61
Photius 84, 93
Phrygianum, on Vatican Hill 15
Piranesi 175 n.61
Plautus 30, 31
   The Braggart Soldier 30
Pliny the Elder 15, 45, 52, 68, 69, 159 n.94
   lost *History* 45
   Natural History 15, 52, 68, 69, 159 n.94
Plutarch 1, 34, 35, 46, 48, 49, 52, 59, 60, 108
   Life of Alexander 48
   Life of Antony 1–2
   Life of Demetrius 108
   Life of Galba 34
Polemo 56, 57, 59, 60–1, 62, 63, 67, 70
   Physiognomy 61, 61–2, 66, 70
Polycrates, bishop of Ephesus 103
Pompey the Great 2
Pope, Alexander 40, 150 n.49
Porphyry, bishop of Gaza 92–3
Posides, eunuch freedman of Claudius 52, 153 n.142
Pothinus, eunuch of Ptolemy XIII 2
Probatius, eunuch of Jovian 163 n.88
Procopius 69, 82, 119, 120–1, 122, 122–3, 123, 126, 127–33, 133–4
   Buildings 173 n.8
   Secret History 120, 173 n.8
   Wars 120, 122, 123
prodigies/portents 67–9, 70
Prosperina/Persephone 34, 43, 45, 50
Prudentius, Christian poet 53
Pseudo-Zachariah, *Church History* 179 n.180
Ptolemaeus, *miles stabuli* 90
Ptolemy I 2, 108
Ptolemy III 42
Ptolemy V 2, 135
Ptolemy VI 2, 31
Ptolemy XIII 2

Quadratus, proconsul of Asia 59
Quintilian 48, 52, 70–1
   Training in Oratory 48, 52, 70–1
Quintus Curtius Rufus 47–8
   Histories of Alexander the Great 47–8

Ragnaris, Hun 123
Ravenna 122, 123, 126, 127, 175 n.61
   church of San Vitale 175 n.61
Reifenstein's syndrome 66–7
Renault, Mary 2
   The Persian Boy 2
Romanos II 126
Rufinus 103
   Church History 103, 168 n.34
Rufinus, Praetorian Prefect 91, 92
Rufinus, uncle of Gallus 84

Sabas 114, 115
Sabinianus 85, 86
Sacchias, king 110
Sagaritis, nymph 10
Samosata 63
Sangarius
   king 12
   river 10, 12, 13
Saturnalia 41, 44
Sayings of the Fathers 114
Schinegger, Erik/Erika 154 n.2
Scholasticus, eunuch commander 134, 180 n.195
Scipio Africanus 22, 23
Scipio Nasica, Publius Cornelius 8
Sclaveni 122, 133, 134
Sejanus, Praetorian Prefect of Tiberius 52
Seleucus I 108
Semenya, Caster 4, 154 n.2
Semiramis, Assyrian queen 2
Seneca the Younger, *Moral Letter to Lucilius* 52
Septimius Severus 100
Septuagint 110
Sergius, nephew of Solomon 180 n.189
Severus Alexander 81
Shakespeare, William 1, 22
   Antony and Cleopatra 1
Sigillaria 34, 41, 44, 45
Silvanus 85

Sindual, king of Heruli 124, 125, 128, 177 n.138
Skoptsy 16, 99, 117
Smyrna 57
Socrates 57, 58, 59, 64, 72
Socrates, *Church History* 82, 92, 93
softness 19, 143 n.106
Solomon, eunuch general 69, 120, 133–5, 179 n.180 and n.182, 180 n.185 and n.191
Sophronius, Patriarch of Jerusalem 114
Souda 59
Sozomen, *Church History* 82, 84, 89, 91, 93, 94, 113
Sporus 3, 5, 33–5, 40–51, 53
   name of 44, 45, 49, 50
Statius 6, 35–6, 41–2, 42, 43, 44, 45, 48, 50, 51
   poem on hair of Earinus 6, 35–8, 43
   Silvae 36
Stephanus, commander 127
Stilicho 89–90, 91–2, 97
Subarmachius 92
Sudan 108, 169 n.65
Suetonius 22, 23, 33–4, 41, 43, 44, 46, 49, 51, 51–2
   Life of Domitian 51
   Life of Nero 33–4, 41, 43
   Lives of the Poets 22–3
Synesius of Cyrene 92
   On Kinghip 92

Tacitus 41, 46, 49, 51–2
   Annals 46
   Histories 46
Tarbigilus/Tribigild, Gothic general 90, 93
Tatianus, Praetorian Prefect 105
taurobolium 15, 141 n.67
Teias, king of Ostrogoths 123, 125
Terence 3, 22–3
   The Eunuch 3, 5, 6, 21–32, 33, 48, 82, 106
   illustrated manuscripts of plays 28
Tertullian 2–3, 15, 103, 105
   Against Marcion 105
   Exhortation to Chastity 3
   On Monogamy 103
Thelys, eunuch 143 n.107
Theodoret of Cyrrhus 89, 110–11

Church History 89
Commentary on Daniel 110–11
Theodosius I 79, 82, 89, 90, 91, 97, 102, 105, 114, 168 n.44
Theodosius II 83, 106, 161 n.24, 172 n.129, 173–4 n.22
Theodosius, Patriarch of Alexandria 121
Theophilus, Patriarch of Alexandria 92
Theophylact Simocatta, *History* 179 n.180
Theudebald, Frankish king 123, 124
Theudebert 131–2
Thubursicum Numidarum (Khamissa) 146–7 n.57
Tiberius 10, 18, 41, 44, 46, 52, 53
Tiberius II 124
Tibullus 159 n.92
Tigellinus, Praetorian Prefect of Nero 34
Tigrius, eunuch presbyter 113
Timasius, general 91
Timocrates, teacher of Polemo 61
Timotheus, on the Great Mother 11
Titus 40, 45, 52, 100
    baths of 73
Totila, king of Ostrogoths 122–3, 124, 125, 129–30
Trajan, Forum of 75
transsexual 49
transvestite 49
'transvestite nuns' 114, 117
Trier 82
Trimalchio, eunuchs of 52

Troy 9, 139 n.20
Tyre 69, 111

Uranus, castration of 17, 46
Ursicinus, general 84–5, 85–6, 87

Valens 90
Valentinian II 105
Valerian, general 123
Valerius Maximus, *Memorable Doings and Sayings* 10, 15, 18
Valesians 102, 104, 105, 167 n.23
Vandals 133, 180 n.184
Vardanes, Parthian king 106
Varro 9, 17
Vatican Hill 15
Vatican Terence (Codex Vaticanus Latinus 3868) 145–6 n.26, 146–7 n.57
Venus 36–8, 46, 50, 51
Vespasian 40, 47, 110
Victor, bishop of Rome 103
Vigilius, Pope 124
Virgil, *Aeneid* 9
Vitalian 177 n.108
Vitalis, bishop of Altinum 125
Vitellius 35, 43, 44, 45, 46, 49, 51, 52

Widin, Goth 124, 125
Wilde, Oscar 4, 56

Zheng He, Chinese eunuch admiral 135
Zosimus, *New History* 82, 91, 92, 93

www.ingramcontent.com/pod-product-compliance
Lightning Source LLC
Chambersburg PA
CBHW072233290426
44111CB00012B/2076